Quality by
Experimental Design

QUALITY AND RELIABILITY

A Series Edited by

Edward G. Schilling
Center for Quality and Applied Statistics
Rochester Institute of Technology
Rochester, New York

1. Designing for Minimal Maintenance Expense: The Practical Application of Reliability and Maintainability, *Marvin A. Moss*

2. Quality Control for Profit, Second Edition, Revised and Expanded, *Ronald H. Lester, Norbert L. Enrick, and Harry E. Mottley, Jr.*

3. QCPAC: Statistical Quality Control on the IBM PC *Steven M. Zimmerman and Leo M. Conrad*

4. Quality by Experimental Design, *Thomas B. Barker*

In preparation

Integrated Product Testing and Evaluating, *Harold L. Gilmore and Herbert C. Schwartz*

Applications of Quality Control in the Service Industry, *A. C. Rosander*

Quality Management Handbook, *edited by Loren Walsh, Ralph Wurster, and Raymond J. Kimber*

Quality by Experimental Design

Thomas B. Barker

Center for Quality and Applied Statistics
Rochester Institute of Technology
Rochester, New York

MARCEL DEKKER, INC.   **New York and Basel**

ASQC QUALITY PRESS   **Milwaukee**

Library of Congress Cataloging in Publication Data

Barker, Thomas B., [date]
  Quality by experimental design.

  (Quality and reliability ; 4)
  Includes index.
  1. Quality control–Statistical methods.
2. Experimental design. I. Title. II. Series: Quality
and reliability ; vol. 4.
TS156.B375 1985   658.5'62   85-20444
ISBN 0-8247-7451-5

MARCEL DEKKER, INC.
270 Madison Avenue, New York, New York 10016

Current printing (last digit):
10 9 8 7 6 5 4 3 2 1

PRINTED IN THE UNITED STATES OF AMERICA

To Mason E. Wescott,
a teacher of teachers

"... the engine was a better engineer than the engineers. It told us what kind of piston rings it liked! We just ran errands for it, bringing it a variety to choose from."

—*Charles F. Kettering*
(on the development of the diesel engine by empirical methods)

Preface

There have been a great many textbooks and reference manuals on the subject of statistically designed experiments. The great work by Owen Davies is still considered a classic by this author. Why then a new book to crowd others on the shelves of the professional statistician? Mainly because this book is written to introduce the *nonstatistician* to the methods of experimental design as a philosophical way of life. It is intended to bridge the gap between the experimenter and the analyst, and break down the aura of mystery created by so many statisticians. In short, this is a short book (as contrasted with Davies' encyclopedia) that lays the foundation for logical experimental thinking, the efficient means to implement the experiment, the statistical methods of sorting signal from noise, and then the proper methods of utilizing the information derived in the experiment.

To present the reasoning behind each concept and yet allow the book to stand as a reference, a unique format has been created. For each chapter there are two parts. In the main text we present the entire story complete with examples. An extract is then made of the key concepts in the appendix for each chapter. This serves as a handy reference after the learning is over and the concepts are put to practical use. After all, experimental design is not an academic subject, but a down-to-earth, practical method of getting necessary information.

Throughout this book, we shall rely upon modern computer techniques to perform the tedious arithmetic sometimes associated with large scale experimentation. The appendix of each chapter also contains the BASIC language versions of the programs needed to complete the computing.

The method of presenting material is based on the discovery and building block approach to learning. No new concepts are thrown out without a basis on previous information. When a new idea is presented it is developed in such a way that the reader has the thrill of discovery. I believe that the learning will last longer if he or she is able to *develop* the concept rather than have it given from memory.

I would like to thank all the people who have been associated with the preparation of this book. At Xerox Corp., Doug Boike, my manager, saw the need for a practical treatment of experimental design and encouraged me to complete the manuscript. The Innovation Opportunity Program provided the resources to allow my scribblings to become the bits and bytes via the Alto work station. Karen Semmler and Mark Scheuer both worked on this transcription and showed me how to format and change these electronic images through the many revisions necessary before a "quality" manuscript was in hand. Loretta Lipowicz and Nuriel Samuel both helped translate the computer programs into the "PC" format from my TRS-80 originals. Without their help the project could never have been finished.

I would especially like to thank all of the many design-of-experiment students at Rochester Institute of Technology who found the "glitches" in the manuscript as they used it as "supplemental notes" for the courses I have taught there over the past 15 years. These students also encouraged me to "finish your book soon" and helped me find the title through a *designed* experiment.

Of course, special thanks are extended to my wife Anne who always has encouraged my writing and aided the content by making sure it was clear and correct. It is fortunate to have such a knowledgeable statistician in the same household. My children Audrey and Greg who grew up as I spent 9 years on this effort must be thanked for allowing me to close the den door and work on "daddy's project."

Thomas B. Barker

How to Use This Book

The chapters of this book have been arranged in a functional rather than chronological reading order. The concepts of experimental design methods and the philosophy behind these methods found in parts one and two can be grasped without the formality of statistical analysis. However, the reader/student will eventually *want* to know how to separate the information (signal) from the random error (noise). It is suggested that this learning take place via excursions into the third part of the book as outlined in the following diagram.

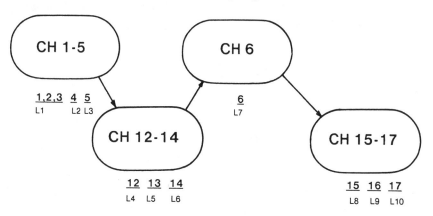

The above would serve as a first quarter course in Experimental Design with the appropriate reading assignments shown underlined and in the small type below the boxes. The appropriate lectures are shown below the chapters (L1.10). The 11 week quarter would entail 10 lectures and allow time for a final exam. Of course the reader who is working alone would also find this path useful and the final exam would be a real problem in need of solution.

For a second quarter course, a similar outline is found below. In this quarter, the "specialized" designs used when randomization is not possible and other topics like components of variance are explored. It is suggested that a class project be utilized in the last 4 weeks of the quarter to put the concepts of the *entire* course to work.

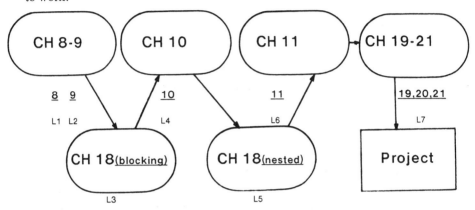

For a semester course, the outline for the first quarter plus the chapters on blocking and the analysis in Chapter 18 for blocking followed by the case history and Monte Carlo would fit into the 15 week format. A two semester enriched course could follow the quarter outline and expand the time on least squares (CH 16 -17) in the first semester while spending more time on the examples and class project in the second semester.

Contents

Preface   *v*
How to Use This Book   *vii*

PART I
The Philosophy of Experimentation

1. Why Design Experiments   3

   Uses of Experimental Designs   3
   Efficiency   4
   First, Experiment   4
   Second, Required Information   5
   Third, Resources   6
   A General Example   6
   Problems for Chapter 1   9
   Appendix 1   9

2. Organizing the Experiment   11

   The Elements of Any Experiment   11
   Prior Knowledge   12
   The Qualities of a Response   13
   Goals and Objectives   13
   Gathering Information   15
   Organizational Psychology   15
   Experimental Phases   16

Problems for Chapter 2   17
Appendix 2   17

PART II
Statistical Experimental Designs

3. The Search for Efficiency   23
    Appendix 3   25

4. The Factorial 2 Level Design   27
    Plotting Interactions   34
    Cost   36
    Problems for Chapter 4   37
    Appendix 4   38

5. Fractional Factorials at 2 Levels   43
    Confounding Rules   47
    Fractionalization Element   47
    More Factors—Smaller Fractions   47
    Logical Approach   50
    Resolution   52
    Problems for Chapter 5   52
    Appendix 5   53

6. Multi-level Designs   62
    A Note on Choosing Levels   70
    Problems for Chapter 6   72
    Appendix 6   72

7. Three Level Designs   74
    3^{k-p} Designs   76
    Generating a 3^{k-p} 77
    Information and Resources   80
    3^{k-p} Design Rules   80
    Larger 3^{k-p} Designs   82
    A Comment on 3 Level Fractions   84
    Problems for Chapter 7   85
    Appendix 7   86

8. Blocking in Factorial Designs   88
    Theory of Blocking   92
    Choice of Primary Blocks   93

	Problems for Chapter 8	96
	Appendix 8	97
9.	Randomized Block and Latin Square	98
	Complete Randomized Block	98
	Generalization of Results	99
	Latin Squares	100
	The Mis-use of the Latin Square	105
	Problems for Chapter 9	107
	Appendix 9	107
10.	Nested Designs	109
	A Nested Design	111
	Coals to Kilowatts	112
	Summary	113
	Problems for Chapter 10	113
	Appendix 10	114
11.	EVOP	115
	The Prime Directive of Manufacturing	115
	Evolutionary Operations	116
	A Slow Experience	118
	Use of the EVOP Worksheet	119
	Signal to Noise in EVOP	121
	Time for Decision	121
	Phase II	124
	Equations from EVOP	124
	EVOP References	129
	Appendix 11	129

PART III
Sorting the Signal from the Noise

12.	Simple Analysis	135
	Hypothesis Testing	136
	Example #1	136
	The Null Hypothesis	137
	The Alternative Hypothesis	137
	Alpha Risk	138
	Beta Risk	138
	Steps in Hypothesis Testing	139
	A Designed Hypothesis Test	141
	Tests Between Two Means	146

Buying a Copier   147
Problems for Chapter 12   152
Appendix 12   153

13.   Analysis of Means by Using the Variance   161

This Remedy Is Spelled A-N-O-V-A   162
Signal/Noise   162
No Difference   162
Big Difference   168
An Apple a Day   170
Comparison of Individual Levels   175
More Conclusions   178
Functional Relationships   179
ANOVA Assumptions   183
Test for Homogeneity of Variance   183
Tests for Normality   185
Problems for Chapter 13   186
Appendix 13   188

14.   YATES Algorithm   197

Application to 2^{k-p} Fractional Designs   201
Deconfounding Effects   203
Problems for Chapter 14   207
Appendix 14   207

15.   Matrix Algebra   212

Matrix Defined   212
Transposition   213
Multiplication   214
Matrix "Division"   216
Problems for Chapter 15   218
Appendix 15   219

16.   Least Squares Analysis   221

Least Squares Developed   221
Using the Formula   230
The Role of the Matrix   231
The Dummy Factor   232
Regression, ANOVA, and YATES   234
Problems for Chapter 16   236
Appendix 16   237

17.   Putting ANOVA and Least Squares to Work   239

Using the Half Effects   241

Plotting Interactions   244
Plotting Curves   246
Problems for Chapter 17   249
Appendix 17   250

18. ANOVA for Blocked and Nested Designs   267

Complete Randomized Block   270
Paired Comparison   273
Latin Square   275
Nested Designs   277
Using the Hierarchy   287
Problems for Chapter 18   288
Appendix 18   290

PART IV
The Derivation of Empirical Equations from
Statistically Designed Experiments

19. A Case History of an Experimental Investigation   297

The Phase Approach   297
Example One—A Popcorn Formula   298
Phase II   306
Example Two—A Photographic Process   310
The Concept Phase   310
Defining the Required Information   312
Adding Levels   316
The Second Phase   319
Plotting the Results   320
Constructing the Model   321
A Final Note   325
Problems for Chapter 19   325

PART V
Utilization of Empirical Equations

20. Monte Carlo Simulation   331

Simulation   331
Combining Simulations and Probabilities   332
Application to More Complex Situations   337

Problems for Chapter 20   340

Appendix 20   341

21. Case History Completed—The Utilization of the Equation   344

Random Method   345

Another Approach   350

ANOVA of the Results   355

Appendix 21   360

Index   381

PART I

The Philosophy of Experimentation

1

WHY DESIGN EXPERIMENTS

In today's industrialized society, almost every product that eventually reaches the market has a long lineage of testing and modification to its design before it sees the light of day. In view of the success of such products, we may ask "Why upset the apple cart? What we are doing now gets the product out. Why change?"

It is always difficult to argue with success, but those of us who are on the inside of industry know that this "success" is a most difficult commodity to come by, especially in the time-frame imposed upon us – a time-frame structured by a customer need or by a competitive threat.

Our customer is more informed today than ever before. Improved products constantly raise the level of expectation for next-generation products. In many cases, technology and invention are moving more rapidly than our ability to do good design engineering and manufacturing by the "old" methods. Quality products that perform as advertised and do so without variation are now part of the informed customer's expectation. In many cases, only testing can give us the information necessary to determine the quality of a product or service.

It is our job as experimenters to find the most efficient schemes of testing, and apply such schemes to as broad a gamut of applications as possible to obtain the information required to make a successful product.

USES OF EXPERIMENTAL DESIGNS

Now that we have demonstrated a need for testing, the question of where experimental designs are used is likely to arise. The prime application area, and the area we shall emphasize in this book, is the *characterization* of a process. [A process is broadly defined as <u>any</u> phenomenon that is worthy of investigation.   A process could be the way we assemble a copy machine in a manufacturing environment or the way banking is practiced in the world of finance.]   In this very general use, we study the result of making purposeful changes in the way the process is operated and watch the way the results (or responses) of the process change.

Another application utilizes experimental designs to <u>troubleshoot</u> a problem by interchanging components.   In this way, we can induce a failure at will and understand the source of this failure.   <u>Routine</u> analytical <u>errors</u> may be accessed by proper experimental designs.   Instead of just watching the variation in our data by a so-called "random process," we trace the sources of changes in the numbers so we may gain <u>control</u> of the overall variance and improve the quality of our product, process or service.

Now, the above applications are not all-inclusive, but represent the main areas of use. The common connection between these applications is the fact that we study the change <u>we</u> induce rather than merely trying to study a change induced by fate.

Purposeful change is the important part of experimental design.   Efficiency is the added value provided by a statistical approach to experimentation.

EFFICIENCY

A good experiment must be efficient.

EFFICIENT: AN <u>EXPERIMENT</u> THAT DERIVES THE
                    <u>REQUIRED</u> INFORMATION AT THE
                    <u>LEAST</u> EXPENDITURE OF <u>RESOURCES</u>.

The above is a very precise definition and is about the only aspect of the techniques of designing experiments that should be committed to memory.   Let's take the definition apart and see what it means.

FIRST, EXPERIMENT

First, we speak of an <u>experiment</u> and not a single, isolated test. A "test" merely looks at a problem as a "go" – "no-go" situation. It does not answer why. The <u>experiment</u> goes far beyond the "test" by drawing the reasons for the "go" or the "no-go" in a series of ordered tests. While a test is success-oriented, an experiment is information-oriented. An experiment gets to <u>why</u> something works, rather than if it works. When we know why, we can make it work!

It is unfortunate that many of us spend much of our time testing rather than experimenting and then try to let mathematics (in the form of multiple regression) do the organizing that should have been done before the testing, but is left until after the fact. This commonly reduces our scientific endeavors to the not-so-scientific ground of "the lure of accumulated data".

All too often the tester laments the fact that after a number of years of work trying "a little of this and some of that" he is no further ahead than when he started. Worse yet, he doesn't have any chance of reconstructing the data into anything that could guide him to his next endeavors.

While a set of properly-designed experiments may not produce the exact result wanted, the information derived along the way will point in the correct direction to what must be done to achieve the goals.

The first order of business, as we strive for efficiency, is a well-planned experiment and not just some disjointed testing. An experiment is a structured set of coherent tests that are analyzed as a whole to gain understanding of a process.

SECOND, REQUIRED INFORMATION

Before we can plan the tests that build into our experiment, we need to decide firmly on what we are looking for. This may sound like a trivial task, but it is one of those deceptive essentials that usually gets by the experimenter. Motivated by a real need, he rushes off into the lab to get quick results (see figure 1). In his zeal, he misses the fundamental understanding that lasting results will be built upon.

The information that we need to define before we begin our experiment is not necessarily every component attributable to the process under study, but just the required information needed to answer our questions. This is both fortunate and unfortunate. It is fortunate since we need only to isolate a handful of components from the virtual bag of causes that exist on a typical problem to get an adequate understanding. It is unfortunate since many times the vital few components are quite difficult to characterize or even recognize. Since the investigator is human, he will often select the easiest or more obvious parameters from the trivial many, and by throwing these into an experiment he misses the heart of the understanding, even though he conducts a good experiment from a procedures viewpoint.

This type of work has in the past given statistical design techniques a bad name since the experiment was a success, but the patient died.

The region between what is easy to define and what is difficult or impossible to identify is the territory of required information. The exploration of this region requires one skilled in the disciplines of the process under study. A neophyte will fall into the many traps set along the way. An understanding of the nature of the process under study is essential for a good experiment. In chapter 2 we will show how to avoid such problems by proper pre-experiment organization.

THIRD, RESOURCES

The final part of our definition of efficiency concerns the area of resources. Resources can be money, people, buildings, prototype machines, chemicals and, in every experiment, <u>time</u>. In most industrial experimentation, management can provide enough of the material resources of an experiment, but time is costly, and large quantities are usually unavailable at any price. Here is where the statistical design shines, for it strikes a balance between what is defined as needed and the way to get there at the least cost. We will show in later chapters how statistical design is inherently more resource-efficient.

When we realize that every piece of experimental data we gather is merely a statistic (that is a sample, subject to variability) then it becomes clear why we need a body of methods called STATISTICS to treat these statistics. By using statistical methods, we will obtain the required information to do the job in a systematic and controlled manner.

A GENERAL EXAMPLE

Unfortunately, most experimenters do not realize that a short term investment in a good experiment is actually more cost effective than a series of "shot in the dark" attempts to fix problems. Figures 1-1 and 1-2 contrast the usual method of testing (1-1) and the statistical experimental design method (1-2). These examples are further enhanced by the assignment of chances of success based on actual experience. This general example shows that there is much better control and lower overall cost with the statistical approach to the design and analysis of experiments.

In figure 1-1, the chance of solving the problem is only about 20%. The chance of solving the right problem is only 30%. There is also a high probability that a new problem will be created as a result of the "solution" to the first problem! It takes a long time to get a reward for a good job in figure 1-1 because we are constantly going back to a previous step. There is an old saying that is still very true today. "There is never enough time to do the job right, but lots of time to do it over." This is the unfortunate problem with the approach in figure 1-1 we do it over too much. A computer simulation of this "Jump on the Problem" method shows that there is a high cost (59 days) with a very high uncertainty (44 days) by using this faulty

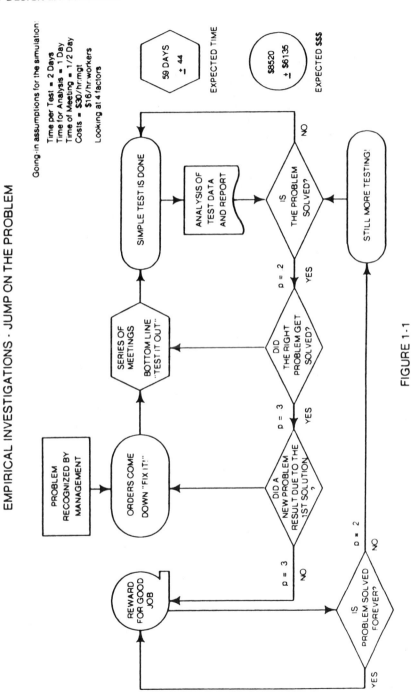

SYSTEM FLOW DIAGRAM

EMPIRICAL INVESTIGATIONS - JUMP ON THE PROBLEM

Going-in assumptions for the simulation:

Time per Test = 2 Days
Time for Analysis = 1 Day
Time of Meeting = 1/2 Day
Costs = $30/hr.mgt
$16/hr.workers
Looking at 4 factors

FIGURE 1-1

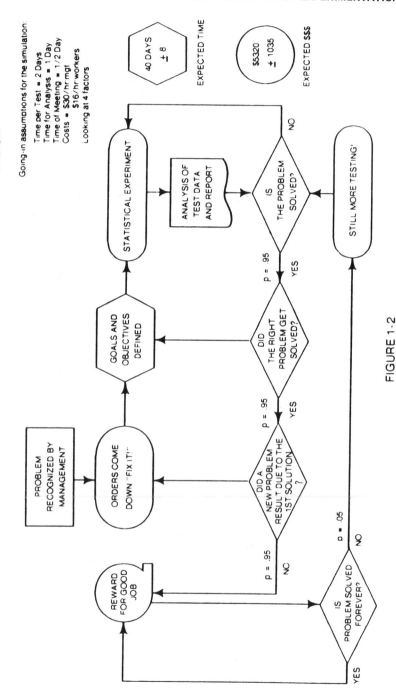

SYSTEM FLOW DIAGRAM

EMPIRICAL INVESTIGATIONS USING STATISTICAL EXPERIMENTAL DESIGN

Going-in assumptions for the simulation:

Time per Test = 2 Days
Time for Analysis = 1 Day
Time of Meeting = 1/2 Day
Costs = $30/hr mgt
        $16/hr workers
Looking at 4 factors

40 DAYS ± 8   EXPECTED TIME

$5320 ± 1035   EXPECTED $$$

PROBLEM RECOGNIZED BY MANAGEMENT

ORDERS COME DOWN "FIX IT"

GOALS AND OBJECTIVES DEFINED

STATISTICAL EXPERIMENT

ANALYSIS OF TEST DATA AND REPORT

IS THE PROBLEM SOLVED? NO

DID THE RIGHT PROBLEM GET SOLVED? p = .95 YES

DID A NEW PROBLEM RESULT DUE TO THE 1ST SOLUTION? p = .95 YES

IS PROBLEM SOLVED FOREVER? p = .05 NO

REWARD FOR GOOD JOB

STILL MORE TESTING!

p = .95 NO

p = .95 YES

FIGURE 1-2

approach to problem solving. In figure 1-2 we need only to include a statistically designed experiment as the investigation methodology. Now the chances are much higher for solving the problem the first time. We are almost certain (95%) to solve the problem on only one try and we will solve the right problem. The problem also stays solved without creating new problems. This is because the statistical approach looks at the whole situation and not just a fragmented segment. Now the time to do the job is reduced to 40 days and the variation is reduced to only 8 days. An experimental design is more than an engineering tool. It is a necessary part of the management of the engineering process. Of course, as we do not restrict the meaning of the word "process", we should not restrict the word "engineering" to only industrial/manufacturing structures. The engineering concept can be expanded to include any process that needs to be improved to meet the quality requirements of our customers. It is possible, then, to engineer medicine, banking, baking, airline service as well as the obvious manufacturing methods.

PROBLEMS FOR CHAPTER 1

1. Define a problem that you have encountered in you work experience or any related experience that could or did require an experiment.

2. a) if an experiment was performed on the problem in #1 above, determine if it was efficient,

   and/or

   b) set down what is required information in regard to the problem in #1 and what resources are available to perform the experiment. Is this the most efficient approach?

3. a) Given an example of a test.

   b) Give an example of an experiment.

Figures 1-1 and 1-2 show a simulation of two approaches to solving a typical industrial problem. In both cases the orders come down from above to fix a problem. In the usual case, (figure 1-1) the workers jump on the job without too much consideration of what they are doing! In the case that employs SED, (figure 1-2) the predictability of the time necessary to accomplish the task and the overall cost are both more reasonable than in the "jump on the problem" approach.

APPENDIX 1

<u>USES</u>:

1. Characteristics of a process
2. Trouble shooting
3. Quantification of errors.

<u>EFFICIENCY</u>:

An experiment that derives the required information at the least expenditure of resources.

<u>TEST</u> --- One shot go, no-go. Usually success oriented. (ie: make the thing work).

<u>EXPERIMENT</u> ---   leads to understanding via a structured set of <u>coherent</u> tests that are analyzed as a <u>whole</u>. Always information oriented.

<u>REQUIRED INFORMATION</u> --- that which is necessary and sufficient to accomplish our goals.

<u>RESOURCES</u> --- what we have to derive the required information. Time is the most valuable and costly.

<u>WHY STATISTICAL EXPERIMENTAL DESIGN?</u>

a) A structured plan of attack
b) more efficient
c) meshes with powerful analysis tools
d) FORCES EXPERIMENTER TO ORGANIZE

2

ORGANIZING THE EXPERIMENT

If a designed experiment does anything at all, it should force the experimenter to organize his thoughts. In many situations, pressures to produce a result cause ill-planned, premature experiments. In a great number of these cases there is not enough prior or "lab bench" knowledge available to formulate the proper questions that need to be studied. Here we fall into the human trap of investigating the obvious. In doing so, we violate our prime directive of efficiency by not deriving the required information.

In a great many ill-planned experiments we generate an impressive array of purposeful changes, but neglect to define a meaningful measure of the results of these changes. Again, we miss the required information.

The most flagrantly violated area involved in designing experiments is also the most trivial sounding. There are so many situations in which the experimenter has confused Goals with Objectives and in doing so has failed to identify the problem. It often has been observed that if the real problem can be identified, half the work is completed.

THE ELEMENTS OF ANY EXPERIMENT

The three items essential for a successful, efficient experiment are then:

1. Knowledge of the process.
2. A response variable.
3. Clear goals and objectives.

Without sufficient knowledge of the process, we are completely halted in any good thinking. We tend to grasp onto the obvious. There is no rule of thumb relating to how long the preliminary study should be before going into a full experiment, but the Experimental Design organizational form (in 2B) is a help. If any part of this form cannot be completed, you need to go back to the bench for more preliminary information.

PRIOR KNOWLEDGE

One of the major requirements for efficient experimentation is a solid prior knowledge of the process under investigation. This may seem to be contradictory, since we are experimenting to gain knowledge! While it may appear to be circular thinking, the logic dictates that we can't run an experiment if we don't know what we are doing!

So where does the prior knowledge come from? There are many sources, but the following are the primary ones available to the average experimenter.

- School
- On The Job Training (OJT)
- Small Less-Structured Experiments
- A Regression Analysis Of Accumulated Data

Most of us have obtained our prior knowledge in the formality of college and bring this knowledge to the job. While college has trained us in general thinking about a discipline, we learn to apply our knowledge while on the job and enrich our basic information with the particular nuances (and nuisances!) of the application under study. While working on a problem, we often try small experiments. These "lab bench" trials form the substance for our more structured efficient experimentaiton. There is nothing wrong with a little fiddling around before the main event.

The final possible source of prior knowledge comes from the "lure of accumulated data." Many times, there has been an effort to solve a problem in a less than efficient manner and records of this work may sometimes yield enough information to structure a proper investigation. There are a number of good books that describe the care required in using the methods of regression.

We can see that those who scoff and are skeptical at the need for knowledge to build knowledge need not fear. Again we only call upon common sense to build on what we know to gain more of what we need to know. A good experiment will ask more probing questions while it answers the needs of the present.

THE QUALITIES OF A RESPONSE

The response variable is unfortunately the most neglected variable in many experiments. The attitude is usually, "Oh, we can think of what to measure after the process has produced the product.". Anyone who has a working knowledge of basic statistics knows the fallacy behind this statement, since to specify how many samples from the process are sufficient to find an important difference, we need to know the variability of the response or responses (yes, there are cases involving more than one dependent variable). We must be sure that these response variables are:

1. Quantitative
2. Precise
3. Mean something

Some examples of responses include such quantitative measures as % contamination, customer satisfaction, product wear out, and time to failure. Qualitative responses give us trouble since a "good" or "bad" response will not "compute".

If the response is not quantitative, it will be impossible to perform the arithmetic operations of the statistical analysis. There are arbitrary numerics that can be applied to qualitative data. In the case of a binomial response such as "good" or "bad" a "0" or "1" can be used. An ascending order counting scale can be used to quantify qualitative responses. These scales, of course, are arbitrary and all attempts should be made to quantify a qualitative response on a physical basis. This quantification is much of the work of the fundamental sciences.

To get sensitivity in our experiment, it is essential that our response is repeatable or precise. If it is not, we end up with so much noise due to our measurements, that nothing of value emerges from the experimental work.

Finally, the response must have a meaning related to the subject under investigation. Studying an effect for its own sake adds nothing to the efficiency of our experiment. There are a great number of responses that are quantitative and precise, but don't relate to the problem. We should not run an experiement under such conditions.

GOALS AND OBJECTIVES

It is surprising how many experimenters go off and try to solve a problem without first understanding the roots behind it. This mistake is a matter of confusing goals with objectives.

A Goal is the ultimate end result of a task. (ie: "make it work")

An Objective is a statement of how the task will be accomplished. (ie: "understand how it works")

For example:

We may want to make a disabled car work. However, before we can fix the car we must present some hypothesis about what is broken. We then test this hypothesis and if we are correct, we can then accomplish the goal and apply the repair. Figure 2-1 shows this process in action. Sometimes it takes a number of cycles from the conjecture stages to the final solution of the problem. These cycles form the scientific method of conjecture-deduction, information-inference.

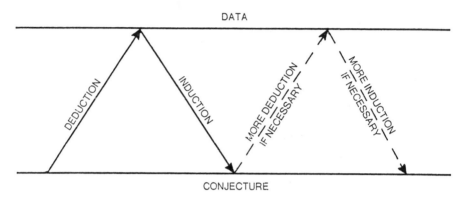

FIGURE 2-1

There is often a hierarchy of goals and objectives in an industrial organization that could look like this:

GOAL *end result*

Corporate: $$$$$
Marketing: Sell a product.
Manufacturing: Have a good product.
Development: Make it work.

Objective *how*

Sell a product.
Have a good product.
Make it work.
Test the hypothesis that a functional relationship exists between a response and some independent factors.

What becomes obvious from the outline above is that what is one organization's goal becomes another's objective. In the area of experimental design, our objectives must be defined carefully so as to state the problem clearly in scientific terms.
Stating the objective in the form of testing the hypothesis that a response is a function

of a variable is convenient and has proven its value in the past. By using this form of stating the GOAL separately from the OBJECTIVE, we are able to avoid confusion and solve the problem through understanding. "Goal words" include "fix", "improve", "make less costly". An objective searches for understanding by testing a change in a response as a function of changes in control factors.

GATHERING INFORMATION

The "Experimental Design Form" - Page 19 - is a useful way to organize the information needed to design your experiment. This form provides questions on all the input or independent variables, as well as the responses.

It is best to organize an experiment as a team effort and use the "brainstorming" technique to scope the entire problem. From the list of many control variables gathered at the brainstorming session, select those that should have the greatest impact (based on prior knowledge) on the system under study. The team effort assures that there is a good probability that we do not miss any factors. A team has a positive synergistic effect on the quality of the factor selection process, since more than one or two opinions are responsible for picking the control factors and response variables.

The example of a designed experiment in Chapter 19 shows the process in action, and illustrates the concept of the phased approach to design. Brainstorming is an uninhibited method of creating ideas that can be later rationalized.

Use brainstorming and a team effort up front to do the planning of an experimental design, and your experiment will have a greater chance of producing the required information. By using a statistical approach to your experiment, you will get this information at the least expenditure of resources. Proper organization and statistical methods will assure success.

ORGANIZATIONAL PSYCHOLOGY

The prime reason for the brainstorming session is to determine the possible sources of influence on the possible responses. However, a designed experiment is not run to just come up with understanding of the process under study. Once the objective of understanding is achieved, we will use this knowledge to modify the process and produce a better quality product.

If we include the people who have the responsibility to implement the changes at the beginning of the planning stages and keep them informed all along the experimental path, we will have a much better chance of watching the changes take place. Don't work in a vacuum, include the implementers in the brainstorming* session.

Another group that should be included in planning is the technical people who will be running the experiment. They often can lend a wealth of ideas to the effort. At the end of the experiment when the analysis is completed, be sure to report <u>first</u> to these knowledgeable workers for they will be able to see any big problems with the analysis since they have been intimate with the data.

EXPERIMENTAL PHASES

Once we have selected the factors for our experiment and written the goals and objectives, it is important that we embark on the experiment in phases or stages. If we were to put all our experimental resources into one basket and we discovered a hole in that basket near the end of the effort, we will have lost a quantity of resources; obtained poor (if any) information; and probably alienated our management against using experimental design techniques again.

The Phases Of Experimentation

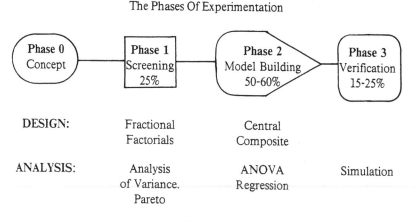

Figure 2-2

*Note on brainstorming: While the technique is simple, there have been a number of systems established to guide the process. You should have at least 4 or 5 people involved. Someone should take notes on a large pad so everyone can see. Don't use a chalkboard, since you will want to use the written information later. All people contribute and present one idea per round. If no ideas are available from a person on his or her round, a "pass" is an acceptable response. When everyone passes, then the session is considered over. The rules during brainstorming require that any idea is valid. No judgments may be made on the worth of an idea. After the brainstorming is over, the group can pass judgment and reduce the number of ideas to a workable handful. Other helps to brainstorming, such as "fish-bone" diagrams and "synectics" (The Practice of Creativity, by George M. Prince, Collier Books, 1972) provide a structure that enhances the basic technique.

The trick is to plan the experiment in phases. Each phase builds on the prior information of the earlier phase. A general rule of thumb says that no more than 25% of the total experimental resources should be spent in the first phase of experimentaiton. Figure 2-2 shows the phases of experimentation and indicates the possible experimental designs to be used in each phase. We will devote the remainder of this book to the "how-to" aspect of designing these experiments with the help of established statistical experimental designs (SED). The general approach to the phases of experimentation includes: CONCEPT; SCREENING; MODEL BUILDING; VERIFICATION.

PROBLEMS FOR CHAPTER 2

1. Pick an experimental situation from your experience (or invent one) and state the goal and objective.

2. List three quantitative response variables.

3. List three qualitative response variables. Attempt to quantify them.

APPENDIX 2

Essential for an experiment:

1. Knowledge of the process,
2. A response variable,
3. Clear GOALS and OBJECTIVES.

A response is what we measure and it must be:

1. Quantitative
2. Precise
3. Meaningful

A GOAL is the end result of a study applied to get results.
An OBJECTIVE is a statement of how the task will be accomplished.

EXAMPLE:

GOAL: Improve the life of an 80 grit sandpaper.
OBJECTIVE: To test the hypothesis that grit adhesion, grit wear, and paper wear are functions of adhesive type, adhesive thickness, grit size distribution, and paper basis weight.

The general form of an objective:

To test the hypothesis that (response(s)) is a function of (control variable(s))

GUIDELINES FOR BRAINSTORMING.

Suspend judgment

Strive for quantity

Generate wild ideas

Build on the ideas of others

Leaders Rules for Brainstorming

Be enthusiastic

Capture *all* the ideas

Make sure you have a good skills mix

Push for quantity

Strictly enforce the rules

Keep intensity high

Get participation from everybody

TEAM MAKE-UP

The Leader

Experts

"Semi" experts

Implementers

Technical staff who will run the experiment

EXPERIMENTAL DESIGN

OBJECTIVE OF EXPERIMENT:___To test the hypothesis that (response(s)) is/are a function of_____
 _(control variables)._____

_____

_____

DATE EXPERIMENT IS TO START_____

       END_____

1) How many independent factors are to be studied?_____

FACTOR	TYPE*	DIMENSIONS	RANGE OF INTEREST	LEVELS
1.				
2.				
3.				
4.				
5.				
6.				
7.				

2) How many Responses (dependent variables) are to be measured?_____

  List responses in order of importance as follows:

RESPONSE	TYPE*	DIMENSIONS	SIGNIFICANCE DIFFERENCE YOU WANT TO DETECT	αRISK	ESTIMATE OF STD. DEV.
1.					
2.					
3.					
4.					
5.					
6.					
7.					

3) How many runs do you want to make?_____maximum allowable?_____

4) How long does it take for one run?_____

5) Can all the treatment combinations be randomized?_____

  If not, which factors can't be?_____

*Put Q for qualitative (attibute) and C for quantitative.

## PART II

Statistical Experimental Designs

3

THE SEARCH FOR EFFICIENCY

So far, all we've said about an experiment is that it should be efficient and well thought out before execution. Since most people will buy this concept, where does statistical experimental design have any advantage over the basic, normal way experimenters have been doing business for centuries? Let's look at a long-established method (usually called the "classical one-factor-at-a-time" [1-F.A.T.] technique) and then see if it fits our definition of efficiency.

Suppose we have a chemical process that needs to be studied to improve the level of contamination in the end product. Our goal is to reduce the contaminants. There are three factors which we have good reason to believe are the main contributors to the contamination in the process. These are:

	Low Level	High Level
Pressure (P)	100 psi (P_0)	200 psi (P_1)
Temperature (T)	70 degrees (T_0)	90 degrees (T_1)
Time (t)	10 minutes (t_0)	20 minutes (t_1)

Our objective is to test the hypothesis that % contaminants is a function of pressure, temperature and time.

In running the individual tests in the experiment, we might follow this line of thinking. First, get a base line on the low values of each of the three factors and then make systematic changes to each of the factors, one-at-a-time. By taking the difference between the base case and each change, we can assess the effect of each factor on our response. Let's watch that process in action and observe the results.

23

The first test we run is the base line where all three factors are at their low values. The statistical jargon for this would say "run at their low <u>levels</u>". So a *level* is a value at which you set each of the factors in your experiment. The test that you run with each of the factors at each of its levels is called a **treatment combination** of factors or tc for short.

The next treatment combination we encounter would be to change one of the factors, say pressure, to its high level (while leaving the others at their low levels) and observe the % contamination. We would make similar one-at-a-time changes to the remaining two factors and end up with 4 treatment combinations which when analyzed in a simple manner will give the answers we wanted.

However, we do have a little bit of knowledge of statistics, and remembering from a long time ago, that it is better to look at average values, rather than single isolated points, we decide to repeat the experiment and produce the set of results shown in Table 3-1. We run the 4 treatments in 4 trials.

Table 3-1

Treatments			Trail 1	Trial 2	Trial 3	Trial 4	Average
P_0	T_0	t_0 #1	2.2	2.8	3.2	3.6	2.95
P_1	T_0	t_0 #2	3.4	3.9	4.3	4.7	4.07
P_0	T_1	t_0 #3	4.6	5.0	5.4	5.8	5.20
P_0	T_0	t_1 #4	3.7	4.1	4.5	4.9	4.30

If we look at the average difference between each of the changed treatments (#2,3,4) and the base case (#1) we observe the following:

The effect of pressure is 4.07 −2.95 = 1.12   ie: #2 − #1

The effect of temperature is 5.20 −2.95 = 2.25   ie: #3 − #1

The effect of time is 4.30 −2.95 = 1.35   ie: #4 − #1

The only statistics we have used so far is a simple average. Nothing too powerful, nor complicated. The real question is, have we designed our experiment efficiently? Did we get the required information? At this point we really can't judge the information part of the efficiency definition, since we haven't tried the results in a production situation. However, it looks like we are pretty close to learning how to control the process. It appears that we should stay at the low levels of each of the factors to keep the contamination to a low level since increasing each factor increased contamination.

What about the "least cost" aspect of efficiency? The least cost would have been to run only 4 treatment combinations and take the differences between single value responses. However, we notice that a strange thing is happening in this process. As we run more trials, the contamination builds up. Notice that the base case trial #4 is over 1.5 times as high in contamination as the first run. (i.e. 3.6 versus 2.2).

Checking into the actual records of the experiment, we find that the reaction container was too large and difficult to clean out between runs and thus the material that stuck to the walls of the container became part of the next batch that was run. This type of chemical reaction has the tendency to spill-over contamination into the next batch. What we are observing is a systematic build-up of contamination merely caused by not starting with a clean reactor. Since we ran our experiment in a systematic order of one complete trial, we have mixed up (or in the statistical jargon "confounded") the effect of cleaning (or not cleaning as in this case) with the factors under study. If cleaning has a large effect, as it seems to have here, the signal we wish to observe could be obliterated by the noise of the way we ran the experiment. What's worse, is the fact that the factor "time" is always last in the order of testing, and this is the condition when the worst carry-over contamination is present. Therefore, the effect of time on the contamination will be made up of any effect time really has and the accumulated effect of not cleaning the reaction container. Now do you think we have the *correct* required information?

To draw that conclusion we shall have to try another method of experimentation. Let us say for now, that the classical one-factor-at-a-time approach even with replicated trials is probably not the most efficient method of experimentation. We will have to discover efficiency in the next chapter.

APPENDIX 3

Definitions:

FACTOR	An item to which you make purposeful changes and observe a change in the response variable.
LEVEL	The value assigned to the changes in the factor.
TREATMENT COMBINATION	The levels of all of the factors at which a test run is made or simply the set of conditions for a test in an experiment. Abbreviation: tc.

REPLICATE   A repeat of a set of experimental conditions.
                                  Not a re-reading of a value, but an entire new
                                  run.

4

THE FACTORIAL 2 LEVEL DESIGN

In the one-factor-at-a-time (1-F.A.T.) experiments we looked at in Chapter 3, the analysis is performed on each result independently of the other results. This is an intuitive and logical approach to the assessment of changes in our responses as a result of the changes we make to the control factors we are studying. While this is ostensively logical, we still wonder if this 1-F.A.T. experimental approach obtains the required information.

The class of experimental designs we will investigate in this chapter may at first look complex in comparison with the 1-F.A.T.s, but we shall see that they are a simple extension of basic testing concepts. Let's look at the structure of the two level factorials and compare them with the 1-F.A.T. designs.

A set of experimental designs that can look at k factors in n observations, with each factor at two levels, is called the two level factorial design. In such a design the observations are not analyzed separately, but as an experimental unit to provide independent (or "orthogonal") assessments of the effects of each of the factors under study. The number of observations (tc) in such an experiment is given by taking the number of levels (2) to the power of the number of factors (k):

$$tc = 2^k \qquad (4\text{-}1)$$

Thus for a 3 factor experiment, there would be 2^3 or 8 observations (or in statistical terms, there would be 8 treatment combinations (tc). For 5 factors there would be 32 treatment combinations. In these designs we look at all possible combinations of the two levels.

Besides the formalities in naming the components of the experiments (factors, levels, treatment combinations, etc.) there are some conventions which are widely accepted for describing the experimental runs or treatments. In the last chapter, we used the very simple notation of a subscript to indicate the low (we used 0) and the high (we used 1) levels for the factors under study. Since we wish to obtain an analysis that will provide mathematically independent assessments of the effects of each of the factors and we would also like this analysis to be fairly easy to perform, we now introduce the concept of the orthogonal design. By properly coding the levels of our experiment into what we call "design units", we can accomplish our goals of having independent assessments and an easy analysis. The design units are mathematically coded values related directly to the physical values of the factors under study.

The coding method is not difficult. What we require is an experimental design in which the covariance of any pair of columns is zero. Covariance is a measure of the relationship between two variables. The larger the covariance, the more the variables are related to each other. If there is independence between a set of variables, then we observe zero covariance between the variables. This does not necessarily mean that the factors under study are physically independent. It only means that the mathematical analysis will produce independent results for each variable. The covariance looks much like the variance in its definition, but involves two variables rather than just one as with the variance.

Variance: $s^2 = \dfrac{\Sigma(x_i - \bar{x})^2}{n-1}$ n = # of x's   (4-2)

Covariance: $s_{xy} = \dfrac{\Sigma(x_i - \bar{x})(y_i - \bar{y})}{n-1}$ n = # of pairs of y's and x's   (4-3)

$\bar{x}$ is the average x
$\bar{y}$ is the average y

Note: These are defining formulas. There are easier calculation methods.

The method used to code the levels produces a set of **design** unit values consisting of − and + signs. These really represent the values −1 and +1 and are devised by taking the physical values of the factors under study and transforming them using the following method:

$$\frac{X - \bar{X}}{(X_{hi} - X_{lo})/2} \qquad (4\text{-}4)$$

Where: X is the value of the level, X_{hi} is the high level; X_{lo} is the low level and $\bar{X}$ is the average of X_{lo} and X_{hi}.

Thus by using 4-4 we can change the physical values of the factor under study to independent (mathematically) design unit values.

This coding works every time and as long as you have only two levels, the results will always be the same. You will get a -1 for the low level and a $+1$ for the high level of X. Let's illustrate the method with the factors in the experiment on % contamination from Chapter 3.

For the pressure factor, there were two levels, 100 and 200 psi. The average of these is 150 and the difference between the high and the low levels is 100. Therefore if we substitute these values into 4-4:

For the low level:
$$\frac{100-150}{(200-100)/2}$$

$$\frac{-50}{50} = -1$$

For the high level:
$$\frac{200-150}{(200-100)/2}$$

$$\frac{50}{50} = +1$$

This coding process begins to become trivial as soon as we realize that the values will always become $+1$ and -1, but upon analysis (as covered in Chapter 14) you will see that this coding will help us obtain that easy analysis we desire.

From the coding we have just developed, the convention of using the $-$ and $+$ signs has emerged. We can code (see problems) the other two variables similarly and thus produce an experimental design matrix. The matrix (Table 4-1) begins at first to look much like the design of a one-factor-at-a-time experiment. We note that there is a treatment combination with all the factors at their low levels (indicated by a row of minus signs). Next we change the first factor to plus while leaving the others at minus. Then we change the second factor to plus with the others at minus. But the next treatment combination is different! Here we change two factors at the same time. An engineer once remarked to me that everyone who knows anything about engineering realizes that in a test, you don't change two things at the same time, since you won't be able to discover which one make the change. How close to the truth and far from discovery was this poor chap. The truth is that in any single isolated test, my engineer friend is correct, but in an orthogonal, experimental design, we are not interested in the results of one treatment combination, but in the average change in the response over a number of experiments. Remember: An experiment is a set of coherent tests that are analyzed as a WHOLE to gain understanding of the process.

Table 4-1

A Pressure	B Temperature	C Time
−	−	−
+	−	−
−	+	−
+	+	−
−	−	+
+	−	+
−	+	+
+	+	+

Note the pattern in the columns of Table 4-1. The first column varies the plus and minus alternately, while the second column varies them in pairs and the third in fours. In general, we can reduce the pattern of − and + signs in any column to a formula:

The number of like signs in a set $= 2^{n-1}$ (4-5)

Where n is the column #

$$for\ n\ =\ 1,\ 2^{1-1}\ =\ 2^0\ =\ 1$$
$$for\ n\ =\ 2,\ 2^{2-1}\ =\ 2^1\ =\ 2$$
$$for\ n\ =\ 3,\ 2^{3-1}\ =\ 2^2\ =\ 4$$
$$for\ n\ =\ 4,\ 2^{4-1}\ =\ 2^3\ =\ 8$$
$$etc.$$

The convention of alternating − 's and + 's produces an order in the experimental design which is useful in the design and analysis. It is called Yates order after the British statistician. There are other conventions in such designs that we shall study. The next convention helps us identify each run or treatment combination.

We can identify each of the treatment combinations with a unique letter or combination of letters (Table 4-2). To do so, we name each column by an upper case letter of the alphabet. Whenever there is a plus sign appearing in a row under a letter, we bring that letter over to the left to create a new column called the treatment combination (tc) identity column. To illustrate, for the first treatment combination (row), there are no + signs and just to show that we observed this, we put a 1 in the tc identifier column. The next row has a + in the A column, so an "a" (lower case by convention) goes in the tc column. The next entry is a "b", while the fourth row is both "a" and "b" to give "ab". The remainder of the entries follow the same pattern.

Table 4-2

tc	A	B	C	Row
1	−	−	−	1
a	+	−	−	2
b	−	+	−	3
ab	+	+	−	4
c	−	−	+	5
ac	+	−	+	6
bc	−	+	+	7
abc	+	+	+	8

By using the logic behind the construction of the tc identifier column in reverse, we can produce the plus and minus table when given just the identifiers in the proper Yates order. The Yates order for the tc's can also be generated without the plus and minus matrix. To do so, first place a "1" at the top of a column. Now multiply the first letter of the alphabet by this "1" to produce the second entry. The scheme repeats by multipling each new entry (letter of the alphabet) by the existing entries. The next letter of the alphabet (b) is multiplied by 1 to get "b" and then by "a" to get "ab". We now have 1, a, b, ab which when multiplied by the next letter, "c", produces c, ac, bc, abc and this then completes the tc column of the table (4-2).

In many publications (Reference 1) on two level factorial designs, the treatment combination identifiers are the only pieces of information given and the designs are completed by the user who places + signs in the columns of the letters that appear in the tc identifier for that particular row of design, and − signs in all other positions. Therefore, if I have "acd" for my identifier, there will be a + in the A, C, D columns for that treatment combination, and a − in the B column.

	A	B	C	D
acd	+	−	+	+

The treatment combination identifiers have a practical, mundane aspect also. They uniquely identify the experimental run you are making. Therefore, in labeling the results of the run (the label on the sample bottle, the marking on the test copy, etc.) you should use the tc identifier rather than the sequence number (which is not necessarily unique) or the full description of the run (which is cumbersome). An entire experiment worth 1/2 million dollars was almost lost by using sequence numbers as identifiers. The experimenters changed the sequence and a lot of scrambling was required to reconstruct the true identity of the tests!

Thus far, we have merely shown the mechanics of the construction of the two level factorial designs. It certainly looks like more work to build and understand these designs than the simple one-factor-at-a-time types shown before. What is the gain in efficiency in using these designs?

The first thing you may notice as a difference between the design in Table 4-1 and the design in Table 3-1 is that there are 4 more treatment combinations in the factorial (Table 4-1) than in the one-at-a-time design (Table 3-1). Certainly, from a resources viewpoint, the factorial is less efficient. We have questioned the efficiency of the one-at-a-time method for its ability to get the required information. Let's see if the four extra resource units in the more "expensive" factorial really get us any more information over the simpler method.

If you recall, there was a problem with residual contamination build-up in the chemical reaction example we were studying. Therefore, in this factorial experiment, we will not use the set of treatments in the order of the design, but <u>randomize</u> the running of the experiment. This randomization will assure that any treatment combination has an equally likely change of appearing first in the running order and that the remaining tc's are equally likely to appear in any subsequent run order positions. Randomization can be done by simply creating a lottery by writing the tc identifiers on pieces of paper and drawing them from a "hat", or by using a table of random numbers or a random order program as supplied in the appendix. By randomizing, we now have the original tc's in the order of Table 4-3 for the actual running of the experiment. To run the experiment, read the conditions row wise. For Run #1, the c condition, we would have Low Pressure (A), Low Temperature (B), and high time (C). (See Table 4-2 to confirm these levels).

Table 4-3

Random Order	tc	% Contamination
1	c	4.1
2	1	2.6
3	a	3.9
4	abc	3.2
5	ac	1.7
6	b	4.4
7	ab	8.0
8	bc	7.8

After the actual running of the experiment, we must put the results back into Yates order for our analysis. We shall go through a simple analysis at this point, and in Chapter 14 show a more analytical approach to separating the signal from the noise.

For this analysis we shall write (in Table 4-4) the entire + and − matrix which will include all of the factors we are able to draw conclusions about from the design. You

THE FACTORIAL 2 LEVEL DESIGN

will easily recognize the first three factor columns, but the last 4 are new. In setting up a design, we do not write any columns beyond the main factors. These "new" columns are only needed for the analysis.

Table 4-4

Random Order	tc	SINGLE FACTORS			INTERACTIONS				% Contamination
		A	B	C	AB	AC	BC	ABC	
2	1	−	−	−	+	+	+	−	2.6
3	a	+	−	−	−	−	+	+	3.9
6	b	−	+	−	−	+	−	+	4.4
7	ab	+	+	−	+	−	−	−	8.0
1	c	−	−	+	+	−	−	+	4.1
5	ac	+	−	+	−	+	−	−	1.7
8	bc	−	+	+	−	−	+	−	7.8
4	abc	+	+	+	+	+	+	+	3.2

Let's look at the first three Single Factor columns since these produce a direct comparison with the resuls in the one-at-a-time-design. First, notice that there is more than only one change from the "base case" for each of the factors. Factor C, the time, is found at its high level 4 times and at its low level 4 times also! Looking a little closer, we see that the pattern of + and − signs for factors A and B is exactly the same for the 4 low C's (−) and the four high C's (+). If we first assume that the effects of A and B are exactly the same over the two levels of C and secondly C is mathematically independent of factors A and B, then we can "sum over" factors A and B (treat them as if there were no variation induced by them) and then find the average difference between the low level of C and its high level. The first assumption depends upon the physical reality of the situation. For the moment we shall make this assumption and return to a verification later. The second assumption is easy to check and the results are general for all the two level factorial designs (even the fractional factorials in the next chapter). Recall, that mathematically independent factors demonstrate this quality by having zero covariance . By using equation 4-3 we can show that there is zero covariance between all the factors (see homework problem 4-9).

The same logic concerning independence that we just applied to factor C applies to factors A and B so we now can find the average differences for the three single factors by summing the responses at the low levels (−'s) and the high levels (+'s) and take the difference of the average.   To illustrate, we will continue using factor C since in this design it is the most clear-cut example. (All the minus signs are grouped together and all the plus signs are grouped together).

C low (−)	C high (+)
2.6	4.1
3.9	1.7
4.4	7.8
8.0	3.2
18.9	16.8

Average = 4.73   4.20

Difference in averages (4.20 − 4.73) is −0.53 (for C).
For Factor A (Pressure) the difference −0.53.
For Factor B (Temperature) difference 2.77.

These results are different from the result we calculated in the one-at-a-time design in Chapter 3.   The effects of pressure and time are reversed and the effect of temperature is just a bit greater. But there is even more to look at. Now is the time to inspect   the "interaction" columns which contain the remaining required information in this experiment.

PLOTTING INTERACTIONS

We can compute effects for interactions in the same way we compute effects for main factors. Simply add up the responses at the plus levels and at the minus levels for the interactions, find the averages, and take the differencs of these averages. Since there seems something unusual in the way factors A and C work together, let's take the AC interaction column and find the effect of the AC interaction.

This AC interaction column is generated by taking the algebraic product of column A times column C. The first entry is a + which is the product of a − times a −. The remaining 7 signs of AC are created in the same way. The sum of the responses at the plus values for the AC interaction is 11.9 and the sum of the responses at the minus values is 23.8. This produces an average difference of 2.98 which is an even greater effect than that Factor B which was the largest of the single factors. Indeed, there is something going on with the combination or "interaction" of factors A and C.

The easiest way to understand an interaction is to plot the results in an interaction graph which is an iso-plot of the response variable for one of the factors over changes in the other factor. To plot figure 4-1 we build a two-way table (4-5) for the interaction factors.

Table 4-5

Factor A

	Low Level —		High Level +	
Low Level —	2.6		3.9	
		3.50		5.95
	4.4		8.0	
Factor C				
High Level +	4.1		1.7	
		5.95		2.45
	7.8		3.2	

The underlined values are the averages of the cells which are made up of the responses corresponding to the combination of Factors A and C. For instance, the entry in Table 4-5 with the average of 2.45 (high A & high C) comes from the responses in Table 4-4. The value 1.7 is the "ac" treatment and corresponds to the event when A and C are both at their + levels. The 3.2 value is the second time in this experiment that A and C are both + together. The interaction graph can be plotted with either factor as the iso-level factor and in some cases it is informative to plot two graphs as shown in Figure 4-1 using each factor as the iso-level.

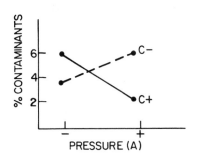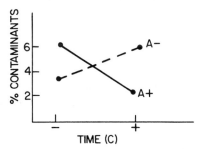

Figure 4-1

In this case, the plots are quite similar in shape. Both have been plotted to show the method. More important than the method of plotting, is the result of this experiment. The discovery made in this experiment is graphically displayed in the interaction plots (Figure 4-1). The level of contamination varies with both pressure and the time of the reaction. Increasing one factor by itself while the other stays at a low level gives a higher level of contamination than if both factors are increased. The type of interaction or superadditivity shown is common in physical and chemical ractions and is a very important piece of information. Since we never ran the treatment combinations which involved the changing of two factors at the same time in the one-at-a-time design in Chapter 3, the opportunity to make this discovery was passed by. Thus, the one-at-a-time experiment did not produce the required information.

COST

There is still the other half of the definition of efficiency related to cost. The factorial design in this particular experiment gives the effects of a factor for the average difference. This average is made up of 4 items in this particular 3 factor investigation. If we wanted to get the same degree of certainty in the results from the one-factor-at-a-time experiment it would be necessary to replicate the experiment 4 times so when we looked at average differences, we would have 4 items involved in the average. In Chapter 3 we did just that and it took 16 treatment combinations to get the job done. That is, there were 4 different set-ups (the base case and the one change each in each of the 3 factors) which had to be repeated 4 times each to get the averages. In the factorial design we make more efficient use of the tc's by using the runs more than once in our computations. We are allowed to do this because the factors are mathematically orthogonal (independent) and balanced. Based on the criterion of resources alone, the work in the one-at-a-time experiment is 16 units while the work in the factorial is 8 units. This means that the factorial is twice as efficient as the 1-fat. In general, as the number of factors increases the efficiency factor goes up. Table 4-6 shows efficiencies for up to 7 factors which is about as many that we can handled in one experiment without resorting to other methods we shall study in Chapter 5.

Table 4-6

# Factors	Factorial # tc's	# tc's Times # In Average	One-At-A-Time Factorial # In Average	Efficiency
3	8	4	$4*4 = 16$	2
4	16	8	$5*8 = 40$	2.5
5	32	16	$6*16 = 96$	3
6	64	32	$7*32 = 224$	3.5
7	128	64	$8*64 = 512$	4

The two level factorial design is a very efficient method of getting the information we require. It gets the required information at the least expenditure of resources. Besides standing on its own as an excellent method of experimental organization, it forms the backbone of many of the more advanced methods of efficient experimentation which we shall study in the next chapters.

PROBLEMS FOR CHAPTER 4

1. Build a table showing the number of treatment combinations for two level experiments with 3 to 10 factors.

2. Compute the covariance for the following sets of X and Y values:

SET #1		SET #2		SET #3	
X	Y	X	Y	X	Y
−1.0	2	5	3	1	7
−0.5	4	6	1	2	6
0.0	6	8	4	3	5
0.5	8	9	5	4	4
1.0	10	1	6	5	3
				6	2
				7	1

3. Set up the coding for plus and minus signs using expression 4-4 for the following two factors (ie.: change the physical units to design units):

	Low Level	High Level
Temperature	70°	90°
Time	10 min	20 min

4. Set up an experiment in design units for the following problem:

Temperature (A)	90°	200°
Speed (B)	70 ft/min	120 ft/min
Chemical (C)	0.5 grams/liter	40 grams/liter

5. From the following treatment combination identifiers, set up the plus and minus sign table for this two level design:

   1, a, b, ab, c, ac, bc, abc, d, ad, bd, adb, cd, acd, bcd, abcd

6. Put the following tc's in Yates order: ab, b, c, a, 1, abc, bc, ac.

7. Use the results in Table 4-4 to compute the effects of the 4 iteractions.

8. Plot the interaction graph for the BC interaction from Table 4-4.

9. Compute the covariance between all single effects in a 2^3 factorial design.

10. Compute the covariance between the AC interaction and the BC interaction in a 2^3 factorial design.

APPENDIX 4

DEFINITIONS:

Orthogonal	Independent mathematically
Orthogonal Design	An experimental design constructed to allow independent analysis of each single factor and the interactions between all factors.
Coding	A mathematical technique used to force the treatment combinations in a design into orthogonality.
Covariance	The covariation of two factors as defined by the average product of the differences from the mean:

$$s_{xy} = \frac{\Sigma(x_i - x)(y_i - y)}{n-1}$$

Design Units	Mathematical representations of the levels of the factors in an orthogonal design. These are selected to create the orthogonality.

For the 2 level design the coding to give the design units is:

$$\frac{X - \bar{X}}{(X_{hi} - H_{lo})/2}$$

Interaction	A result of the non-additivity of two or more factors on the response variable. The situation where the change in a response (its slope) differs depending on the level of the other factor or factors.

FORMULAS:

There are n treatment combinations in a two level factorial design equal to:

$$tc = 2^k \text{ where k is the number of factors}$$

We use a " $-$ " sign for the low level of a factor and a " $+$ " sign for the high level of a factor.

The columns of $-$ and $+$ signs alternate these signs according to:

$$\text{The \# of like signs in a set} = 2^{n-1}$$
Where n is the column number

RANDOM ORDER PROGRAM

```
110 PRINT "HOW MANY NUMBERS DO YOU WANT IN RANDOM ORDER";
120 INPUT T
125 DIM X(500)
130 FOR I=1 TO T
140 X(I)=0
145 NEXT I
150 L=1
160 U=T
165 PRINT "HERE THEY ARE!!"
170 L=L-1
175 U=U+.5
180 J=INT((RND(-1)*(U-L)))
185 IF J=0 THEN 188
186 J=J+L
187 GO TO 190
188 J=1+L
190 K=J-L
191 IF X(K)=0 THEN 200
195 GO TO 180
200 PRINT J;
201 J=J-L
205 X(J)=1
210 Z=0
212 FOR I=1 TO T
214 Z=Z+X(I)
216 NEXT I
220 IF Z=T THEN 240
230 GO TO 180
240 END
>
```

```
RUN
12:09    FEB 12   RANDOM...
HOW MANY NUMBERS DO YOU WANT IN RANDOM ORDER  ?16
HERE THEY ARE!!
 2    7    12    3    8    11    6    10    9    4    1    13    5    14    15
 16
     240 HALT
>
```

```
RUN
12:09    FEB 12   RANDOM...
HOW MANY NUMBERS DO YOU WANT IN RANDOM ORDER  ?8
HERE THEY ARE!!
 7    1    2    5    3    8    6    4
     240 HALT
>
```

```
RUN
12:10    FEB 12   RANDOM...
HOW MANY NUMBERS DO YOU WANT IN RANDOM ORDER  ?32
HERE THEY ARE!!
 23    6    20    1    11    28    4    25    19    16    27    24    30
 29    2    5    14    12    3    17    15    8    22    9    18    7    10
 31    13    21    26    32
     240 HALT
```

TOKAY   COMPUTER PROGRAM

```
100 DIM N$(10),L$(2,5),               D(32),S(5,32)
105 DIM R(32)
110 I9=0
120 FOR I=1 TO 5
140 READ N$(I)
160 NEXT I
180 DATA A,B,C,D,E
200 PRINT "HOW MANY FACTORS(NO MORE THAN 5)";
220 INPUT N
240 IF N>5 THEN 200
245 PRINT "HOW MANY REPLICATES";
250 INPUT R4
260 FOR I=1 TO N
280 PRINT "WHAT IS THE NAME OF FACTOR";N$(I);"?(USE 6 LETTER ABBREV.)"
300 INPUT N$(5+I)
320 PRINT "WHAT IS THE LOW LEVEL OF";N$(I+5);
340 INPUT L$(1,I)
360 PRINT "WHAT IS THE HIGH LEVEL OF";N$(I+5);
380 INPUT L$(2,I)
400 NEXT I
420 DIM T$(32)
440 FOR I=1 TO 32
460 READ T$(I)
480 NEXT I
500 PRINT
520 PRINT
540 DATA (1),A,B,AB,C,AC,BC,ABC,D,AD,BD,ABD,CD,ACD,BCD,ABCD
560 DATA E,AE,BE,ABE,CE,ACE,BCE,ABCE,DE,ADE,BDE,ABDE,CDE,ACDE,BCDE,ABCDE
580 FOR I=1 TO 5
600 FOR J=1 TO 32
620 READ S(I,J)
640 NEXT J
660 NEXT I
680 DATA -1 +1 -1 +1 -1 +1 -1 +1 -1 +1 -1 +1 -1 +1 -1 +1 -1 +1 -1 +1 -1 +1 -1 +
1 -1 +1 -1 +1 -1 +1 -1 +1
700 DATA -1 -1 +1 +1 -1 -1 +1 +1 -1 -1 +1 +1 -1 -1 +1 +1 -1 -1 +1 +1 -1 -1 +1 +
1 -1 -1 +1 +1 -1 -1 +1 +1
720 DATA -1 -1 -1 -1 +1 +1 +1 +1 -1 -1 -1 -1 +1 +1 +1 +1 -1 -1 -1 -1 +1 +1 +1 +
1 -1 -1 -1 -1 +1 +1 +1 +1
760 DATA -1 -1 -1 -1 -1 -1 -1 -1 +1 +1 +1 +1 +1 +1 +1 +1 -1 -1 -1 -1 -1 -1 -1 -
1 +1 +1 +1 +1 +1 +1 +1 +1
780 DATA -1 -1 -1 -1 -1 -1 -1 -1 -1 -1 -1 -1 -1 -1 -1 -1 +1 +1 +1 +1 +1 +1 +1 +
1 +1 +1 +1 +1 +1 +1 +1 +1
790 PRINT "        2**K FACTORIAL IN YATES ORDER"
800 PRINT
820 PRINT "RUN #   TC  ";
840 FOR I=1 TO N
860 PRINT N$(I+5);
880 NEXT I
900 PRINT
920 PRINT
940 IF I9=1 GOTO 1340
960 GOSUB 1700
965 O1=1
970 FOR K1=1 TO R4
980 FOR I=1 TO 2**N
1000 PRINT TAB(2)""O(O1)""TAB(9)T$(I);
1020 I5=18
1030 O1=O1+1
1040 FOR J=1 TO N
1060 IF S(J,I)=+1 THEN 1120
1080 K=1
1100 GOTO 1140
1120 K=2
1140 PRINT TAB(I5) L$(K,J);
1160 I5=I5+7
```

```
1180 NEXT J
1200 PRINT
1220 PRINT
1240 NEXT I
1250 NEXT K1
1260 PRINT
1280 PRINT
1300 PRINT "          2**K FACTORIAL IN RANDOM ORDER"
1320 I9=1
1325 O1=1
1330 GOTO 800
1340 FOR K1=1 TO R4
1344 FOR I=1 TO 2**N
1345 L=O(O1)
1346 O1=O1+1
1350 R(L)=I
1355 NEXT I
1356 NEXT K1
1380 FOR I=1 TO (2**N)*R4
1400 L=R(I)
1420 PRINT TAB(2) ""I"" TAB(9) T$(L);
1440 I5=18
1460 FOR J=1 TO N
1480 IF S(J,L)=+1 THEN 1540
1500 K=1
1520 GOTO 1560
1540 K=2
1560 PRINT TAB(I5) L$(K,J);
1580 I5=I5+7
1600 NEXT J
1620 PRINT
1640 PRINT
1660 NEXT I
1680 END
1700 REM RANDOM ORDER SUBROUTINE
1720 I4=1
1740 T=(2**N)*R4
1760 DIM X(T)
1780 FOR I=1 TO T
1800 X(I)=0
1820 NEXT I
1840 L=1
1860 U=T
1880 L=L-1
1900 U=U+.5
1920 J=INT((RND(1)*(U-L)))
1940 IF J=0 THEN 2000
1960 J=J+L
1980 GO TO 2020
2000 J=1+L
2020 K=J-L
2040 IF X(K)=0 THEN 2080
2060 GO TO 1920
2080 O(I4)=J
2100 I4=I4+1
2120 J=J-L
2140 X(J)=1
2150 Z=0
2160 FOR I=1 TO T
2165 Z=Z+X(I)
2170 NEXT I
2180 IF Z=T THEN 2220
2200 GO TO 1920
2220 RETURN
```

EXAMPLE OF TOKAY PROGRAM

```
RUN
12:15   FEB 12   TOKAY...
HOW MANY FACTORS(NO MORE THAN 5)   ?3
HOW MANY REPLICATES    ?1
WHAT IS THE NAME OF FACTOR   A    ?(USE 6 LETTER ABBREV.)
?FACT.A
WHAT IS THE LOW LEVEL OF   FACT.A   ?LO
WHAT IS THE HIGH LEVEL OF    FACT.A   ?HI
WHAT IS THE NAME OF FACTOR   B    ?(USE 6 LETTER ABBREV.)
?FACT.B
WHAT IS THE LOW LEVEL OF   FACT.B   ?-
WHAT IS THE HIGH LEVEL OF    FACT.B   ?+
WHAT IS THE NAME OF FACTOR   C    ?(USE 6 LETTER ABBREV.)
?FACT.C
WHAT IS THE LOW LEVEL OF   FACT.C   ?100
WHAT IS THE HIGH LEVEL OF    FACT.C   ?200
```

2**K FACTORIAL IN YATES ORDER

RUN #	TC	FACT.A	FACT.B	FACT.C
6	(1)	LO	−	100
1	A	HI	−	100
4	B	LO	+	100
2	AB	HI	+	100
3	C	LO	−	200
5	AC	HI	−	200
8	BC	LO	+	200
7	ABC	HI	+	200

2**K FACTORIAL IN RANDOM ORDER

RUN #	TC	FACT.A	FACT.B	FACT.C
1	A	HI	−	100
2	AB	HI	+	100
3	C	LO	−	200
4	B	LO	+	100
5	AC	HI	−	200
6	(1)	LO	−	100
7	ABC	HI	+	200
8	BC	LO	+	200

5

FRACTIONAL FACTORIALS AT 2 LEVELS

In Chapter 4 we studied a method of extracting the required information in the form of the main (single) effects of the factors under study and the interactions of these factors. We will now raise a question concerning the cost aspect from our definition of an efficient experiment. We must always keep in mind the balance that must be maintained between information and cost. To develop this point, we shall examine a rather trivial example and then expand into a real, extensive experiment. Before these examples, we will look at the information content of 2^k factorials in general.

If we were to study only 3 factors, then there would be 3 single effects and 4 interactions possible. With 4 factors, there are four single effects and 11 interactions. Table 5-1 shows how the number of treatment combinations and information increases as the number of factors increases.

Table 5-1

k Factors	2k	Single Factors	2 Factor Interactions	3 Factor Interactions	4 Factor Interactions	5 Factor Interactions	6 Factor Interactions
5	32	5	10	10	5	1	—
6	64	6	15	20	15	6	1
7	128	7	21	35	35	21	7
8	256	8	28	56	70	56	28

In general, you find the number of interactions by using the combinations formula:

$$C_h^k = \frac{k!}{(k-h)!(h!)} \qquad (5\text{-}1)$$

Where: k = # of factors
h = # of factors in interaction

Thus for a 10 factor experiment the number of four factor interactions is given by:

$$C_4^{10} = \frac{10!}{(10-4)!(4!)} = 210 \qquad (5\text{-}2)$$

Now that is a lot of information on four factor interactions! However, four factor interactions are quite rare. In such a 10 factor experiment, we need to spend 210 degrees of freedom (each degree of freedom is a measure of work and information) in determining what is most likely zero information!! Now that is not efficient. The most likely interactions expected to take place are some of the 45 two factor, or first order interactions. If we add in the 10 single effects, we find that all we need are 55 degrees of freedom to describe the required information in this situation. The 2^{10} experiment has 1024 treatment combinations or about 18 times the volume of information we need to do the job efficiently.

Results like these lead us to the conclusion that the 2 level factorial is not efficient when the number of factors increases above 5 or 6. Since many of our problems are likely to contain more than 5 factors, we need a method to get at the required information with the least cost. If we can come up with a method that uses a fraction of the treatement combinations we can accomplish that goal. We want to decrease the volume of work and information while still obtaining the required information.

Let us take a very simple example and then expand upon it to the point where we can understand and observe the value of the method. Suppose, that we wish to find the weight of three objects A, B and C. In any normal weighing operation, we would place the objects on the balance one at a time to find the weights. In a full factorial design, however, we would need 2^3 or 8 treatment combinations to accomplish the same goal. However, think about the information that will emerge from the full factorial beyond the "effect" of placing the objects on the scale. We will be able to find the interactions of AB, AC, BC and ABC. Consider the fact that in weighing an object, the weight of that object will not change if it is alone on the balance or if it has other objects with it. Therefore, there can be no interactions in this experiment. If we should run the full experiment, any effects for the interactions can only be attributed to random error, since the effects of these interactions will be zero according to physical laws. If these interactions are zero and we have a fairly errorless system for weighing, what good are these pieces of information? They are actually worthless. It appears that a full factorial is not efficient since we have empty information and the cost is excessive. So how do we become efficient?

First, we determine the number of treatment combinations necessary to obtain the required information. In this case we need to find three weights with a degree of freedom for each weight. Since in every experiment, we need one degree of freedom for the grand mean, the least amount of work to run this experiment is 4 treatments. That just happens to be half the number of weighings needed by the full factorial design. We need a 1/2 fractional factorial design. To set up such a design we revert to the basic building-block of a full factorial design. Table 5-2 shows the matrix for a 2^2 design for Factors A and B. We also show the AB interaction column in this matrix.

Table 5-2

tc	A	B	AB
(1)	–	–	+
a	+	–	–
b	–	+	–
ab	+	+	+

Now the full factorial still shows a two factor interaction (AB). Since we have ruled out all interactions, we still have excess information. Let's turn that excess AB interaction information into something we can use. Since the effect of the AB interaction is zero, we can equate this empty interaction with the information we wish to obtain about Factor C. That is, we will make C equivalent to AB by using the signs of the AB interaction column to describe the presence or absence of object C on the balance just as in the A and B columns. Table 5-3 shows the new design.

Table 5-3

tc	A	B	C
(c)	–	–	+
a	+	–	–
b	–	+	–
ab(c)	+	+	+

Note that the "tc" labels have changed. Instead of the usual "1" in the first entry, we have "(c)". The use of parentheses is a convention to indicate that Factor C is not a part of the full factorial base design, but a part of the fractional design. This convention distinguishes a fractional factorial from a full factorial and in no way means that Factor C is inferior to the other factors with respect to its information detection ability. *The information detection ability of all the factors is equivalent in a fractional factorial design.* We will now introduce an algebraic system which will help to identify the information in the experiment.

Recall how the fractional factorial was created. We made the AB interaction effect equivalent with the factor C effect. That is we have mathematically combined the two effects. The statistical word for this combining is <u>confounding</u>. We can write this as an equivalence:

$$C \equiv AB \qquad\qquad (5\text{-}3)$$

Note that we use triple line sign and not the equal sign. This indicates that the measure of the effects are equivalent, but not necessarily equal. In fact, in some cases, it is possible for one effect to be negative and the other positive and the measured result can be zero, since the measured effect is the algebraic sum or the linear combination of the two independent effects. The effects remain independent physically, but the fractional factorial design has mathematically combined or confounded them in such a way that it is impossible to assess their effects independently. Of course, in the weighing experiment, there are no interactions and thus we are able to extract the physical interpretation out of the confounded mathematical result.

The system which defines all the confounding in a fractional factorial design is based on a modulo 2 algebra system. Relationship 5-3 forms the basis of the fractional factorial or what we shall call the <u>generator</u> of the design. From this generator, we derive a relationship call the <u>defining contrast</u>. We now need to introduce some terms and rules to make the system work.

Define "I" as the identity symbol. (In regular algebra the number 1 is the identity).

Modulo Algebra Rules:

1. The identity (I) symbol appears only on the left side of the equivalence sign.

2. Any even power of a term (modulo 2) becomes the identity (although the symbol (I) never is expressed on the right side of the equivalence).

3. Any terms times the identity (I) is that term. (Same as in regular algebra).

An example will illustrate these rules:

The Generator, $C \equiv AB$
and when multiplied through by C gives: $C^2 \equiv ABC$
Which according to Rule #2 produces $I \equiv ABC$ $\qquad\qquad (5\text{-}4)$

Expression 5-4 is the <u>defining contrast</u> which is used in determining the entire set of confounded effects in the design. We multiply the defining contrast through for each main factor (A, B, C) and apply Rule #3 of the modulo algebra to the left side of the equivalency and Rule #2 to the right side of the equivalency.

$$AI \equiv A^2BC \quad \text{which is } A \equiv BC$$
$$BI \equiv AB^2C \quad \text{which is } B \equiv AC$$
$$CI \equiv ABC^2 \quad \text{which is } C \equiv AB$$

The last result (C $\equiv$ AB) is the generator (5-3) of the design and shows that the algebra works in both directions.

In the above experiment, all main effects are confounded with two factor interactions. In any other experiment, this would be an undesirable situation, since two factor interactions are likely to exist. (Of course in this weighing experiment, the interactions are physically impossible.) In general, we need a set of rules to determine priorities in what may be confounded in fractional designs.

CONFOUNDING RULES

1. Do not confound main factors with each other.
2. Do not confound main factors with two factor interactions.
3. Do not confound two factor interactions with each other.

These rules are listed in descending priority and in many cases, Rule #2 and #3 may sometimes be violated. Rule #1 should never be violated.

FRACTIONALIZATION ELEMENT

Before getting into the larger and more realistic fractional factorial designs, let us present the remaining conventions involved with designating fractional factorials. The name given to this type of design is a "2^{k-p}" where k is the number of factors and p is the fractionalizing element of the design. The result of subtracting p from k gives n the power for the number of Levels (2). The 2^{k-p} gives the number of treatement combinations in the design. Usually we know the number of factors and the maximum number of tc's we can economically afford and thus the p is determined. In the case of the weighing experiment p = 1, and our design was a 2^{3-1}. We can use the p to determine the fraction of the whole factorial we are using by taking $1/2^p$. If we have a 2^{6-2}, then this is a $1/2^2$ or a 1/4 fractional factorial, with 2^4 (16) treatment combinations. Also, there will be p generators for the designs and 2^p terms (counting "I") in the defining contrast. These last two pieces of information are important in designing fractions smaller than the very simple 1/2 fractional factorial where there is only one generator and 2 terms in the defining contrast.

MORE FACTORS - - SMALLER FRACTIONS

The weighing example represents the fewest number of factors and the smallest fractional design possible. For real experimental work this design is not at all good, since it violates the confounding rules. For the most part, a general rule of thumb says that the smallest fractional design that is possible is one that has 8 treatment combinations. The base full factorial for such a design would be a 2^3 with factors A, B, C:

Table 5-4

tc	A	B	C	ABC=D
(1)	−	−	−	−
a	+	−	−	+
b	−	+	−	+
ab	+	+	−	−
c	−	−	+	+
ac	+	−	+	−
bc	−	+	+	−
abc	+	+	+	+

Let us define a new factor D as equivalent to the ABC interaction. The generator of this fractional factorial design is then:

$$D \equiv ABC \tag{5-6}$$

and the defining contrast is:

$$I \equiv ABCD \tag{5-7}$$

In such a design, by using the modulo algebra, we find that:

$$
\begin{array}{ll}
A \equiv BCD & AB \equiv CD \\
B \equiv ACD & AC \equiv BD \\
C \equiv ABD & AD \equiv BC \\
D \equiv ABC &
\end{array}
$$

These are all the effects we may find in this experiment, since there are 8 treatment combinations and thus 7 degrees of freedom for determining effects. Note that the main factors are confounded with three-factor interactions, but the two-factor interactions are confounded with each other. This is the smallest design we may use to determine main effects and is usually reserved for first cut or screening experiments. We can go one step further and add still another factor to this design to create the matrix in table 5-5.

Table 5-5

tc	A	B	C	ABC≡D	BC≡E
(e)	–	–	–	–	+
a(de)	+	–	–	+	+
b(d)	–	+	–	+	–
ab	+	+	–	–	–
c(d)	–	–	+	+	–
ac	+	–	+	–	–
bc(e)	–	+	+	–	+
abc(de)	+	+	+	+	+

This is a 2^{5-2} fractional factorial. Thus with a "p" of 2, the fraction is $\frac{1}{2}^2$ or a ¼ fraction. We can observe in Table 5-5 that there are 2 generators in the design:

$$D \equiv ABC$$
$$E \equiv BC$$

These generators were chosen with little freedom, since the base design is so small. There will be 2^p $(2^2 = 4)$ terms in the defining contrast. Here is where the modulo algebra can get difficult. To determine the terms in the defining contrast, start out as usual by multiplying through by the term in the left side of the equivalency of the generators to make the left side the identity:

$$DD \equiv ABCD \qquad \text{or} \qquad I \equiv ABCD$$
$$EE \equiv BCE \qquad \text{or} \qquad I \equiv BCE$$

Combine to give: $I = ABCD, BCE$ (there is only one "I" per defining contrast).

This gives only 3 terms (I,ABCD,BCE). The fourth term is obtained by multiplying the terms on the right side together.

$ABCD*BCE$ gives AB^2C^2DE or ADE and then $I \equiv ABDC, BCE, ADE$ becomes the 4-term defining contrast for the design in Table 5-5.

Upon examination, we find that in this design we have main factors confounded with two factor interactions and this would only be appropriate as a screening design where we would not expect any interactions. Since interactions are the way of nature, this design is inadequate and we must search for a design that can remain efficient by obtaining the required information.

If we were to continue to design and check for efficiency in a sort of groping manner, we might spend a lifetime searching for that elusive design that is just right for the situation. There is a short-cut that can guide us into the proper area and then after a check-out, give us the answer we desire.

LOGICAL APPROACH

The short-cut makes use of Table 5-1, where we analyzed the information content of various designs. Let us say that we need to characterize a process in which we expect two-factor interactions to be present along with the usual main effects. There are 7 factors that we determine to be important in this process. Table 5-1 shows that a full factorial design would require 128 treatments to get all of the information. We only require a fraction of this information, so we go to a fractional design.

The question is what fraction? A half, a quarter, an eighth? If we look back at Table 5-1 notice that the total degrees of freedom necessary to determine the main effects and two-factor interactions comes to 28. That means we need a design that has 29 treatment combinations rather than 128. The closest design we have in integer powers of 2 is a 2^5 or 32 treatments. Thus, the "p" fractionalizing element of the design is $7-5=2$. We have a ¼ fractional factorial with 2^2 terms in the defining contrast, and two generators. The choice of the generators is important. Table 5-6 shows the base design and some possible generators.

If we were to take $F \equiv ABCDE$ and $G \equiv BCDE$, then the defining contrast will be:

$$I \equiv ABCDEF, BCDEG, AFG$$

We immediately see that in the "AFG" part of the defining contrast, there is main factor and two factor interaction confounding. This generator set is not appropriate for the information we seek. There are adequate degrees of freedom to get main effects free of two-factor interactions. The trick is to use the correct parts of the design to attain this promise.

Let us try another set of generators. Let $F \equiv ABCD$ and $G \equiv BCDE$. Now the defining contrast becomes:

$$I \equiv ABCDF, BCDEG, AFEG \qquad (5-8)$$

This design seems to do the job. The only problem may be with the "AEFG" contrast. In it we have two-factor interactions confounded together. There will be 6 interactions that are confounded:

$$AF \equiv EG$$
$$AE \equiv FG$$
$$AG \equiv FE$$

Table 5-6

A	B	C	D	E	ABCDE	ABCD	BCDE
−	−	−	−	−	−	+	+
+	−	−	−	−	+	−	+
−	+	−	−	−	+	−	−
+	+	−	−	−	−	+	−
−	−	+	−	−	+	−	−
+	−	+	−	−	−	+	−
−	+	+	−	−	−	+	+
+	+	+	−	−	+	−	+
−	−	−	+	−	+	−	−
+	−	−	+	−	−	+	−
−	+	−	+	−	−	+	+
+	+	−	+	−	+	−	+
−	−	+	+	−	−	+	+
+	−	+	+	−	+	−	+
−	+	+	+	−	+	−	−
+	+	+	+	−	−	+	−
−	−	−	−	+	+	+	−
+	−	−	−	+	−	−	−
−	+	−	−	+	−	−	+
+	+	−	−	+	+	+	+
−	−	+	−	+	−	−	+
+	−	+	−	+	+	+	+
−	+	+	−	+	+	+	−
+	+	+	−	+	−	−	−
−	−	−	+	+	−	−	+
+	−	−	+	+	+	+	+
−	+	−	+	+	+	+	−
+	+	−	+	+	−	−	−
−	−	+	+	+	+	+	−
+	−	+	+	+	−	−	−
−	+	+	+	+	−	−	+
+	+	+	+	+	+	+	+

The remaining 15 two factor interactions will be free of each other. Usually, not all the two-factor interactions are likely. Those factors that are unlikely to interact are assigned to the confounded pairs. In this example, factors A,E,F,G would be chosen as non-possible interacting pairs. Even if it is not possible to make this assignment, there are techniques of analysis to separate confounded two-factor interactions. (See Chapter 14).

The type of reasoning used in the example above should be applied to all two-level fractional factorial designs.

- Define required information (k main effects, $k*(k-1)/2$ interactions)
- Determine minimum number of degrees of freedom
- Determine base 2 level design (2^n)

● Compute "p", the fractionalization element ($p = k - n$)
● Select the p generators
● Calculate defining contrast
● Check if required information is attained

RESOLUTION

George Box (Reference 3) has introduced a handy nomenclature for the 2^{k-p} designs. This descriptive label gives an immediate indication of the information capacity of the design. The term "resolution" has been applied to the number of individual letters (or elements) in the <u>shortest</u> "word" of the defining contrast. The lower the resolution, the less information is freely produced (i.e. unconfounded information).

For example, a Resolution IV (Four) has in its defining contrast at least one word with only 4 letters in it. This is exactly like expression 5-8. A Resolution III (Three) design has at least one word with only 3 letters in it and will confound main effects with two factor interactions. According to our rules of confounding, we would ideally like to use only Resolution IV and above designs.

PROBLEMS FOR CHAPTER 5

1. Extend Table 5-1 to 12 factors using relationship 5-1.

2. If we are interested in only main factors and two-factor (first order) interactions, how much excess information in terms of degrees of freedom is there in a full factorial 2^{12} experiment?

3. Show the design matrix for a 2^4 full factorial.

4. Using the 2^4 factorial from #3, add a fifth factor.

   a) What fraction do you have?
   b) What is the generator?
   c) What is the defining contrast?
   d) Is this an efficient design if we need to investigate main effects and first order interactions?
   e) Justify you answer to d.

5. Using the 2^4 factorial in #3 add two more factors, E,F.

   a) What fraction do you have?
   b) What are the generators?
   c) What is the defining contrast?

d) Is this an efficient design if we need to investigate both main effects and two-factor interactions?

e) Justify your answer to e.

6. Show the design for a 2^{8-3} fractional factorial. Include the generators, defining contrast.

7. An engineer has defined a problem that includes 8 factors. He would like to determine the effect of each factor and if any two-factor interactions exist. He also has a resource constraint of 16 weeks. It is possible to run two treatment combinations per week. What would your advice to this person be if you could use a two level design?

APPENDIX 5

Degrees of Freedom:
abbr: df or ν

A counting scheme devised to assess the amount of information contained in an experiment. To get a full degree of freedom, the information must be independent of any other information.

In general each time we compute a mean value, we deduct one degree of freedom from the total available. Thus in a 3 level experiment, upon computing the mean across the three levels (which is done in each analysis) we lose 1 df and have 2 left. In a two level design, we have only one degree of freedom for each factor. Interaction degrees of freedom are determined by the product of the degrees of freedom of the main factors which make up the interaction. Thus, if A has 2 df, and B has 3 df, then AB has 6 df.

Confounding: also aliasing

The linear combination of two or more effects. Factors that are confounded have to share the same degree of freedom and are not independent or orthogonal to each other.

If AB≡CD and the effect found is 10, this could mean that either AB or CD has the effect or the combined effect of both is equal to 10. Some possible combinations of AB and CD are:

AB	CD	Observed Result
0	10	10
10	0	10
5	5	10
-20	30	10
etc.		

Generator: Usually a high order interaction column with which
                                  a factor is equated. There are p generators in the
                                  fractional designs.

Defining Contrast: A relationship used to show the confounded sets of
                                  factors in a fractional design. including the identity
                                  term, there are 2^p terms in the defining contrast,
                                  including the identity term (I).

Computer program for generating 2^{k-p} designs

```
50 CLS
60 PRINT "PLEASE SWITCH PRINTER ON"
65 PRINT:PRINT:PRINT TAB(30)
70 INPUT "IS IT ON? ",Y$
75 IF Y$="Y" THEN GOTO 80 ELSE GOTO 50
80 CLS
85 INPUT "ENTER A NUMBER BETWEEN 5 AND 50";RS
90 RANDOMIZE(RS)
100 DIM M(12,12),N$(24),L$(2,12),O(64),S(12,64)
110 DIM R(64),E(10)
120 I9=0
130 FOR I=1 TO 12
140 READ N$(I)
150 NEXT I
160 DATA A,B,C,D,E,F,G,H,J,K,L,M
170 PRINT "HOW MANY FACTORS(NO MORE THAN 12)";
180 INPUT N
190 IF N>12 THEN 170
200 PRINT "HOW MANY REPLICATES";
210 INPUT R4
220 FOR I=1 TO N
230 PRINT "WHAT IS THE NAME OF FACTOR ";N$(I);"?(USE 6 LETTER ABBREV.)"
240 INPUT N$(12+I)
250 PRINT "WHAT IS THE LOW LEVEL OF ";N$(I+12);
260 INPUT L$(1,I)
270 PRINT "WHAT IS THE HIGH LEVEL OF ";N$(I+12);
280 INPUT L$(2,I)
290 NEXT I
300 DIM T$(64)
310 FOR I=1 TO 64
320 READ T$(I)
330 NEXT I
340 PRINT
350 PRINT "..................INFORMATION ANALYSIS...................."
360 I3=(N*(N-1))/2
370 PRINT "THERE ARE";N;"MAIN FACTORS AND "
371 PRINT I3;"TWO-FACTOR INTERACTIONS AS EXPECTED INFORMATION."
380 IF (N+I3)<= 15 THEN 420
385 IF (N+I3)<=45 THEN 440
390 IF (N+I3)<=78 THEN 445
400 PRINT "YOUR INFORMATION REQUIREMENTS EXCEED THIS AUTOMATED DESIGN";
405 PRINT "GENERATOR. SEE NBS TABLES."
410 END
420 B1=4
430 GOTO 450
440 B1=5
442 GOTO 450
445 B1=6
```

```
450 PRINT "THEREFORE, TO OBTAIN THIS INFORMATION, YOU"
451 PRINT "WILL NEED A MINIMUM BASE DESIGN OF";2^B1;"RUNS"
460 P=N-B1
470 PRINT "THE RECOMMENDED DESIGN IS A: 1   /";2^P;"FRACTIONAL FACTORIAL."
480 PRINT
490 PRINT
500 DATA (1),A,B,AB,C,AC,BC,ABC,D,AD,BD,ABD,CD,ACD,BCD,ABCD
510 DATA E,AE,BE,ABE,CE,ACE,BCE,ABCE,DE,ADE,BDE,ABDE,CDE,ACDE,BCDE,ABCDE
515 DATA F,AF,BF,ABF,CF,ACF,BCF,ABCF,DF,ADF,BDF,ABDF,CDF,ACDF,BCDF,ABCDF
516 DATA EF,AEF,BEF,ABEF,CEF,ACEF,BCEF,ABCEF,DEF,ADEF,BDEF,ABDEF,CDEF
517 DATA ACDEF,BCDEF,ABCDEF
520 FOR I=1 TO 6
530 FOR J=1 TO 64
540 READ S(I,J)
550 NEXT J
560 NEXT I
570 DATA -1,+1,-1,+1,-1,+1,-1,+1,-1,+1,-1,+1,-1,+1,-1,+1,-1,+1,-1,+1,-1
575 DATA +1,-1,+1,-1,+1,-1,+1,-1,+1,-1,+1
576 DATA -1,-1,+1,+1,-1,-1,+1,+1,-1,-1,+1,+1,-1,-1,+1,+1,-1,-1,+1,+1,-1
577 DATA +1,-1,+1,+1,-1,-1,+1,-1,+1,-1,+1
580 DATA -1,-1,+1,+1,-1,-1,+1,+1,-1,-1,+1,+1,-1,-1,+1,+1,-1,-1,+1,+1,-1
585 DATA -1,+1,+1,-1,-1,+1,+1,-1,-1,+1,+1
586 DATA -1,-1,+1,+1,-1,-1,+1,+1,-1,-1,+1,+1,-1,-1,+1,+1,-1,-1,+1,+1,-1
587 DATA -1,+1,+1,-1,-1,+1,+1,-1,-1,+1,+1
590 DATA -1,-1,-1,-1,+1,+1,+1,+1,-1,-1,-1,-1,+1,+1,+1,+1,-1,-1,-1,-1,+1
595 DATA +1,+1,+1,-1,-1,-1,-1,+1,+1,+1,+1
596 DATA -1,-1,-1,-1,+1,+1,+1,+1,-1,-1,-1,-1,+1,+1,+1,+1,-1,-1,-1,-1,+1
597 DATA +1,+1,+1,-1,-1,-1,-1,+1,+1,+1,+1
600 DATA -1,-1,-1,-1,-1,-1,-1,-1,+1,+1,+1,+1,+1,+1,+1,+1,-1,-1,-1,-1,-1
605 DATA -1,-1,-1,+1,+1,+1,+1,+1,+1,+1,+1
606 DATA -1,-1,-1,-1,-1,-1,-1,-1,+1,+1,+1,+1,+1,+1,+1,+1,-1,-1,-1,-1,-1
607 DATA -1,-1,-1,+1,+1,+1,+1,+1,+1,+1,+1
610 DATA -1,-1,-1,-1,-1,-1,-1,-1,-1,-1,-1,-1,-1,-1,-1,-1,+1,+1,+1,+1,+1
615 DATA +1,+1,+1,+1,+1,+1,+1,+1,+1,+1,+1
616 DATA -1,-1,-1,-1,-1,-1,-1,-1,-1,-1,-1,-1,-1,-1,-1,-1,+1,+1,+1,+1,+1
617 DATA +1,+1,+1,+1,+1,+1,+1,+1,+1,+1,+1
620 DATA -1,-1,-1,-1,-1,-1,-1,-1,-1,-1,-1,-1,-1,-1,-1,-1,-1,-1,-1,-1,-1
621 DATA -1,-1,-1,-1,-1,-1,-1,-1,-1,-1,-1
622 DATA +1,+1,+1,+1,+1,+1,+1,+1,+1,+1,+1,+1,+1,+1,+1,+1,+1,+1,+1,+1,+1
623 DATA +1,+1,+1,+1,+1,+1,+1,+1,+1,+1,+1
625 GOSUB 1510
630 LPRINT
640 LPRINT
650 LPRINT"               2**K-P FRACTIONAL FACTORIAL"
660 LPRINT"                   IN YATES ORDER"
670 LPRINT
680 LPRINT "RUN #    TC        ";
690 FOR I=1 TO N
700 LPRINT N$(I+12);"         ";
710 NEXT I
720 LPRINT
730 LPRINT
740 IF I9=1 GOTO 1010
750 GOSUB 1240
760 O1=1
770 FOR K1=1 TO R4
780 FOR I=1 TO 2^B1
790 LPRINT TAB(2)""O(O1)""TAB(9)T$(I);
800 I5=I8
810 O1=O1+1
820 FOR J=1 TO N
830 IF S(J,I)=+1 THEN 860
```

```
840 K=1
850 GOTO 870
860 K=2
870 LPRINT TAB(I5) L$(K,J);
880 I5=I5+7
890 NEXT J
900 LPRINT
910 LPRINT
920 NEXT I
930 NEXT K1
940 LPRINT
950 LPRINT
960 LPRINT "          2**k-P FRACTIONAL FACTORIAL"
970 LPRINT "             IN RANDOM ORDER"
980 I9=1
990 O1=1
1000 GOTO 670
1010 FOR K1=1 TO R4
1020 FOR I= 1 TO 2^B1
1030 L=0(O1)
1040 O1=O1+1
1050 R(L)=I
1060 NEXT I
1070 NEXT K1
1080 FOR I=1 TO (2^B1)*R4
1090 L=R(I)
1100 LPRINT TAB(2)""I""TAB(9)T$(L);
1110 I5=18
1120 FOR J=1 TO N
1130 IF S(J,L)=+1 THEN 1160
1140 K=1
1150 GOTO 1170
1160 K=2
1170 LPRINT TAB(I5)L$(K,J);
1180 I5=I5+7
1190 NEXT J
1200 LPRINT
1210 LPRINT
1220 NEXT I
1230 END
1240 REM RANDOM ORDER SUBROUTINE
1250 I4=1
1260 T=(2 B1)*R4
1270 DIM X(T)
1280 FOR I=1 TO T
1290 X(I)=0
1300 NEXT I
1310 L=1
1320 U=T
1330 L=L-1
1340 U=U+.5
1350 J=INT((RND*(U-L)))
1360 IF J=0 THEN 1390
1370 J=J+L
1380 GOTO 1400
1390 J=1+L
1400 K=J-L
1410 IF X(K)=0 THEN 1430
1420 GOTO 1350
1430 O(I4)=J
1440 I4=I4+1
1450 J=J-L
```

```
1460 X(J)=1
1470 Z=0
1475 FOR I=1 TO T:Z=Z+X(I):NEXT I
1480 IF Z=T THEN 1500
1490 GOTO 1350
1500 RETURN
1510 INPUT "WILL YOU USE THE RECOMMENDED FRACTION";I$
1520 DIM D(128,12)
1523 FOR I=1 TO 128:FOR J=1 TO 12
1525 D(I,J)=0:NEXT J:NEXT I
1530 IF I$="Y" THEN 1570
1540 IF I$="YES" THEN 1570
1550 PRINT "ENTER THE FRACTIONALIZATION ELEMENT FOR THE DESIGN YOU WANT"
1555 PRINT "THIS ELEMENT MUST NOT BE GREATER THAN 6"
1560 INPUT P
1565 IF P>6 GOTO 1550
1570 PRINT "TO BUILD THE THE DESIGN, ENTER THE NUMBER OF LETTERS "
1571 PRINT "IN THE GENERATOR 'WORD'.  THEN WHEN PROMPTED ENTER"
1572 PRINT "THE INDIVIDUAL LETTERS (ONE AT A TIME) IN THE GENERATOR"
1573 PRINT "USING THE NUMERICAL EQUIVALENTS OF THE LETTERS."
1574 PRINT "IE: 1=A,2=B,3=C,4=D,5=E,F=6"
1590 FOR I= 1 TO P
1600 PRINT "ENTER THE NUMBER OF LETTERS IN GENERATOR #";I;
1610 INPUT L1
1615 E(I)=L1
1620 FOR J=1 TO L1
1630 PRINT "ENTER # VALUE FOR LETTER ";J;
1640 INPUT D1:M(I,J)=D1:D(I,D1)=1
1650 NEXT J
1660 NEXT I
1670 B1=N-P
1680 FOR I= 1 TO P
1690 FOR J=1 TO 64
1700 S(B1+I,J)=1
1705 L1=E(I)
1710 FOR K=1 TO L1
1720 L2=M(I,K)
1730 S(B1+I,J)=S(B1+I,J)*S(L2,J)
1740 NEXT K
1760 NEXT J
1770 NEXT I
1775 REM DETERMINING THE DEFINING CONTRASTS
1780 FOR I=1 TO P:J=N-P+I:D(I,J)=1:NEXT
1790 ON P GOTO 3000,2000,2100,2200,2500,2800
2000 REM FOR P=2
2010 FOR J=1 TO N
2020 A1%=D(1,J)+D(2,J)
2030 IF (A1%-INT(A1%/2)*2)=1 THEN D(3,J)=1
2040 NEXT J
2050 GOTO 3000
2100 REM FOR P=3
2105 FOR J= 1 TO N
2110 IN=0
2115 FOR I1=1 TO P-1
2120 FOR I2=2 TO P
2125 IF I1>=I2 GOTO 2145
2130 IN=IN+1
2135 A1%=D(I1,J)+D(I2,J)
2140 IF (A1%-INT(A1%/2)*2)=1 THEN D(P+IN,J)=1
2145 NEXT I2
2146 NEXT I1
2150 NEXT J
```

```
2152 IF P>=4 GOTO 2210
2155 FOR J=1 TO N
2160 A1%=D(1,J)+D(2,J)+D(3,J)
2165 IF (A1%-INT(A1%/2)*2)=1 THEN D(7,J)=1
2170 NEXT J
2175 GOTO 3000
2200 REM FOR P=4
2205 GOTO 2105
2210 FOR J=1 TO N
2214 IF P=4 THEN IN=6
2215 IF P=5 THEN IN=10
2216 IF P=6 THEN IN=15
2220 FOR I1=1 TO P-2
2225 FOR I2=2 TO P-1
2230 FOR I3=3 TO P
2235 IF I1>=I2 GOTO 2260
2240 IF I2>=I3 GOTO 2260
2245 IN=IN+1
2250 A1%=D(I1,J)+D(I2,J)+D(I3,J)
2255 IF (A1%-INT(A1%/2)*2)=1 THEN D(P+IN,J)=1
2260 NEXT I3
2265 NEXT I2
2270 NEXT I1
2275 NEXT J
2277 IF P=>5 GOTO 2520
2280 FOR J=1 TO N
2285 A1%=D(1,J)+D(2,J)+D(3,J)+D(4,J)
2290 IF (A1%-INT(A1%/2)*2)=1 THEN D(15,J)=1
2295 NEXT J
2300 GOTO 3000
2500 REM FOR P=5
2510 GOTO 2105
2520 FOR J=1 TO N
2530 IF P=5 THEN IN=20
2531 IF P=6 THEN IN=35
2540 FOR I1=1 TO P-3
2550 FOR I2=2 TO P-2
2560 FOR I3=3 TO P-1
2570 FOR I4=4 TO P
2580 IF I1=>I2 GOTO 2640
2590 IF I2=>I3 GOTO 2640
2600 IF I3=>I4 GOTO 2640
2610 IN=IN+1
2620 A1%=D(I1,J)+D(I2,J)+D(I3,J)+D(I4,J)
2630 IF (A1%-INT(A1%/2)*2)=1 THEN D(P+IN,J)=1
2640 NEXT I4
2650 NEXT I3
2660 NEXT I2
2670 NEXT I1
2680 NEXT J
2685 IF P=6 GOTO 2820
2690 FOR J=1 TO N
2700 A1%=D(1,J)+D(2,J)+D(3,J)+D(4,J)+D(5,J)
2710 IF (A1%-INT(A1%/2)*2)=1 THEN D(31,J)=1
2720 NEXT J
2730 GOTO 3000
2800 REM FOR P=6
2810 GOTO 2105
2820 FOR J=1 TO N
2830 IN=50
2840 FOR I1=1 TO P-4
2850 FOR I2=2 TO P-3
2860 FOR I3=3 TO P-2
```

```
2870 FOR I4=4 TO P-1
2880 FOR I5=5 TO P
2890 IF I1>=I2 GOTO 2955
2900 IF I2>=I3 GOTO 2955
2905 IF I3>=I4 GOTO 2955
2910 IF I4>=I5 GOTO 2955
2930 IN=IN+1
2940 A1%=D(I1,J)+D(I2,J)+D(I3,J)+D(I4,J)+D(I5,J)
2950 IF (A1%-INT(A1%/2)*2)=1 THEN D(P+IN,J)=1
2955 NEXT I5
2956 NEXT I4
2957 NEXT I3
2958 NEXT I2
2959 NEXT I1
2960 NEXT J
2965 FOR J=1 TO N
2970 A1%=D(1,J)+D(2,J)+D(3,J)+D(4,J)+D(5,J)+D(6,J)
2975 IF (A1%-INT(A1%/2)*2)=1 THEN D(63,J)=1
2980 NEXT J
3000 REM PRINT ROUTINE FOR DEFINING CONTRASTS
3005 LPRINT "DEFINING CONTRAST: I=";
3010 FOR I=1 TO 2^P-1:FOR J=1 TO N
3020 IF D(I,J)=1 THEN LPRINT N$(J);
3030 NEXT J
3040 IF 2^P-1>I THEN LPRINT ",";
3045 IF I-INT(I/8)*8=0 THEN LPRINT
3050 NEXT I
3060 LPRINT
3070 RETURN
```

Illustration of the use of TOKAYMP

Note: The Generators for the 2^{k-p} fractional factorial designs may be found in Table 11, page 378.

```
>LOAD "TOKAYMP"
READY
>RUN
HOW MANY FACTORS(NO MORE THAN 12)? 6
HOW MANY REPLICATES? 1
WHAT IS THE NAME OF FACTOR A?(USE 6 LETTER ABBREV.)
? FACT A
WHAT IS THE LOW LEVEL OF FACT A? LO
WHAT IS THE HIGH LEVEL OF FACT A? HI
WHAT IS THE NAME OF FACTOR B?(USE 6 LETTER ABBREV.)
? FACT B
WHAT IS THE LOW LEVEL OF FACT B? LO
WHAT IS THE HIGH LEVEL OF FACT B? HI
WHAT IS THE NAME OF FACTOR C?(USE 6 LETTER ABBREV.)
? FACT C
WHAT IS THE LOW LEVEL OF FACT C? LO
WHAT IS THE HIGH LEVEL OF FACT C? HI
WHAT IS THE NAME OF FACTOR D?(USE 6 LETTER ABBREV.)
? FACT D
WHAT IS THE LOW LEVEL OF FACT D? LO
WHAT IS THE HIGH LEVEL OF FACT D? HI
WHAT IS THE NAME OF FACTOR E?(USE 6 LETTER ABBREV.)
? FACT E
```

```
WHAT IS THE LOW LEVEL OF FACT E? LO
WHAT IS THE HIGH LEVEL OF FACT E? HI
WHAT IS THE NAME OF FACTOR F?(USE 6 LETTER ABBREV.)
? FACT F
WHAT IS THE LOW LEVEL OF FACT F? LO
WHAT IS THE HIGH LEVEL OF FACT F? HI


..................INFORMATION ANALYSIS...................
THERE ARE 6 MAIN FACTORS AND
 15 TWO-FACTOR INTERACTIONS AS EXPECTED INFORMATION.
THEREFORE, TO OBTAIN THIS INFORMATION, YOU
WILL NEED A MINIMUM BASE DESIGN OF
 32 RUNS.
THE RECOMMENDED DESIGN IS A: 1  / 2 FRACTIONAL FACTORIAL.


WILL YOU USE THE RECOMMENDED FRACTION? NO
ENTER THE FRACTIONALIZATION ELEMENT FOR THE DESIGN YOU WANT
? 3
TO BUILD THE THE DESIGN, ENTER THE NUMBER OF LETTERS
IN THE GENERATOR 'WORD'.  THEN WHEN PROMPTED ENTER
THE INDIVIDUAL LETTERS (ONE AT A TIME) IN THE GENERATOR
USING THE NUMERICAL EQUIVALENTS OF THE LETTERS.
IE: 1=A,2=B,3=C,4=D,5=E
ENTER THE NUMBER OF LETTERS IN GENERATOR # 1 ? 2
ENTER # VALUE FOR LETTER  1 ? 1
ENTER # VALUE FOR LETTER  2 ? 2
ENTER THE NUMBER OF LETTERS IN GENERATOR # 2 ? 2
ENTER # VALUE FOR LETTER  1 ? 1
ENTER # VALUE FOR LETTER  2 ? 3
ENTER THE NUMBER OF LETTERS IN GENERATOR # 3 ? 2
ENTER # VALUE FOR LETTER  1 ? 2
ENTER # VALUE FOR LETTER  2 ? 3


DEFINING CONTRAST: I=ABD,ACE,BCF,BCDE,ACDF,ABEF,DEF


           2**K-F FRACTIONAL FACTORIAL
                IN YATES ORDER
```

RUN #	TC	FACT A	FACT B	FACT C	FACT D	FACT E	FACT F
1	(1)	LO	LO	LO	HI	HI	HI
3	A	HI	LO	LO	LO	LO	HI
2	B	LO	HI	LO	LO	HI	LO
7	AB	HI	HI	LO	HI	LO	LO
6	C	LO	LO	HI	HI	LO	LO
8	AC	HI	LO	HI	LO	HI	LO
4	BC	LO	HI	HI	LO	LO	HI
5	ABC	HI	HI	HI	HI	HI	HI

2**K-P FRACTIONAL FACTORIAL
IN RANDOM ORDER

RUN #	TC	FACT A	FACT B	FACT C	FACT D	FACT E	FACT F
1	(1)	LO	LO	LO	HI	HI	HI
2	B	LO	HI	LO	LO	HI	LO
3	A	HI	LO	LO	LO	LO	HI
4	BC	LO	HI	HI	LO	LO	HI
5	ABC	HI	HI	HI	HI	HI	HI
6	C	LO	LO	HI	HI	LO	LO
7	AB	HI	HI	LO	HI	LO	LO
8	AC	HI	LO	HI	LO	HI	LO

6

MULTI-LEVEL DESIGNS

While the factorial and fractional factorial designs that we have explored in the past chapters are considered the "work horses" of modern empirical investigations, there is still a lingering question that asks if they are efficient. Remember that to be efficient an experiment must get the required information at the least cost. The fractional factorials certainly get the required information in the form of interactions and do so at the least cost, but what if there is a non-linear relationship between the response we are measuring and the factors we are changing in the design? In that case we could be mislead. A classic example is shown in Figure 6-1. Here the levels of the experiment have been set at two extremes and a straight line between them shows that there is no slope. However, the dashed line is the form of the real underlying relationship which is quadratic in nature with the optimum midway between the two levels set in the experiment. Here indeed, we did not get the required information and in fact by using the two level design probably threw out the factor under investigation.

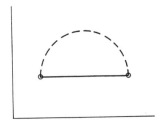

Figure 6-1

Does this condemn to oblivion the two level type design? No, of course not. This is where knowledge of the process comes into play. Remember this knowledge is the main ingredient when any experiment is undertaken. If the factor we were looking at was temperature, and the process was a photographic development investigation, then we should have known that there is a peak temperature level where a response such as quality will be optimized. Therefore, if we see no relationship as a result of the two level experiment we should not throw away prior ideas, but follow on with more extensive investigations. This is one reason for the "25% rule" which states that for the first part of your experimental investigations, you should expend only 25% of the total resources available. This assures that there is enough time and money to complete the work. Remember that a good experiment will probably pose more questions which will lead to more experiments that will lead to the final answer.

One last word of caution before we get into the methods of designing efficient experiments that look at more than two levels. Sometimes an experienced worker will be so convinced of an outcome, he or she will keep testing until by chance the results match that preconceived idea. This kind of narrow thinking will only impede progress. We should be ready and willing to modify our convictions in the light of evidence. Without such a philosophy, we will not advance.

The usual intuitive approach to investigate a curved relationship is to design a 3 level experiment. Such a design is able to investigate up to a quadratic polynomial relationship (i.e., a curve as shown in Figure 6-1). In general, we may determine a polynomial up to one 'order' less than the number of levels in the factor. So, in the case of a two level design, we may investigate first order or linear relationships. For a three level design, we may make inferences about a second order or quadratic relationship. Now, in this case, the phrase 'second order' does not mean "not important" as some researchers imply, but describes the power of the exponent applied to the factor in a polynomial equation. This means that in a simple linear relationship with a straight line fit, the equation is:

$$Y = b * X_1 \qquad \text{where b is the slope} \qquad (6\text{-}1)$$
$$\text{and X is the control factor}$$
$$\text{and Y is the response}$$

With a second order the equation is:

$$Y = b_1 * X_1 + b_{11} * X_1^2 \qquad (6\text{-}2)$$

Notice that the lower order term is retained in the second order polynomial. This is dictated by the polynomial expansion rules for a "proper polynomial". Also, notice the subscript on the second "slope" (b_{11}). This is not read as eleven, but as "one,one". It signifies the fact that X is multiplied by itself (i.e., X^2 is equivalent to $X*X$).

If, in fact, the above equation (6-2) is true, then the second order nature of this relationship is very important and should not be shrugged off as "only a second order effect." It is indeed the mathematical form of the relationship found in figure 6-1. So second order and above can be important and there must be ways of investigating these relationships.

A simple three level design for two factors and three levels is designated by 3^2 where the "3" refers to the number of levels and the "2" is the number of factors. This same notation holds for bigger experiments also. A 5^2 would have five levels and 2 factors under investigation. To find the number of treatment combinations, we simply solve the power relationship. So, a 3^2 design would have 9 treatment combinations. A 5^2 would have 25 treatment combinations.

Now what do we get for all this experimental work? We may quantify the information in an experiment by degrees of freedom as described in the last chapter. So for a 3^2 design, we have 9 treatment combinations from which we lose 1 degree of freedom (df) due to finding the grand mean of the data (this corresponds to the intercept term in regression). This leaves us with 8 df to estimate the effects in the process we are investigating.

The allocation of these 8 df are as follows:

Table 6-1

Measurement Of	df Used Up	Math Form
two main effects (linear)	2	X_1, X_2
two quadratic effects	2	X_1^2, X_2^2
linear interaction	1	$X_1 * X_2$
. . . .		
linear/quadratic interactions	2	$X_1 * X_2^2, X_1^2 * X_2$
quadratic interaction	1	$X_1^2 * X_2^2$
TOTAL	8	

A dotted line is drawn after the linear interaction since the quadratic forms of the interactions do not usually happen. Therefore, we have 3 degrees of freedom that will estimate effects that are equal to zero. This is not a big problem and does not violate our quest for efficiency. However, in the next sized design, (a 3^3) with three factors, we see less pay-back for the experimental resources spent.

Table 6-2

Measurement Of	df Used Up	Math Form
three main effects (linear)	3	X_1, X_2, X_3
three quadratic effects	3	X_1^2, X_2^2, X_3^2
linear interactions	4	$X_1{}^*X_2, X_1{}^*X_3$ $X_2{}^*X_3, X_1{}^*X_2{}^*X_3$
linear/quadratic interactions and quadratic interactions	16	complex!

With the 26 df in this experiment, 16 df or 61% of the expensive information will probably not be needed since such complex interactions do not exist in nature. These are the so-called "second order" effects that inefficient experiments will seek to discover and only waste resources on.

So how can we produce efficient experiments on multi-level problems with more than 3 factors? This is a most likely field of investigation. To answer that question let us

perform a sleight of hand trick with the 3^2 experiment we looked at just a moment ago. The geometric form of this experiment is:

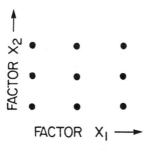

Figure 6-2

Now if we rotate the design 45°, while leaving the factor axis alone, the pattern becomes:

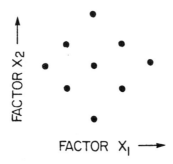

Figure 6-3

To take the design out of the abstract and into the real world, we add names to the factors and put levels along the axis. At the same time, we recognize a familiar geometric pattern in the middle of all this. it is the 2^k (in this case 2^2) factorial!

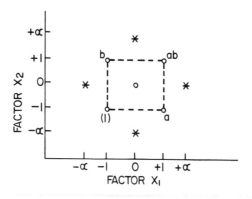

Figure 6-4

Along with the two levels of this design (2^k) that allows us to investigate the required interactions, we have a center point (at zero) and two extreme points on each factor which are shown in figure 6-4 as stars. Counting up the number of levels in the new design was seen that instead of the original three levels, we now have 5 levels for each factor. This will allow curvilinear investigations up to fourth order or a quartic relationship. While quartics are not too common, the real value of the design is the increased scope of the experiment. We have expanded the "volume" of the design by expanding the levels over a wider inference space. So now if we see a curvilinear relationship of second order, we have not used up all the degrees of freedom in fitting this equation as is necessary in the three level design.

Now we can't get something for nothing. What is the price in this design? After all, we have 5 levels for 2 factors. In the usual factorial design (which will be balanced), there are 25 treatment combinations (5^2). The above design has only 9! If we compare the information in the 5^2 from a "degrees of freedom" view to our cut down version, we see that all is not lost---actually we only lose the non-essential information that we would have thrown away anyway. Table 6-3 shows that only 7 df are neded to capture the essential information from a 5^2 design. This amount of information is more closely matched by the design shown in Figure 6-4 which produces 8 df worth of understanding.

Table 6-3

Analysis of 5^2 Information Content

Measurement of	df used up	math form
two linear main effects	2	X_1, X_2
two quadratic main	2	X_1^2, X_2^2
one interaction	1	$X_1 * X_2$
two cubic main effects	2	X_1^3, X_2^3
. . . .		
two quartic main effects	2	X_1^4, X_2^4
various quadratic & cubic interactions that are unlikely to happen	15	complex

The design shown in figure 6-4 is called a central composite design (CCD) for it is made up of a central point and the optimal joining of the 2^k factorial designs with (of all things!) a one-factor-at-a-time (1-fat) design. This joining is permissible here since the factorial design gives the interactions (linear ones that are likely to happen) and the linear main effects, while the 1-fat expands the volume of the inference space for curvilinear effects. The central composite design obtains all the information above the dotted line in table 6-3. We cannot (because there are not enough degrees of freedom) pick up the information below the line. So, what is given up in the CCD is exactly the information we would have thrown away from the full factorial experiment!

Therefore, the CCD is efficient since it gets just the required information and, in comparison with the 5^2, does this with about 1/3 the work. Central Composite designs are easy to construct since they are based on two level factorials and one-factor-at-a-time techniques. The general designation of the design is:

$$\# tc's = 2^{k-p} + (2*k) + 1 \qquad \text{where } k = \# \text{ of factors} \qquad (6\text{-}3)$$
$$p \text{ is the fractionalization element}$$

Table 6-4 gives the number of treatment combinations and the <u>distance</u> from the center to the "star" positions for various values of k and p. These distances will allow the design to be orthogonal (or independent) in design units and also assures us that the error in predicition remains constant (rotatable) around the design. These points will be fully covered in Chapter 16 when we learn to apply the proper analysis to this design.

TABLE 6-4

SOME ORTHOGONAL DESIGNS FOR THREE TO EIGHT FACTORS

Number of Factors:	2	3	4	5	5	6	6	7	7	8
Size of Factorial:	full	full	full	full	½	full	½	full	½	¼
# of Points in 2^{k-p}:	4	8	16	32	16	64	32	128	64	64
# of Star Points:	4	6	8	10	10	12	12	14	14	16
Length of star points from center: (α)	1.414	1.682	2.0	2.378	2.0	2.828	2.378	3.363	2.828	2.828
Total tc's including center point:	9	15	25	43	27	77	45	143	85	81

While each of these designs can get by with a single center point, we will see in the analysis that the center point plays a pivotal role in deriving our equations. Therefore, to assure the intergrity of the data from this treatement (the zero point) it is prudent to replicate it between 3 and 5 times. This replication also provides a measure of experimental error. We may consider the 3 to 5 replicates as cheap insurance against experimental hazards.

Table 6-4 will probably be sufficient to satisfy most of the design requirements encountered in normal experimental situations. If it is necessary to build larger designs, the length of the distance from the center of the design to the star points may be calculated according to expression 6-4.

$$\alpha = \sqrt[4]{2^{(k-p)}} \qquad \text{or} \qquad \alpha = 2^{(k-p)/4} \qquad (6\text{-}4)$$

To use these α distances, we simply extend the design from the two level factorial's -1 and $+1$ distances in proportion to the size of the alpha star lengths. So if we decide that 3 factors will be studied in this experiment the design in <u>design</u> units will be as follows:

TABLE 6-5

tc	A	B	C
(1)	-	-	-
a	+	-	-
b	-	+	-
ab	+	+	-
c	-	-	+
ac	+	-	+
bc	-	+	+
abc	+	+	+
$-\alpha_a$	-1.682	0	0
$+\alpha_a$	+1.682	0	0
$-\alpha_b$	0	-1.682	0
$+\alpha_b$	0	+1.682	0
$-\alpha_c$	0	0	-1.682
$+\alpha_c$	0	0	+1.682
zero	0	0	0

Since we usually can't work in design units in a physical world, this design shown in table 6-5 will have to be converted to physical units. So we'll add some substance to the problem and talk about the factors we are working with.

Consider a study of a polymer process where the yield is measured by taking the ratio of the product produced to the raw materials put into the reactor. The closer this ratio comes to 1, the higher the yield. The three control factors under study are temperature, pressure, and time of reaction. Therefore, the goal of this project is to increase yield and the objective is to test the hypothesis that yield is a function of temperature, pressure, and time of reaction. Table 6-6 shows the "working ranges" for the factors under study.

Table 6-6

Factor	Range of interest
Temperature	100° - 200°
Pressure	20 psi -50 psi
Time	10 min - 30 min

If we pick the extremes of the ranges for the -1 and +1 levels of our factorial portion of the CCD, then there is no room to move to the alpha star points. So in this case, if we wish to utilize the entire range, we will assign the end points of the ranges to the alpha distances. This means that the -1 and +1 levels of the factorial must be moved in proportionally from the 1.682 distances as prescribed in table 6-5.

To do this we set up a proportion of the distance from the center point to the star (call this the delta-star) to the distance from the center point to the -1 and +1 positions (call this the delta factorial). On a number line it looks like this:

Table 6-7

	-1.682	-1	center	+1	+1.682
Temperature	100		150		200
Pressure	20		35		50
Time	10		20		30

the proportion for temperature is:

$$\frac{50(\text{delta star})}{1.682} = \frac{x(\text{delta factorial})}{1}$$

so: $1.682x = 50$
and: $x = 29.73$
this is the distance from the center to the + and− temperature positions.
so the level of " − " temperature is $150 - 29.73 = 120.27$
and the level of " + " temperature is $150 + 29.73 = 179.73$

The completion of the calculation of the levels for pressure and time is left as an exercise (problem #1).

While the *exact* values of temperature have been computed, it would be silly to try to set them to the level of precision suggested by this design. It would be better from an experimental operations point of view to set the temperature at 120° and 180°. This slight excursion will not destroy the mathematical integrity of the design.

A NOTE ON CHOOSING LEVELS

The choice of levels in an experiment is critical to the success of execution and analysis of the treatment combinations. Should we pick levels so close together that the noise of the system swamps the information we are seeking, then we will get nothing for our efforts. On the other hand, if we spread the levels so wide across the possible range of investigation, we will most certainly get measurable effects, but these

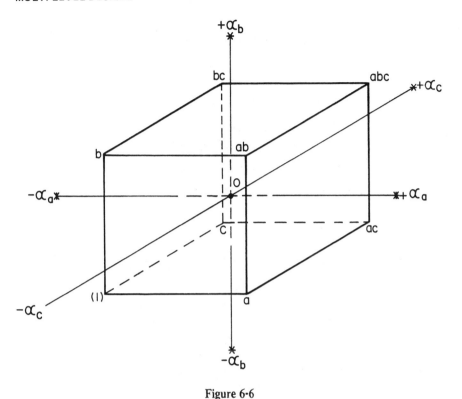

Figure 6-6

Diagram of a CCD for 3 Factors

effects could be an artifact of the choice of levels and not an indication of the importance of the factor under study. Another problem in choosing levels that are too far apart is the fact that when in combination with other widely spaced levels of other factors, we may have a treatment combination that utterly fails to produce any product. In the case of the polymer process, this usually is termed an experimental treatment that has produced "glop"!

The CCD is able to help us choose levels that will be mathematically independent with errors that will not be inflated by the addition of higher order polynomial terms, but is *not* able to tell us how far to set these levels apart. This is where prior knowledge of the process (a necessary ingredient for any successful experiment) must be used. For this reason, the CCD should *not* be used until there is sufficient information to assure us that the levels we pick will not lead us into the dangers outlined above. It is very tempting to apply the CCD on a new problem right at the beginning without the up-front work of fractional factorial screening designs. As we have outlined in the first chapters, it is important to build on prior experimental knowledge before putting all our eggs in one experimental basket that may have holes in it.

PROBLEMS FOR CHAPTER 6

1. Complete the calculation of the physical levels for the problem outlined in the text using the working ranges found in table 6-6. Compute the levels for pressure and time that are set for the -1 and +1 design unit positions.

2. With the results from problem #1, build the randomized treatment combination table that would be used to run the experiment with temperature, pressure and time.

3. Compute the alpha star distances for the following designs:

# of Factors	Type of Factorial
5	1/4 fractional
6	1/4 fractional
9	FULL
12	1/64 fractional

4. Set up a CCD for the following problem:

Factor	Working Range	
Screw Speed	10	25 ips
Temperature	300^{0}	400^{0}
Holding Time	30 sec	90 sec
Feed Particle Size	.5 mm	5mm

APPENDIX 6

Philosophy: There is a balance between skepticism and learning. We should always be skeptical of results that are counterintuitive, but we must also be willing to modify our convictions in the light of experimental evidence. So if a two level experiment seems to indicate no difference in a factor under study, we may still want to study this factor further in a multi-level design.

CCD: Center Composite Design

● An efficient design that allows investigation of interactions (two level) and curvilinear main effects.

● The number of treatment combinations in a CCD

$$\#tc's = 2^{k-p} + 2*(k) + 1$$

where $k = \#$ of factors

p is the fractionalization element

while the "1" is the center point, in practice this point is usually replicated to obtain an estimate of experimental error. The number of replicates is dependent on the cost of experimentation, but should be at least 3 but needs to be no more than 5 or 6.

Some Functions:

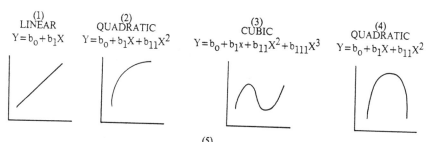

(1)
LINEAR
$Y = b_0 + b_1 X$

(2)
QUADRATIC
$Y = b_0 + b_1 X + b_{11} X^2$

(3)
CUBIC
$Y = b_0 + b_1 x + b_{11} X^2 + b_{111} X^3$

(4)
QUADRATIC
$Y = b_0 + b_1 X + b_{11} X^2$

(5)
QUADRATIC
$Y = b_0 + b_1 X + b_{11} X^2$

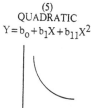

7

THREE LEVEL DESIGNS

In Chapter 6 we showed how three level designs are inherently inefficient due to the volume of information generated at a relatively high cost. There are some modifications of the basic three level designs that can be efficient by giving the required information at a low cost. The 3^2 design with its three levels and only two factors fits into this category as we showed in chapter 6. We also showed that for 3 level designs with more than 2 factors, the efficiency degraded rapidly. The solution to this problem was to use the central composite design which has 5 levels. Sometimes it is not possible to obtain the required 5 levels for the CCD. We could run a "modified" CCD with most of the factors at 5 levels and a few at 3 levels. Such a design would not be orthogonal, but would not suffer terribly in the analysis. An outline of such a design for 4 factors using a 1/2 fractional factorial as the base would be as follows given that only 3 of the factors could be run at 5 levels:

Table 7-1

tc	A	B	C	D
(1)	-	-	-	-
a(d)	+	-	-	+
b(d)	-	+	-	+
ab	+	+	-	-
c(d)	-	-	+	+
ac	+	-	+	-
bc	-	+	+	-
abc(d)	+	+	+	+
$-a_a$	-1.682	0	0	0
$+a_a$	+1.682	0	0	0
$-a_b$	0	-1.682	0	0
$+a_b$	0	+1.682	0	0
$-a_d$	0	0	0	-1.682
$+a_d$	0	0	0	+1.682
zero	0	0	0	0

In this design, we have simply left the alpha star positions out for factor C. This ommission of the alpha star levels could be taken to the extreme by leaving out all the alpha star positions for all the factors and simply run the center point with a 2^{k-p} factorial. This is a good thought at first, but leads to confusion in the analysis since we don't know which center point of which factor is causing the curvilinearity to take place. This confusion called "Confounding" has appeared in fractional factorials and is common in designs that lack control. We shall avoid such designs. While the modified CCD is a viable alternative to investigating reduced multi-levels, it still can be improved upon when we use three levels exclusively.

One class of designs that will investigate three levels with a minimum of work is called the "Box-Behnken" three level designs. The concept makes logical use of the 2^k factorial. To build a Box-Behnken (B-B) design, take the factors and build a 2^2 factorial for all pairs of them while holding the other factors at a center point. So, for an example of the four factor experiment, this is how a Box-Behnken three level would look:

Table 7-2

A	B	C	D	
-	-	0	0	
+	-	0	0	
-	+	0	0	A&B Together in a 2^2
+	+	0	0	
-	0	-	0	
+	0	-	0	
-	0	+	0	A&C Together in a 2^2
+	0	+	0	
-	0	0	-	
+	0	0	-	
-	0	0	+	A&D Together in a 2^2
+	0	0	+	
0	-	-	0	
0	+	-	0	
0	-	+	0	B&C Together in a 2^2
0	+	+	0	
0	-	0	-	
0	+	0	-	
0	-	0	+	B&D Together in a 2^2
0	+	0	+	
0	0	-	-	
0	0	+	-	
0	0	-	+	C&D Together in a 2^2
0	0	+	+	
0	0	0	0	Zero Point

In comparing the design in table 7-1 with the design in Table 7-2, we can see that there is a greater expenditure of resources in the B-B design when compared with the CCD. The B-B requires 47% more work than the CCD and the CCD operates at five levels while the B-B only operates at 3. However, the B-B design is still more efficient then the comparable 3^4 full factorial that would require 81 treatment combinations.

To determine how many "sets" or sub-designs in a B-B, we need to find the number of pairs of factors for the problem at hand. This is the combination of k factors taken 2 at a time. or:

$$C_2^k = \frac{k!}{(k-2)!\, 2!} \tag{7-1}$$

where k = # of factors

this reduces to: $C_2^k = \frac{k(k-1)}{2}$ (7-2)

for this special case of pairs

Therefore the number of treatment combinations in a B-B design will be equal to the number of pairings of factors times the number of treatments in the sub-design (which will always be 4) plus the zero or center point.

$$\#tc = 4* \frac{k(k-1)}{2} + 1 \tag{7-3}$$

As in any experimental design, the tc's are randomized and run in random order. While the B-B designs are not as efficient as the CCD, they fill a gap between the 2^{k-p} and the larger, multi-level full factorial designs and certainly are far more efficient than the full 3^k factorials.

Once again, from a degree of freedom analysis, we can see that the B-B designs use up fewer df and in turn give up information on higher order interactions that would not likely occur. We do not obtain information on quadratic interactions from a B-B design. We do, however, get information on main linear and main quadratic effects along with the two factor linear interactions.

3^{k-p} DESIGNS

While the Box-Behnken design is an appropriate, clever and useful approach to solving the problem of investigating non-linear effects, some researchers and engineers prefer to use fractions of the 3^k factorial designs. These 3 level designs are completely balanced with all levels of all factors found in combination with all other factor's levels. In contrast, the central composite design has its extreme low and high levels "orphaned" off the axes of the main part of the design and not in balance. The B-B design does not combine more than 2 factors at a time (beyond the zero point). While we have shown how these "flaws" in the CCD and B-B designs are really virtues from an information theory perspective, there is still a controversy in the field of statistics over the merits of the alternative approaches to the investigation of curvilinear functions. The CCD and B-B designs were specifically engineered to fit the criteria outlined in the paper by Box and Wilson (1951). It has been said that the three-level factorial and fractional factorial designs are "methods searching for an application." We shall see one possible application in Chapter 20 of the controversial three level fractional factorial. For now, we will study this class of experiments to understand their nature.

As we present the methods for constructing the 3^{k-p} fractions, we will also see some of the problems encountered in the application of such designs to building response surfaces and writing equations on an unknown process.

GENERATING A 3^{k-p}

To build three-level fractional factorials we shall use some of the same thinking that was used in Chapter 5 to construct the 2^{k-p} designs. As you shall see, the 3^{k-p} are more complex and the interpretation of the physical nature of the interactions is somewhat obscure in the 3^{k-p} designs. Also, to handle the three level designs, we will change our notation from the -1, $+1$ coded levels of the 2 level designs to a 0,1,2 notation designating the low, mid, and high levels of the 3^k factorials. We will also need to expand our modulo arithmetic from base 2 (used in the 2^{k-p}) to base 3. In base 3 modulo arithmetic, any modulus of 3 becomes zero. Therefore, $3=0$, $6=0$, $9=0$, etc. The "remainder" of any modulus of 3 keeps its identity. This gives us the following:

MOD 3

$0=0$	$7=1$
$1=1$	$8=2$
$2=2$	$9=0$
$3=0$	$10=1$
$4=1$	$11=2$
$5=2$	$12=0$
$6=0$	etc...

Let's look at a simple 3^2 design with two factors at three levels and partition the degrees of freedom. This design has 9 treatment combinations and after accounting for the grand mean, we have 8 degrees of freedom to measure effects.

Table 7-3

Row	A	B	AB	$AAB \equiv A^2B$	$ABB \equiv AB^2$	$AABB \equiv A^2B^2$
1	0	0	0	0	0	0
2	1	0	1	2	1	2
3	2	0	2	1	2	1
4	0	1	1	1	2	2
5	1	1	2	0	0	1
6	2	1	0	2	1	0
7	0	2	2	2	1	1
8	1	2	0	1	2	0
9	2	2	1	0	0	2
	L1	L2	L1+L2	L1+L1+L2	L1+L2+L2	L1+L1+L2+L2
	2df	2df	1df	1df	1df	1df

In Table 7-3 we have labeled the columns at the top with both conventional and unconventional notation. The usual notation for effects is seen in the first three columns, but the quadratic interaction effects have been noted first in the unconventional manner (ie: AAB) of multiplying out the quadratic function and then in the conventional manner (ie: A^2B) of showing the exponent. This notation should help to show how the _name_ of the effect is related with the linear combinations that create the entries in each column. At the base of each column, we have defined the linear combinations (L) in terms of the basic L1 and L2 columns which represent the A and B effects respectively.

Let's use our Mod3 algebra and derive the values in the fourth column (AAB or A^2B). We see at the bottom of this column, the linear combination rule is to take $(L1+L1+L2)$ mod$_3$. For the first row, the values of L1 and L2 are both zero, so the entry in the fourth column, first row is also a zero. In the second row, we take two L1's which when added give a 2 and L2 is still zero, so we end up with a 2 in the second row, fourth column. We can continue down the column row by row in a similar manner. The sixth row is interesting. We take L1 twice which gives 4 and add on L2 to give 5, which in mod3 produces a 2 which is entry in column 4, row 6.

Besides the unconventional column heading notation for the interactions, we have also represented the components of the interaction unconventionally. The 4df for the _general_ AB interaction have been split into 4 parts instead of 2 parts with 2df each which is the usual custom. We have gone one division step further to observe how a notation convention evolved.

Let us combine the interaction columns in pairs. Since there are 4 columns, we can combine them in pairs in 6 different ways. Table 7-4 shows the 6 linear combinations possible.

Table 7-4

Col:	I AB+ AAB	II AB+ ABB	III AB+ AABB	IV AAB+ ABB	V AAB+ AABB	VI ABB+ AABB
	0	0	0	0	0	0
	0	2	0	0	1	0
	0	1	0	0	2	0
	2	0	0	0	0	1
	2	2	0	0	1	1
	2	1	0	0	2	1
	1	0	0	0	0	2
	1	2	0	0	1	2
	1	1	0	0	2	2

Columns III and IV come up "empty", that is with no pattern of variation. We call this "emptiness" the Identity (I). This is the same identity that we used in the 2^{k-p} designs of Chapter 5. Column III is the linear combination of AB and AABB which leads to A^3B^3. In mod3, this turns into I since any power that is a modulus of 3 becomes the identity and $I*I=I$. By stretching this point further and realizing the underlying concept of the identity, we conclude that the AB interaction is no different from the A^2B^2 interaction. This lead to the convention that of the 4 df available in 3^k designs for 2-factor interactions, we will only break them down into two components with 2df each. The reason for no further breakdown of the df is the redundancy that we have seen in Columns III and IV of Table 7-4.

The convention in deciding which part of the 2df is used as standard notation is arbitrary, but the choice results in a neater notation than the alternative. The convention requires that the first term (or letter) of the interation "word" is raised to the first power only. Therefore A^2B^2 and A^2B are eliminated as viable choices for notation, not because they can't exist physically, but because they are redundant with AB and AB^2.

A further inspection of Table 7-4 reveals that the pattern of levels of Columns V and VI are the same as A and B respectively. If we look at the column headings we see that the linear combination of V is $A^2B+A^2B^2$ which in Mod3 reduces to A (ie: A^4B^3). Similarly Column VI produces B (ie: A^3B^4). Thus the pattern of "Confounding" is predicted by the linear combination.

The first two columns (I and II) present at first a more obscure relationship, but the linear combination gives us a clue. Column I's linear combination is A^3B^2 which reduces to B^2. Now B^2 is found from L_2+L_2 which is exactly the pattern in Column I. Column II follows the same concepts (see homework Problem #5).

INFORMATION AND RESOURCES

All of the above insights derived from Tables 7-3 and 7-4 help in the sorting of information available in the 3 level designs. We are also able to balance our resources with knowledge of the effects that can be expected in a particular experimental situation. We will now regroup the 3^2 experimental table into the four 2df columns that are not redundant.

Table 7-5

A	B	AB	AB^2
0	0	0	0
1	0	1	1
2	0	2	2
0	1	1	2
1	1	2	0
2	1	0	1
0	2	2	1
1	2	0	2
2	2	1	0

If we do not expect an interaction, then we may use one of the interaction columns as a third factor much as we did in 2 level fractional factorials.

In doing this we step into the realm of the 3^{k-p} fractional factorial. The k refers to the number of factors and the p is a fractionalization element as before. Since each 3 level factor requires 2df, we may add as many as 2 factors when we have 9 treatments. Let's add at first a third factor C and equate it with the AB column. In doing so, we have established a confounding pattern that can be determined using defining contrasts similarly to the 2^{k-p} designs. Because of the extra information content of the 3^{k-p} designs, the rules for their construction are a bit more complex.

3^{k-p} DESIGN RULES

1. There is a fractionalization element $p = k - n$ where k is the number of factors under study and n is the nth root equal to 3 of the number of treatment combinations in the base design.

2. There will be p generators chosen from the available 2df positions of the interactions in the base design.

3. The fraction of the full design is $1/3^p$.

4. There are $(3^p-1)/2$ terms in the fundamental defining contrast (FDC). If p is greater than 1, then the FDC is generated by finding all the

non-redundant (in Mod3) multiples of the of the first-found terms (Groups) of the FDC using up to a square power in these group multiplications.

5. Use the FDC and its square to determine the pattern of confounding in Mod3.

Let's continue the example from Table 7-5 and apply the above rules to complete the generation of the 3^{k-p} design.

1. Our base design has 9 tc's since $k=3$ (factors A,B,C) and $n=2$ ($3 = \sqrt[n]{9}$) then $p=1$.

2. We have 1 generator, the AB interaction.

3. The fraction is $1/3^1 = 1/3$.

4. There will be $(3^1-1)/2=1$ term in the FDC which is $I \equiv ABC^2$ (Don't count I).

5. $I \equiv ABC^2$ (FDC) , A^2B^2C (FDC)^2

$A \equiv A^2BC^2 \Rightarrow AB^2C$, $A^3B^2C \equiv B^2C \Rightarrow BC^2$
$B \equiv AB^2C^2$, $A^2B^3C \equiv A^2C \Rightarrow AC^2$
$C \equiv ABC^3 \Rightarrow AB$, $A^2B^2C^2 \equiv ABC$
$AC \equiv A^2BC^3 \Rightarrow A^2B \Rightarrow AB^2$, $A^3B^2C^2 \equiv B^2C^2 \Rightarrow BC$

Summary of Confounding:

$A \equiv AB^2C$, BC^2
$B \equiv AB^2C^2$, AC^2
$C \equiv AB$, ABC
$AC \equiv AB^2$, BC

The implication of the confounding in this design is that the two factor interactions are linearly combined with each other and with factor C (because of the generator).

Even if we had picked the alternative generator ($C \equiv AB^2$) we would have run into the same difficulty (see homework Problem #6).

Because of the extent of the confounding, this 9 tc, 1/3 fraction can be considered only as a main effect design. The AB interaction which is confounded with C certainly is not allowed since we would not be able to distinguish which effect was causing the change in our response.

LARGER 3^{k-p} DESIGNS

Since powers of 3 grow very rapidly, there are only two 3^{k-p} base designs that are useful. The 9 tc (3^2) has a limited application when a curved effect is suspected, but it is unable to detect interactions. The next size design is a 27 tc (3^3). We will look at this design in detail. The 81 tc (3^4) is much too large for most budgets and fails as an efficient design from the excess cost criterion. So we really only have a 9 tc or a 27 tc base design to fractionalize. Since we will confound main effects and two factor interactions in a 9 tc design, there is really only one useful 3 level fractional factorial design. Of course, the degree of fractionalization will produce a number of 27 tc configurations. We will look at a 3^{5-2}.

In the base 3^3 design there are 26 df. Table 7-6 shows these 26 degrees of freedom broken down into the 2df segments for the main effects, 2 factor interactions and 3 factor interactions.

While there are a large number of possible combinations of defining contrasts, the "best" from a confounding standpoint is:

$$D \equiv AB^2C^2 \qquad (7-5)$$

$$E \equiv AB^2C \qquad (7-6)$$

The FDC is found by clearing the generators in the usual way:

$$I \equiv AB^2C^2D^2, AB^2CE^2 \qquad (7-7)$$
$$\quad (G_1) \qquad (G_2)$$

and then multiplying G_1 (Group 1) times G_2 (Group 2) and G_1 times $(G_2)^2$. This gives all the possible non-redundant multiples of G1 and G2 up to the second power. If there had been a G3, we would have had to find all *pairs* of multiples and *triples* of multiples.

$$AB^2C^2D^2*AB^2CE^2 = A^2B^4C^3D^2E^2 \Rightarrow AB^2DE \qquad (7-8)$$

and

$$AB^2C^2D^2*A^2BC^2E = A^3B^3C^4D^2E \Rightarrow CD^2E \qquad (7-9)$$

TABLE 7-6

Row	A	B	C	AB	AB²	AC	AC²	BC	BC²	AB²C	AB²C²	ABC²	ABC
1	0	0	0	0	0	0	0	0	0	0	0	0	0
2	1	0	0	1	1	1	1	0	0	1	1	1	1
3	2	0	0	2	2	2	2	0	0	2	2	2	2
4	0	1	0	1	2	0	0	1	1	2	2	1	1
5	1	1	0	2	0	1	1	1	1	0	0	2	2
6	2	1	0	0	1	2	2	1	1	1	1	0	0
7	0	2	0	2	1	0	0	2	2	1	1	2	2
8	1	2	0	0	2	1	1	2	2	2	2	0	0
9	2	2	0	1	0	2	2	2	2	0	0	1	1
10	0	0	1	0	0	1	2	1	2	1	2	2	1
11	1	0	1	1	1	2	0	1	2	2	0	0	2
12	2	0	1	2	2	0	1	1	2	0	1	1	0
13	0	1	1	1	2	1	2	2	0	0	1	0	2
14	1	1	1	2	0	2	0	2	0	1	2	1	0
15	2	1	1	0	1	0	1	2	0	2	0	2	1
16	0	2	1	2	1	1	2	0	1	2	0	1	0
17	1	2	1	0	2	2	0	0	1	0	1	2	1
18	2	2	1	1	0	0	1	0	1	1	2	0	2
19	0	0	2	0	0	2	1	2	1	2	1	1	2
20	1	0	2	1	1	0	2	2	1	0	2	2	0
21	2	0	2	2	2	1	0	2	1	1	0	0	1
22	0	1	2	1	2	2	1	0	2	1	0	2	0
23	1	1	2	2	0	0	2	0	2	2	1	0	1
24	2	1	2	0	1	1	0	0	2	0	2	1	2
25	0	2	2	2	1	2	1	1	0	0	2	0	1
26	1	2	2	0	2	0	2	1	0	1	0	1	2
27	2	2	2	1	0	1	0	1	0	2	1	2	0

L_1 L_2 L_3 $L_4 = L_1+L_2$ $L_5 = L_1+2L_2$ $L_6 = L_1+L_3$ $L_7 = L_1+2L_3$ $L_8 = L_2+L_3$ $L_9 = L_2+2L_3$ $L_{10} = L_1+2L_2+L_3$ $L_{11} = L1+2L_2+2L_3$ $L_{12} = L_1+L_2+2L_3$ $L_{13} = L_1+L_2+L_3$

So the FDC is:

$$I \equiv AB^2C^2D^2, AB^2CE^2, AB^2DE, CD^2E \qquad (7\text{-}10)$$

And the square of this FDC is:

$$I^2 \equiv A^2BCD, A^2BC^2E, A^2BD^2E^2, C^2DE^2 \qquad (7\text{-}11)$$

Now we can use the FDC and its square to determine the pattern of confounding in our $3^{5\text{-}2}$ design. For the main effects and selected 2 factor interactions we can see the results in Table 7-7. Only factors A and B are clear of 2 factor interactions and the 2 factor interactions are confounded among themselves. This design could be used with prior knowledge of likely and unlikely interactions.

TABLE 7-7

	FDC	$(FDC)^2$
$I = $	$AB^2C^2D^2, AB^2CE^2, AB^2DE, CD^2E;$	$A^2BCD, A^2BC^2E, A^2BD^2E^2, C^2DE^2$

A	=	$ABCD, ABC^2E, ABD^2E^2, ACD^2E, BCD, BC^2E, BD^2E^2, AC^2DE^2$
B	=	$AC^2D^2, ACE^2, ADE, BCD^2E, ABC^2D^2, ABCE^2, ABDE, BC^2DE^2$
C	=	$AB^2D^2, AB^2C^2E^2, AB^2CDE, CDE^2, AB^2CD^2, AB^2E^2, AB^2C^2DE, DE^2$
D	=	$AB^2C^2, AB^2CDE^2, AB^2D^2E, CE, AB^2C^2D, AB^2CDE^2, AB^2E, CDE$
E	=	$AB^2C^2D^2E, AB^2C, AB^2DE^2, CD^2E^2, AB^2C^2D^2E^2, AB^2CD^2E^2, AB^2D, CD^2$
A B	=	$ACD, AC^2E, AD^2E^2, ABCD^2E, BC^2D^2, BCE^2, BD^2E^2, ABC^2DE^2$
CD	=	$AB^2, AB^2C^2DE^2, AB^2D^2E, CE^2, AB^2CD, AB^2D^2E^2, AB^2C^2E, DE$

A COMMENT ON 3 LEVEL FRACTIONS

It is appropriate to end this chapter in a comparison of the efficiency of $3^{k\text{-}p}$ versus $2^{k\text{-}p}$ designs. A direct comparison of a 5 factor, 2 level design to the above 5 factor, 3 level design shows that a $1/2 \, (2^{5\text{-}1})$ fraction with 16 tc's will give the main effects and the 2 factor interactions with no trouble at all. (The defining contrast is $I = ABCDE$). However, the 2 level design can't get at curved effects. The $3^{k\text{-}p}$ design can get the curved effects, but can't get the 2 factor interactions. This conflict between information and resources and the balance required for efficiency drives the important axiom home that no experiment can be undertaken without sufficient prior knowledge of the process. Because interactions are often so important in the processes we study, we may conclude that the inability of $3^{k\text{-}p}$ designs to detect interactions makes them a class of designs searching for an application. In Chapter 20 we will discuss an application that just may be the answer to that search.

PROBLEMS FOR CHAPTER 7

1. Set up a B-B design for the following problem:

Factor	Working Ranges	
Screw Speed	10	25ips
Temperature	300^0	400^0
Holding Time	30 sec	90 sec
Feed particle size	.5mm	5mm

2. Compare the design from #1 above to the CCD design you developed as an answer to problem #4 in chapter 6. Comment on the efficiency. What if 3 levels were the maximum available?

3. How many tc's in a B-B for 6 factors? Compare this with a fractional factorial based CCD that will obtain all main effects and two factor interactions

4. A food engineer wishes to study the effect of changing the amount of ingredients in a pancake mix. He expects curvilinearity and wants to use a 3 level design. Resource constraints will hold the number of treatment combinations to 30 or fewer. Design a 3^{k-p} for this engineer. (Not a B-B.)

Factor	Range
Flour	3/4 cup to 1 cup
Sugar	1-1/2 T to 2-1/2 T
Salt	1/4 t to 3/4 t
Baking Powder	1-1/2 t to 2-1/2 t
Milk	1 cup to 1-1/2 cups
Eggs	1 to 3
Shortening	1-1/2 T to 2-1/2 T

a. Be sure to write a goal and objective and show the design in random order.

b. Show the confounding pattern in this design.

5. By taking the proper linear combination, show that Column II of Table 7-4 is indeed A^2. Make the comparison using the 0,1,2 levels.

6. Design a 3^{3-1} using the generator $C \equiv AB^2$. Work out the summary of confounding and comment on the precautions necessary in the application of this design.

7. Complete the computation of the defining contrast (I and I^2) for the following 3^{5-2} design given the following generators. Comment on the confounding pattern.

$$D \equiv ABC^2 \qquad\qquad E \equiv AB^2C$$

8. Answer Question #7 again using the following generators:

$$D \equiv AB^2C^2 \qquad\qquad E \equiv ABC$$

9. Use the defining contrast generated in #8 to determine the confounding for the main effects (A, B, C, D, E) and these interactions:

$$AB \qquad\qquad AD \qquad\qquad DE$$

Comment on the confounding.

APPENDIX 7

Box-Behnkin Design (B-B):   A three level fractional factorial that is built on sub-assembly 2^2 factorials while all other factors are held at a mid-point. There will be as many sub assemblies in the B-B design as there are pairs of factors. The number of treatment combinations is equal to:

$$\#tc's = \frac{k*(k-1)}{2} * 4 + 1$$

where k = # of factors.

A Box-Behnken for 3 factors would be as follows:

A	B	C
-	+	0
+	-	0
-	+	0
+	+	0
-	0	-
+	0	-
-	0	+
+	0	+
0	-	-
0	+	-
0	-	+
0	+	+
0	0	0

3^{k-p} Design Rules:

1. There is a fractionalization element $p = k - n$ where k is the number of factors under study and n is the nth root equal to 3 of the number of treatment combinations in the base design.

2. There will be p generators chosen from the available 2df positions of the interactions in the base design.

3. The fraction of the full design is $1/3^p$.

4. There are $(3^p-1)/2$ terms in the fundamental defining contrast (FDC). If p is greater than 1, then the FDC is generated by finding all the non-redundant (in Mod3) multiples of the of the first-found (Group) terms of the FDC using up to a square power in these group multiplications.

5. Use the FDC and its square to determine the pattern of confounding in Mod3.

8

BLOCKING IN FACTORIAL DESIGNS

During the early development of experimental design and analysis techniques, it was recognized that some of the assumptions that were required to perform a proper analysis of data from a designed experiment could not be fulfilled. The main assumption that was in jeopardy was the assumption of independence of the error through-out the experiment.

An early application of statistical experimental design was in the field of agriculture. We find many of the terms applied to that science have filtered their way into the words statisticians use to describe the procedures in use today. One such term is "blocking".

If we were to reconstruct the early days (in the 1920's and 30's), with an experiment, we can see the logic and methods used to remove some confusion from the results of an experiment that was constructed to study the effect of fertilizer on plant growth.

Table 8-1

Factors Under Study	Levels	
Fertilizer Nitrogen	10%	20%
Fertilizer Phosphor	5%	10%
Fertilizer Potash	5%	10%
Plant Type	Corn	Tomatoes

In this 2^4 design there will be 16 treatment combinations. To get a precise measure of yield (our reponse variable) is it necessary to plant at least 1/4 acre per treatment combination. To do all 16 treatments, we will neet 4 acres of land.

Table 8-2 shows the 16 treatment combinations for this experiment. Good experimental procedure dictates that we give some consideration to the assignment of the 4 acres of land. Should it be done at random? If not randomly, then in what systematic manner? Let's look at some alternatives:

Assign Acreage: a) At Random
                 b) First 4 tc's to acre #1, second 4 to acre #3, etc.
                 c) Some other manner.

Let's look at the implications of each of these proposed methods of assigning the acreage to the experiment. In Table 8-2, the random run order has been used to assign the proper acre at random. Runs number 1-4 have been assigned to acre #1; runs 5-8 are with acre #2; runs 9-12 are assigned acre #3; and runs 13-16 go with acre #4. To get an even better idea of the physical implications of these assignments, figure 8-1 shows how the plantings and fertilizations will look if viewed from an aerial photograph.

Table 8-2

RUN#	TC	NITRO%	PHOS%	POTSH%	TYPEPL	ACRE#
12	(1)	10	5	5	Corn	3
2	a	20	5	5	Corn	1
13	b	10	10	5	Corn	4
8	ab	20	10	5	Corn	2
14	c	10	5	10	Corn	4
4	ac	20	5	10	Corn	1
1	bc	10	10	10	Corn	1
9	abc	20	10	10	Corn	3
11	d	10	5	5	Tomato	3
3	ad	20	5	5	Tomato	1
10	bd	10	10	5	Tomato	3
15	abd	20	10	5	Tomato	4
16	cd	10	5	10	Tomato	4
6	acd	20	5	10	Tomato	2
5	bcd	10	10	10	Tomato	2
7	abcd	20	10	10	Tomato	2

Assigning the plants and the fertilizer at random is probably not a bad idea, for if there are any acre-to-acre differences, these differences are not confused or confounded with the factors under study as in the design found in Figure 8-2 and Table 8-3. Let's see what is improper or bad about the design using a systematic assignment of the acres.

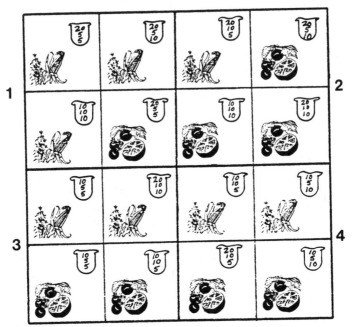

Figure 8-1
Fertilizers and Plantings Over A Four Acre Plot
(randomly placed)

In the 8-3 design, all the corn is systematically planted in acres designated as #1 and #3, while the tomatoes are systematically planted in the #2 and #4 acres. On top of that, notice that acres #1 and #2 all have 5% potash while acres #3 and #4 have the 10% potash. We can't tell if it is the natural fertility of the land or the fertilizer that is inducing the change in the growth of the plants in this confounded design.

We have used the word "confounded" before in Chapter 5. Recall that one of the rules of confounding was to not confound main effects with each other. We have done exactly that in the design of Table 8-3. We have in fact double-confounded type of plant and potash concentration with the land fertility. So to use the systematic approach of assigning the 4 acres of this example is not good practice and can lead to incorrect conclusions.

But what about the randomized design in Table 8-2? If there are acre-to-acre differences, then these differences will not show up as systematic effects, but as random effects. In our analysis, any differences between acres will be part of the error (our ability to repeat the measurements). This could be as undesirable as confounding

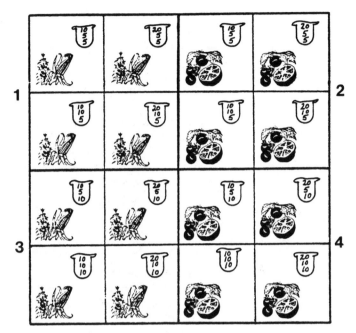

Figure 8-2
Fertilizers and Plantings Over a Four Acre Plot
(systematically placed)

Table 8-3

RUN#	TC	NITRO%	PHOS%	POTSH%	TYPEPL	ACRE#
12	(1)	10	5	5	Corn	1
2	a	20	5	5	Corn	1
13	b	10	10	5	Corn	1
8	ab	20	10	5	Corn	1
14	c	10	5	10	Corn	3
4	ac	20	5	10	Corn	3
1	bc	10	10	10	Corn	3
9	abc	20	10	10	Corn	3
11	d	10	5	5	Tomato	2
3	ad	20	5	5	Tomato	2
10	bd	10	10	5	Tomato	2
15	abd	20	10	5	Tomato	2
16	cd	10	5	10	Tomato	4
6	acd	20	5	10	Tomato	4
5	bcd	10	10	10	Tomato	4
7	abcd	20	10	10	Tomato	4

the main effects, since any increase in experimental error would decrease the sensitivity of the experiment which is our ability to find differences between effects. (For an expansion of this concept see Chapter 18).

THEORY OF BLOCKING

The solution to this dilemma is to systematically assign the acres as "blocks" in the experiment. However, the assignment is not made in the simple manner first tried in Table 8-3 where main effects are confounded with the acres, but in a more clever manner. Recall how in Chapter 5 we were able to confound a new main effect with a high order interaction and create the fractional factorial designs. The same thinking takes place in blocked factorial designs. We will confound the blocked "factor" with a higher order interaction. We use quotes on the word factor since we are not really studying the acres. It is a nuisance that we can't run the whole experiment on a homogeneous piece of land. Therefore, we call the variation between acres a "nuisance factor" which we do not study, but remove from the experiment.

A blocked experiment will need to take place in cases where there is a potential or real source of variation creeping into our experiment. We do not wish to study this source of variation, but must remove it from the results so the random error is not inflated. There are other reasons for blocking and other methods, but for now let's solve this agriculture problem and take a look at the general method of approaching blocking in 2^k factorials.

The idea is to confound the blocks (acres in this case) with higher order interactions. To construct the design, we need to know the number of blocks and from this number compute the number of primary or generating blocked effects. This is a concept similar to the fractionalization element of fractional factorial designs. We will use the symbol "p" to indicate the number of primary blocks. "p" is computed by finding the pth root of n (the number of blocks) that will produce 2.

$$^p\sqrt{n} = 2 \qquad\qquad (8\text{-}1)$$

or,

$$p = \frac{\ln (n)}{\ln (2)} \qquad\qquad (8\text{-}2)$$

Where: n represents the number of blocks
              p represents the number of primary blocks
              ln is the natural log functions.

How does a "primary block" differ from an ordinary block? In choosing the interactions to be confounded with the blocks, we have a limited free choice. Once we have decided upon the p primary blocks, the remaining blocks are determined. We must choose these primary blocks with great care so that the secondary or resulting blocks are not main effects or two-factor interactions. Let's return to our example and what see all this theory means.

CHOICE OF PRIMARY BLOCKS

In the 2^4 design we are working on, we have a four factor interaction ABCD that seems to be a likely candidate as an interaction to be confounded with the blocks. According to expression 8-1 we will need 2 primary blocks (i.e., $2\sqrt{4} = 2$) with 4 blocks representing the 4 acres of the land in this experiment. We need to pick another interaction to confound with the acres. We decide on a three factor interaction and select ACD from the 4 three factor interactions that are available.

The resulting secondary block is determined by using the same modulo (2) algebra system as used in Chapter 5. We multiple the two primary blocks together and any even power terms drop out.

$$ABCD * ACD = A^2BC^2D^2 = B \tag{8-3}$$

This result is not very acceptable. It says that one of the blocks will be confounded with a main effect (B, which is the nitrogen concentration). It is clear that our initial choice of primary blocks was not wise.

In general, we should choose primary blocks with the least number of common letters among them. The choice of the ABCD interaction was not keeping with this concept. Let's examine all the higher order interactions from this 2^4 design and see what we have to work with.

3-factor interactions:

A B C
A B   D
A   C D
B C D

4-factor interations:

A B C D

Setting the interactions down in the above staggered form is often a help in identifying the overlap and the resulting secondary blocks. From the above layout, we can see that if we use the 4-factor interaction, we will always get confounding with a main effect if we use one of the 3-factor interactions. We can also see that in this case, the best we can achieve in the secondary block is a 2-factor interaction as a result of the combination of two 3-factor interactions. Let's pick ABC and BCD. This gives us the 2-factor resultant of AD in the secondary block.

Now we have all the information necessary to complete the design. Table 8-4 is our original design with the appropriate signs of the two primary blocks added at the end. The combination of these signs shows us which block (or acre of land in this case) goes with each treatment combination. You will notice that we do not need to use the secondary block in our determination of the arrangement of block numbers. The combination of the two interactions with two levels gives us exactly the four blocks we need. If we were to add the secondary block, AD, as a column, we would see it would add no further information and only be redundant. (See problems).

To use the primary block columns in determining the proper block for each treatment, we observe the combination of signs. There are four unique combinations among the 16 tc's. There is a " − − ", a " + − ", a " + + ", and a " − + ". We will assign a block to each of these unique combinations. For example, block #1 is assigned to tc #(1), bc, abd, and acd, since each of these treatements have a " − − ". Similar assignments are made for the other 3 blocks as shown in Table 8-4.

While we have shown the logic behind the mechanics of building the blocked factorials, there are still a few loose ends left. We have not discussed degrees of freedom in these designs. In the original design, there are 15 df. By blocking, we are essentially adding another "factor". We do not want to study this "factor", but only remove its effect from the analysis. Our scheme is to keep the unwanted factor from inflating the experimental error, while not getting mixed up with the main effects under study. If this factor (or any factor, for that matter) has four levels, then we need three degrees of freedom to estimate its effect. The four blocks correspond to the four levels and consume three degrees of freedom. We get these three degrees of freedom from the interactions ABC, BCD, and AD.

In our analysis of this experiment (found in Chapter 18) any effects found with the ABC, BCD, or AD interactions will not be these interactions alone, but the linear combination of the blocked effect and the interaction effect. Since we don't know and can't know each component's contribution to this linear combination, we are unable to draw any conclusion about the "effect" of blocks or the effect of the interactions. In combining the blocks with these interactions, we give up our ability to draw inferences about either. We lose our degrees of freedom for the analysis in this part of the experiment. However, the remainder of the experiment is clear of any other confounding and we may draw conclusions about all the main effects and the remaining interactions.

Figure 8-3 shows the schematic diagram of the final experiment. Now we can see where the term "BLOCKED" comes from. The 4 acres of land have been divided up into uniform blocks of land and the appropriate treatment combinations have been

Table 8-4

RUN#	TC	NITRO%	PHOS%	POTSH%	TYPEPL	ABC	BCD	BLOCK#
12	(1)	10	5	5	Corn	−	−	1
2	a	20	5	5	Corn	+	−	2
13	b	10	10	5	Corn	+	+	3
8	ab	20	10	5	Corn	−	+	4
14	c	10	5	10	Corn	+	+	3
4	ac	20	5	10	Corn	−	+	4
1	bc	10	10	10	Corn	−	−	1
9	abc	20	10	10	Corn	+	−	2
11	d	10	5	5	Tomato	−	+	4
3	ad	20	5	5	Tomato	+	+	3
10	bd	10	10	5	Tomato	+	−	2
15	abd	20	10	5	Tomato	−	−	1
16	cd	10	5	10	Tomato	+	−	2
6	acd	20	5	10	Tomato	−	−	1
5	bcd	10	10	10	Tomato	−	+	4
7	abcd	20	10	10	Tomato	+	+	3

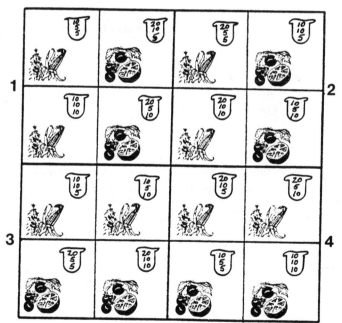

Figure 8-3
Fertilizers and Plantings Over A Four Acre Plot Using A Blocked Factorial

assigned to each block. Within each block we should assign the four treatment combinations at random. We can see why by looking at Figure 8-3. The boundaries we have set up are by measurement. Nature will impart her own differences in fertility across the land. There could be a diagonal swath of barren land running from the upper left corner to the lower right corner. While any such pattern of fertility could exist, our design can cope with it, and will be able to remove its influence on the factors under study to give us the sensitivity we need to complete the analysis.

PROBLEMS FOR CHAPTER 8

1. Compute the number of primary blocks in the following designs:

   a) a 2^6 with 4 treatments per block
   b) a 2^5 with 8 treatments per block
   c) a 2^4 with 4 treatments per block
   d) a 2^6 with 8 treatments per block

2. Select the primary blocks and compute the secondary blocks for the following designs:

   a) a 2^4 with 8 treatments per block
   b) a 2^6 with 16 treatments per block
   c) a 2^6 with 8 treatments per block

3. An experiment was designed to determine the effects of electrical coil breakdown voltage (i.e. when the coil shorts out). There were 6 factors under study, but the experiment could not be completely randomized due to changing environmental conditions. It is possible to make 8 runs under the same conditions, so the experiment was run in 8 blocks. Set up a reasonable design for this problem.

FACTORS	LEVELS		
1) Firing Furnace	#1	or	#3
2) Firing Temperature	1650°	or	1700°
3) Gas Humidification	Present	or	Absent
4) Coil Outer Diameter	.0300"	or	.0305"
5) Artificial Chipping	Yes	or	No
6) Sleeve	#1	or	#2

APPENDIX 8

BLOCKING:

A design method that allows the experimenter to remove an unwanted source of variation from the data.

Blocked Effect:

The source of variation being removed from the experiment. We do not "study" this effect, but rather determine its quantitative contribution to the variation and remove it from the noise or error.

Primary Block(s):

Higher order interaction effects that we have free choice in determining. We will choose p primary blocks where:

$$p = \frac{\ln(n)}{\ln(2)}$$

where ln is the natural log and n is the # of blocks.

Number of Blocks:

There will be n blocks in a blocked 2^k design where n will be an integer power of 2 and determine by the experimental conditions. If there are 32 treatments and it is possible to run only 8 treatments under uniform conditions, then there will be 4 blocks in the design.

Secondary Blocks:

Resulting interactions derived by multiplying the primary blocks together using the modulo 2 algebraic system. So, if we selected 2 primary blocks (ABC, BCDE) from a 2^5 with 4 blocks, then the secondary block would be ABC $*$BCDE = AB^2C^2DE = ADE.

Degrees of Freedom:

For blocks, there will be one less than the number of blocks degrees of freedom for the blocks. df $= n-1$ where n is the number of blocks.

9

RANDOMIZED BLOCK AND LATIN SQUARE

Although the blocked 2^k factorial design is a common type of approach to compensating for non-uniformities in the experimental conditions, there are other forms of the blocked experimental design. While the underlying concept remains the same in all blocked designs, particular restrictions on randomization have resulted in some very clever schemes and treatment combination patterns to overcome the problem of not being able to randomize completely. Picking the proper design almost becomes automatic and intuitive once the concept is understood. The analysis and interpretation is where the difficulties arise. In this chapter, we shall look at some of the other blocked designs. Chapter 18 will then show how to properly analyze the data from these designs.

It is interesting that this particular aspect of experimental design (blocking) has attracted much attention in other books and in many papers, while it probably is used less than 20% of the time! However, if the difficulty associated with the inability to randomize an experiment arises, it is mandatory that blocking methods be used if we want valid results.

COMPLETE RANDOMIZED BLOCK

In this family of designs, all of the possible treatment combinations are present. The blocked 2^k designs belong to this group. The design is quite simple, but the analysis requires care. In such designs, it is possible to block on only one effect while looking at another factor. The usual type of nuisance effects that we block on include day-to-day variation, operator to operator differences, lot to lot raw material changes, and other sources of variance that we do not wish to study, but which must be considered as potential sources of error.

The following example shows the effect of day-to-day variation on the density of a black and white photographic film. The factor under study in this experiment is the type of developer solution. The objective is to test the hypothesis that density (how black the image gets) is a function of the type of developer. From some preliminary information, it is determined that 8 samples from each type of developer are necessary to control the risks in the experiment. Because of the time necessary to process the film, only 8 runs may be made in a single day. It is also well-known that there can be day-to-day differences in developing film using this process. If we were to use only developer A on the first day and only developer B on the second day, we would not know if we were observing a developer change or a day-to-day change. In statistical words, we would have confounded days with developers. To block this day-to-day problem out of the experiment, we run half of the tc's with developer A on day 1 and the other half on day 2. We do the same for developer B. Now, we have 4 runs from each type of developer within a single day. Since there could be some variation induced during a day, we randomize the order of running the 8 treatments within each day. Our design would look like this (the values in parentheses are the density readings):

Table 9-1

	Developer A		Developer B	
	tc#3	(1.1)	tc#6	(1.2)
Day #1	tc#7	(1.0)	tc#2	(1.3)
	tc#1	(1.1)	tc#8	(1.2)
	tc#4	(1.3)	tc#5	(1.1)
	$\bar{X} = 1.125$		$\bar{X} = 1.20$	
	tc#4	(1.2)	tc#7	(1.4)
Day #2	tc#8	(1.4)	tc#1	(1.5)
	tc#5	(1.3)	tc#6	(1.4)
	tc#2	(1.2)	tc#3	(1.5)
	$\bar{X} = 1.275$		$\bar{X} = 1.45$	

We can see from the averages ($\bar{X}$'s) that there is a difference between days and also between developers. We shall see in a more extensive analysis in Chapter 18 how the day-to-day differences could have clouded the results if not analyzed in a blocked design. The blocked design allows us to remove a source of nuisance variation while still running a minimum of treatment combinations. We shall complete this analysis in Chapter 18 via Analysis of Variance.

GENERALIZATION OF RESULTS

Up to now, we have blocked our experiments to remove unwanted sources of variation. There is another reason to block in experimental design. The following example illustrates that concept.

A major energy company wants to test the effectiveness of a new additive on automobile gasoline efficiency. The pilot plant prepares a quantity of unleaded gasoline and adds 10% alcohol to half of the batch. The objective of the experiment is to test the hypothesis that miles per gallon is a function of type of gasoline. Since the results of this experiment could be used in a national advertising campaign, the test engineer wants to be sure that there is sufficient evidence to support a claim that gas-o-hol increases mpg. Considering the diversity of automobiles on the road, she decides to run the experiment not with just one automobile, but with a variety of automobiles. By doing this, the inference space is not restricted to only one make and model of vehicle, but is opened up to include the range of cars found on the road.

By looking at sales figures of domestic and foreign cars, the engineer picks the top five models that make up almost 65% of automobiles being driven, and adds five other models selected for their inherent efficiency. We now have a sufficient inference space capable of supporting any claims about the fuels. Table 9-2 shows the 10 cars and the results of fuel performance using the two types of gasoline in each automobile. We could look at the average of the mpg over the 10 cars for each type of fuel and do a simple "t" test of the difference between two means as outlined in Chapter 12. However, since there are 10 different types of cars in each average, with a wide range of inherent mpg capabilities, the variation in the data would lead us to conclude that there is no signification difference between the fuels. We can get around this problem of inflated variance by a simple trick in the analysis. Instead of trying to draw an inference about the difference between the two means, we will find the differences between each pair of fuelings for each car and test to see if these differences, when averaged over the 10 cars, produce a value significantly different from zero. This method, which is the very simplest of blocked designs, is called the "paired comparison" method or sometimes the "correlated pair".

The experiment in table 9-2 illustrates again that it is not so much the design, but the analysis, that is key in the understanding of information from experiments that are *blocked.* Chapter 18 will complete the analysis of this randomized block experiment to see if the gas-o-hol is indeed significantly better than plain unleaded fuel.

LATIN SQUARES

We have seen that blocking in experimental design can remove an unwanted source of nuisance variation and can also help expand the inference space of our conclusions to generalize the results. In all of the examples so far, we have blocked on only one

Table 9-2

Car Type	Plain Unleaded	Gas-o-hol	Difference
Chevette	31	34	3
Escort	33	37	4
Toyota	39	38	−1
T-2000	28	30	2
Reliant K	26	27	1
Rabbit	39	43	4
Coup DeVille	18	21	3
Regal	23	26	3
Firebird	14	18	4
Fairmont	18	20	2
	$X = 26.9$	29.4	2.5
	$s = 8.75$	8.46	1.58

effect. It is possible to block on two effects in a single experiment by using a design called the Latin Square. This design has attracted a lot of attention from the field of mathematics, and it has been studied by mathematicians for its pure structure, for there are only a finite set of Latin Squares. However, if blocked designs are used only 20% of the time, the Latin Square is used even less than that (possibly only 5%), and this design, although important, does not deserve this extensive publicity.

As the name implies, this design must be a square. That is, there are as many levels in the factor we are investigating as there are items in the two blocked "factors". The quotes on the word "factor" are important since we cannot study a blocked "factor", but only remove its effect from the analysis. This is a very important concept that is sometimes violated in a mis-application of the Latin Square.

Since there must be an equal number of levels among the factor under study and the blocks, it is sometimes difficult to apply the Latin Square to ordinary problems. This is one of the reasons that the use of this type of design is limited.

To build a Latin Square, we first usually identify the number of levels in the factor under study. Then we match the number of levels in the blocked "factors" to this number. Traditionally, the blocks are assigned to the rows and columns of the square and the factor under study is put into the body of the matrix. To create a three-dimensional matrix in only two dimensions, we superimpose letters of the Latin alphabet on the two-dimensional matrix. Table 9-3 shows a 5 x 5 Latin Square.

Block #1 runs across the top and block #2 runs along the side. The factor under study is identified by the letters A to E in the body of the experiment.

Table 9-3

BLOCK #1

		1	2	3	4	5
	1	A	B	C	D	E
	2	B	C	D	E	A
BLOCK #2	3	C	D	E	A	B
	4	D	E	A	B	C
	5	E	A	B	C	D

In superimposing the letters on the two-dimensional matrix, we have cycled them so that no row or column has the same letter in the intersection more than once. In running the experiment, we follow the conditions set by the row and column block levels and the letter identifies the level of the factor under study.

Now let's look at a Latin Square with six levels in the factor under study. We need to investigate the quality of photographs taken on 6 different color films that are on the market. Since we are interested in consumer opinion in a part of this assessment of quality, we will go directly to the customers and ask their opinion of the pictures. We carefully control the lighting, camera, and subject movement conditions in the creation of the pictures so these factors do not influence the judgement. We do, however, use 6 different picture content scenes, since it is a well-known fact that picture content can influence the opinion of an observer. By including various picture content scenes, we can expand our inference space beyond only one type of picture. We also know that different observers could inflate the error in our determinations of picture quality and render our experiment useless. Therefore, we will block this nuisance factor out of the analysis. The design for this doubly-blocked experiment is found in Table 9-4.

There are two possible approaches to randomization of the Latin Square design. The simpler approach is to assign random orderings to each treatment combination and execute the runs in that order. Another approach is to assign a random number to each column and reorder the columns, and then do the same thing to the rows. To illustrate this approach, we will reorder Table 9-4 first by column and then by row to obtain the final random order. Table 9-5 reorders the columns and Table 9-6 reorders the rows.

Table 9-4

Block #1 - Picture Content (For Generality)

		Rural	Portrait	Child	Old Man	Model	Food
	1	Fuji	Kodak	Fotomat	Kmart	Ilford	Agfa
	2	Kodak	Fotomat	Kmart	Ilford	Agfa	Fuji
Block #2	3	Fotomat	Kmart	Ilford	Agfa	Fuji	Kodak
Observer	4	Kmart	Ilford	Agfa	Fuji	Kodak	Fotomat
(nuisance)	5	Ilford	Agfa	Fuji	Kodak	Fotomat	Kmart
	6	Agfa	Fuji	Kodak	Fotomat	Kmart	Ilford

Table 9-5

Block #1 - Picture Content

		Child	Model	Rural	Portrait	Old Man	Food
	1	Fotomat	Ilford	Fuji	Kodak	Kmart	Agfa
	2	Kmart	Agfa	Kodak	Fotomat	Ilford	Fuji
Block #2	3	Ilford	Fuji	Fotomat	Kmart	Agfa	Kodak
Observer	4	Agfa	Kodak	Kmart	Ilford	Fuji	Fotomat
	5	Fuji	Fotomat	Ilford	Agfa	Kodak	Kmart
	6	Kodak	Kmart	Agfa	Fuji	Fotomat	Ilford

Now we take Table 9-5 and rewrite it with the observers in random order.

Table 9-6

Block #1 - Picture Content

		Child	Model	Rural	Portrait	Old Man	Food
	3	Ilford	Fuji	Fotomat	Kmart	Agfa	Kodak
	6	Kodak	Kmart	Agfa	Fuji	Fotomat	Ilford
Block #2	1	Fotomat	Ilford	Fuji	Kodak	Kmart	Agfa
Observer	4	Agfa	Kodak	Kmart	Ilford	Fuji	Fotomat
	5	Fuji	Fotomat	Ilford	Agfa	Kodak	Kmart
	2	Kmart	Agfa	Kodak	Fotomat	Ilford	Fuji

Before we begin gathering the data in the above experiment, we should review the reasons for running such a study. Many times, in such a detailed experiment, we become so involved with the design, we forget the reason for the work! To bring us back to reality, we need to understand the goal and the objective in this study of film types.

The goal is to find the best film for the purposes we have identified and the applications we specify. An experiment of this nature could be the basis of a report in a consumer magazine. The goal in this instance would be to make a valid recommendation on film type.

The objective of the experiment is to test the hypothesis that judged image quality is a function of film type. Notice that we are not interested in studying differences in picture content or differences between observers. There is only one factor under study. That factor is the film type. The picture content is included in the design to expand the inference space and the observer "factor" is merely a method of replicating the work to give it greater statistical validity.

Now it's time to gather some data. We start in the upper left corner of the design with Observer #3. Actually in selecting observers, we have "natural" randomization, since the selection process is a random process. However, given that we have the 6 observers in the room, we will take them in the order the design dictates. While there are a number of methods of attaching a numerical value to a psychological response, we will use the psychometric method called "magnitude estimation" as developed by S. S. Stevens. In this method the observer reports a numerical value that he or she associates with the "goodness" of the picture. In this case, the scale runs from 0 (poor) to 100 (good). We will present the pictures one at a time to the observer and obtain the responses as shown in Table 9-7.

Table 9-7

Block #1 - Picture Content

		Child	Model	Rural	Portrait	Old Man	Food
	3	75(I)	85(Fj)	80(Ft)	50(Km)	65(A)	88(EK)
	6	97(EK)	43(Km)	73(A)	85(Fj)	60(Ft)	65(I)
Block #2	1	82(Ft)	67(I)	87(Fj)	97(EK)	37(Km)	75(A)
Observer	4	82(A)	87(EK)	42(Km)	67(I)	72(Fj)	65(Ft)
	5	95(Fj)	70(Ft)	65(I)	80(A)	80(EK)	43(Km)
	2	57(Km)	77(A)	92(EK)	77(Ft)	57(I)	85(Fj)

We can find the average values for the 6 types of films from the body of the table. We can also find the average values of the picture content by finding the averages of the columns. The row averages give the differences between observers. These last two "factors" show a difference, but since these were added merely to increase the inference space of the experiment, we don't read any meaning into the differences. The only factor under study in this experiment is the film.

Film averages:

Table 9-8

Ilford	Fuji	Fotomat	Kmart	Agfa	Kodak
66	80.7	70.7	45.3	75.3	90.2

In Chapter 18 we will carry the detailed analysis of this Latin Square to completion.

THE MIS-USE OF THE LATIN SQUARE

We have emphasized the fact that in a Latin Square design, there is only one source of variation that can be studied as a true factor. The other two "factors" are merely removed from the analysis to reduce the noise portion of the variation. There are some experimenters who do not realize that in blocked designs there is an underlying assumption that there is no possibility of any interactions taking place between the nuisance factors and the factor under study. Since the Latin Square design is capable of handling a multi-level situation, there is an appeal to use it as a three-factor multi-level fractional factorial design. Such a use would be contrary to the assumption of no possible interactions, and we shall show in the following example that this is a complete mis-use of the Latin Square.

While the example is a simple 2-level design, the consequences can be expanded to the multi-level situation. Table 9-9 shows a Latin Square for the study of three factors. We have coded the levels with the conventional " − " and " + " signs used in Chapters 4 and 5 to indicate the low and high levels of the factors.

Table 9-9

Factor A

		−	+
Factor B	−	C (+)	C (−)
	+	C (−)	C (+)

Since this is a 2-level design, we can put it in YATES order in a different tabular form that conforms to the conventions shown in Chapters 4 and 5. Reconstructing Table 9-9, we get Table 9-10.

Table 9-10

A	B	C	AB	AC	AB
−	−	+	+	−	−
+	−	−	−	−	+
−	+	−	−	+	−
+	+	+	+	+	+

By observing the matching patterns in the signs of the main effects and the interactions in Table 9-10, we can readily see why interactions are not allowed in a Latin Square design. The main effects are completely confounded with the interactions! Another way of showing that the information in a Latin Square is limited in scope is to look at the degrees of freedom. As we showed in Chapter 5, this is a quantitative way of measuring the volume of information in an experiment.

In the above design, there are 3 degrees of freedom (one less than the total number of observations). We will require one degree of freedom for each main effect since there are two levels in each factor. We "use up" all the available(3) degrees of freedom immediately with the main effects. There are no degrees of freedom left for the interactions. From an information content, we cannot investigate interactions in a Latin Square; therefore, this design cannot be used as a factorial design where the intent is to be able to obtain information on interactions.

The concept of information content as measured by degrees of freedom can be applied to even larger Latin Squares. For example, a 5 x 5 Latin Square has 24 degrees of freedom. The 3 main effects require 12 degrees of freedom, which leaves 12 degrees of freedom. However, each two-factor interaction uses 16 degrees of freedom (4 x 4). There are 3, two-factor interactions among the three factors, and if we were to measure them, we would require 48 degrees of freedom, which is 36 more than we have left after measuring the main effects! Since degrees of freedom cannot be created out of thin air, we can see that, again, interactions are not possible in a Latin Square. What is worse is the fact that, if interactions exist between the factors under study, their effects will be confounded with the main effects, which will bias the conclusions.

The solution to the multi-level fractional factorial is the central composite design (CCD) that we studied in Chapter 6. A three-factor central composite design requires even less work than a 5 x 5 Latin Square (there are 15 treatment combinations in the CCD with 3 factors). It is the allocation of the degrees of freedom in the CCD that makes the difference between the good information it obtains and the mis-information a Latin Square used as a factorial confers upon us.

PROBLEMS FOR CHAPTER 9

1. An assembly line process is conducted in two plants and there is a suspicion that the two plants do not produce the same level of quality. Because of the nature of the response variable, it is necessary to have a relatively large sample to draw the conclusions with low risk. The required sample size is 250 units per line. However, the assembly process is slow, and each line can make only 10 units per day. If there is evidence from the control charts on the lines that there is a hefty amount of day-to-day variation, then how would you design such an experiment to see if the lines differ? State the goal and objective for this experiment and propose a design that will handle the nuisance of day-to-day variation.

2. There is a suspicion, but no evidence, that two methods of analysis produce different results, although they are supposed to be identical. Propose an experiment that will settle the argument.

3. If I have four different copiers and wish to study the image quality produced by these devices, how many observers and test patterns will I need if I want to generalize the results with respect to test patterns, and remove the effect of the observers?

4. Show the design for the problems in #3 above. Put it in random order in readiness for running.

5. Consider an example of a situation from your experience that would require a blocked experimental design. Show the general design for this situation.

APPENDIX 9

Blocking: A technique used to remove an unwanted source of nuisance variation from an experiment or to expand the inference space of an experiment by generalizing over a set of conditions.

Randomized Block: One of the types of blocked experiments in which a block or condition is identified and within which the treatement combinations are randomized as if there were a "mini experiment" taking place in that block alone. However, there will be more than one block in the whole experiment which is considered in the total analysis.

Paired Comparison or   The simplest of the ramdomized block experiments
Correlated Pairs: where there are only two levels of the factor under
                                study. A "t" test on the average of the differences
                                between individual paired observations is used to
                                remove the unwanted source of variation.

Latin Square: An incomplete randomized block design that blocks
                                on two sources of nuisance variations (or two
                                generalizing variables; or one of each). In the Latin
                                Square there must be as many levels in each of the
                                two blocks as there are in the factor under study.
                                Each level of the factor under study is combined once
                                and only once with the intersections of the levels of
                                the two blocking effects.

Interactions and Blocks: There can be no interactions between the block effect
                                and the factor under study for valid conclusions to
                                hold.

10

NESTED DESIGNS

One of the uses of experimental design suggested in Chapter 1 was the "quantification of errors." All of the designs we have used so far have been concerned with the determination of a factor's functional effect on a response in a mechanistic or "fixed" sense. In addition to this fixed way of looking at the mechanism, we also set up the design to allow each of the levels of a factor to be present and in combination with the levels of all other factors. These factorial designs "cross" all the factors and levels. Table 10-1 shows a typical multi-level factorial experiment with replication. Observe how the levels of Factor #1 combine or cross with the levels of Factor #2.

Table 10-1

Temperature
Factor #1

		100°	200°	300°	400°
	10 psi	R1 R3 R2	R2 R1 R3	R1 R3 R2	R3 R2 R1
Pressure Factor #2	15 psi	R3 R1 R2	R1 R2 R3	R1 R3 R2	R1 R3 R2
	20 psi	R3 R1 R2	R3 R2 R1	R2 R1 R3	R1 R3 R2

In the above design, with the two factors of temperature and pressure, we find that for the 10 psi pressure setting, there are all the four temperature levels present. This allows us to study the effect of temperature at a specific level of pressure, and in fact do so at more than one level of pressure as we see in the rest of the experiment for the pattern of temperature change repeats over all three levels of pressure. Similarly, we can see from Table 10-1 that the pressure is studied (or changed) over all levels of temperature.

The "crossed" factorial experiment has an important place in experimental techniques and has been the subject of most of this book, for it allows us to study and make inferences about the interactions between factors.

However, as we look further into the design in Table 10-1, we find another "factor" with three "levels". This "factor" is not really a factor at all, but the replication used to determine the error or noise in the experiment. We have already discovered that the replicates must be randomly placed through-out the experiment. Therefore, each replicate has an equally likely change of appearing anywhere in the experiment at any time. Because of this randomness, we ask the question, "Does it make sense to compare the replicates' "levels" as we make comparisons across the temperature and pressure?" Of course, the answer is no. The three "levels" of the replication cannot be combined to study the "effect" of R1 or any interaction between R1 and the other true factors of temperature and pressure.

The replicates are included in the experiment for the single reason of quantifying the random error involved in setting up the control factors and measuring the response variable. The labels R1, R2, R3 are mere conveniences in the outline of our design. The set of three replicates contained in each treatment combination is complete in itself. The only remote relationship between each replicated cell we would like to see is that the amount of variation in each cell does not differ significantly from the variation in any of the remaining cells.

In the analysis of variance as shown in Chapter 13, we compute the pooled (or averaged) variance across the replicated cells. We can look at the error variance in each cell as contained or "nested" in that cell.

Figure 10-1 shows the way the cross experiment involving temperature and pressure would look in a diagramatic form. In this diagram, a line is drawn from each level of Temperature to each level of Pressure and represents a single treatment combination or run in the experiment. Notice how the lines cross. This type of design is called the "crossed" factorial.

If we were to take one of the treatment combinations from the factorial and extend the diagram to include the replicates, then we would obtain the picture in Figure 10-3.

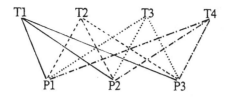

Figure 10-1

Notice that the three replicates do not cross over into another cell. This method of configuration is called "nesting" and can be extended to designs beyond the simple application of replication.

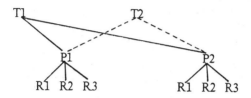

Figure 10-2

A NESTED DESIGN

In many manufacturing situations, we may have a process producing a product that is experiencing a greater degree of variation than can be tolerated by the functional specifications. The control chart may be in control, but the overall level of variance is too high. By merely taking the product as it emerges off the end of the line and measuring the response, we can compute the mean level of the quality parameter and its variance. This variance is probably the result of many influential sources. We would like to find the key source or sources of variance that contribute most to the overall observed variation. If we are able to do this detective work, we than have a good change of controlling the overall variation and producing a product that is fit for use. (That is, it meets the functional specifications).

Identifying and quantifying the sources of variation in an efficient manner is the job of the nested experimental design. In its most fundamental application, the concept of nesting is used in all replicated experiments to quantify the error variance. We have just shown in the previous example (Table 10-1) that even in a fully crossed, fixed factorial experiment, the error is always nested within the cells created by the combinations of the factors under study. We can extend the nesting concept upward to all of the factor in the experiment and study the effect of the variation as well as the effect of the change in overall mean values.

COALS TO KILOWATTS

To illustrate the concept of a nested design, let's look at an example from the electric power industry. The problem is centered around the level of polution-producing components in solid fossil fuel (coal) used for producing steam to generate electricity.

The coal comes from strip mines and is loaded into hopper cars directly from the mine. The electric utility is able to sample the coal before it leaves the mine site. If the sulphur content is below 5%, the EPA will allow the coal to be burned. The electric company has observed a high degree of variation in past shipments of coal from this mine, and wants to locate the sources of variation. The possible variance inducing factors are hopper car-to hopper car, samples within hopper cars, and analyses within samples. Figure 10-3 shows the diagram of this experiment which is a completely nested design.

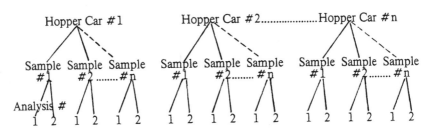

Figure 10-3

Each hopper car constitutes an experiment in itself. We can sample each car and find the variation induced in sulphur % from the chemical analysis. We can also find the variation from sample to sample taken within the car. If we look across many hopper cars, we can identify the amount of variation caused by car-to-car differences. Of course, all of the variation we observe is a function of the way the coal was formed in the ground, for the hopper cars only represent the loading of the coal from the mining operation. The nested design breaks the loading process down into a hierarchy of levels that can be isolated to pinpoint the sources of variation. The nested design is sometimes called a hierarchical experiment due to its ordered structure.

Getting back to the example, let's say that we randomly pick 3 hopper cars and take 4 samples per car. We will split the samples into two parts and replicate the measurements to quantify the levels of variation induced by the chemical analysis technique. Table 10-2 shows the data for this nested experiment.

Table 10-2

	HOPPER CAR # 1				HOPPER CAR # 2				HOPPER CAR # 3			
SAMPLE	1		2		3		4		1		2		3		4		1		2		3		4	
ANALYSIS	1	2	1	2	1	2	1	2	1	2	1	2	1	2	1	2	1	2	1	2	1	2	1	2
SULPHUR CONTENT	2	3	4	4	2	2	2	4	4	4	4	5	3	3	3	5	6	7	5	6	4	6	5	7

The average sulphur content across the 24 observations is 4.17 and the standard deviation is 1.52. If we can assume a normal distribution, then there is a portion of the coal that will be expected to have a sulphur content above the 5% EPA limit. Based on the normal distribution model, we can expect that 30% of the coal from this mine to be in excess of the EPA standard for sulphur content. Since we have exceeded the specification, the real question is where are the major sources of variation? Or, is it the chemical analysis that is causing the variance to be so large? The samples we have taken in the above nested design can answer these questions, since the structure of this design allows us to split the overall variance into its component parts. In Chapter 18 we will complete the analysis of this experiment and pinpoint the likely sources of variation. We will also show what to do with this knowledge of the variance in controlling the differences between cars, samples, and chemical analyses.

SUMMARY

The nested experimental design allows us to structure the treatment combinations into homogeneous groups that can be treated as separate sources of variation. In this way, we can dissect an overall source of variation into its component parts. With the knowledge of the major sources of variation, we can control the overall variance by controlling the individual components of variance.

PROBLEMS FOR CHAPTER 10

1. Show in a schematic outline an experimental design to study the components of variance for a chemical process which produces a granular product (1−5mm beads). The process is run in batches which are determined by the raw material. The product is packaged in large barrels with over 100 barrels per batch. The property under study is the viscosity of the material when heated and extruded through a small orifice.

2. A product that is being produces on an "around the clock" production schedule is experiencing a greater than expected reject rate. How would you begin to attack this problem? What questions could be asked to identify the sources of variation?

3. A chemist has developed a new analytical method to determine the concentration of a harmful chemical in fish. Suggest a nested design for the following possible variance contributors. Between sampling locations (lakes), between batches of reagents, between fish.

4. A market researcher wants to determine the best sampling scheme that will produce the lowest variance with the least cost. She expects to find sample-to-sample variance due to cities, states, counties, and people. What type of experiment could help determine which source of variation is the biggest? Outline such an experiment.

APPENDIX 10

Fixed Effect: We study only the levels present in the design to determine their mechanistic influence on the response. We may interpolate between levels, but do not make any general statement about the variance inducing properties of the factor as we may with the random effect.

Random Effect: We are less interested in measuring a mechanistic effect and more emphasis is placed on the general influence of this type of factor on the overall variation imposed on the response. Instead of being picked at specific levels, the random factor's levels are chosen by chance from a large array of possibilities.

Nested Factor: A set of treatments that are complete in themselves and do not cross into another set of treatments. Random error found by replication is always nested within the treatment combination.

Crossed Factor: The levels of this type of factor combine with all the levels of other factors.

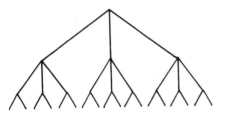

Nested Factors

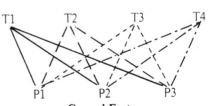

Crossed Factors

11

EVOP

All of the experimental designs we have studied so far have been "revolutionary" in their nature. In our study of process behavior or product characteristics, we have made rather large changes to the control factors to allow the observation of wide changes in the response variables. These experiments have revealed much information about the process or product, but the techniques have caused big changes to take place. Sometimes our experiments produce treatment combinations that actually make bad or less than desirable levels of the response variable's requirement. In such experiments, we welcome such "negative" information since it tells us how a process works. The contrast between the low level of a response and its higher level provides the information necessary to gain insight and understanding.

In two respects, then these designs are revolutionary. First of all there is a great "revolt" or change in the levels of the factors under study. Because of this revolt, we are able to "reveal" great quantities of information . Such revealing designs with "revolting" levels are useful in research projects, development endeavors, pilot plant trials and just about any experimental situation where we can and may make wide changes to the control factors under study.

THE PRIME DIRECTIVE OF MANUFACTURING

There is, however, a situation where wide ranging changes in the control variables are not allowed for fear of producing "bad product". If a product is already being manufactured and has not had the advantage of a good history of experimentation during its development cycle, then it may be advantageous to improve the process via some type of systematic investigation. The problem, however, in such a situation is

115

the fact that revolutionary changes will probably cause the process to go out of control and worse yet, produce some bad product.

The prime directive of a production line is not to produce any more bad product than would be expected based on past history.

Due to the nature of revolutionary types of experimentation, it is clear that such designs are incompatible with the basic goals of a manufacturing situation.

EVOLUTIONARY OPERATIONS

Instead of applying the relatively swift methods of a revolutionary experiment, we use the slow, systematic technique that allows us to evolve into improved process conditions. This methodology, called "Evolutionary Operations", or EVOP for short follows the following concepts and allows us to explore the terrain of a response surface.

1. PRIME DIRECTIVE: No interruption of the process.   No increase in defective production.

2. The investigation is based on small changes to the control factors under study.

3. The design is a two-level factorial plus a center point.

4. Work is conducted in phases with a change to new conditions (a new phase) taking place only when we have statistical evidence of a better set of conditions.

The four EVOP concepts mesh together to form a closed loop. The small changes in the control factors assure us that the prime directive will not be violated. (If it were violated, we would soon be "out of the factory on our ear"). The systematic approach in our study of a response surface utilizes the tried-and-true 2^k factorial with the added benefit of a center point to allow for the investigation of curvilinear effects.

Figure 11-1 shows a picture of a response surface. This particular surface represents the yield of a process as a function of temperature and pressure. The higher the "mountain", the greater the yield. If we were to take a "slice" of the mountain parallel with the ground, we would obtain an iso-yield section. That is, all around the perimeter of the slice we would observe the same level of the response. We would continue to take slices of the mountain and much like a contour map transfer these sections to a two-dimensional plot (as shown in Figure 11-2) that shows the relationship between yield and the two control variables of pressure and temperature.

To use the information in the response surface diagram, we find the intersection of the pressure and temperature that produces a given yield. We would probably be

Figure 11-1
A response surface.

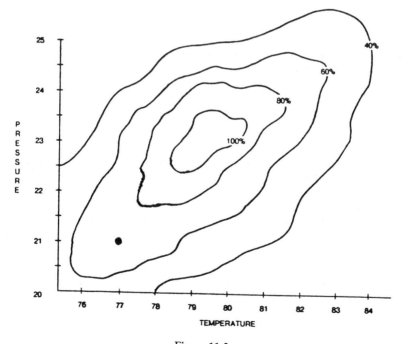

Figure 11-2

interested in obtaining the highest yield, so we find that where the temperature is between 79 and 81 and the pressure is between 22 and 23, we get a region that gives 100% yield. However, the surface is not parallel to the temperature axis and some of the combintaions of temperature and pressure points will not give 100% yield. To be exact, the 81°, 22psi combination gives only a 67% yield. The slope of the surface is very steep in this part of the drawing as indicated by the closeness of the contours.

On the other end of the yield range, we find that there are many combinations of pressure and temperature that give us the lowest reading of 40% yeild. Some of these are:

81°	21 psi
84°	22.75 psi
76°	22.75 psi
77°	23.75 psi

One feature of this process is the large changes in yield as a function of the changes in temperature and pressure. The manufacturing process must be kept in tight control to hold any specific yield at all. Let's say that we are obtaining yields between 60% and 70% for a set point of 77°, 21 psi with tolerances of ±1° and ±.5 psi. If we were to experiment and make large changes (say 2 to 3 degrees and 1 to 2 psi) we would certainly get into the 100% yield region, but we would also fall into the 40% or less region. Remember, this is a process that **must** continue to put out a product!

Because we may not disrupt the process, we resort to the EVOP method to guide us up the slope of the surface to the higher yield region. Of course, we don't know what the shape of the surface looks like, so we must grope around and find the proper vector from our current set point. To do so, we set up a small 2^2 factorial design with a center point. The center point is, in fact, the current operating conditions of 77° and 21 psi. We stay within the tolerances of the process and use temperature excursions that range only over ±.5°. This means that our low level of temperature is 76.5°, while the high is 77.5°. The pressure is changed only ±.25 psi. This produces levels of 20.75 psi and 21.25 psi.

While we attempt to set and hold the process conditions, we realize that such exact settings are probably impossible and combined with the natural measurement error in the response, we find that while we do our best, the yield is a random variable that shows some fluctuations. To compensate for this variation and to characterize the variance, we replicate the conditions. Replication is no problem, since we are in a production situation and we take advantage of the many times the process is run in a day.

A SLOW EXPERIENCE

To take advantage of the EVOP method, we must be very patient. The purposeful modifications in the manufacturing conditions will produce changes in the response that are very close to changes induced by random noise. However, by taking many observations, the noise can be reduced by the "law of large numbers" which assures us of reduced noise when we compare mean values. Of course, by taking more and more samples, we build up enough data to create mean values that begin to stabilize. If there are differences between the means, then we will be able to detect them when the sample size gets big enough. EVOP has its own analysis technique which we shall watch as we complete this example involving yield.

Table 11-1 is an EVOP worksheet that allows us to gather data and complete the analysis at the same time. This form has been set-up for a two factor EVOP and the proper factors apply to only this type of design. Most EVOPs are limited to only two factors, so this form and the following example will handle most of the situations encountered. A blank form is found in the appendix of this chapter.

USE OF THE EVOP WORKSHEET

Remember, EVOP takes a long time. For this reason, we first fill out the phase and cycle numbers. The phase refers to the set of conditions we will use in the factorial design. The phase will not change until we have evidence of a better set of operating conditions. The cycle is another name for a replicate. We will perform as many cycles as necessary to reduce the error limits to the point where the signal is big enough to be seen. Table 11-1 indicates that we are in Phase I, Cycle 1. The response is yield and it is a good idea to fill in the date.

The pictorial diagram in the upper left corner helps us keep an account of the five treatment combinations in the EVOP. We fill in the levels of temperature and pressure and now we are ready to begin the exploration of our process.

Each of the five treatment combinations are run in random order as in any experiment. The values are filled in on Line iii, the new observation. Since Cycle #1 has no replication, we move directly into Cycle #2 in Table 11-2. We transcribe the information from the previous worksheet before starting Cycle #2. The previous sum and the previous average are merely the first observations from cycle #1. We obtain new observations and now we can find the differences between the new observations and the previous average. This difference is placed in Line iv. We scan the range of differences and find the smallest difference is −2. Note that we watch the algebraic signs in our finding of the differences. The largest difference is 2. The range of differences (4) is recorded just to the right of Row iv. We will use this shortly to compute the standard deviation or noise in the experiment. We enter the sum of the observations in Row v and be dividing by n, the cycle number, we get the average in Row vi. The effects are computed by filling in the values of the new average at the appropriate points in the formulas below the data table. These formulas merely find the average contrast or change from the high level of the factor to the low level of the factor. So, for Factor A (temperature) we find the sum of the responses for the high levels of A (ie: a + ab) and subtract from it the low levels of A (ie: (1) + b). Taking half of this value gives us the average effect of Factor A. Similar calculations are made for B and the AB interaction.

The calculation of the effect for the center point may look complicated, but it is conceptually equivalent to finding the average of the four pieces of data in the factorial design and subtracting the zero point from this average.

$$\frac{1}{5} \, ((1) + a + b + ab - 4* \, (zero)) \qquad (11\text{-}1)$$

The value calculated in expression 11-1 provides us with information on the "curviness" of the response surface in the region of experimental investigation. If the region is curved, then we will observe a large difference between the "conceptual average" obtained by taking the four corners of the factorial design and the actual zero data point in the center of the design. If there is no curvature, then the two values are the same (within experimental error). Because of the way we subtract the zero from the average of the factorial points, a negative value indicates that the zero point is near a maximum, and a positive indicates that the zero is near a minimum. Figure 11-3 illustrates this concept by showing a side view of the surface with the average of the factorial and the zero point.

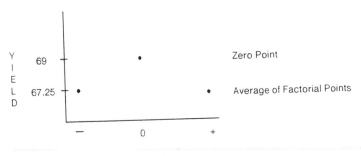

Figure 11-3

If we subtract the zero point from the average of the factorial we get a negative value for this example indicating what is illustrated in Figure 11-3 that the zero point is higher than the rest of the experimental values. Now, we don't really make such a simple subtraction of the average and the zero point, but weight the 5 points according to expression 11-1. We look at the average of the whole set of five values (that's why a divisor of 5) with the zero point multiplied by 4 to balance it against the four points of the factorial.

The reason for the measure of the position of the center point with respect to the total experiment is to tell us if we should stop the EVOP process because of a maximum or minimum value in the region of investigation. In our example we have an indication of being in a maximum region, but we need to now compute the noise in the data to see if there is a real change taking place.

SIGNAL TO NOISE IN EVOP

To make the calculations of the variation encountered in an EVOP as easy as possible for the production people using the technqiue, the standard deviaiton is derived from a simple range calculation.

Again, Table 11-2 has the details. Since we are only in Cycle #2, there are no previous sum of the standard deviations (Σs) nor a previous average standard deviation (ave s). We can compute a new standard deviation (new s) on the third line (just across from Row iii). The difference range of 4 for this example is multipled by the $f_{k,n}$ from the table at the lower right corner of the worksheet. This factor $f_{k,n}$ is the multiplier that will convert a range statistic into a standard deviation. The k subscript refers to the number of treatment combinations in the EVOP (5 in our example) and the n is the cycle number (2 in this case). The appropriate $f_{k,n}$ number is then 0.30. This gives us a new standard deviation of 1.2, which is also the new sum of the standard deviation (new ss) and new average standard deviation. Now, some "purists" will argue that you can't average a standard deviation, but for the type of inference we are working with in this EVOP system, the fact is, the method works. We will not go into the theory in this chapter, but further details are available in reference 1 by Box and Draper.

TIME FOR DECISION

With measure of the effects and armed with a standard deviation, we have all the elements for making a statistical inference via a signal to noise ratio. We will make this process even easier by calculating the "error" limits for the effects under study. If the effect exceeds the error limit, then we can safely say (at a 95% level) that there is more than just chance influencing the response variable.

The error limits for the averages and the effects are calculated alike by taking twice the standard deviation and dividing it by the square root of n. This gives us an error limit of 1.7. The error limit for the change in the center effect is only slightly different. The standard deviation is multiplied by 1.78 since there are 5 values in the computation of the center point value. The error limit for the center point is 1.5.

If we compare the error limits to the effects calculations, we find that all the effects are greater than the error limits. This indicates that there is a significant change in the response due to the changes in temperature and pressure. However, the change in the center effect is less than (in absolute value) error limit for the change in the center effect and we are neither at a maximum nor at a minimum. We have the "GO"

Table 11-1

EVOP WORKSHEET

CYCLE n =	1				
PHASE =	I				
RESPONSE =	Yield				

CALCULATION OF AVERAGES						CALCULATION OF STD. DEV.
TREATMENT COMBINATION	0	(1)	a	b	ab	
(i) PREVIOUS SUM						PREVIOUS Σs =
(ii) PREVIOUS AVERAGE						PREVIOUS AVERAGE $\bar{s}$ =
(iii) NEW OBSERVATION	70	65	65	63	75	NEW s = RANGE • $f_{k,n}$ =
(iv) DIFFERENCE ii-iii						DIFFERENCE RANGE =
(v) NEW SUM i + iii	70	65	65	63	75	NEW Σs =
(vi) NEW AVERAGE $\frac{V}{N}$	70	65	65	63	75	NEW AVERAGE s = $\frac{NEW \ \Sigma s}{n-1}$ =
DATE	11/15	11/15	11/15	11/15	11/15	FOR 2^2 EVOP
TIME	1 PM	10 AM	3 PM	11 AM	9 AM	

EFFECTS:

$A = \frac{1}{2}((a + ab) \cdot ((1) + b))$ =

$B = \frac{1}{2}((b + ab) \cdot ((1) + a))$ =

$AB = \frac{1}{2}(((1) + ab) \cdot (a + b))$ =

EFFECT OF THE CHANGE IN THE CENTER*

$\frac{1}{5}((1) + a + b + ab-4 \text{*}(zero))$ =

*IF NEGATIVE-CENTER IS NEAR MAX.
*IF POSITIVE-CENTER IS NEAR MIN.

ERROR LIMITS: n = # OF CYCLES

FOR AVERAGES: $2\bar{s}/\sqrt{n}$ =

FOR NEW EFFECTS: $2\bar{s}/\sqrt{n}$ =

FOR CHANGE IN THE
CENTER EFFECT: $\frac{1.78\bar{s}}{\sqrt{n}}$ =

TABLE OF $f_{k,n}$

CYCLES	$f_{k,n}$ for k = 5
1	..
2	.30
3	.35
4	.37
5	.38
6	.39

Table 11-2

EVOP WORKSHEET

CYCLE n =   2

PHASE =   I

RESPONSE =   Yield

CALCULATION OF AVERAGES						CALCULATION OF STD. DEV.
TREATMENT COMBINATION	0	(1)	a	b	ab	
(i) PREVIOUS SUM	70	65	65	63	75	PREVIOUS Σs = None
(ii) PREVIOUS AVERAGE	70	65	65	63	75	PREVIOUS AVERAGE s̄ = None
(iii) NEW OBSERVATION	68	67	65	64	74	NEW s = RANGE *f $_{k,n}$ = 4*.3 = 1.2
(iv) DIFFERENCE ii-iii	2	-2	0	-1	1	DIFFERENCE RANGE = 4
(v) NEW SUM i + iii	138	132	130	127	149	NEW Σs = 1.2
(vi) NEW AVERAGE $\frac{V}{N}$	69	66	65	63.5	74.5	NEW AVERAGE s = $\frac{\text{NEW } \Sigma s}{n-1}$ = 1.2
DATE	11/17	11/17	11/18	11/17	11/18	FOR 2^2 EVOP
TIME	10 AM	1 PM	10 AM	3 PM	3 PM	

EFFECTS:

$$A = \frac{1}{2} ((a + ab) - ((1) + b)) \quad = 5$$

$$B = \frac{1}{2} ((b + ab) - ((1) + a)) \quad = 3.5$$

$$AB = \frac{1}{2} (((1) + ab) - (a + b)) \quad = 6$$

EFFECT OF THE CHANGE IN THE CENTER*

$$\frac{1}{5} ((1) + a + b + ab - 4*(zero)) \quad = -1.4$$

*IF NEGATIVE-CENTER IS NEAR MAX.
*IF POSITIVE-CENTER IS NEAR MIN.

ERROR LIMITS: n = # OF CYCLES

FOR AVERAGES: $2\bar{s}/\sqrt{n}$ = 2.4/1.44 = 1.7

FOR NEW EFFECTS: $2\bar{s}/\sqrt{n}$ = 1.7

FOR CHANGE IN THE
CENTER EFFECT: $\frac{1.78\,\bar{s}}{\sqrt{n}}$ = 1.5

TABLE OF f $_{k,n}$

CYCLES	$f_{k,n}$ for k = 5
1	..
2	.30
3	.35
4	.37
5	.38
6	.39

signal from these results and should move to a new phase of investigation. the
direction that gives us the highest yield is toward the ab treatment combination. The
difference between our current zero point and the best experimental point is (74.5-69)
5.5 yield units which is in excess of the error limit for an average. therefore, we can
make the move to the ab (77.5 temp., 21.25 pressue) treatment combination and use
this as our new zero point in Phase II.

PHASE II

In phase II our new conditions are moved up in both temperature and pressure. In
the second cycle (Table 11-4) we observe large effects for all the factors and the
interaction, but while these effects are greater than the error limits, the difference
between the current set-point (the zero point) and the next higher contender (the ab
treatment combination) is only 1.5 (absolute) yield units. This is not enough to
consider a change to the next phase since the 1.5 is not greater than the error limit for
averages of 2.97. We therefore, go to another cycle and gather 5 more data points.

In Cycle 3, the error limits are reduced by both better repeatability and because the
divisor in the computation of this factor is increased. Now we can see how EVOP gets
its sensitivity by many replicates. The error limits are of sufficient size to allow us to
decide that the "ab" treatment is significantly larger than the "zero" treatement.

There is one slight problem with a decision to move to another set of operating
conditions. The effect of the change in the center indicates that the center is near a
maximum. If we did not have the basic knowledge of the response variable, we might
be inclined to halt the EVOP process here. However, we know that yield can reach
100%, so we move on to a third phase with the conditions of the old "ab" treatment
becoming the conditions for the new center point in the third phase.

By now you should get the idea that EVOP is a slow process. We have spent about
two weeks in only two phases and there is a lot more work to accomplish before we
can reach our goal of 100% yield. Figure 11-6 is a summary of the completion of this
EVOP. Notice how the technqiue follows a clear path up the side of the response
surface and reaches the top without any detours.

EQUATIONS FROM EVOP

With the large quantity of data after an EVOP has been run, the experimenter might
be tempted to load all the information into a regression computer program and create
an equation of the surface. While this is a good thought, remember that the scope of
the EVOP experiment is very narrow. The equation would be valid only in that
portion of the response surface that was explored. Therefore, the equation would not
be general enough to perform the robust predicitons expected of it. It would be
sufficient to help control the process in the region of interest. It could be used to help

Table 11·3

EVOP WORKSHEET

CYCLE n = ___1___

PHASE = ___II___

RESPONSE = ___Yield___

CALCULATION OF AVERAGES						CALCULATION OF STD. DEV.
TREATMENT COMBINATION	0	(1)	a	b	ab	
(i) PREVIOUS SUM						PREVIOUS Σs =
(ii) PREVIOUS AVERAGE						PREVIOUS AVERAGE $\bar{s}$ =
(iii) NEW OBSERVATION	74	68	69	68	78	NEW s = RANGE *$f_{k,n}$ =
(iv) DIFFERENCE ii-iii						DIFFERENCE RANGE =
(v) NEW SUM i + iii	74	68	69	68	78	NEW Σs =
(vi) NEW AVERAGE $\frac{V}{N}$	74	68	69	68	78	NEW AVERAGE s = $\dfrac{NEW\ \Sigma s}{n-1}$ =
DATE	11/20	11/19	11/20	11/20	11/19	FOR 2^2 EVOP
TIME	3 PM	1 PM	11 AM	9 AM	9 AM	

EFFECTS:

$A = \frac{1}{2} ((a + ab) - ((1) + b)) =$

$B = \frac{1}{2} ((b + ab) - ((1) + a)) =$

$AB = \frac{1}{2} (((1) + ab) - (a + b)) =$

EFFECT OF THE CHANGE IN THE CENTER*

$\frac{1}{5} ((1) + a + b + ab - 4*(zero)) =$

*IF NEGATIVE-CENTER IS NEAR MAX.
*IF POSITIVE-CENTER IS NEAR MIN.

ERROR LIMITS: n = # OF CYCLES

FOR AVERAGES: $2\bar{s}/\sqrt{n}$ =

FOR NEW EFFECTS: $2\bar{s}/\sqrt{n}$ =

FOR CHANGE IN THE CENTER EFFECT: $\dfrac{1.78\,\bar{s}}{\sqrt{n}}$ =

TABLE OF $f_{k,n}$

CYCLES	$f_{k,n}$ for k = 5
1	··
2	.30
3	.35
4	.37
5	.38
6	.39

Table 11-4

EVOP WORKSHEET

CYCLE n =   2

PHASE =   II

RESPONSE =   Yield

CALCULATION OF AVERAGES						CALCULATION OF STD. DEV.
TREATMENT COMBINATION	0	(1)	a	b	ab	
(i) PREVIOUS SUM	74	68	69	68	78	PREVIOUS Σs = None
(ii) PREVIOUS AVERAGE	74	68	69	68	78	PREVIOUS AVERAGE $\bar{s}$ = None
(iii) NEW OBSERVATION	77	67	69	64	76	NEW s = RANGE *f $_{k.n}$ = 7*.3 = 2.1
(iv) DIFFERENCE ii-iii	-3	1	0	4	2	DIFFERENCE RANGE = 7
(v) NEW SUM i + iii	151	135	138	132	154	NEW Σs = 2.1
(vi) NEW AVERAGE $\frac{V}{N}$	75.5	67.5	69	66	77	NEW AVERAGE s = $\frac{NEW \Sigma s}{n-1}$ = 2.1
DATE	11/23	11/23	11/24	11/24	11/23	FOR 2^2 EVOP
TIME	11 AM	3 PM	9 AM	11 AM	9 AM	

EFFECTS:

$A = \frac{1}{2} ((a + ab) - ((1) + b)) = 6.25$

$B = \frac{1}{2} ((b + ab) - ((1) + a)) = 3.25$

$AB = \frac{1}{2} (((1) + ab) - (a + b)) = 4.5$

EFFECT OF THE CHANGE IN THE CENTER*

$\frac{1}{5} ((1) + a + b + ab - 4*(zero)) = 4.75$

Δ BETWEEN "0" and "ab" = 75.5 - 77 = -1.5

*IF NEGATIVE-CENTER IS NEAR MAX.
*IF POSITIVE-CENTER IS NEAR MIN.

ERROR LIMITS: n = # OF CYCLES

FOR AVERAGES: $2\bar{s}/\sqrt{n}$ = 2.97

FOR NEW EFFECTS: $2\bar{s}/\sqrt{n}$ = 2.97

FOR CHANGE IN THE
CENTER EFFECT: $\frac{1.78\,\bar{s}}{\sqrt{n}}$ = 2.64

TABLE OF f $_{k.n}$

CYCLES	$f_{k.n}$ for k = 5
1	..
2	.30
3	.35
4	.37
5	.38
6	.39

Table 11-5

EVOP WORKSHEET

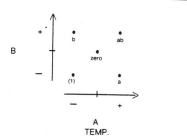

B

A
TEMP.

CYCLE n =   3

PHASE =   II

RESPONSE =   Yield

CALCULATION OF AVERAGES						CALCULATION OF STD. DEV.
TREATMENT COMBINATION	0	(1)	a	b	ab	
(i) PREVIOUS SUM	151	135	138	132	154	PREVIOUS Σs = 2.1
(ii) PREVIOUS AVERAGE	75.5	67.5	69	66	77	PREVIOUS AVERAGE $\bar{s}$ = 2.1
(iii) NEW OBSERVATION	75	68	67	66	79	NEW s = RANGE *$f_{k,n}$ = 4*3.5 = 1.4
(iv) DIFFERENCE ii-iii	.5	-.5	2	0	-2	DIFFERENCE RANGE = 4
(v) NEW SUM i + iii	226	203	205	198	233	NEW Σs = 3.5
(vi) NEW AVERAGE $\frac{V}{N}$	75.3	67.7	68.3	66	77.7	NEW AVERAGE s = $\dfrac{\text{NEW } \Sigma s}{n-1}$ = 1.75
DATE	11/30	12/1	11/30	12/1	11/30	FOR 2^2 EVOP
TIME	9 AM	1 PM	1 PM	9 AM	11 AM	

EFFECTS:

$A = \frac{1}{2} ((a+ab) \cdot ((1)+b))$ = 6.15

$B = \frac{1}{2} ((b+ab) \cdot ((1)+a))$ = 3.85

$AB = \frac{1}{2} (((1)+ab) \cdot (a+b))$ = 5.55

ERROR LIMITS: n = # OF CYCLES

FOR AVERAGES: $2\bar{s}/\sqrt{n}$ = 2.02

FOR NEW EFFECTS: $2\bar{s}/\sqrt{n}$ = 2.02

FOR CHANGE IN THE
CENTER EFFECT: $\dfrac{1.78\,\bar{s}}{\sqrt{n}}$ = 1.8

EFFECT OF THE CHANGE IN THE CENTER*

$\frac{1}{5} ((1)+a+b+ab-4*(zero))$ = -4.3

Δ BETWEEN "0" and "ab" = 75.3 - 77.7 = -2.4

*IF NEGATIVE-CENTER IS NEAR MAX.
*IF POSITIVE-CENTER IS NEAR MIN.

TABLE OF $f_{k,n}$

CYCLES	$f_{k,n}$ for k = 5
1	..
2	.30
3	.35
4	.37
5	.38
6	.39

get a sick process back to health should it wander from the path worn in the mountainside by the EVOP investigation. If you look at the response surface, you will see that there are many possible paths to the top. The path that is taken depends on where we start the process. We started in the South-West corner and get to the top. We could have just as easily started in the North-East corner and moved down in temperature and pressure to reach the same peak.

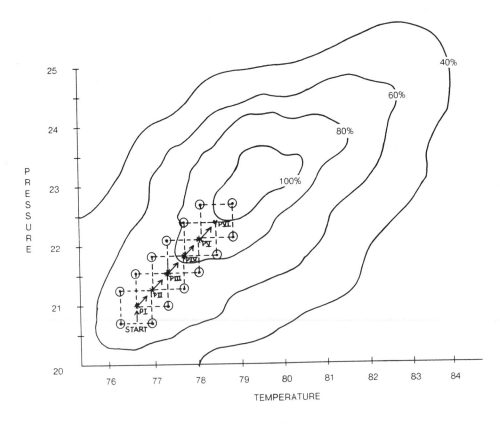

Figure 11-6

Completion of the EVOP. The phases of the process are shown by the corners of the 2^2 factorial designs.

EVOP REFERNCES

1. Box, George E.P.; Draper, Norman R., Evolutionary Operation, John Wiley & Sons, Inc., 1969.

2. Bingham, Richard S., Try EVOP for Systematic Process Improvement, Industrial Quality Control, Vol XX, No. 3, September 1963.

3. Box, G.E.P., and Hunter, J.S., Condensed Calculations for Evolutionary Operation Programs, Technometrics, Vol. 1, No. 1, pages 77-95, February, 1959.

APPENDIX 11

EVOP:

EVolutionary OPeration: a method that allows improved product or process performance while maintaining the uninterrupted flow of a production line.

RULES OF EVOP:

1. No interruption of the process or increase in % defective.
2. Make small changes to the factors under study.
3. Use a two level factorial with a center point.
4. Work in phases with a shift to a new phase only when there is evidence of a statistically significant improvement in the response.

STATISTICAL SIGNIFICANCE:

Statistical Significance is demonstrated when the error limits as calculated from the standard deviation are smaller than the effect being studied.

See next page for EVOP Worksheet.

There are no problems in this chapter.

EVOP WORKSHEET

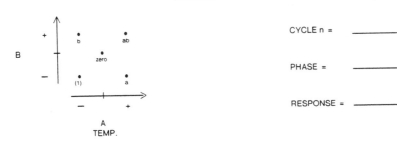

B

A
TEMP.

CYCLE n = _____

PHASE = _____

RESPONSE = _____

CALCULATION OF AVERAGES						CALCULATION OF STD. DEV.
TREATMENT COMBINATION	0	(1)	a	b	ab	
(i) PREVIOUS SUM						PREVIOUS Σs =
(ii) PREVIOUS AVERAGE						PREVIOUS AVERAGE $\bar{s}$ =
(iii) NEW OBSERVATION						NEW s = RANGE * $f_{k,n}$ =
(iv) DIFFERENCE ii-iii						DIFFERENCE RANGE =
(v) NEW SUM i + iii						NEW Σs =
(vi) NEW AVERAGE $\dfrac{V}{N}$						NEW AVERAGE s = $\dfrac{\text{NEW } \Sigma s}{n \cdot 1}$ =
DATE						FOR 2^2 EVOP
TIME						

EFFECTS:

$A = \dfrac{1}{2}((a + ab) \cdot ((1) + b))$ =

$B = \dfrac{1}{2}((b + ab) \cdot ((1) + a))$ =

$AB = \dfrac{1}{2}(((1) + ab) \cdot (a + b))$ =

EFFECT OF THE CHANGE IN THE CENTER*

$\dfrac{1}{5}((1) + a + b + ab \cdot 4 \cdot (zero))$ =

*IF NEGATIVE-CENTER IS NEAR MAX.
*IF POSITIVE-CENTER IS NEAR MIN.

ERROR LIMITS: n = # OF CYCLES

FOR AVERAGES: $2\bar{s} / \sqrt{n}$ =

FOR NEW EFFECTS: $2\bar{s} / \sqrt{n}$ =

FOR CHANGE IN THE
CENTER EFFECT: $\dfrac{1.78 \bar{s}}{\sqrt{n}}$ =

TABLE OF $f_{k,n}$

CYCLES	$f_{k,n}$ for k = 5
1	..
2	.30
3	.35
4	.37
5	.38
6	.39

```
100 REM EVOP PROGRAM FOR 2X2 WITH CENTER POINT
101 S1=0
102 S2=0
103 S3=0
104 S4=0
105 S5=0
106 S6=0
110 PRINT "ENTER CYCLE #"
120 INPUT C
130 PRINT "ENTER VALUES FOR TREATMENTS: 0,(1),A,B,AB"
135 INPUT Z,O,A,B,A1
140 IF C=1 THEN 150
141 D1=S1/(C-1)-Z
142 D2=S2/(C-1)-O
143 D3=S3/(C-1)-A
144 D4=S4/(C-1)-B
145 D5=S5/(C-1)-A1
150 S1=Z+S1
160 S2=O+S2
170 S3=A+S3
180 S4=B+S4
190 S5=A1+S5
195 IF C=1 THEN 110
250 X1=S1/C
260 X2=S2/C
270 X3=S3/C
280 X4=S4/C
290 X5=S5/C
295 PRINT
300 PRINT "AVERAGES: 0=";X1;"(1)=";X2;"A=";X3;"B=";X4;"AB=";X5
310 PRINT
320 PRINT "DIFFERENCES:";D1;D2;D3;D4;D5
330 PRINT
340 PRINT "ENTER DIFFERENCE RANGE AND F(KN)"
350 INPUT R,F
360 D=R*F
370 S6=D+S6
380 D6=S6/(C-1)
385 PRINT
390 PRINT "STANDARD DEVIATION=";D6
400 E1=.5*((X3+X5)-(X2+X4))
410 E2=.5*((X4+X5)-(X2+X3))
420 E3=.5*((X2+X5)-(X3+X4))
430 C1=.2*(X2+X3+X4+X5-(4*X1))
440 PRINT "EFFECTS: A=";E1;"B=";E2;"AB=";E3
450 PRINT "CENTER EFFECT=";C1
460 PRINT
470 PRINT "ERROR LIMITS:";(2*D6)/(C**.5)
480 PRINT "CENTER ERROR LIMITS=";(1.78*D6)/(C**.5)
490 PRINT "ANOTHER CYCLE?  ENTER 1 IF SO"
500 INPUT Y
510 IF Y = 1 THEN 110
520 END
>
```

PART III

Sorting the Signal from the Noise

12

SIMPLE ANALYSIS

In any and all experimental work, the results we observe are subject to variation. If there were no variation, then the discipline of statistical analysis would not exist. It is interesting to speculate on the origin of the word "statistic" and how the science evolved from uses in early feudal kingdoms. There are three roots to the word. The first, "stat ", refers to the state. The second, "ism", is a root that can take on the meaning of fact or condition. The third part, "ist", is a suffix meaning the practice of, or discipline. So, the word "statistic" first meant a discipline to understand the condition of the state. Indeed, in the early days of statistics, the prime duty of the royal statistician was to report population, wealth and all the other important information that would help the kingdom gather the correct taxes. Today we still have our demographers and actuarians who "write about people" and gather facts for the state. Every 10 years, a national census of the population is taken at great cost, and sometimes with controversial results.

While the counting of people and wealth is still practiced, it is the discipline of statistical analysis that we shall treat in the third part of this book, for it is a necessary ingredient in the understanding of the results of our experimental designs. The analysis we shall investigate is called "statistical inference". This branch of mathematics that does something useful for people consists of a body of methods for making wise decisions in the face of uncertainty. We shall assume that the reader has a rudimentary idea of probability. You have undoubtedly gained such knowledge of probability from betting on the weekly football pool or from listening to the weatherman talk about "chances of rain".

To understand the uses of probability in statistical inference, we need go no further than to say that we would like to have a high probability (close to 1) of making the "correct decision". (For those who are in need of a quick review of some basic probability axioms, Appendix 12 is appropriate reading.) The "correct decision" is a wise decision based on the application of the methods of statistical inference.

Before we can look at the methods, we need to define how much of a chance we can take in making a wrong decision. This is called our "risk" and the inverse of the risk (1-"risk") is the probability of being correct. Ideally, we would like the risk to be zero. Practically, it is impossible to make the risk zero as long as there is variation in our data, but the risk can be reduced to levels as low as .05 (5%) or even .01 (1%) depending on the quality of the information obtained from the experiment. This is why the design of the experiment is very important.

HYPOTHESIS TESTING

The cornerstone of statistical inference is the discipline known as "hypothesis testing". The hypothesis test stems directly from our prior knowledge of the process and the objective we write before we even gather one iota of information. In simple experiments, the hypotheses are stated about differences between mean values and also about differences in the variation. We shall treat the mean value hypotheses in the following examples before getting into the methods for testing variation.

EXAMPLE #1

Let's assume that a production line has been routinely making a piece-part with a dimension of 10 inches. We know that this value of 10 inches is an average value

Table 12-1

10.06	9.76	10.07	10.15	9.85
10.02	9.85	10.03	10.16	10.12
10.08	9.98	10.04	10.15	9.95
9.98	9.82	9.92	9.95	9.81
9.84	10.08	9.76	9.93	9.81

measured over the long run (many years). If we were to take a random sample from the production line at any time and measure, say, 25 parts, we would hope to find a mean value of 10. However, not all the parts would be exactly the same size because of process variation. Table 12-1 shows what 25 parts would look like from such a process. Notice that the parts are all near the 10-inch mark, but very few, if any, actually are at 10 exactly.

THE NULL HYPOTHESIS

Since we do not know any better, we will form a hypothesis of optimism and say that there is no difference between the long term mean (which we shall call μ_O) and the current production population (which we shall call μ). (Note these Greek letters represent the population parameters and are pronounced "mu"). The formal statement of the "null hypothesis" is:

$$H_O: \mu = \mu_O \qquad (12\text{-}1)$$

THE ALTERNATIVE HYPOTHESIS

Now, what can we say about the alternative to this null hypothesis? Without any extra knowledge of the process, we can only say that there is a difference between the all-time average and the value for the current production. This is stated as the "alternative hypothesis" or the hypothesis of difference as follows:

$$H_1: \mu \neq \mu_O \qquad (12\text{-}2)$$

Together, the null and alternative hypotheses form what is called hypothesis testing using "t" tests. In such "t" tests, we are comparing two populations of items and we have the simplest experiments with the simplest methods of analysis. While these are simple tests, the concept behind these tests is the same concept that applies to all statistical inference. We look at a signal and compare this signal to the noise observed as we measure this signal.

In the case of the simple "t" test of $\mu = \mu_O$, the signal is the difference between the two mean values and the noise is the uncertainty of the measurement expressed as the standard deviation. (For those in need of a review of the mean and standard deviation, please refer to Appendix 12).

When the signal is smaller than the noise, it is obvious that there is no signal of a significant nature. When the signal is vastly larger than the noise we again see no difficulty in deciding that the signal is significantly bigger than the noise. It is in the region where the signal and noise are nearly the same, or when the signal is only two or three times as big as the noise, that there is uncertainty in our decision. This is where probability-based decision rules help us make the wise decisions we wish to make consistently.

Let's look at the possible outcomes of our simple experiment which compares the mean with the all time output of the piece-part process. Since we are taking only a sample in time (a sort of a snapshot) we need to know how the information in this sample could compare to the truth of the situation.

Table 12-2

Sample says:

		Reject Null: Parts Differ	Do Not Reject Null: Parts are Same
Truth	parts differ	want to be here if parts differ	error if parts are really different Type II error
	parts are same	error if parts are really the same Type I error	want to be here if parts are the same

ALPHA RISK

In table 12-2 there are four alternatives <u>before</u> we make a decision based on the evidence before us. Two of the alternatives are good and we would like to land in one of those boxes of the truth table most of the time. However, the lower left box, where the truth is that no difference exists between the parts (but our sample says that there is a difference), leads to an error of "the first kind". Before we make the decision leading to this error, we have a risk associated with this error. This risk is named the alpha (α) risk after the first letter of the Greek alphabet.

BETA RISK

The box in the upper right corner of the truth table again presents us with an error if we fall into it. Here we sit back and say there is no difference, when in truth there is a difference. This is a "lazy" person's error and is an error of the second kind. Associated with this error is the risk we take in committing this error <u>before</u> we make any decision. This risk is called the beta (β) risk after the second letter of the Greek alphabet. If you want to be able to remember the difference between these risks in a simple memonic manner, think of the somewhat lazy looking letter beta that is relaxing while it should be out finding differences. Since there are only two risks, the other must be alpha!

The Lazy Beta

Figure 12-1

No matter what we call the risks and the errors, the real lesson to be learned is that when faced with uncertainty, there is a risk that our decision will be in error due to the variation in the numbers we are working with. There are two ways to combat this error. 1) We could attempt to improve the physical nature of the variation by working on the response variable to "clean it up." 2) Usually, we take a bigger sample and make use of "the law of large numbers." This general "law" can be reduced in particular to a very useful concept called the "central limit theorem". Among other things, the central limit theorem assures us that no matter what the original distribution of the X_i values, if we take samples from this population of size n, then the distribution of averages formed from these samples will converge to a normal distribution. This result is handy, since we will be using probability models based on the normal distribution to help separate our signal from the noise. However, the real point of the central limit theorem comes from another of its properties that says that the variance of the resulting distribution of averages will be equal to the variance in the original data divided by (or reduced by) the number of samples (n) used to form the averages! In algebraic form this is:

$$s_{\bar{X}}^2 = \frac{s_X^2}{n} \tag{12-3}$$

And of course if we are dealing with the standard deviations, this equation becomes:

$$s_{\bar{X}} = \frac{s_X}{\sqrt{n}} \quad \text{called the standard error of the mean} \tag{12-4}$$

So if we compute the standard error of the mean for the data in table 12-1 we get:

$$X = 9.967 \quad s_X^2 = 0.01621 \quad s_X = 0.1273 \quad n = 25$$

$$s_{\bar{X}} = \frac{0.1273}{\sqrt{25}} = 0.0255$$

Which means that by taking 25 samples, we have effectively reduced the uncertainty in the hypothesis test by a factor of 5. This result shows why an average value is better than a single observation.

STEPS IN HYPOTHESIS TESTING

Now how do all these concepts we have discussed come together? We want to make wise decisions in the face of uncertainty. We now have a mean value from the sample that we hypothesize to be a representation of the population mean of 10 inches. We realize that we could make an error in the decision and that the central limit theorem helps reduce the variation in this decision.

Let's follow a formality of steps and put the pieces together.

Step 1)   State the Null and alternative hypotheses:

$$H_0: \mu = \mu_0 = 10 \text{ inches}$$
$$H_1: \mu \neq \mu_0$$

Step 2)   Understand that the errors are independent and normally distributed. (The errors we speak of here happen to be the "noise" we refer to and measure by the standard deviation.)

Step 3)   State the level of alpha and beta risks:

alpha = 0.05
beta = ? (as we shall see beta is dependent upon other considerations)

Step 4)   Select a critical region based on the alpha risk and the sample size:

To complete step 4 we need to look at the "Student t" table in the back of this book. With 25 samples we have 24 degrees of freedom (df). Our risk for this test which can reject the null hypothesis if the mean is smaller or larger than the standard (a "two tail test") is 0.05 which gives a "t" critical value of ± 2.06.

Step 5)   Compute $\bar{X}$, s^2, and s

Step 6)   Calculate the "t" value for this problem based upon the statistics in hand:

$$t = \frac{\bar{X} - \mu_0}{s/\sqrt{n}} \qquad (12\text{-}5)$$

$$\text{so: } t = \frac{9.967 - 10}{0.1273/\sqrt{25}}$$

$$t = -0.033/0.0255$$

$$t = -1.304$$

Step 7)   Draw conclusions in ordinary language: (For this case) we cannot reject the null hypothesis. There is no evidence that the process has changed.

Let's look at our decision in the light of the risks involved. Is it possible to commit a type I error? If you look back at Table 12-2, you will note that the only time you can commit a type I error is when you reject the null hypothesis. So we can't make a type I error in the above conclusion. However, we have not rejected the null, and this decision has the type II error associated with it. But we have not stated a beta risk which is the risk of making a type II error! Unfortunately this is a common mistake in hypothesis testing of data that does not come from a designed experiment. The "design" in this experiment should have been to select a sample size sufficient to control both the type I error <u>and</u> the type II error.

A DESIGNED HYPOTHESIS TEST

Let us revisit our problem once again and see how a simple design can be meshed with a "t test" to produce a wise decision.

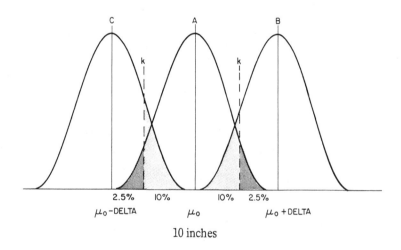

10 inches

Figure 12-2

Figure 12-2 shows the piece-part problem in terms of the possible distribution patterns we could encounter in our experiment. If there is no difference from the hypothesized true mean of 10 inches, then we will be in distribution "A" with the μ of our sampled population no different from the μ_0. If the population of parts has shifted upward from the 10 inch all-time average, then we would be in the "B" distribution. If the average has shifted down, then we are in the "C" distribution. The problem is to determine if we have made a "significant" move from A to somewhere else. Since we are using the sampling distribution of the mean and the properties of the central limit theorem we should realize that the distributions we are looking at are distributions of $\overline{X}$'s, (which are normal). However, we only have one $\overline{X}$

in our sample and it has a probability of being anywhere in each of the three distributions. If the $\overline{X}$ we observe as a result of our data is really in the "A" distribution then it could be right on the 10 inch (μ_0) point or to the right or left of the μ_0. There is a small but measurable chance that the $\overline{X}$ we observe could be so far over in the "A" distribution that it is overlapping into the "B" or "C" distributions. This is a result of the fact that there is a distribution of $\overline{X}$'s and not a single point that keeps coming up over and over again. But we know the shape of this distribution. It is the normal distribution (because of the central limit theorem) and we know that between +2 and –2 standard deviations of the mean, this distribution will encompass 95% of the possible occurrences of the placements of samples of $\overline{X}$ if they are indeed a part of the "A" distribution. But what about the other 5%? In figure 12-1 there are lines drawn designated by the letter k at the upper 2 standard deviation and lower 2 standard deviation points in the "A" distribution which leaves a total of 5% cut off of "A". The placement of k puts 2.5% in each "tail" of the "A" distribution. When we set our alpha risk at 5% in such a "two-tail" test of hypothesis, we create such a picture. This means that should the $\overline{X}$ of our sample fall into the lower or upper 2.5% tail of the "A" distribution (it's still really a part of "A") then we would erroneously say it was not a part of "A" in our rejection of the null hypothesis! This is of course an error of the first kind. You can see that the chance of committing such an error is small, so we make a wise decision most of the time. But what if the $\overline{X}$ of our sample really comes from either the "B" or "C" population? Note that it can come only from one or the other at one time. It is impossible for $\overline{X}$ to be a part of both "B" and "C" at the same time. Let's say that the sample ($\overline{X}$) really comes from the "B" distribution. This sampling distribution of the mean will be a "delta" away from the "A" distribution point by point, so the mean of B (μ_0 + delta) will be a distance delta from μ_0. How much will delta be? That really depends upon the actual shift in the "B" distribution. How much of a shift in "B" is important to detect? That depends upon our judgment of the importance of the shift. In other words, we must bring some prior knowledge to the situation in the form of "how much of a difference makes a difference" to us. This difference is not based on statistics, but on our knowledge of the process. So, if the piece-part must be held to a tolerance of ± 0.015 inches without any adverse consequences, then we may say that we have an indifference zone up to 0.015 inches. The difference that makes a difference is 0.015 inches. Therefore, if we have a shift in the mean of the "A" distribution as great or greater than 0.015 inches, we want to do something about it. How do we make this wise decision? Recall an important promise of the central limit theorem that the standard error of the mean ($s_{\overline{x}}$) will shrink by the inverse of the square root of n, the sample size for the sampling distribution of the mean. This is where our design comes in. We will select a sample size sufficient to control the risks of both types of errors to predetermined levels. These levels again depend on the knowledge we bring to the situation. For now we will pick an alpha of 5% and a beta of 10% to continue our example. There is a 10% chance that we will erroneously think we are in the "A" distribution when we really are in the "B" distribution. This is the lightly shaded area of Figure 12-2 to the left of k in the "B" distribution. Given the above picture of the situation, we are in a position to calculate the placement of k on the number line and at the same time compute the number of samples that will satisfy the risk levels we have set.

Looking at the "A" distribution, k will be 1.96 standard deviations away from the μ_O point, so using the t transformation: (t with **indefinite df**).

$$t = \frac{k - \mu_O}{s/\sqrt{n}} \qquad \therefore \qquad 1.96 = \frac{k - 10}{0.1273/\sqrt{n}} \qquad (12\text{-}6)$$

Now in equation 12-6 we do not insert the original sample size of 25 because we do not know if this sample size is sufficient to control the alpha <u>and</u> beta risks.

By rearranging equation 12-6 we obtain:

$$1.96\,(0.1273/\sqrt{n}) = k - 10 \qquad (12\text{-}7)$$

Now let's look at the "B" distribution and the placement of k with respect to it. k will be located at a point where 10% of the lower tail of "B" is less than k. According to the normal distribution, this is a point −1.28 standard normal units away from the mean of "B". So we substitute this information into the t transformation as we did in 12-6 and get:

$$-1.28 = \frac{k - 10.015}{0.1273/\sqrt{n}} \qquad (12\text{-}8)$$

> Note that 10.015 is μ plus the delta of 0.015. This is the location of the mean of the "B" distribution.

Which when rearranged is:

$$-1.28(0.1273/\sqrt{n}) = k - 10.015 \qquad (12\text{-}9)$$

By combining equations 12-7 and 12-9, we have two equations in two unknowns which are easily solved by eliminating k as follows:

subtract 12-9 from 12-7:

$$1.96(0.1273/\sqrt{n}) = k - 10$$

(change signs) $+\ \underline{1.28(0.1273/\sqrt{n}) = -k + 10.015}$

and we get: $3.24(0.1273/\sqrt{n}) = 0.015 \qquad (12\text{-}10)$

with a little simple algebra:

$$\sqrt{n} = 3.24(0.1273)/0.015$$
$$\sqrt{n} = 27.4968$$
$$n = 756.07$$

Round up to 757 samples to detect a .015 difference with a standard deviation of .1273 for the levels of alpha and beta risk we have set. Now that's a hefty sample size. It might make you believe that statistics makes more work! Let's analyze the problem once again and see why the 757 samples are required. Notice that the sample size formula can be reduced to a general form from equation 12-10.

$$n = \left[\frac{(t_\alpha + t_\beta)(s)}{delta} \right]^2 \qquad (12\text{-}11)$$

Observe in equation 12-11 that as delta becomes small, n gets larger and larger. Also, if s is large in comparison with delta, then n also gets larger. In our example, we have a large s (with respect to delta) and a small delta (with respect to s). We are trying to find differences smaller than the "natural variation" in the process and this takes an enormous sample to accomplish. Could we back off on the risks? Let's say that we set the beta risk at 50% (or as good as a coin toss). Then the t value for beta would be zero and the sample size would be

$$n = (2(0.1273)/0.015)^2 = 288.$$

Which is still a big sample, and when we are finished, and make a decision not to reject the null hypothesis, there is still a 50% chance of sitting back and saying that there is no change in the population based on this sample when there really is a change! So the original sample of 25 that we took is a drop in the bucket compared with the necessary sample to make a wise decision with this data that is so variable.

If we were to back off on the difference (delta) that makes a difference to us, then the sample size will shrink. Let's say that we make delta as large as the standard deviation of the data we have. Equation 12-11 then becomes:

$$n = ((t_\alpha + t_\beta)1/1)^2 = (t_\alpha + t_\beta)^2 \qquad (12\text{-}12)$$

For our example with alpha = 0.05 and beta = 0.10, the sample size is merely the t_α = (1.96) and t_β = (1.28) added together and squared! This gives us a sample size of 11. But there is a hitch. The t distribution is based on the degrees of freedom in the sample you have. The original values we put into equation 12-12 assumed a large sample size was needed (large samples with a t distribution is usually above 30). But we have only 11 samples when s = delta! So we must modify our sample size by recalculating the sample size based on the first determination. The values for t_α and t_β becomes 2.281 and 1.37 respectively for 10 degrees of freedom. This set of new t values produce a sample size of $(2.281 + 1.37)^2$ or 13.32. This is rounded up to 14 (since we can't have a fraction of a sample). Once more we go through the computation to find that with 14 samples (giving 13 degrees of freedom), we get a sample size of $(2.16 + 1.35)^2 = 13.32$, which rounds up to 13. One more iteration gives a sample size of 12.52 which is the same as 13 in our always round up mode.

This is the same as the last computation and thus the sample size has converged for the case when delta = the standard deviation. Since the ratio of various deltas to standard deviations will always produce the same sample size, it is not necessary to go through this iterative procedure to find a sample size in designing an experiment. Table 3 gives the sample size for levels of alpha and beta for values of delta divided by the standard deviation.* To illustrate the use of table 3 let's find the sample size for a situation where the standard deviation as calculated from a preliminary sample of five observations is 22.68. The difference we want to detect (this is the minimum difference) is 14.17. The ratio (D) of delta to standard deviation is then:

$$D = 14.17/22.68 = 0.6247$$

The closest value in table 3 is 0.60. If we set our alpha risk at 0.01 and our beta risk at 0.1, then the sample size will be found at the intersection of the D = 0.60, alpha = 0.01, and beta = 0.1. The value is 45 at this point (bracketed value in Table 12-3).

Let's investigate the effect of the risks on the sample size in the following table given that the D is a constant 0.60:

Table 12-3

Alpha risk

		0.01	0.05	0.10
	0.01	71	53	46
Beta	0.05	53	38	32
Risk	0.10	{45}	32	26
	0.20	36	24	19
	0.50	22	[13]	9

There is a mildly popular opinion that the beta risk controls the sample size. If we examine table 12-3, we can see that both alpha and beta have the same effect on the sample size for equal risk levels. There must be a basis for this erroneous concept and it rises from the fact that we can always state a level of the t test at which we reject the null hypothesis (which is the alpha risk). If we reject the null hypothesis, then there is no beta risk! So, if we took a small sample and rejected, we could not make an error of the second kind. If we did not reject with a too small sample, then the beta risk would force us to a larger sample. To illustrate this point, let's say that we set an alpha at 5% and take 13 samples (value in square of Table 12-3) with the same D of .6. If we reject the null hypothesis, then we are home free. But if we do not reject the null hypothesis, we are stuck with a 50% beta risk! To obtain a lower level of beta, we need to increase the sample size to 32 or even 38 for a 0.1 or 0.05 probability of not sitting back and saying there is no difference when there is indeed a difference.

---

*The procedure used to derive Table 5 is the same in principle as the rough method just shown, but is based on the more accurate non-central t distribution.

One last thought on risks and errors before we look at other types of hypothesis tests. In all formulations of the risks, we have stated the risk value as if it were the <u>actual</u> risk involved in our hypothesis test. The numerical value of the risk we have stated is actually the <u>worst</u> (or highest) level of probability of making an error in the decision we make. Depending on the actual information we gather, this risk can be less than the value stated. A sort of "what if" diagram called an operating characteristic curve shows the actual risks for different levels of deviations from the mean in question. The appendix of this chapter shows the construction of this risk defining tool.

TESTS BETWEEN TWO MEANS

Our first example looked at the difference between an "all-time" average level and a sample from a recent trial. What do we do if we want to compare two trials that could be different due to some process modifications? In this case, the null hypothesis would look like:

$$H_o: \mu_A = \mu_B$$

and the alternative would be:

$$H_1: \mu_A \neq \mu_B$$

To establish a proper design for this experiment, we need to look at the four items we freely select to establish the sample size which controls the maximum risks involved in making our decision.
These four items are:

~ alpha risk
~ beta risk
~ the amount of difference that makes a difference (important difference)
~ the standard deviation

Given these four pieces of information, we may enter Table 4 on page 366 to determine the sample size that will assure us of conformance to the stated risks.

A more realistic question is, how do we set up the risk levels, determine the important difference, and find the standard deviation? The levels of risk as well as the important difference are both functions of the problem we are working with. The amount of difference we need to detect depends on our prior knowledge of the process. This must be a finite value different from zero, for if any difference is intolerable (i.e., we want zero difference between means), then the sample size must be infinite or equal to the whole population sample. Sometimes this unreasonable request is made in the field of health where any difference from a standard or from a control group would mean that a medical problem could arise. From a theoretical point of view, this is a proper way to treat the subject, but it causes sample sizes to grow to huge quantities, especially when the risks are set at very low levels. In such cases a compromise can be reached by establishing the difference that makes a difference as a fraction of the standard deviation involved in making the measurements. This brings in the subject of the standard deviation. While we have a somewhat free choice of the risks and difference, the standard deviation is a function of the measurement system we are working with. Therefore, while it appears to be one of our free choice items, it is really dependent on the way we do our experimental work. If the variation is excessive, then it might be worth the effort to examine the sources of variation using the methods of Chapter 10 and the analysis techniques of Chapter 18.

With the above general concepts behind us, let us watch the thought process for statistical inference unfold in the following example.

BUYING A COPIER

We have narrowed our choices from a field of many brands of copiers to two particular devices that are priced within a few hundred dollars of each other. Brand A and brand B sales offices will agree to go along with our experiment and allow us to sample the output of a number of their machines so we may evaluate the quality of the output. Since we will be placing a large order for copiers from either of the vendors, we want to make sure that the quality will be good in the device we choose. Using a national standard of measurement of quality and an appropriate test pattern, we will canvass a number of sites where the copiers are working on a day-to-day basis. If there is no significant difference between the copy quality of the two devices, we will purchase the less expensive one. If there is a big enough difference in the quality between the machines, then we will purchase the copier with the better quality. Since this is not a life-or-death problem, we will set our maximum risks as follows. The chance of saying that there is a difference when there really is no difference (alpha risk) will be limited to no more than 5% (0.05). This means that one time in 20 we will not go for the less expensive machine (assuming that it comes up with lower copy quality) when we should. This is a risk that will cost us some immediate resources, but will not have a long-term impact. The chance of getting stuck with a poor performer over a number of years is associated with the beta risk. If we decide from the sample that there is no difference between the copiers, and there really is a difference, then we could buy the wrong device based on price (assuming that the low price device actually has lower quality). So we want to protect ourselves from such a long-term risk and set the beta at 1% (0.01). This means that one time in a hundred we will say the devices are the same when they are really different.

The amount of difference that makes a difference in the metric under study (copy quality value) depends on how fussy we are. This response is measured on a 0 to 100 scale with just perceptible differences equal to 2 units. That means that if shown a copy, a person could not distinguish a 78 from an 80. This gives us some insight into the difference we wish to detect. Obviously a difference of 2 units or less is beyond our ability to see any difference. Being a fussy company, we decide that a difference of 5 units (or 2.5 times the perception limits) will be the amount of difference that is important to us.

What about the standard deviation? Since we have no prior knowledge in this situation, we must take a preliminary sample. A rule of thumb suggests that the sample size for such a preliminary sample should be at least 2 (the fewest samples that will give a std. dev.) but no more than 5. For this example, we will go to installations of 5 devices at random and get the samples. Now all five of these samples must come from the same brand of copy machine, for if there were a difference between brands, this difference would inflate the variation. We will tentatively assume that the variation between brands is the same and use the estimate of the standard deviation from only one brand to set up our sampling scheme. We will choose the brand to be sampled preliminarily by tossing a fair coin. Let's say that brand A gets the toss and we obtain the five samples as follows:

$$82.3 \qquad 72.4 \qquad 67.9 \qquad 86.2 \qquad 72.9$$

which give a standard deviation of 7.6.

Now we calculate the ratio of the important difference to the standard deviation:

$$D = 5/7.6 = 0.658$$

The closest entry in table 4 is 0.65 and the intersection of D, alpha (0.05), and beta (0.01) is at a sample size of 88 copies from each population of devices. Now this may appear to be a large sample, but look at the calculation of D. We are trying to find a difference that is 2/3 as small as the "natural" variation in the process. This is the price of being fussy.

Before we go out and gather this data in a random fashion, let's see where we are.

$$\text{alpha} = 0.05$$
$$\text{beta} = 0.01$$
the difference is 5 that makes a difference
$$s = 7.6 \text{ (preliminary)}$$
$$H_0: \mu_A = \mu_B$$
$$H_1: \mu_A \neq \mu_B$$

Now we actually collect the copy quality samples from randomly selected machines as follows:

Table 12-3

Machine Type #1(A)   Price: $1995

71.4	65.2	74.9	84.2	80.0	75.7	77.1	75.2	79.4	77.0	92.6	71.9
62.1	61.6	80.0	78.2	76.9	74.6	73.3	86.5	74.9	78.3	76.2	81.9
82.6	76.6	73.5	71.8	73.5	76.9	87.9	86.3	73.9	64.3	81.9	72.8
65.2	79.9	93.0	83.9	77.3	86.5	83.6	74.5	83.9	53.7	61.2	74.7
70.0	83.1	78.4	76.9	80.8	69.5	63.9	81.2	63.5	80.4	70.2	83.8
70.8	74.6	82.3	84.7	76.5	82.2	81.4	82.6	91.6	58.0	82.6	81.4
78.8	65.9	70.8	80.9	64.3	72.1	64.9	67.5	74.4	72.8	79.8	74.9
82.8	86.9	81.7	76.8							

Machine Type #2 (B)   Price: $2395

80.4	86.8	85.5	85.0	89.3	88.3	86.5	94.8	81.9	76.3	70.9	85.2
91.1	90.1	80.9	83.3	80.9	87.4	89.5	82.9	81.3	83.4	75.8	75.3
86.4	87.1	84.7	96.2	84.2	80.3	77.3	85.8	92.6	96.2	89.5	86.1
81.6	80.8	82.4	81.9	87.3	94.0	91.8	85.5	82.6	90.9	87.9	96.6
76.5	86.3	82.7	85.4	84.1	92.5	85.2	84.9	93.3	91.2	83.2	88.9
80.2	88.6	82.9	82.7	80.8	84.7	78.2	84.1	82.9	76.4	90.2	78.1
92.7	81.7	91.8	85.7	95.1	91.6	89.1	85.9	87.2	76.3	72.9	81.9
101.9	83.5	76.5	91.5							

Using the computer program "TTEST" from appendix 12 we obtain the following information on the statistics of the data from the two machines:

$$\bar{X}_1 = 76.3 \qquad \bar{X}_2 = 85.4$$
$$s_1 = 7.79 \qquad s_2 = 5.85$$
$$s_1^2 = 60.700 \qquad s_2^2 = 34.209$$
$$n_1 = 88 \qquad n_2 = 88$$

While the TTEST computer program will calculate the appropriate test statistic, let's see what is going on in that program by looking at the "road map" of significance tests also found in Appendix 12. We start at the branch of the decision tree marked "testing means." From there we branch off to the type of hypothesis which in this case is "$\mu_1 = \mu_2$". The next branch asks a question we are not yet prepared to answer with the knowledge we have obtained thus far. We need to know if the variances between the two populations are significantly different from each other. (We can see that there is a difference between s_1^2 and s_2^2, but is this a real difference or just by chance?)

To answer this important question, we divert from our comparison of means momentarily and set up a test on variances using the "F" statistic. This is a simple hypothesis test that looks at the ratio of the two variances. By convention, we put the larger variance in the numerator of the ratio which will always give us F values greater than 1. This convention is used since the F table of critical values is compiled with only values equal to or greater than one. The "F" test is a formal hypothesis test with a null and alternative hypothesis as follows:

$$H_o: \quad \sigma_1^2 = \sigma_2^2$$

$$H_1: \quad \sigma_1^2 \neq \sigma_2^2$$

σ^2 is the population variance we are inferring about. (Note that "σ" is the Greek letter (lower case) "sigma"). The test of this hypothesis shows that there is no significant difference between the two variances.

$$F = 60.70/34.21 = 1.77 \qquad\qquad F_{0.01,\ 87,\ 87} = 1.81$$

Since the variances are not significantly different, we move back to the portion of the flow diagram in our test of means. The test statistic for this situation looks somewhat complex, but it is merely the same signal-to-noise ratio we encountered in the simpler hypothesis test of the mean. The signal part is the difference between the means. The noise part is the standard error of the means. Now it is the noise portion of the formula that seems to have grown more complex. Actually it is merely an expression that takes into account all the data we have gathered in this experiment and puts this good work to use.

The denominator consists of two parts. The first part is the computation of the "pooled" standard deviation. The second merely divides this pooled standard deviation by the total number of samples we have obtained. Let's look at the pooled standard deviation first. The computation simply takes the variance of each set of data and multiplies by n-1. This turns the variance back to a "sum of squares". Recall the formula for standard deviation is:

$$s = \sqrt{\frac{\Sigma(X - \bar{X})^2}{n - 1}}$$

The expression $\Sigma(X - \bar{X})^2$ is the sum of the squares and if we multiply the variance by $n - 1$ we can reconstruct these sums of squares. The reason for reconstructing the sums of squares lies in the fact that while variances are additive when the sample sizes are equal, they are not when there is a different sample size involved in each variance. Therefore this general pooling formula (12-13) will apply in any sample size situation.

$$s_p^2 = \frac{(n_1 - 1) s_1^2 + (n_2 - 1) s_2^2}{(n_1 + n_2) - 2} \qquad (12\text{-}13)$$

Applying 12-13 we find that the pooled variance is 47.45 and the square root of this (the pooled standard deviation) is 6.89. If we divide this by the square root of the sum of the sample sizes from the two populations of copiers we obtain the standard error of the mean ($S_{\bar{x}}$). The formula in the road map actually multiplies by the square root of the inverse of the sample sizes, but this is a completely equivalent mathematical expression and makes the formula easier to express in printed form.

Now the moment we have been waiting for. Are the populations of copiers the same? We calculate the test statistic as follows:

$$t = \frac{X_1 - X_2}{sp * \sqrt{1/n_1 + 1/n_2}} = \frac{76.3 - 85.4}{6.89 \sqrt{1/88 + 1/88}} = -8.76$$

With a calculated t of -8.76 compared to the two sided critical t for 174 degrees of freedom (87 df + 87 df) which is ± 1.96, we reject the null hypothesis and conclude that there is a difference between the copy quality of the two machines. We also note that Machine #2 gives better quality. While the prices are sufficiently different ($400) to warrant buying the cheaper one, we will choose the copier (Brand #2) based on the quality difference demonstrated in this experiment.

Before we leave this chapter on "simple analysis", let's ask what the risk is in making the last decision. Remember that we rejected the null hypothesis. Therefore, while there was the potential of making either a type one error or a type two error before we made the decision, we can only make one error given that we have made one decision. In this case, since we rejected the null hypothesis, we can only make a type I error.

The maximum risk involved with that error is the alpha risk that we designed into our experiment at 5%. With the amount of difference we observe between the two copiers, we can be quite sure that we have made the correct decision on the purchase of the "Brand 2" copy machine. If we were to do this same experiment over and over again our chances would be that in 20 repeats we would make the wrong decision only once. Those are pretty good odds.

One last note. If our variances had not been "equal", then the pooling of variances is not allowed. You can make the calculation, of course, but you get an incorrect representation of the variation in the pooled value. To skirt this problem and still allow an inference to be made, an approximate "T" statistic is calculated. This is the formula in the flow diagram called the Fisher-Behrens "T". To use this approximate "T" test, you simply find the square root of the two variances divided by their sample sizes and use this as the standard error of the mean. However, due to the lack of similarity between the variances, the degrees of freedom are adjusted downward in proportion to the difference between the variances. So the greater the difference in the variances, the fewer degrees of freedom. This test will give just as good validity as the "true" T test especially when the sample size is large (say over 30 in each population). As the sample does get smaller, however, the approximate "T" begins to lose sensitivity due to the reduction in the degrees of freedom.

PROBLEMS FOR CHAPTER 12

1) The following data represent the force required to break a bond between two cemented metal parts. Two methods were used to joing these parts together. Method A used one drop of adhesive which was applied after thoroughly buffing the two mating surfaces. Method B used two drops of adhesive after the surfaces were wiped clean with a dry rag. Method A requires 20 seconds of operator time per assembly; method B requires 7 seconds of operator time.

Method A	Method B
227	233
235	215
225	202
237	202
237	226
239	224
226	222
220	219
244	217
228	235

Test the hypothesis that the two methods need the same average force to break the bond using a t-test, assuming that the variances are equal.

2) A modification is planned to an existing process. The average, long-term output from this process has been 9.37. A pilot run with the change produces an average of 10.42 with a standard deviation of 1.22. 25 samples were taken to obtain the average and the distribution does not differ from a normal distribution.

Set up the appropriate hypotheses and test them.

3) Two production lines produce the "same" part. The samples from these lines give statistics as follows:

	Line A	Line B
$\overline{X}$	2.54 cm	2.83 cm
s	0.04 cm	0.03 cm
n	14	10

Set up the appropriate hypothesis test and answer the question if the two lines differ significantly.

4) A development engineer wants to try out a new toner. He wants the particle size to be different by at least 2 microns. A preliminary sample shows that the standard deviation of the measurement is 0.5 microns. Given that he wants to limit his errors as follows, how many samples will be necessary to tell the difference between two batches of toner? (Limit the risk of saying toners are the same when they differ to 5% and the risk of finding differences when there is no difference to 10%.)

5) Construct an OC curve for the copier quality example (data on page 151).

APPENDIX 12

SOME BASIC RULES OF PROBABILITY

1) The sum of the probabilities in a single cause system must equal one. There may not be any negative probabilities.

2) If two events are mutually exclusive then the probability that one or the other will occur equals the sum of their probabilities.

3) For independent events, the probability that all the events will occur is the product of all the event's probabilities.

4) Odds may be related to probabilities by the following rule:

For odds a to b and probability p

$$a/b = p/(1 - p)$$

and $p = a/(a + b)$

BASIC STATISTICAL FORMULAS

1) The mean or average

$$\bar{X} = \frac{\sum\limits_{i=1}^{n} X_i}{n}$$

2) The standard deviation

$$S = \sqrt{\frac{\sum\limits_{i=1}^{n} X_i^2 - (\sum\limits_{i=1}^{n} X_i)^2/n}{n-1}}$$

STEPS IN HYPOTHESIS TESTING

1) State the Null and alternative hypotheses

   ie:

Population	Population
vs.	vs.
Standard	Population

   H_0: $\mu = \mu_0$ H_0: $\mu_A = \mu_B$

                                                    Double Sided

   H_1: $\mu \neq \mu_0$ H_1: $\mu_A \neq \mu_B$
   -

   H_0: $\mu = \mu_0$ H_0: $\mu_A = \mu_B$

   H_1: $\mu > \mu_0$ H_1: $\mu_A > \mu_B$

      or   or   Single Sided

      $\mu < \mu_0$ $\mu_A < \mu_B$

2) Decide upon the risks you are willing to live with.

   alpha risk (risk of rejecting H_0 falsely) = _____
   beta risk (risk of not rejecting H_0 when we should) = _____
   set critical "t" value based on alpha risk = _____

3) Determine how much of a difference is important in terms of physical variables involved.

   delta = _____

4) Take a preliminary sample to determine the variation in your data, or use a previously determined value of the standard deviation.

   Preliminary Std. Dev. = _____

STEPS IN HYPOTHESIS TESTING (CONTINUED)

5) Determine the sample size based on the above criteria by using the appropriate table (Table 3 or 4, depending on your hypothesis)

$$\text{Sample size} = \underline{\hspace{2cm}}$$

6) Gather your data and compute statistics:

$$\bar{X} = \underline{\hspace{1.5cm}} \qquad s^2 = \underline{\hspace{1.5cm}} \qquad s = \underline{\hspace{1.5cm}}$$

$$(\text{for } \mu_A = \mu_B) \quad \bar{X} = \underline{\hspace{1.5cm}} \qquad s^2 = \underline{\hspace{1.5cm}} \qquad s = \underline{\hspace{1.5cm}}$$

7) Compute test statistic based on the "road map" and draw conclusions. Always remember to use non-statistical words in your conclusion.

ROAD MAP OF SIGNIFICANCE TESTS

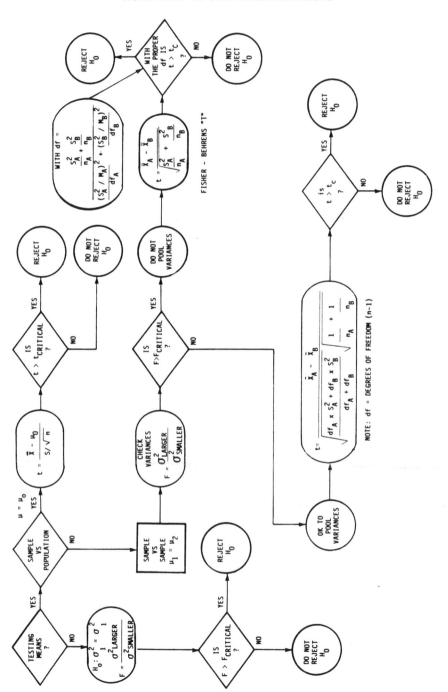

QUANTIFYING RISKS AND ERRORS

Example: A developer is planning a new shopping center and wants to check that the average annual income in the area is $8400. He selects at random 200 families and he will accept the claim (of $8400) if the sample mean falls between $8300 and $8500.

Realize that there is a probability that the average will exceed or be lower than the limits even when the true mean is at $8400! Also, it is probable that the mean will fall within the indifference zone even if the true mean is not $8400.

The first type of error is the Type I and has an associated α risk.

The second type of error is the Type II and has a β risk attached.

We can quantify the α risk by knowing the variation in the data, the indifference points, and the sample size.

To quantify the β risk, we need to know the variation, the indifference points, the sample size, <u>and</u> we need to hypothesize where the true mean lies.

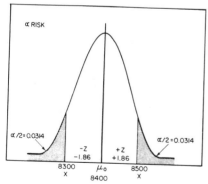

$\sigma = 760 \qquad n = 200$

$$z = \frac{x - \mu_0}{\sigma / \sqrt{n}}$$

$$z = \frac{8300 - 8400}{760 / \sqrt{200}} = -1.86$$

Area to z is:
$1 - .9686 = .0314$

$$z = \frac{8500 - 8400}{760 / \sqrt{200}} = +1.86$$

Area to z is:
$1 - .9686 = .0314$

The Alpha Risk is the sum of the areas in the two tails.

$.0314 + .0314 = .0628$

OPERATING CHARACTERISTIC CURVE

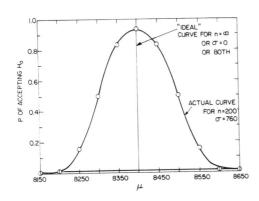

$$\sigma = 760 \qquad \sigma_{\bar{x}} = \frac{760}{\sqrt{200}} = 53.7$$
$$n = 200$$
$$\mu_0 = 8400$$

$$z = \frac{x - \mu}{\sigma_{\bar{x}}}$$

The Operating Characteristic (OC) Curve is a type of "What If?" exercise. It shows the risk of accepting (or more properly, not rejecting) the null hypothesis for various levels of possible location of the true mean.

To construct the OC curve, we ask what if the mean were at a certain point and then simply find the area or probability up to that point. This is done for many points and then the smooth curve is plotted.

This is the OC Curve for the example.

HERE'S WHERE IT CAME FROM:

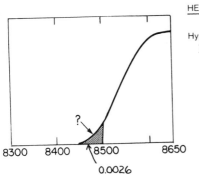

Hypothesized Value of the "True" Mean	Calculation of Probability

8650

Find area in tail of the 8650 distribution that is less than 8500 (indifference).

$$z = \frac{8500 \cdot 8650}{53.7} = -2/793$$

The area up to this point is 0.0026.

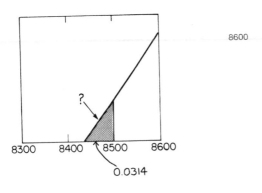

8600

Find the area in tail of the 8600 distribution that is less than 8500 (indifference).

$$z = \frac{8500 \cdot 8600}{53.7} = -1.862$$

The area up to this point is 0.0314.

	Hypothesized Value of the "True" Mean	Calculation of Probability

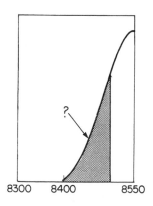

8550

Find area in tail of the 8550 distribution that is less than 8500 (indifference point on high end).

$$z = \frac{8550 - 8500}{53.7} = -.93$$

Area up to -.93 is .1762.

Is there any area from the 8550 distribution beyond 8300 (the lower indifference point?).

$$z = \frac{8300 - 8500}{53.7} = -4.66$$

Which is a very small area! So we conclude that there is none.

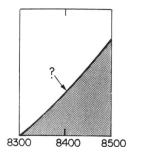

8500

Find area in tail of the 8500 distribution that is less than 8500 (indifference point on high end).

$$z = \frac{8500 - 8500}{53.7} = 0$$

Area for 0 is .50.

Is there any area beyond 8300?

$$z = \frac{8300 - 8500}{53.7} = -3/72$$

Which gives a very small area! So we conclude that there is none.

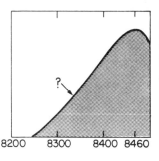

8450

Find area between 8300 and 8500 for the 8450 distribution.

Since the normal curve is symmetrical, we can use the areas already found that "reflect" from the other side for:

$$z_1 = \frac{8500 - 8450}{53.7} = .93$$

Area to .93 is .8238.

$$z_2 = \frac{8300 - 8450}{53.7} = -2.793$$

Point	Area
8350	.8212
8300	.5000
8250	.1762
8200	.0314
8150	.0026

Area to -2.793 is .0026.

Area between z_1 and z_2 is the difference:

$$.8238 - .0026 = .8212$$

```
95 CLS
100 DIM X(2),S(2),N(2)
120 PRINT TAB(20) "<MENU>"
130 PRINT TAB(10) "1. T TEST OF MEAN MU=MU ZERO"
140 PRINT TAB(10) "2. T TEST BETWEEN MEANS. MU1=MU2"
150 PRINT TAB(10) "3. END"
160 PRINT "MAKE SELECTION"
170 INPUT Z
180 ON Z GOTO 600,200,660
185 PRINT "TRY AGAIN"
190 GOTO 160
200 REM T TEST BETWEEN TWO MEANS
210 PRINT "ENTER XBAR1,S1,N1"
220 INPUT X(1),S(1),N(1)
230 PRINT "ENTER XBAR2, S2,N2"
240 INPUT X(2),S(2),N(2)
250 REM TEST FOR VARIANCES
260 F = S(1)^2/S(2)^2
265 IF F>1 GOTO 290
270 F=1/F
275 PRINT "F=";F;"WHAT IS THE CRITICAL F FOR:";N(2)-1;N(1)-1;"DF";
285 GOTO 300
290 PRINT "F=";F;"WHAT IS THE CRITICAL F FOR:";N(1)-1;N(2)-1;"DF?"
300 INPUT F1
310 IF F>F1 GOTO 440
320 PRINT "VARIANCES DO NOT DIFFER"
330 PRINT "ENTER CRITICAL T FOR:";N(1)+N(2)-2;"DF"
340 INPUT T1
350 S1=SQR(((N(1)-1)*S(1)^2+(N(2)-1)^2)/((N(1)-1)+(N(2)-1)))
360 N1=SQR(1/N(1)+1/N(2))
370 S2=S1*N1
380 T=(X(1)-X(2))/S2
390 IF ABS(T)>T1 GOTO 420
400 PRINT "WITH A T VALUE OF";T;"WE CANNOT REJECT THE NULL HYPOTHESIS"
405 PRINT "DIFFERECNE=";X(1)-X(2)
410 GOTO 430
420 PRINT "WITH A T VALUE OF";T;"WE REJECT THE NULL HYPOTHESIS"
425 PRINT "DIFFERENCE=";X(1)-X(2)
430 GOTO 160
440 PRINT "VARIANCES DIFFER FOR AN F=";F;"DO YOU OPT FOR THE FISHER-BEHRENS FID
CIAL T TEST? 1=NO,2=YES"
450 INPUT Z
460 ON Z GOTO 330,480
465 PRINT "TRY AGAIN"
470 GOTO 440
480 REM FIDUCIAL T
490 D=(S(1)^2/N(1)+S(2)^2/N(2))^2
500 S4=(S(1)^2/N(1))^2/(N(1)-1)
505 S5=(S(2)^2/N(2))^2/(N(2)-1)
506 D=D/(S4+S5)
508 T=(X(1)-X(2))/(SQR((S(1)^2/N(1))+(S(2)^2/N(2))))
509 D=INT(D)
510 PRINT "ENTER CRITICAL T VALUE FOR";D;"DF"
520 INPUT T1
530 IF ABS(T)>T1 GOTO420
540 GOTO 400
600 REM T TEST OF MEAN
610 PRINT "ENTER MU ZERO,XBAR,S,N,CRITICAL T VALUE"
620 INPUT X(2),X(1),S(1),N(1),T1
630 T=(X(1)-X(2))/(S(1)/(SQR(N(1))))
640 IF ABS(T)>T1 GOTO 420
650 GOTO 400
660 END
```

13

ANALYSIS OF MEANS BY USING THE VARIANCE

While we were able to make wise decisions in the face of uncertainty using the simple analysis techniques of Chapter 12, the real problems we encounter are often of a more complex nature, and require analysis techniques beyond simple "t" tests.

It's easy to see how the "t" test works, with its signal-to-noise ratio concept. The difference between the means is the signal in the numerator, and the variation is the noise in the denominator. But what do we do when there are more than two means to compare? We could set up a "t" test that looks at only the extreme values, but this would waste a lot of the information we had paid valuable resources for. We could run "t" tests on all possible pairs of means in question, but we shall see this leads to a problem in making correct decisions. Let's look at a specific example with three means under comparison. If we were to use a "t" test on the following null hypothesis, we wouldn't have one "t" test, but a series of tests depending on the number of ways the means can be paired together.

$$H_0: \mu_1 = \mu_2 = \mu_3$$

Now, if the risk is 0.05, then the probability of being correct (or level of confidence) is 1 minus the risk, or in this case, $1 - .05 = 0.95$. If each "t" test is an independent test and the rules of probability state that for independent events, the probability of all events taking place is the product of the individual probabilities. This means that for all the decisions to be correct in our example, the first decision and the second decision and the third decision must be correct. Applying these rules of probability, we state our example as follows:

$$0.95 * 0.95 * 0.95 = 0.857375$$

Now, this resulting probability (.857) is considerably less than the 0.95 level of confidence we had specified in any one single test.

If we were to use the multiple "t" test method, we would not be making very wise decisions.

THIS REMEDY IS SPELLED A·N·O·V·A

So what do we do? Pack up and quit? No, what we need to develop is a hypothesis that tests multiple means, but does it with a single risk. The only way to have a single risk is to have a single test. To accomplish this goal we set up the same null hypothesis as in the multiple "t" test situation, but the alternative hypothesis is changed. Instead of having many alternatives that spell out which means differ from each other in pairs, as in the "t" test, we make one blanket statement that says the means differ. Now for the moment this may be a relatively unsatisfactory alternative hypothesis, since we really want to know which means differ; but as we progress, we will see that all our burning questions will be answered, and will be answered with control over the probability of making the correct decision.

To see how we can control our fate, let's return to the original example and try to compare three populations. This is a single-factor, three-level experiment, and is commonly called a "one-way-ANOVA". ANOVA is an acronym for "ANalysis Of VAriance" which is the name of the technique we are about to develop. While the name says "analysis of variance", we are really making inferences about means by using variances.

SIGNAL/NOISE

This analysis of means via variances may sound like a round-about method, but it accomplishes our goal of single risk inference in a multi-level experiment. The concept is to compute the variance within the means under investigation (the noise) and compare this with the variance between the means (the signal). If the resulting signal-to-noise ratio exceeds that which is expected by chance, we say that there is a difference between the means. The test statistic used in ANOVA is the same simple "F" ratio which we used to test differences between variances in Chapter 12. To illustrate the concept of ANOVA, let's look at two numerical examples. The first will show a situation in which we know that the population means are not different, and the second will illustrate a situation where the means are different.

NO DIFFERENCE

Let's take 15 random, normal numbers all from the same source population (factor), and divide them into three equal portions (levels) at random.

Table 13-2

	Portion #1	Portion #2	Portion #3	
	17.47	22.43	18.80	
	21.25	19.12	16.72	
	18.87	17.65	19.99	
	23.76	23.72	23.08	
	21.88	19.29	21.67	
$\bar{X}$:	20.646	20.442	20.052	$\bar{\bar{X}} = 20.38$
s^2:	6.206	6.392	6.115	
Σx:	103.23	102.21	100.26	Grand Total = 305.70

Looking at the averages, we see that there is very little difference between them. This is not unexpected, since the total of 15 numbers were randomly divided into three parts. We would expect any one randomly-selected portion to represent the whole. We also notice that the variation within each of the portions is fairly consistent. This is an important consideration, and, as we shall see later, is an assumption necessary in using ANOVA properly.

The noise we calculate is the pooled variance over the three portions. The calculation is similar to that used in a simple "t" test.

While it is easy to see where the noise comes from in the ANOVA calculations, the source of the signal is a bit more obtuse. To find the signal variance, we need to go back to our null hypothesis and do what it says.

$$H_0: \quad \mu_1 = \mu_2 = \mu_3 \qquad (13\text{-}2)$$

Expression 13-2 suggests that all of the means are the same. If this is so, and we were to put all of the data together as if it came from one population, then the variance we would observe would be no greater than the variance observed within any portion of the data. These "any portion" variances are the variations within each of the individual populations we are studying. We recognize these variations as the lowest order noise.

To compute the signal, we put the populations in the null hypothesis together as if they came from only one larger population and compute the variance of this population. If there are no differences between the populations, then the variance we observe will be no different from the variance we observe in the smaller "within" populations. If there is a difference between the populations under study, then the variance we compute when we put the populations all together will be larger than the variance computed within the individual populations. Figure 13-1 illustrates the concept of the Analysis of Variance in the form of population diagrams.

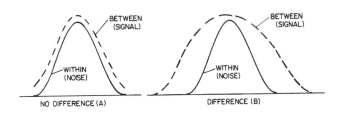

Figure 13-1

In Figure 13-1(A) the signal and noise populations are not different. Since they are the same, when we perform an "F" test we find that the signal to noise ratio, F, is only a chance happening and does not exceed the "critical" value in the table. In Figure 13-1(B), the spread of the "between" population is much greater than the spread of the "within" population. Here an "F" test shows that the between variance is indeed larger than the within variance. In our second numerical example, we shall see how this (13-1(B)) takes place. But, for the moment, let's concentrate on a numerical evaluation of the "A" portion of Figure 13-1 by going back to the data in Table 13-2.

We need to compute two variances for this example. Recall that the formula for variance may be expressed as follows:

$$s^2 = \frac{\Sigma x_i^2 - ((\Sigma x_i)^2/n)}{n-1} \tag{13-3}$$

This formula says to take each x value, square it and add it to the rest of the x-squared values; then find the sum of all the x values and square this quantity, and then divide by n (the number of x's). Take the difference between the two quantities and divide by n-1 (the degrees of freedom).

If we apply this formula to portion #1 of the example in Table 13-2 we get:

$$\Sigma x_i^2 = 17.47^2 + 21.25^2 + 18.87^2 + 23.76^2 + 21.88^2 = 2156.1123 \tag{13-4}$$
$$(\Sigma x_i)^2 = (17.47 + 21.25 + 18.87 + 23.76 + 21.88)^2 = (103.23)^2 = 10656.433$$
$$\text{and } (\Sigma x_i)^2/n = 10656.433/5 = 2131.2866 \tag{13-5}$$

When we find the difference between 13-4 and 13-5 we have the numerator of the expression for finding the variance. This is called the "sum of squares corrected for the mean". The "correction" is not to make up for any mistakes, but to center the variance over a mean of zero. The sum of the x's, quantity squared, divided by n is called the "correction factor". Without this correction factor, the sum of squares would be dependent upon the magnitude of the mean of numbers we were using. By correcting for the mean, we are able to look at only the true magnitude of the variation without the extra confusion of the mean level.

Continuing with the numerical example, we obtain the difference between 13-4 and 13-5 which is:

$$2156.1123 - 2131.2866 = 24.8257 \qquad (13\text{-}6)$$

If we were now to divide this result by the degrees of freedom $(5 - 1 = 4)$ we would get 6.206 which is the variance reported in Table 13-2. However, we do not choose to divide at this point, but to hold the "Sum of Squares" of the first portion and go on to compute the sum of squares for the two other portions in the same way.

For portion #2 the sum of squares is 25.568, and for portion #3 the sum of squares is 24.460.

Now, why did we hold off in the computation of the variance? Since the "within" variation is really made up of the three portions of the data from the experiment, we should use all three in our calculation of the noise variation. To use all three, we must pool the variances together. This is the same operation we performed in Chapter 12 in equation 12-13. In this operation of pooling, we had to multiply the variance by n-1 and turn it back to a sum of squares. To save this multiplication step, we simply leave all calculations of variances in the ANOVA system in terms of sum of squares until the last possible moment and save redundant operations. As mentioned before in Chapter 12, sums of squares are always additive, while variances are additive only when their sample sizes are the same.

So now let's add up our "noise" sums of squares.

$$
\begin{array}{ll}
24.8257 & \text{portion \#1 noise} \\
25.5680 & \text{portion \#2 noise} \\
\underline{24.4600} & \text{portion \#3 noise} \\
74.8537 & = \text{"noise" } \Sigma \text{ sq over all 3 portions}
\end{array}
$$

This is only one part of the sources of variation in our data. We still need to compute the "signal" portion. To do this, we need to put together the three portions (levels) as if they came from one population. We could take the averages of the three portions and compute the variance between them, but this leads to a computational problem if the sample sizes are different in each portion. Instead, we square the totals of each portion. Then we divide each of these squares by the number of items that went into the total we squared. Then we sum these three terms. This is the sum of squares between means, but still needs to be "corrected" to account for the grand mean, so we take the grand total squared, divided by the total number of samples, and subtract this from the "raw" sum of squares for the means. Symbolically:

$$\text{"Signal" } \Sigma sq = \frac{X_{p1}^2}{n_{p1}} + \frac{X_{p2}^2}{n_{p2}} + \frac{X_{p3}^2}{n_{p3}} - \frac{\text{Grand Total}^2}{n \text{ Total}} \qquad (13\text{-}7)$$

and with the numbers from Table 13-2:

$$\text{"Signal" } \Sigma sq = \frac{103.23^2}{5} + \frac{102.21^2}{5} + \frac{100.26^2}{5} - \frac{305.70^2}{15} = 0.9109$$

We can see that this is a very small sum of squares. It is in fact the extra sum of squares that would be induced into the data if there were a difference between the means of the three portions. However, in <u>this</u> example we obtained the data from one source of random normal numbers, and we would not expect to see any extra variation due to the pieces we broke out of the sample except by chance. The amount we got by chance in this case was a mere 0.9109.

As a final check, let's see if the two components we have just computed add up to the total sum of squares. The "noise" was equal to 74.8537 and the "signal" was 0.9109. Together this adds up to a total of 75.7646.

To check this sum, we will simply take each individual observation, square it and add all these squares together (there will be 15 items). Then remove the correction factor from this raw sum of squares. You will probably recognize this as the same set of calculations we would do if we were to compute the simple variance of the 15 pieces of data!

so: $(17.47^2 + 21.25^2 + 18.87^2 + \ldots\ldots 21.67^2) - \frac{305.7^2}{15} = 6305.9304 - \frac{93452.49}{15}$

Total $\Sigma sq = 6305.9304 - 6230.166 = 75.7644$

Which is pretty close to the result we obtained (off by 0.0002!) from the sum of the parts. This amount of rounding error can be expected when using even large scale computers. All the calculations for this example were made using a pocket calculator that has the facility to compute means and standard deviations and display the sum of the x's and the sum of the x^2's. This is a handy tool to use for such computations.

Now with all the necessary calculations finished, it is time to put the information in order and draw the conclusions about the data we have been looking at. The formality for this is to construct an "ANOVA Table" as follows:

Table 13-3

ANOVA	Source	Sum of Squares	df	Mean Square	F	$F_{critical}$ (0.05,2,12)
"SIGNAL"	Between portions	0.9109	2	0.4555	0.073	3.89
"NOISE"	Within portions (pooled)	74.8537	12	6.2378		
	TOTAL	75.7644	14	--------		

In Table 13-3 we record and identify the sums of squares as computed. The next column contains the degrees of freedom (df) for each source of variation. Let's see where these come from. Starting at the bottom of the table, we find the df for the total by taking one away from the total number of observations in the data. Since there were 15 observations, we get 14 degrees of freedom. The concept behind these degrees of freedom is exactly the same as discussed in previous chapters. Whenever we compute a mean value (which we must do to compute a variance) we lose a degree of freedom. Going up to the top of the table, we look at the number of levels in the "between portions" source of variation and from our data table (Table 13-2) we observe that there were three levels. Since we put these levels together to compute an overall mean, we lose a degree of freedom from the number of levels, so there are 2 degrees of freedom for the "between portions" source. In general, there will be degrees of freedom equal to the number of levels in the factor under study minus one. So if there were 6 levels then there would be 5 df.

Now for the last source of variation. You could use an "easy-out" method and say that the within portion source must be the remaining 12 degrees of freedom. This is correct, but it is worth the effort to see where the 12 df come from in this case and in general. Let's look into each of the portions in Table 13-2. There are 5 pieces of data in each portion. When we compute the variance in each portion, we lose a degree of freedom and have 4 df left. We do this in each portion and therefore the degrees of freedom for the "within" (our "noise" source) is equal to the sum of the degrees of freedom from all portions, or 12 df for noise.

Now we take the sum of squares and turn it into a variance by dividing by its df. In our ANOVA table this is called the "Mean Square" (i.e., average square), but is actually a variance that will be used in an F ratio. The calculation of the Mean Square completes the job outlined in equation 13-3. Notice that we saved the division by n-1 until last, when we had all the pieces of the sums of squares computed. This was to take advantage of the additivity of the sums of squares.

The final computation is the F test which is done by comparing the signal (between portions) in the numerator with the noise (within portions (pooled)) in the denominator.

$$F = \frac{0.4555}{6.2378} = 0.073$$

This comparison is made using the ratio of mean squares which are variances. We now compare this calculated F with the critical F in Table 5 for 2 numerator degrees of freedom and 12 denominator degrees of freedom. At the 0.05 risk level, this is 3.89. Since the computed F is far less than the critical F, we do not reject the null hypothesis. We conclude that the three portions all came from the same cause system. This confirms the fact that we knew all along in this set of data, since we drew our sample from the same source.

BIG DIFFERENCE

While the last example showed how to compute all the pieces of the ANOVA table, the data did not show differences. This next example will draw its samples from three different populations of normal random numbers. Let's see if the ANOVA technique can discover these differences. This example will produce a situation as pictured in Figure 13-1 (B) where the between level variance is much greater than the within level variance.

Table 13-4

	Level #1	Level #2	Level #3	
	20.23	30.85	26.27	
	20.71	28.96	25.76	
	20.05	29.71	24.83	
	21.47	29.55	24.33	
	20.67	31.68	25.60	
$\bar{X}$	20.625	30.150	25.358	$\bar{\bar{X}} = 25.378$
s^2	0.302	1.20	0.597	
Σx	103.13	150.75	126.79	Grand Total $= 380.67$

We will first compute the noise sum of squares for the difference between the levels under study. This is done by finding the sum of the squares of the five observations in each of the levels and then subtracting the sum of the five observations squared divided by 5 from this.

$$\Sigma x_i^2 - (\Sigma x_i)^2/5$$

for level 1: 2128.3693–2127.1594 = 1.2099
for level 2: 4549.9131–4545.1125 = 4.8006
for level 3: 3217.5283–3215.1408 = 2.3875

Now we sum the above results:

$$1.2099 + 4.8006 + 2.3875 = 8.398$$

which is the sum of the squares for error or noise.

Next we find the sum of squares for the difference between the levels under study. This is done by squaring each total for the three levels and then dividing by the number of observations in each of the squared totals, and then subtracting the "correction factor" from this. The "correction factor" is the grand total squared and divided by the grand number of observations.

$$\frac{103.13^2}{5} + \frac{150.75^2}{5} + \frac{126.79^2}{5} - \frac{380.67^2}{15} = 226.7695$$

Then, to check our arithmetic, we finally compute the total sum of squares. Take each observation, square it and sum all these squares. Subtract the "correction factor" from this sum of squares and the value we get is equal to the sum of the two parts, the noise and the signal sum of squares.

so we take: $20.23^2 + 20.71^2 + \ldots\ldots\ldots 24.33^2 + 25.60^2 = 9895.8107$

then, $9895.8107 - \frac{380.6722}{15} = 235.1675$

The Analysis of Variance table is now constructed from these calculations.

Table 13-5

ANOVA

	Source	Sum of Squares	df	Mean Square	F	$F_{critical}$ (0.05,2,12)
"SIGNAL"	Between portions	226.7695	2	113.385	162.02	3.89
"NOISE"	Within portions (pooled)	8.398	12	0.700		
	TOTAL	235.1675	14	------		

In the above example we can see that the calculated F vastly exceeds the tabulated value, so we conclude that the difference between the means of the levels is not a chance occurrence, but a real indication that the means differ. Now you could say, "Of course the means differ. I could see that without any ANOVA calculations!" Let's just look once more at what the ANOVA is saying. While there will probably always be differences observable (even in the first example there were differences), the real question is: "Are the differences we observe bigger than the natural variation within the data?" If the variation in the repeated measurements is greater than the differences in the means in the hypothesis, then we are unable to believe that there are any more differences between the means than within the means and must conclude that the means are all the same. However, if the differences between the means are greater than can be expected by chance, we are inclined to believe that the means do differ. This is what we mean by a "significant" difference. The word "significant" does not mean big or important in a physical sense, but simply from a statistical/probability stance, that the signal is greater than the noise. Many researchers often get the meaning wrong and equate practical importance with statistical significance. A result may be "significant", meaning it has a greater signal to noise ratio (F) than expected by chance, but the differences between the means under study may not amount to anything practically important. Therefore, when the researcher draws the conclusions, both the statistical and the practical implications should be addressed. Let's take one more example of ANOVA and expand the problem to a real-life situation to illustrate the point of significance vs. importance.

AN APPLE A DAY

Apple growing is an important upstate New York industry. The farmers harvest the crop in the late summer and early fall. However, people like to eat apples all year round. While there is an abundance of apples at low prices in the fall, the winter and spring bring higher and higher prices to the consumer. Besides being a supply and demand situation, one price-inflating factor is storage. There are different kinds of apples grown and there are different types of storage methods. In this problem, a large apple co-op is experimenting to determine optimum storage conditions. The response to be measured is the time to spoilage as measured in months. Table 13-6 shows the data that shall be analyzed by ANOVA.

Now in this set of data we have introduced a second source of variation in contrast to the one-way ANOVA. We look at the storage conditions (columns) as we did before, and find the sum of squares between conditions by squaring the sum in each column and adding these squares together. We divide this sum by the number of items that went into the squared value (which is six in this case). From this result, we subtract the "correction factor" to obtain the sum of squares due to conditions.

Table 13-6

Storage Condition

		36°	38°	40°	42°	44°	Row Totals
A	Ida Red	6.5	7.5	8.0	7.5	5.0	
p		6.0	8.0	8.5	7.0	4.5	68.5
p							
l	McIntosh	7.5	8.5	9.5	9.5	7.5	
e		8.0	9.0	9.0	9.0	7.0	84.5
T	Delicious	5.0	6.0	7.0	6.0	5.0	
y		4.5	6.5	7.5	5.5	4.5	57.5
p							
e							
Column Totals:		37.5	45.5	49.5	44.5	33.5	210.5

$$\Sigma sq_{cond.} = \frac{37.5^2 + 45.5^2 + 49.5^2 + 44.5^2 + 33.5^2}{6} - \frac{210.5^2}{30}$$

$$= \frac{9029.25}{6} \quad -1477.0 = 27.875$$

Now, you might ask, how can we sum over the types of apples as if they didn't exist in this calculation? You will notice that the experiment is balanced with as many (and the same type) kinds of apples in each storage condition. Because of this balance, we may ignore the effect of the types of apples as we study the temperatures of the conditions independently. We will do the same "summing over" with the apple types. We will sum over the temperatures of storage as if they did not change since the same change in temperature takes place over all types of apples. The sum of squares for apple types is obtained in the same manner.

$$\Sigma sq_{type} = \frac{68.5^2 + 84.5^2 + 57.5^2}{10} - \frac{210.5^2}{30} = 1513.875 - 1477.0 = 36.875$$

Notice here that we divide the sum of the squares of the types by 10, since there were 10 items (or apples) that went into each sum that was squared.

Next we compute the sum of squares due to the noise or lack of sameness in each treatment combination. Notice that in each cell or treatment, the difference in storage life is exactly one-half a month. We may simplify the arithmetic in this example by finding the sum of squares in one of the treatments and then extend this by multiplying by the number of treatment combinations (which is 15 in this case).

The sum of squares in each cell is: $\dfrac{6.5^2+6.0^2-\underline{12.5^2}}{1\qquad\quad 2}$ = 0.125
(the same as in the first cell)

so the entire sum of squares for error (or noise) is 0.125 times 15 = 1.875.

Now we will compute the total sum of squares and see if it checks out. To do this, simply find the square of each individual data point and sum over all these. Then subtract the correction factor.

$$6.5^2+6.0^2+7.5^2+8.0^2+\ldots\ldots\ldots 5.0^2+4.5^2=1546.75$$

$$1546.75-\dfrac{\underline{210.5^2}}{30}=69.75$$

When we add up the pieces, we get:

Conditions + Apples + Error

27.875 + 36.875 + 1.875 = 66.625!!!!

Which is not the total we computed from the individual pieces of data. The individual pieces sums of squares are short by a little more than 3 units. So where is the "lost" sum of squares?

There is one last source of variation that we have not accounted for. This is the source that accounts for the lack of similarity of behavior to temperatures by the different types of apples. If all the apples behaved the same to the storage conditions we would say that the storage condition effect was a simple linear additive effect over the types of apples. If this linearly additive effect does not take place, then we have an interaction between conditions and apples. This interaction is the source of the "lost" sum of squares that is included in the total, but not yet calculated as an individual contributor.

To compute the interaction sum of squares, we need to look into each cell of the data matrix. In Table 13-6 there are two observations per cell and there are 15 cells which are made up of the intersections of the five columns of storage conditions with the three rows of apple types. So the first intersection is with the 36° temperature and Ida Red apple which shows values of 6.5 and 6.0 months to spoilage. We take these values and sum them to obtain the cell total. In the case of the first cell, the total is 12.5. In the second column, first row the cell total is 15.5. We continue with this summing within cells for all 15 cells. Now take each cell total, square it and add all these squares together. We now have the sum of squares for the interaction.

$$Ssq_{interaction} = \frac{12.5^2 + 15.5^2 + 16.5^2 + 14.5^2 + 9.5^2 +}{2} \quad \text{(first row)}$$

$$\frac{15.5^2 + 17.5^2 + 18.5^2 + 18.5^2 + 14.5^2 +}{2} \quad \text{(second row)}$$

$$\frac{9.5^2 + 12.5^2 + 14.5^2 + 11.5^2 + 9.5^2}{2} \quad \text{(third row)}$$

$$= 1544.875$$

We of course divide by the number of observations in the sum we are squaring, which is 2 in this case. Then subtract the correction factor and obtain the interaction sum of squares.

$$1544.875 - \frac{210.5^2}{30} = 67.867$$

But now this sum of squares is too big, since the total sum of squares is only 69.75 and we already have 66.625 in the two main effects and the error. The reason for this "extra" sum of squares lies in the way we computed the interaction sum of squares. We have actually recomputed the sum of squares due to the storage conditions and the apple types in our computation of the interaction. To fix this problem, we subtract these two main effect sources of variation from the interaction sum of squares and we get the real interaction sum of squares all by itself.

$$67.867 - (27.875 + 36.875) = 3.117$$

Now we will put it all together to be able to draw our inferences.

Table 13-7

ANOVA

Source	Sum of Squares	df	Mean Square	F	$F_{critical}$	
Storage Conditions	27.875	4	6.97	55.76	3.0556	(0.05,4,15)
Type Of Apple	36.875	2	18.44	147.52	3.6823	(0.05,2,15)
Interaction	3.117	8	0.39	3.12	2.6408	(0.05,8,15)
Error	1.875	15	.125	---		
Total	69.75	29	---			

The degrees of freedom for the storage conditions and the types of apples are one less than the number of levels in the factors as before. The degrees of freedom for error accumulate as before with one degree of freedom lost for each cell mean computed. Since there were only two observations per cell, there is only one degree of freedom per cell. With 15 cells, then we have 15 df for error. The interaction degrees of freedom is found by taking the product of the df for each of the interacting main factors. So in this case, we multiply the degrees of freedom for conditions (4 df) times the degrees of freedom for types (2 df) and get 8 df.

From the table of critical F values we obtain the F value which, when exceeded by a calculated F from the experiment, tells us that this is not a chance happening, but the result of an outside-cause system. In this case we see that all the critical F values have been exceeded, and we conclude that there is a difference between storage conditions and between types of apples, and that the interaction is also a significant effect. The significant interaction tells us that different apples store differently, and do not behave the same under all storage conditions.

Now let's look at where the differences lie and if there is enough of a difference to warrant changes in the storage of the apples. To do this, we will compute the averages of each treatment combination in the experiment.

Table 13-8

Storage Condition

	36°	38°	40°	42°	44°
Ida Red	6.25	7.75	8.25	7.25	4.75
McIntosh	7.75	8.75	9.25	9.25	7.25
Delicious	4.75	6.25	7.25	5.75	4.75

If we plot the results of the computation of the averages vs. temperature in Table 13-8 we get a better picture of the way the storage conditions influence each type of apple's life.

From the plot of the data (plot of averages) we see that there is a difference between each of the apple types with the McIntosh exhibiting the longest storage life followed by Ida Red and Delicious. There also appears to be an optimum temperature for storage. However, some of the differences we see may not be significantly different with the amount of error or noise in this data. We cannot use a graphic display to draw our final conclusions, but must revert to another test of the data using methods that will go beyond ANOVA and tell us which levels are different.

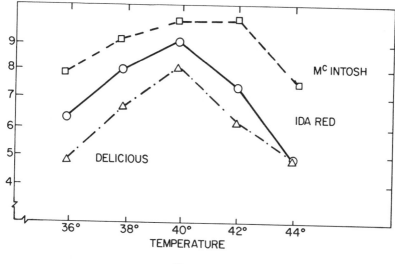

Figure 13-2

COMPARISONS OF INDIVIDUAL LEVELS

There are a number of different methods to compare the individual means after an ANOVA has indicated that there is a difference between the means. In general, the technique used in all of them is to first rank order the means from lowest to highest and then compute a statistic that is related to the standard error of the mean. This statistic is usually called the shortest significant range (SSR) and represents the smallest difference that is statistically different when comparing different mean values that have been ranked. Since we purposely rank the values, the probability increases in finding differences as we compare ranks that are farther apart. Therefore, the SSR gets larger for each comparison we make across ranks that are further apart.

In the case of the apple experiment, we will look at the effect of each apple type at only one level of temperature at a time, since there was a significant interaction in the results of our analysis. If there had been no interaction, then we would have compared the the apple types over all storage conditions averaged together.

In Table 13-9 we order the three types of apples in increasing average months to spoilage. We'll use abbreviations to simplify labeling the types of apples. McIntosh will be abbreviated to M; Ida Red's abbreviation is I; and Delicious is D.

Table 13-9

Temperature	Rank 1	Rank 2	Rank 3
36°	4.75(D)	6.25(I)	7.75(M)
38°	6.25(D)	7.75(I)	8.75(M)
40°	7.25(D)	8.25(I)	9.25(M)
42°	5.75(D)	7.25(I)	9.25(M)
44°	4.75(D) tie	4.75(I)	7.25(M)

We next compute the Shortest Significant Range (SSR) by finding the standard error of the mean from the mean square for error as follows:

$$s_{\bar{X}} = \sqrt{\frac{0.125}{2}} \qquad (13\text{-}8)$$

$$= .25$$

The divisor in the calculation of the standard error is simply the number of observations in the means we are comparing. In this case, there are only two observations per mean. If we had summed over the 5 different storage conditions, then the divisor would have been 10 since there are 2 replicates per cell. We did not sum over the temperatures because of the significant interaction.

Now we find the SSR by taking the $s_{\bar{X}}$ and multiplying it by the upper points of the Studentized Range q found in Table 6.   To enter Table 6, we need to know the df for the error which comes from our ANOVA table and the number of means over which we are making the comparisons. In our case, the df for error is 15 so we move down to the row headed by 15 and then read across the maximum number of means in the rank. In our case this is 3. The q values then are: 3.01 and 3.67 for the 5% level.

Therefore the SSR's are:

Table 13-10

Means in range (p)

	2	3	
$s_{\bar{X}}$	0.25	0.25	
q	3.01	3.67	SSR = q*$s_{\bar{X}}$
SSR	0.7525	0.9175	

We now set up a difference table to be able to compare the actual differences in our data with the SSR's of Table 13-10.

We can see from table 13-11 that all the apple types are different except for the Ida Red and Delicious at the 44° storage condition. This inconsistency is probably the greatest contributor to the interaction. We also observe that the smallest differences occur at the 40° condition. This leads to the practical implication and conclusion that this is probably the best all-around condition for the storage of apples considering that

Table 13-11

DIFFERENCE TABLE

	comparison of adjacent ranks	comparison over 3 ranks
@36°	6.25(I)–4.75(D) = 1.5* 7.75(M)–6.25(I) = 1.5*	7.5(M)–4.75(D) = 3.0*
@38°	7.75(I)–6.25(D) = 1.5* 8.75(M)–7.75(I) = 1.0*	8.75(M)–6.25(D) = 2.5*
@40°	8.25(I)–7.25(D) = 1.0* 9.25(M)–8.25(I) = 1.0*	9.25(M)–5.75(D) = 3.5*
@42°	7.25(I)–5.75(D) = 1.5* 9.25(M)–7.25(I) = 2.0*	9.25(M)–5.75(D) = 3.5*
@44°	4.75(I)–4.75(D) = 0.0 7.25(M)–4.75(I) = 2.5*	7.25(M)–4.75(D) = 2.5*

*indicates significant differences

we could not afford to set up different conditions for different apples. We also note that the 40° condition is also the condition that produces the longest storage life. This is a fortunate happening which makes the choice of storage conditions easier in this situation.

Let's look at some more practical implications of the data we have just analyzed. The difference table confirms that the results plotted in Figure 13-2 are not just numerically different, but statistically different. That is, the signal we observe is greater than the noise encountered. Since we have no control over the apples' inherent spoilage, and we see that the Ida Red and Delicious spoil sooner than the McIntosh, we can use this information to our advantage and attempt to "push" the quicker spoiling apples to market or use them in other ways such as cider production. In this way, we can maximize our profit. We also notice that the McIntosh apples store as well at 42° as they do at 40°. Since the McIntosh will last a full month longer than the other two types, we could allow the temperature to rise a couple of degrees and save refrigeration costs in the last month of storage of the McIntosh apples.

The above insights are based on the practical importance of the data. Such practical conclusions must always be thought of and stated in any statistical analysis. All too often, the analyst will merely state the facts about the statistics and forget the reason for the experimentation in the first place. Always draw conclusions in words that relate to the problem at hand.

MORE CONCLUSIONS

While it appears that we have completed the analysis of the apple data, there are a few fine points yet to be covered. We drew some general conclusions about the storage temperatures, but did not back them up with any statistical tests. We will do so by applying the SSR concept to the temperatures to see which of them are different. From the table of means (13-8) we will rank the average time to spoilage for different levels of temperature. Again, we will do so for isolated levels of apple type since there is an interaction between type and temperature. (i.e. The apples respond differently to storage). Since there are 5 levels of temperature in the storage condition factor, there will be 5 ranks.

Table 13-12

Apple Type	Rank 1	Rank 2	Rank 3	Rank 4	Rank 5
Ida Red	4.75(44°)	6.25(36°)	7.25(42°)	7.75(38°)	8.25(40°)
McIntosh	7.25(44°)	7.75(36°)	8.75(38°)	9.25(40°)	9.25(42°)
Delicious	4.75(26°)	4.75(44°)	5.75(42°)	6.25(38°)	7.25(40°)

The $s_{\bar{x}}$ is the same value we computed for the apple differences since the averages in the above Table (13-11) are also from two observations. We obtain the q values in the same way as before, but go out to a p of 5 since there were 5 levels of temp. So the SSR's are:

Table 13-13

Means in range (p)

	2	3	4	5
$s_{\bar{x}}$	0.25	0.25	0.25	0.25
q	3.01	3.67	4.08	4.37
SSR	0.75	0.92	1.02	1.09

The critical question in the storage temperature information is which condition produces the longest storage. If two conditions are not significantly different, then we would pick the condition that is less costly to attain, which is a higher temperature. Looking back to Figure 13-2, which plots the spoilage data vs temperature, we would look at the peak storage life and ask if there is any difference between the peak and the next higher temperature. In this plot, the peak storage condition is at 40°. The next condition (42°) shows a drop in life for two apple types, but no drop for the McIntosh type. From this we may conclude that there is no difference between 40° and 42° for the McIntosh apples and use the lower cost alternative. For the Ida Red and Delicious we go to the SSR's in Table 13-12 to decide if there is enough difference to warrant a significant difference between the temperatures. For both types of apples, the 40° condition is ranked highest and the 42° temperature is ranked third. This gives us a difference range over three items and a SSR of 0.92. The difference between the 40° condition and the 42° condition for the Ida Red apple is 8.25–7.25 or just greater than the SSR, so we conclude that there is a significant difference and that the 40° condition should be used to store the Ida Red apples.

For the Delicious apples the difference between the 42° and the 40° conditions is 7.25–5.75 = 1.5 which is greater than the SSR of 0.92, so again we conclude that there is a significant difference between conditions, and that we should use 40° for the storage of the Delicious apples.

We could have set up a difference table as was done with the apple types, but the extra work is not really necessary, since only certain questions needed to be answered in light of the practical implications of this study. The difference table for storage conditions would have been a complex set of numbers, and just might have confused the issue. A general rule in reporting results is to keep the analysis as simple as possible while still answering the questions that need to be answered.

FUNCTIONAL RELATIONSHIPS

The analysis of variance techniques is a very powerful method for answering questions involving comparisons of multi-levels in an experiment. While we have shown how to compute the appropriate sums of squares, and build the information into an ANOVA table from which we draw our conclusions, and then go beyond this table to actually compare individual means with a single risk, there is still more that can be extracted from the data in hand.

The storage condition factor in our example is a quantitative factor with equally spaced temperature conditions. This was done in a fully-planned manner when the experiment was designed. When we have a quantitative factor at equally-spaced intervals, we may apply a method to investigate the polynomial functional nature of the data. That is, we may determine the shape of the cruve represented by our data. There is a set of coefficients called "orthogonal polynomials" that, when used to weight the computation of the sums of squares, will reveal from our ANOVA the curved or straight line nature of the data. We shall now apply this concept to the example on storage of apples.

To do so, we will recompute the sum of squares due to storage conditions by breaking up the 4 degrees of freedom into four individual effects. There will be the linear (straight line) effect; the quadratic effect (one hump curve); the cubic (double hump curve); and quartic (triple hump curve). A table of correct weightings for the orthogonal polynomials may be found in table 7   page 372.   Before we use these orthogonal polynomial coefficients, we should look into their nature.

For our example the values of the coefficients are as follows.

Table 13-14

X:	1	2	3	4	5
Linear	-2	-1	0	1	2
Quadratic	2	-1	-2	-1	2
Cubic	-1	2	0	-2	1
Quartic	1	-4	6	-4	1

If we plot these on an <u>equally spaced</u> x axis we get the following:

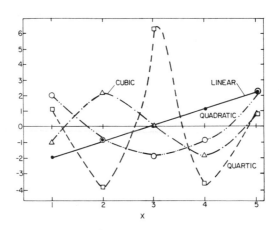

Figure 13-3

So we can see that these coefficients plot out as polynomial relationships. What about the "orthogonal" part of the name? The word orthogonal is used to indicate independence. If the coefficients are independent then there will be no covariance between any of the coefficients. A simple check for this condition is to impose the following rules on the creation of the coefficients. The first rule will require that the sum of any row of the polynomial is equal to zero. The second rule requires that the sum of the cross products of any two rows is also equal to zero. Let's check this out with the coefficients in Table 13-14.

The sum of the linear is: $\quad -2 + (-1)+0+1+2=0$
The sum of the quadratic is: $\quad 2+(-1)+(-2)+(-1)+2=0$
The sum of the cubic is: $\quad -1+2+0+(-2)+1=0$
The sum of the quartic is: $\quad 1+(-4)+6+(-4)+1=0$

So the first condition is met. Now we need to find the cross products of all the combinations of pairs of the 4 rows of coefficients. There will be 6 such pairs.

$$
\begin{array}{l}
\text{L x Qd: } -2*2 + -1*-1 + 0*-2 + 1*-1 + 2*2 \\
\qquad\quad\; -4 \;+\; 1 \;+\; 0 \;+\; -1 \;+\; 4 \quad = 0
\end{array}
$$

$$
\begin{array}{l}
\text{L x C: } -2*-1 + -1*2 + 0*0 + 1*-2 + 2*1 \\
\qquad\quad\; 2 \;+\; -2 \;+\; 0 \;+\; -2 \;+\; 2 \quad = 0
\end{array}
$$

$$
\begin{array}{l}
\text{L x Qt: } -2*1 + -1*-4 + 0*6 + 1*-4 + 2*1 \\
\qquad\quad\; -2 \;+\; 4 \;+\; 0 \;+\; -4 \;+\; 2 \quad = 0
\end{array}
$$

$$
\begin{array}{l}
\text{Qd x C: } 2*-1 + -1*2 + -2*0 + -1*-2 + 2*1 \\
\qquad\quad\; -2 \;+\; -2 \;+\; 0 \;+\; 2 \;+\; 2 \quad = 0
\end{array}
$$

$$
\begin{array}{l}
\text{Qd x Qt: } 2*1 + -1*-4 + -2*6 + -1*-4 + 2*1 \\
\qquad\quad\; 2 \;+\; 4 \;+\; -12 \;+\; 4 \;+\; 2 \quad = 0
\end{array}
$$

$$
\begin{array}{l}
\text{C x Qr: } -1*1 + 2*-4 + 0*6 + -2*-4 + 1+1 \\
\qquad\quad\; -1 \;+\; -8 \;+\; 0 \;+\; 8 \;+\; 1 \quad = 0
\end{array}
$$

So we can see that we have fulfilled the requirements of the orthogonality for these coefficients. This assures us that the sums of squares we obtain in the next step will be independent estimates of the effects.

To obtain the sums of squares for the polynomial relationship, we will compute the sums of squares for storage conditions summed over types of apples, but this time we will <u>weigh</u> the computation by the polynomials found in Table 13-14.

$$
\text{Sum Sq linear} = \frac{(-2(37.5)+-1(45.5)+0(49.5)+1(44.5)+2(33.5))^2}{((-2)2 + (-1)2+(0)2+12+22)*(6)} \tag{13-9}
$$

Let's look at expression 13-9 and see where the numbers come from. In the numerator, the values in parens. are the totals of the temperature conditions from Table 13-6. These are multiplied by the linear orthogonal polynomial coefficients. We would normally divide this sum of squares by the number of observations in the sum being squared and this is the "6" in the denominator. The other part of the denominator is merely the orthogonal polynomial coefficients squared and summed to compensate for their inclusion in the numerator. So, in general, we will find the weighed sum of the factor under study using the weighings of the orthogonal polynomials; then square this sum. Next find the sum of squares of the polynomial coefficients and multiply this sum of squares by the number of observations in each total that is found in the numerator. In this manner, we are able to find a weighed sum of squares and the weighing is based on the polynomial used. For the quadratic term:

$$\text{Sum Sq quadratic} = \frac{(2(37.5)+-1(45.5)+-2(49.5)+-1(44.5)+2(33.5))^2}{(2^2+(-1)^2+(-2)^2+(-1)^2+2^2)*(6)} \quad (13\text{-}10)$$

Similar computations are done for the cubic and quartic to produce the sum of squares for these components. With this information we create a new, revised ANOVA table. In each case, for the factor being broken down into its polynomial parts, there is only one degree of freedom for each polynomial sum of squares.

The revised ANOVA table now includes the sums of squares for the four polynomial effects.

Table 13-15

ANOVA

Source	Sum of Squares	df	Mean Square	F	$F_{critical}$	
Storage Conditions						
Linear	1.35	1	1.35	10.80	4.5431	(0.05,1,15)
Quadratic	26.30	1	26.30	210.40	4.5431	(0.05,1,15)
Cubic	0.07	1	0.07	0.56	4.5431	(0.05,1,15)
Quartic	0.15	1	0.15	1.20	4.5431	(0.05,1,15)
Type Of Apple	36.875	2	18.44	147.52	3.6823	(0.05,2,15)
Interaction	3.117	8	0.39	3.12	2.6408	(0.05,8,15)
Error	1.875	15	.125			
Total	69.75	29				

With calculated F's exceeding the critical F values in both the linear and quadratic effects, we conclude that a polynomial of second order is the appropriate functional form for this data. Notice that the sum of the four polynomial effects add up to the sum of squares for storage conditions (27.87) found in the previous ANOVA (Table 13-7). In computing the polynomial sums of squares, we have simply done a partitioning of the effects into their functional form.

We will leave this ANOVA now, but return in Chapter 16 to further investigate this technique and show how it is a special case of the general linear model problem.

ANOVA ASSUMPTIONS

While we have gone off and computed the sums of squares for the Analysis of Variance, we must realize that there are three underlying assumptions that need to be observed in order that the conclusions we draw are valid in any analysis of variance.

Since we are pooling the error variances together, we must make sure that these variances do not differ significantly from each other. If there is a large amount of difference between the variances we are pooling, then we could get a biased pooled variance and our signal-to-noise ratio would become meaningless. So the first assumption for a valid conclusion to be drawn from an ANOVA is the fact that the variances are homogeneous.

The second assumption for a valid ANOVA is based on the fact that the Normal distribution function is used indirectly in the computation of the critical levels. Therefore, the error variances must be distributed as a normal variate.

The final assumption is more than an assumption; it is a requirement that influences the way we conduct our experiment. The assumption is that the error variances are independent. That is, each test in the experiment should not have an effect on any other test. While this is an assumption, we can accomplish the result by running the entire experiment in a random order to assure that any treatment combination has an equally likely chance of happening anywhere in the sequence of our testing. Therefore, any systematic variation outside the realm of the factors under study will not bias or be confounded with the functional results.

While this third assumption is related to experimental conduct, the first two assumptions will have to be tested. The following statistical tests show how to check for homogeniety of variance and normality.

TEST FOR HOMOGENEITY OF VARIANCE

While there are many tests for checking homogeneity of variance, the Burr-Foster Q test has an advantage inasmuch as it is not sensitive to departures from normality. Therefore it may be applied before a normality test without fear of drawing the incorrect conclusion.

To show how the test works, we will run through the following example of a 4 level one-way ANOVA with 5 replicates per treatment.

Table 13-16
Temperature

100°	200°	300°	400°
90	150	250	400
100	175	300	300
85	125	325	500
110	180	250	450
90	150	225	375

		100°	200°	300°	400°	
s^2	=	100	492.5	1687.5	5750.0	$s^2 = 8030$
s^4	=	10000	242556.25	2847.656.25	33062500	$(s^2)^2 = 36162712$
$\bar{X}$	=	95	156	270	405	
s	=	10	22.19	41.1	75.8	

The test statistic is the value q which is found by taking the ratio of the sum of the variances squared to the sum of the variances quantity squared.

$$q = \frac{\displaystyle\sum_{i=1}^{p} (s_i^2)^2}{(\Sigma s^2)^2}$$

where s^2 is the variance of each population (p).

p is the number of populations.

In our example p is equal to 4 (the 100°, 200°, 300°, 400° populations) so we sum the squared variances for the numerator then square the sum of the variances for the denominator. The q value is the ratio of these two quantities. Table 13-16 shows these values and the value of q is:

$$q = 36162712/8030^2 = 36162712/64480900 = 0.5608 \qquad (13-11)$$

The critical value of q which, if exceeded, signifies that there is nonhomogeneity in the variances is found in table 8 on page 388. We enter the table with degrees of freedom for the populations under study. In this case there are 5 observations in each population, so there are 4 df. Note there must be equal numbers of observations in all the populations for this test. The other parameter of the q value is the number of populations we are investigating. In this example there are 4 populations (p). Therefore, the critical value of q for df=4 and p=4 is 0.549 at an alpha risk of 0.01. It is usual to use very small alphas for this test, since slight departures from homogeniety do not cause great consequences. ANOVA's with variances in a 9 to 1 ratio have been run with little change in the alpha risk (the change has been from 0.05 to 0.06!) (Box,1954). In this example, we have exceeded the critical value of q and reject the hypothesis of homogeniety of variances.

Also in this example, we see a typical problem that creeps into experimental data. If we look at the percentage error as calculated by taking the standard deviation over the average for each population, we see that there is a relatively constant percentage error (averaging about 14%) over all populations. However, as the temperature increases, the size of the response increases, which leads to the non-homogeniety of the errors. To combat this, we need to make a mathematical transformation of the data to compress all the values together. A simple compressing transformation is a log. So in this example we take the log of each value and then compute the ANOVA. The only problem with a transformation is that we lose touch with the data. This explains why we transform only when there is excessive heterogeniety in the data.

TESTS FOR NORMALITY

The second assumption for drawing valid conclusions from an ANOVA is centered around the normality of the error distribution. There are many tests for normality, but the following Shapiro-Wilk test will be most useful for small samples found in ANOVA problems. We will illustrate the procedure by testing for the normality of the errors in the 100° temperature level of the example in Table 13-16.

The hypothesis under study in this normality test is as follows:

$$H_0: \text{ Non-Normal distribution}$$
$$H_1: \text{ Normal distribution}$$

This is somewhat backwards from the usual hypothesis set-up, but is constructed in favor of finding normality with an alpha risk when we reject the null hypothesis. If the hypotheses were reversed, then the normal distribution (which would probably come up most of the time) would have a beta risk attached to it. The beta risk is not defined in this test, so by setting the hypotheses up as shown above, we can cleverly avoid this risk when we have a normal distribution!

The first step in the procedure is to place the data being studied in ascending order.

For the data in our example this will produce:

$$85 \qquad 90 \qquad 90 \qquad 100 \qquad 110$$

Next, we compute the sum of squares of this set of data:

$$(85^2 + 90^2 + 90^2 + 100^2 + 110^2) - 475^2/5 = 45525 - 45125 = 400$$

Now, calculate a value b which is found by taking the difference between the farthest extremes and multiplying this difference by a coefficient from Table 9 on page 390 . Then continue to find the differences between extremes and multiply by the coefficient.

$$\text{For our example: } b = \sum_{i=1}^{k} a_{n-i+1}(x_{n-i+1} - x_i)$$

where $k = (n-1)/2$ for odd n or $k = n/2$ for even n.
n is the number of items being tested
x is the value of the item in the ascending order
a_{n-i+1} is the factor from table

For our numerical example:

$$b = 0.6646 *(110-85) + 0.2413 *(100-90) = 19.028$$

We now compute the test statistic, W which is the ratio of b^2 to the Sum of square of x.

$$W = b^2/SSx \qquad\qquad W = 19.0282/400 = 0.905$$

The critical value from Table 10 on page 392 is 0.762 for alpha equal to 0.05 for n equal to 5 (the number of items in the test).

Since we have a calculated value greater than the critical value, we reject the null hypothesis and conclude that the data shows no departure from normality.

PROBLEMS FOR CHAPTER 13

1) A process engineer has set up the following experiment to determine if there is any difference between four methods of fastening two parts together. The methods are assigned in a random order to the design with as many samples per methods as in affordable. The results are as follows. Complete the ANOVA and test for differences between means using the SSR. Draw all conclusions. The response is breaking strength.

Cyanoacrylaye Adhesive	"Contact" Cement	Hot Melt Glue	"Du Co" Cement
20	16	24	12
18	14	26	14
24	12	25	13
17	15	25	12
20	17	26	13
21	16	25	12.

2) A public relations person wants to test the effect of a series of letters explaining the company's stand on a recent "accident" at an atomic power station. The response is the reaction, measured in number of angry letters sent back to the company protesting the event. Four different letters of explanation were published in local newspapers. The distance for the power plant was classified for each protest letter received. Complete the ANOVA on this data and draw conclusions on the letter and the distance factors.

DISTANCE (Miles)

		0.5	1.0	2.0	4.0	8.0	16.0
	A	20	10	5	2	1	0
LETTER	B	50	24	10	5	2	1
	C	15	6	3	1	1	0
	D	100	49	20	10	2	1

3) Perform an Analysis of Variance (ANOVA) on the following Data:

VENDOR

Kodak	Ricoh	Xerox	Savin	Minolta
90	55	85	60	85
85	60	90	55	88
88	54	88	50	80
91	50	90	54	87
90	56	90	55	84

Is there a difference between the 5 levels of Copy Quality?

If so, which Vendors are different?

4) What can we conclude about the following skew data? (Skew is coded to produce whole numbers).

Run-Out Level

		A	B	C	D	E
	5 ips	2	3	5	7	9
		1	5	6	6	8
Speed	10 ips	4	5	7	9	9
		5	7	6	9	10
	15 ips	1	5	7	6	10
		2	4	6	7	8

After running the ANOVA, test individual differences between levels of run-out and set up the orthogonal polynomials for the speed. Do not forget to state your conclusions.

5) Perform an Analysis of Variance (ANOVA) on the following data:

VENDOR

	A	B	C	D	E
P	2	2	3	2	3
a	3	3	2	3	4
r	3	2	3	3	4
t	2	2	2	2	4
	3	2	3	4	3

Is there a difference between the 5 vendors for this measurement?

APPENDIX 13

Multiple t tests should not be performed since the risk is inflated as follows:

$$\text{inflated risk} = 1 - ((1-\text{risk})^t)$$
$$\text{where } t = n*(n-1)/2$$

ANOVA is the analysis of Variance - it really is an analysis of means by using variance.

Steps in computing an ANOVA:

1) Find the total sum of squares by taking each single piece of data, square it, and add it to the rest of the squared data. From this sum, subtract the grand total squared, divided by the total number of data points.

$$\Sigma x_i^2 - (\Sigma x_i)^2/n \qquad \text{where } x_i \text{ represent each data point.}$$

2) Find the sum of squares for each effect in the experiment by first summing the values for the effect over all other effects ("summing over" means to sum as if the other factors did not exist). Now take each sum and square it. Divide this square by the number of items that went into the sum being squared. Sum all these squares and subtract the grand total squared divided by the total number of data points.

$$\Sigma x_{j.}^2/n - (\Sigma x_i)^2/N \qquad \begin{array}{l}\text{where } x_{j.} \text{ represents the sum over}\\ \text{all other factors and } x_i \text{ represents}\\ \text{each data point.}\end{array}$$

3) Find the error sum of squares by extending the above concept into each treatment combination cell where there is replication to find the sum of squares in each cell, i.e. Find the Σsq of each cell element and subtract the sum of the cell elements squared, divided by n from this.

4) Construct an ANOVA table with the sums of squares you have computed. There will be degrees of freedom for each effect equal to the number of levels in the factor less one. Any interaction will have degrees of freedom equal to the number of degrees of freedom in the interacting terms multiplied together. The degrees of freedom for error will be the sum of the degrees of freedom from each cell where each cell will have one less df than the number of items in the cell.

The table looks like this:

ANOVA Source	Sum Of Squares	df	Mean Square	F	Fcricital
Factor 1					
Factor 2					
Interaction					
Error					
Total					

For "fixed factor" designs, the F is the ratio of the factor Mean square to the error mean square.

Mean Square: Sum of squares divided by degrees of degrees of freedom.

Fixed Factor: The levels of this factor are selected from only those that are available and include all the levels of interest.

Random Factor: As opposed to a fixed factor, the levels are picked at random from a population. See Chapter 18 for more details.

SSR: Shortest Significant Range - a range statistic that helps determine which means differ after we have rejected the null hypothesis in an ANOVA. Any difference that is equal to or greater than the SSR is considered a significant difference.

Orthogonal Polynomial Coefficients: A set of values that are polynomial in nature and also dependent. They are used after rejecting the null hypothesis in ANOVA to determine the functionality of quantitative factors. To be applied properly, the levels of the quantitative factor must be equally spaced in the design.

ANOVA Assumptions: Homogeneous error variances; normal distribution of error variances; error variances are independent.

ANOVA1 COMPUTER PROGRAM

```
90 CLS
95 DIM Y(25),R(25),Z(25,25),U(25)
100 PRINT TAB(20);"ONE-WAY ANALYSIS OF VARIANCE"
105 PRINT:PRINT:PRINT
110 INPUT "DO YOU WANT TO PRINT RESULTS ON LINE PRINTER?";LP$
120 REM ONE-WAY ANALYSIS OF VARIANCE FOR EQUAL OR UNEQUAL
140 REM NUMBER OF REPLICATES PER LEVEL
180 S1=0
200 REM S2=SUM OF X(I) SQUARED
220 S2=0
240 REM S3=LEVEL TOTAL SQUARED DIVIDED BY # REPLICATES
260 REM IN LEVEL
280 S3=0
300 REM R1=TOTAL # OBSERVATIONS
320 R1=0
340 PRINT "WANT DATA ON FILE";
360 INPUT W$
380 IF W$="Y" THEN 440
400 IF W$="YES" THEN 440
420 GOTO 1420
440 PRINT "NAME OF FILE";
460 INPUT B$
480 PRINT"DOES THIS FILE EXIST ALREADY <INDICATE--OLD>"
490 PRINT "OR ARE YOU CREATING IT FOR THE FIRST TIME <INDICATE--NEW>";
500 INPUT I$
520 IF I$="OLD" THEN 580
540 OPEN "O",1,B$
560 GOTO 1420
580 OPEN "I",1,B$
600 INPUT #1,L1
620 PRINT "DO YOU WANT TO EDIT THE DATA";
640 INPUT W$
660 IF W$="Y" THEN 720
680 IF W$="YES" THEN 720
700 GOTO 1500
720 FOR I=1 TO L1
740 INPUT #1,U(I)
760 R2=U(I)
780 FOR J=1 TO R2
800 INPUT #1,Z(I,J)
820 NEXT J
840 NEXT I
860 PRINT "TO CHANGE DATA"
880 PRINT "ENTER THE LEVEL #";
900 INPUT L5
920 PRINT "AND THE REPLICATE # IN THAT LEVEL";
940 INPUT L7
960 PRINT"THE OLD VALUE OF YOUR DATA FOR LEVEL:";L5;"AND REP. #";L7;"IS";Z(L5,L
7)
980 PRINT "ENTER NEW VALUE";
1000 INPUT X
1020 Z(L5,L7)=X
1040 PRINT "MORE EDITING";
1060 INPUT W$
```

```
1080 IF W$="Y" THEN 860
1100 IF W$="YES" THEN 860.
1120 PRINT "EDIT STOPPED. REVISED FILE SAVED. NEW ANOVA BEING COMPUTED."
1140 CLOSE
1160 OPEN "O",1,B$
1180 PRINT #1,L1
1200 FOR I= 1 TO L1
1220 R2=U(I)
1230 PRINT #1,R2
1240 FOR J=1 TO R2
1260 PRINT #1,Z(I,J)
1280 NEXT J
1300 NEXT I
1320 CLOSE
1340 OPEN "I",1,B$
1360 PRINT
1380 INPUT #1,L1
1400 GOTO 1500
1420 PRINT "HOW MANY LEVELS IN YOUR EXPERIMENT?"
1440 REM L1= # LEVELS IN EXPERIMENT
1460 INPUT L1
1500 IF I$="NEW" THEN 1540
1520 GOTO 1560
1540 PRINT #1,L1
1560 FOR L=1 TO L1
1580 IF I$="OLD" THEN 1680
1600 PRINT "HOW MANY REPLICATES IN LEVEL";L;"?"
1620 REM R2=# OF REPLICATES IN LEVEL
1640 INPUT R2
1660 GOTO 1700
1680 INPUT #1,R2
1700 R1=R1+R2
1720 IF I$="NEW" THEN 1760
1740 GOTO 1800
1760 PRINT #1,R2
1780 REM S4=SUM OF X(I) FOR LEVEL
1800 S4=0
1820 IF I$="OLD" THEN 1860
1840 PRINT "ENTER X VALUES OF LEVEL";L;"ONE PER LINE"
1860 FOR R=1 TO R2
1880 IF I$="OLD" THEN 1960
1900 PRINT "REPLICATE";R
1920 INPUT X
1940 GOTO 1980
1960 INPUT #1,X
1980 S4=S4+X
2000 IF I$="NEW" THEN 2040
2020 GOTO 2060
2040 PRINT #1,X
2060 S2=S2+X^2
2080 NEXT R
2100 S3=S3+(S4^2)/R2
2120 S1=S1+S4
2140 Y(L)=S4/R2
2160 NEXT L
2180 CLOSE
2200 REM C=CORRECTION FACTOR
2220 C=(S1^2)/R1
2240 REM T=TOTOL SUM OF SQUARES
2260 T=S2-C
2280 REM T1=TREATMENT SUM OF SQUARES
2300 T1=S3-C
2320 REM T2=RESIDUAL SUM OF SQUARES
2340 T2=T-T1
2360 REM D=TOTAL DEGREES OF FREEDOM
2380 D=R1-1
2400 REM D1=TREATMENT DEGREES OF FREEDOM
2420 D1=L1-1
```

```
2440 REM D2=RESIDUAL DEGREES OF FREEDOM
2460 D2=D-D1
2470 A$="#####.####      ##      #####.####     ###.##"
2471 CLS
2473 IF LEFT$(LP$,1)<>"Y" THEN GOTO 2496
2474 LPRINT:LPRINT:LPRINT "DATA: ";B$:LPRINT:LPRINT
2475 LPRINT "ANOVA":LPRINT
2486 LPRINT "SOURCE       SUM SQ      DF        MS              F"
2487 LPRINT "TREATMENT" USING A$;T1;D1;T1/D1;(T1/D1)/(T2/D2)
2488 LPRINT "RESIDUAL " USING A$;T2;D2;T2/D2
2489 LPRINT "TOTAL    " USING A$;T;D
2495 LPRINT:LPRINT
2496 PRINT "DATA: ";B$:PRINT:PRINT
2497 PRINT "ANOVA":PRINT
2500 PRINT "SOURCE       SUM SQ      DF        MS              F"
2520 PRINT "TREATMENT" USING A$;T1;D1;T1/D1;(T1/D1)/(T2/D2)
2540 PRINT "RESIDUAL " USING A$;T2;D2;T2/D2
2560 PRINT "TOTAL    " USING A$;T;D
2565 PRINT:PRINT
2570 INPUT "F CRITICAL FOR 90% CONFIDENCE: ",CR1
2575 INPUT "F CRITICAL FOR 95% CONFIDENCE: ",CR2
2577 INPUT "F CRITICAL FOR 99% CONFIDENCE: ",CR3
2580 IF LEFT$(LP$,1)<>"Y" THEN GOTO 2600
2585 LPRINT:LPRINT
2586 LPRINT "F CRITICAL FOR 90% CONFIDENCE: ";CR1
2587 LPRINT "F CRITICAL FOR 95% CONFIDENCE: ";CR2
2588 LPRINT "F CRITICAL FOR 99% CONFIDENCE: ";CR3
2600 PRINT:PRINT:PRINT "PRESS <RETURN> TO CONTINUE";
2605 MASK$=INKEY$:INPUT " ",MASK$
2606 IF LEFT$(LP$,1)<>"Y" THEN GOTO 2610
2607 LPRINT:LPRINT:LPRINT "AVERAGES:":LPRINT
2608 FOR L=1 TO L1:LPRINT "LEVEL:";L;Y(L)
2609 NEXT L
2610 PRINT:PRINT:PRINT "AVERAGES:":PRINT
2620 FOR L=1 TO L1
2640 PRINT "LEVEL:";L;Y(L)
2660 NEXT L
2680 PRINT
2700 PRINT "DO YOU WANT TO DO A SSR TEST";
2720 INPUT W$
2740 IF W$="Y" THEN 2860
2760 IF W$="YES" THEN 2860
2780 END
2860 FOR I=2 TO L1
2880 PRINT "ENTER STUDENTIZED RANGE VALUE Q FOR P=";I;"AND DF=";D2;
2900 INPUT R(I)
2920 NEXT I
2940 S8=SQR((T2/D2)/(R1/L1))
2945 IF LEFT$(LP$,1)<>"Y" THEN GOTO 2953
2948 LPRINT:LPRINT:LPRINT  "SHORTEST SIGNIFICANT RANGE TEST"
2950 LPRINT
2951 LPRINT "SSR'S"
2952 LPRINT "RANGE        SSR"
2953 CLS
2955 PRINT:PRINT:PRINT "SHORTEST SIGNIFICANT RANGE TEST"
2956 PRINT
2960 PRINT "SSR'S"
2980 PRINT "RANGE        SSR"
3000 A$="##        ####.###"
3010 IF LEFT$(LP$,1)<>"Y" THEN GOTO 3020
3012 FOR I=2 TO L1
3013 LPRINT USING A$;I;S8*R(I)
3014 NEXT I
3015 LPRINT
3020 FOR I=2 TO L1
3030 PRINT USING A$;I,S8*R(I)
3040 NEXT I
3180 END
```

ANOVA2 COMPUTER PROGRAM

```
90 CLS
100 PRINT TAB(10);"ANALYSIS OF VARIANCE FOR 2 FACTORS"
110 PRINT:PRINT
120 INPUT "DO YOU WANT TO PRINT THE RESULTS ON LINE PRINTER?";LP$
140 REM S1=SUM OF X
160 S1=0
180 REM S2=SUM OF X'S SQUARED
200 S2=0
220 S4=0
240 PRINT "WANT DATA ON FILE";
260 INPUT W$
280 IF W$="Y" THEN 340
300 IF W$="YES" THEN 340
320 GOTO 1340
340 PRINT "NAME OF FILE";
360 INPUT B$
380 PRINT "IF THE FILE EXIST <INDICATE--OLD> OR"
390 PRINT "IF THIS FILE IS TO BE CREATED <INDICATE--NEW>"
400 INPUT I$
420 IF I$="OLD" THEN 480
440 OPEN "O",1,B$
460 GOTO 1340
480 OPEN "I",1,B$
500 INPUT #1,L1,L2,R1
520 PRINT"THERE ARE:";L1;"LEVELS IN FACTOR #1 AND";L2;"LEVELS IN FACTOR #2 WITH"
;R1;"REPLICATES"
540 PRINT "DO YOU WANT TO EDIT THE DATA";
560 INPUT W$
580 IF W$="Y" THEN 640
600 IF W$="YES" THEN 640
620 GOTO 1520
640 E1=L1*L2
660 DIM Z(E1,R1)
680 FOR I=1 TO E1
700 FOR J=1 TO R1
720 INPUT #1,Z(I,J)
740 NEXT J
760 NEXT I
780 PRINT "TO CHANGE DATA:"
800 PRINT "ENTER THE LEVEL OF FACTOR 1";
820 INPUT L5
840 PRINT "ENTER THE LEVEL OF FACTOR 2";
860 INPUT L6
880 PRINT "ENTER THE REPLICATE #";
900 INPUT L7
920 L8=(L5-1)*L2+L6
940 PRINT "THE OLD VALUE OF F1 LEVEL";L5;"F2 LEVEL";L6;"REP#2";L7;"IS";Z(L8,L7)
960 PRINT "ENTER NEW VALUE";
980 INPUT X1
1000 Z(L8,L7)=X1
1020 PRINT "MORE EDITING";
1040 INPUT W$
1060 IF W$="Y" THEN 780
1080 IF W$="YES" THEN 780
1100 PRINT "EDIT STOPPED. REVISED FILE SAVED. NEW ANOVA BEING COMPUTED"
1120 CLOSE
1140 OPEN "O",1,B$
1145 PRINT #1,L1,L2,R1
1160 FOR I=1 TO E1
1180 FOR J=1 TO R1
1200 PRINT #1,Z(I,J)
1220 NEXT J
1240 NEXT I
1260 CLOSE
1280 OPEN "I",1,B$
```

```
1300 PRINT
1310 INPUT #1,L1,L2,R1
1320 GOTO 1520
1340 PRINT "TYPE THE # OF LEVELS IN FACTOR 1"
1360 INPUT L1
1380 PRINT "TYPE THE # OF LEVELS IN FACTOR 2"
1400 INPUT L2
1420 PRINT "AND THE # REPLICATES PER TC"
1440 INPUT R1
1460 REM L1=# LEVELS FACTOR 1 (ROWS)
1480 REM L2=# LEVELS FACTOR 2 (COLUMNS)
1500 REM R1=# REPLICATES
1520 DIM X(L1),Y(L2)
1540 IF I$="NEW" THEN 1580
1560 GOTO 1600
1580 PRINT #1,L1;L2;R1
1600 FOR I=1 TO L1
1620 X(I)=0
1640 NEXT I
1660 FOR I=1 TO L2
1680 Y(I)=0
1700 NEXT I
1720 FOR I=1 TO L1
1740 FOR J=1 TO L2
1760 IF I$="OLD"THEN 1820
1780 PRINT "ENTER RESPONSES FOR FACTOR 1-LEVEL";I
1800 PRINT "                    FACTOR 2-LEVEL";J
1820 S3=0
1840 FOR I1=1 TO R1
1860 IF I$="OLD" THEN 1980
1880 PRINT "REPLICATE";I1;
1900 INPUT X1
1920 IF I$="NEW" GOTO 1940
1930 GOTO 2000
1940 PRINT #1,X1;
1960 GOTO 2000
1980 INPUT #1,X1
2000 S1=S1+X1
2020 S2=S2+X1^2
2040 S3=S3+X1
2060 NEXT I1
2080 X(I)=X(I)+S3
2100 Y(J)=Y(J)+S3
2120 S4=S4+S3^2
2140 NEXT J
2160 NEXT I
2180 C=(S1^2)/(L1*L2*R1)
2200 T=S2-C
2220 S3=0
2240 FOR I=1 TO L1
2260 S3=S3+X(I)^2
2280 NEXT I
2300 T1=S3/(L2*R1)-C
2320 S3=0
2340 FOR I=1 TO L2
2360 S3=S3+Y(I)^2
2380 NEXT I
2400 T2=S3/(L1*R1)-C
2420 T3=S4/R1-T1-T2-C
2440 IF R1>1 THEN 2500
2460 T4=T-T1-T2
2480 GOTO 2520
2500 T4=T-T1-T2-T3
2520 D=(L1*L2*R1)-1
2540 D1=L1-1
2560 D2=L2-1
2580 D3=D1*D2
2600 IF R1>1 THEN 2660
```

```
2620 D4=D-D1-D2
2640 GOTO 2665
2645 IF LEFT$(LP$,1)<>"Y" THEN GOTO 2860
2646 LPRINT "AVERAGES:"
2647 LPRINT "FACTOR 1"
2648 FOR I=1 TO L1
2649 LPRINT "LEVEL:";I;X(I)/(R1*L2)
2650 NEXT I
2651 LPRINT
2652 LPRINT "FACTOR 2"
2653 FOR I=1 TO L2
2654 LPRINT "LEVEL:";I;Y(I)/(R1*L1)
2655 NEXT I
2660 D4=D-D1-D2-D3
2665 CLS
2670 A$="  #####.####      ##       #####.####      ####.##"
2680 IF LEFT$(LP$,1)<>"Y" THEN GOTO 2700
2683 LPRINT "DATA: ";B$
2684 LPRINT:LPRINT
2685 LPRINT "ANOVA":LPRINT
2687 LPRINT "ANOVA":PRINT
2689 LPRINT "SOURCE        SUM SQ        DF        MS              F"
2690 LPRINT "FACTOR 1" USING A$;T1;D1;T1/D1;(T1/D1)/(T4/D4)
2692 LPRINT "FACTOR 2" USING A$;T2;D2;T2/D2;(T2/D2)/(T4/D4)
2693 IF R1=1 THEN 2695
2694 LPRINT "INTERACT" USING A$;T3;D3;T3/D3;(T3/D3)/(T4/D4)
2695 LPRINT "RESIDUAL" USING A$;T4;D4;T4/D4
2696 LPRINT "TOTAL   " USING A$;T;D
2697 LPRINT
2700 PRINT "DATA: ";B$
2705 PRINT:PRINT
2707 PRINT "ANOVA":PRINT
2710 PRINT "SOURCE        SUM SQ        DF        MS              F"
2720 PRINT "FACTOR 1" USING A$;T1;D1;T1/D1;(T1/D1)/(T4/D4)
2740 PRINT "FACTOR 2" USING A$;T2;D2;T2/D2;(T2/D2)/(T4/D4)
2760 IF R1=1 THEN 2800
2780 PRINT "INTERACT" USING A$;T3;D3;T3/D3;(T3/D3)/(T4/D4)
2800 PRINT "RESIDUAL" USING A$;T4;D4;T4/D4
2820 PRINT "TOTAL   " USING A$;T;D
2840 PRINT:PRINT
2845 INPUT "ENTER 'F' CRITICAL FOR 90% CONFIDENCE: FACTOR-1: ",CR11
2846 PRINT TAB(40);:INPUT "FACTOR-2: ",CR12:PRINT TAB(40);:INPUT "INTERACT: ",CR
13
2847 INPUT "ENTER 'F' CRITICAL FOR 95% CONFIDENCE: FACTOR-1: ",CR21
2848 PRINT TAB(40);:INPUT "FACTOR-2: ",CR22:PRINT TAB(40);:INPUT "INTERACT: ",CR
23
2849 INPUT "ENTER 'F' CRITICAL FOR 99% CONFIDENCE: FACTOR-1: ",CR31
2850 PRINT TAB(40);:INPUT "FACTOR-2: ",CR32:PRINT TAB(40);:INPUT "INTERACT: ",CR
33
2851 IF LEFT$(LP$,1)<>"Y" THEN GOTO 2858:LPRINT:LPRINT
2852 LPRINT "F CRITICAL FOR 90% CONFIDENCE: FACTOR-1: ";CR11;" FACTOR-2: ";CR12;
2853 LPRINT "  INTERACT: ";CR13
2854 LPRINT "F CRITICAL FOR 95% CONFIDENCE: FACTOR-1: ";CR21;" FACTOR-2: ";CR22;
2855 LPRINT "  INTERACT: ";CR23
2856 LPRINT "F CRITICAL FOR 99% CONFIDENCE: FACTOR-1: ";CR31;" FACTOR-2: ";CR32;
2857 LPRINT "  INTERACT: ";CR33
2858 PRINT "PRESS <RETURN> TO CONTINUE";
2859 MASK$=INKEY$:INPUT " ",MASK$
2860 IF LEFT$(LP$,1)<>"Y" THEN GOTO 2870
2863 LPRINT:LPRINT:LPRINT "AVERAGES:"
2865 LPRINT "FACTOR 1"
2867 FOR I=1 TO L1
2868 LPRINT "LEVEL:";I;X(I)/(R1*L2)
2869 NEXT I
2870 PRINT:PRINT:PRINT "AVERAGES:"
```

```
2880 PRINT "FACTOR 1"
2900 FOR I=1 TO L1
2920 PRINT "LEVEL:";I;X(I)/(R1*L2)
2940 NEXT I
2960 IF LEFT$(LP$,1)<>"Y" THEN GOTO 2980
2965 LPRINT:LPRINT "FACTOR 2"
2970 FOR I=1 TO L2
2973 LPRINT "LEVEL:";I;Y(I)/(R1*L1)
2975 NEXT I
2980 PRINT:PRINT "FACTOR 2"
3000 FOR I=1 TO L2
3020 PRINT "LEVEL:";I;Y(I)/(R1*L1)
3040 NEXT I
3060 PRINT:PRINT:PRINT "DO YOU WANT TO DO A SSR TEST";
3080 INPUT W$
3100 IF W$="Y" THEN 3220
3120 IF W$="YES" THEN 3220
3140 END
3220 IF L1>=L2 THEN 3280
3240 E5=L2
3260 GOTO 3300
3280 E5=L1
3300 FOR I=2 TO E5
3320 PRINT "ENTER STUDENTIZED RANGE POINT Q FOR P=";I;"AND DF=";D4;
3340 INPUT R(I)
3360 NEXT I
3380 PRINT "IS THERE AN INTERACTION";
3400 INPUT W$
3420 IF W$="YES" THEN 3480
3440 IF W$="Y" THEN 3480
3460 GOTO 3520
3480 S3=SQR((T4/D4)/R1)
3500 GOTO 3541
3520 S3=SQR((T4/D4)/(L2*R1))
3540 S4=SQR((T4/D4)/(L1*R1))
3541 IF LEFT$(LP$,1)<>"Y" THEN GOTO 3560
3542 LPRINT:LPRINT:LPRINT "SHORTEST SIGNIFICANT RANGE (SSR) TEST":LPRINT
3543 LPRINT "SSR'S FOR FACTOR #1"
3544 LPRINT "RANGE         SSR"
3546 FOR I=2 TO L1
3547 LPRINT I;S3*R(I)
3548 NEXT I
3549 LPRINT
3550 LPRINT "SSR'S FOR FACTOR #2"
3551 LPRINT "RANGE         SSR"
3552 FOR I=2 TO L2
3553 IF W$="Y" GOTO 3557
3554 IF W$="YES" GOTO 3557
3555 LPRINT I;S4*R(I)
3556 GOTO 3558
3557 LPRINT I;S3*R(I)
3558 NEXT I
3560 PRINT:PRINT:PRINT "SHORTEST SIGNIFICANT RANGE (SSR) TEST":PRINT
3570 PRINT "SSR'S FOR FACTOR #1"
3580 PRINT "RANGE         SSR"
3600 FOR I=2 TO L1
3620 PRINT I;S3*R(I)
3640 NEXT I
3660 PRINT
3680 PRINT "SSR'S FOR FACTOR #2"
3700 PRINT "RANGE         SSR"
3720 FOR I=2 TO L2
3730 IF W$="Y" GOTO 3750
3731 IF W$="YES" GOTO 3750
3740 PRINT I;S4*R(I)
3745 GOTO 3760
3750 PRINT I;S3*R(I)
3760 NEXT I
3860 END
```

14

YATES ALGORITHM

In our daily lives we use many algorithms to simplify the way we do business. An algorithm has been defined as a method that simplifies a calculation, but mystifies understanding. The analysis of variance we studied in Chapter 13 can lead to some involved arithmetic. Fortunately, for the types of experiments that are used most of the time and prove to be most efficient, there is a simplified algorithm for ANOVA. In Chapters 4 and 5 we learned how to design the two-level factorial and fractional factorial experiments. Because of the two level characteristic of these experiments, we may use the YATES method to compute the sums of squares. While the YATES method may at first seem like a strange exercise, we will see that it produces the same results as a conventional ANOVA method, and gives us a bonus piece of information. This bonus information will prove to be very valuable in the interpretation and presentation of the results from 2^k and 2^{k-p} designs.

In this chapter, we will learn how to make the computations for ANOVA using the YATES method. In Chapter 15 we will review the essential elements of matrix algebra to set the stage for Chapter 16 where we will demonstrate the common bond between ANOVA and the general linear model.

The YATES algorithm is quite simple. Here are the rules.

1) Place the response variable information from the 2^k or 2^{k-p} design in YATES order. (For a review of this, see Chapter 4). If the experiment is fully replicated, sum the replicates first.

2) Set up n columns where $n = k-p$. Label these columns with Roman Numerals (a convention).

3) a. Create entries for the first column by adding adjacent pair-wise sets of data from the response variable column.

b. Complete the first column by going back to the start of the response variable column and subtracting adjacent pair-wise entries. Subtract the first response from the second response as they appear in YATES order.

4) Continue the pair-wise addition and subtraction using the newly created columns until you reach the last column (n).

5) Compute the sum of squares by taking the individual entries in the last column (n) and square each of them. Divide this square by 2^n*r where $n = k-p$ and r is the number of replicates. There is no "correction factor" needed in the YATES ANOVA since the algorithm is a "self-correcting" method.

6) Compute the "half-effects" for quantitative factors by taking the last column (n) and dividing it by 2^n*r ($r = \#$ of replicates). If the factor is of a qualitative nature, then a "half-effect" would be meaningless and a "full-effect" should be calculated by dividing the last column by $2^{n-1}*r$ ($r = \#$ of replicates). The "half-effect" is defined as the change in response over half the range in the factor under study. We shall treat this further in Chapter 16.

The above rules give the method for computing the ANOVA. We shall now look at a numerical example and show how to interpret the results of such an analysis.

For our example, we will use the data from Table 4-4 on page 27. In Chapter 4 we performed an "intuitive" analysis and now by using the YATES ANOVA we will obtain the same results, but with a bit more insight.

The experiment in Chapter 4 investigated the effect of pressure, temperature, and time on the contamination of a polymer product. The response we are looking at is percent contamination.

The results from the experiment as run in random order are:

Table 14-1

Run #	tc	%contamination
1	c	4.1
2	1	2.6
3	a	3.9
4	abc	3.2
5	ac	1.7
6	b	4.4
7	ab	8.0
8	bc	7.8

Step 1 puts the responses in YATES order:

Table 14-2

tc	%contamination
1	2.6
a	3.9
b	4.4
ab	8.0
c	4.1
ac	1.7
bc	7.8
abc	3.2

In this experiment there were three factors, so it was a 2^3 factorial with no fractionalization. Therefore, $n = 3-0$ or 3 and we set up 3 columns in the YATES. We will do so in table 14-3 and complete the pair-wise addition and subtraction for the first column in this table.

Now we complete the table by filling out columns II and III. In doing the arithmetic, be sure to watch the signs of the terms. If you do the work on a pocket calculator, choose a calculator that has the change sign key to make this job easier.

Table 14-3

tc	%cont.	I	II	III
1	2.6	6.5		
a	3.9	12.4		
b	4.4	5.8		
ab	8.0	11.0		
c	4.1	1.3		
ac	1.7	3.6		
bc	7.8	-2.4		
abc	3.2	-4.6		

Add ——————————————
Subtract------------------

Table 14-4

tc	%cont	I	II	III
1	2.6	6.5	18.9	35.7
a	3.9	12.4	16.8	-2.1
b	4.4	5.8	4.9	11.1
ab	8.0	11.0	-7.0	0.1
c	4.1	1.3	5.9	-2.1
ac	1.7	3.6	5.2	-11.9
bc	7.8	-2.4	2.3	-0.7
abc	3.2	-4.6	-2.2	-4.5

We will now take the last column of values and square them and then divide each squared value by 2^n (which is 8 in this case) to produce the sum of squares. We also will take each value in the last column and divide it by 2^n to obtain the "half effects".

Now that we have done all the calculations, let's look into table 14-5 to see what it all means. Each row of the table identifies an effect. We can pick out which effect is which by looking at the treatment combination identifier. The "a" identifier has the sum of squares and half effect for the "A" factor of pressure next to it. The other effects are identified similarly.

Table 14-5

tc	Observation	Sum Square	Half Effect	Measures
(1)	2.6	159.311	4.4625	Average
a	3.9	0.55125	−0.2625	A (pressure)
b	4.4	15.4013	1.3875	B (temperature)
ab	8.0	1.24998E-03	0.0124999	AB (press.–temp. int)
c	4.1	0.55125	−0.2625	C (time)
ac	1.7	17.7013	−1.4875	AC (time-press. int)
bc	7.8	0.0612501	−0.0875001	BC (time-temp. int)
abc	3.2	2.53125	−0.5625	ABC (time-press.-temp. int)

In the above experiment, there was no replication, so unless we can come up with a measure of error, we cannot perform an F test to determine if there is a significant signal-to-noise ratio for the effects. It is sometimes possible to use an "outside" estimate of error. This error estimate would come from previously run experiments or from long-term historical records. Let's assume that we have an outside estimate of error variance (σ^2) for this experiment of 0.9 with 20 degrees of freedom. Therefore, the critical F for 1 and 20 df at the 0.05 level is 4.35. Since in a 2-level experiment there is only one degree of freedom for each effect, the mean square is the same value as the sum of squares. The F's for each effect are computed by dividing the sum of squares from table 14-5 by the 0.9 error mean square.

Table 14-6

Effect Measured	F	
pressure	0.61	not significant
temperature	17.11	significant**
press x temp	0.001	not significant
time	0.61	not significant
press x time	19.67	significant**
temp x time	0.07	not significant
press x temp x time	2.81	not significant

Therefore we conclude that there is a significant temperature effect and a significant pressure-time interaction.

APPLICATION TO 2^{k-p} FRACTIONAL DESIGNS

The YATES method is completely applicable to fractional factorial designs. The method of computing the sums of squares is general enough to allow all the computations to be made as in the full factorial designs. The only difference comes in the interpretation.

In setting up the "measures" column at the end of the YATES ANOVA, we treat the effects based upon the treatment combination identifiers from the base design used to generate the fractional factorial. For a review of this concept see Chapter 5 pages 46-48. For the simplest 2^{k-p} design where $k=3$ and $p=1$ the ANOVA would look like this:

Table 14-7

tc	Sum Of Squares	Measures	
1(c)		---	
a		A, BC	for a 2^{3-1}
b		B, AC	
ab(c)		AB,C	I = ABC

A more complex 1/4 fractional factorial as described on page 48 in Chapter 5 has a much more complicated "measures" column. It is still built on the base design which is a 2^5 in this case. Table 14-8 shows the outline of the YATES ANOVA for this design.

Table 14-8

tc	response	Sum/Diff. Columns I	II	III	IV	V	Sum of Squares	Half Effect	Measures
(gh)									---
a(fh)									A,BCDF,ABCDEG,FEG
b(f)									B̄,ACDF,CDEG,ABFEG
ab(g)									AB,CDF,ACDEG,BFEG
c(f)									C̄,ABDF,BDEG,ACFEG
ac(g)									AC,BDF,ABDEG,CEFG
bc(gh)									B̄C̄,ADF,DEG,ABCFEG
abc(fh)									ABC,D̲F̲,ADEG,BCEFG
d(f)									D,ABCF,BCEG,ADEFG
ad(g)									A̲D̲,BCF,ABCEG,DEFG
bd(gh)									B̄D̄,ACF,CEG,ABDEFG
abd,(fh)									ABD,C̲F̲,ACEG,BDEFG
cd(gh)									C̲D̲,ABF,BEG,ACDEFG
acd(fh)									ACD,B̲F̲,ABEG,CDEFG
bcd(f)									• BCD,A̲F̲,E̲G̲,ABCDEFG
abcd(g)									ABCD,F̲,AEG,BCDEFG
e(fg)									E,ABCDEF,BCDG,AFG
ae									• A̲E̲,BCDEF,ABCDG,F̲G̲
be(h)									B̄Ē,ACDEF,CDG,ABF̄Ḡ
abe(fgh)									→ ABE,CDEF,ACDG,BFG
ce(h)									CE,ABDEF,BDG,ACFG
ace(fgh)									→ A̲C̲E̲,BDEF,ABDG,CFG
bce(fg)									BCE,ADEF,D̲G̲,ABCFG
abce									→ ABCE,DEF,A̲D̲G̲,BCFG
de(h)									D̲E̲,ABCEF,BCG,ADFG
ade(fgh)									→ A̲D̲E̲,BCEF,ABCG,DFG
bde(fg)									BDE,ACEF,C̲G̲,ABDFG
abde									→ ABDE,CEF,A̲C̲G̲,BDFG
cde(fg)									CDE,ABEF,B̲G̲,ACDFG
acde									→ ACDE,BEF,A̲B̲G̲,CDFG
bcde(h)									BCDE,AEF,G̲,ABCDFG
abcde(fgh)									• ABCDE,E̲F̲,A̲G̲,BCDFG

the defining contrast is : I=ABCDF,BCDEG,AEFG

Of the 28 degrees of freedom needed to supply information on the 7 main effects and the 21 two-factor interactions, this design affords only 22 independent or orthogonal degrees of freedom. Three df are confounded for 6 of the two-factor interactions (indicated with dots) and there are 6 df that measure three-factor interactions (indicated with arrows). We may use these three-factor interactions to measure the experimental error.

The usual practice in the analysis of fractional factorial designs is to use the defining contrast to determine the measured effects for those effects that are significant. This saves a lot of extra effort in computing the confounding pattern from the defining contrast.

While the outline of a design shows the effects identified by code letters of the alphabet, in a real experiment, it is difficult to follow the physical reality of the situation by using this alphabetical code. Therefore, it is recommended that the actual names of the factors be substituted for the letters when communicating results.

DECONFOUNDING EFFECTS

In the example above and in many experiments, the resources do not match the required information and we end up with two-factor interactions confounded with each other. There are three methods of attack to resolve this problem.

1) Use prior knowledge to pick the likely interaction.

2) Run a subset experiment.

3) Run the rest of the fraction of the experiment.

The next example will illustrate these methods. We are investigating four factors in a 1/2 fractional factorial experiment with 8 treatment combinations. The factors are: Temperature, Pressure, Time, and Concentration. Using the ABC interaction from the base 2^3 design we obtain a defining contrast of: $I = ABCD$ from which we can see that all of the two-factor interactions are confounded together.

$$ie: \quad AB = CD$$
$$AC = BD$$
$$AD = BC$$

To understand the consequence of this confounding, let's take the first confounded pair of interactions and see exactly what is the meaning of $AB = CD$. We can be very mathematical and state that the effect we observe for AB,CD is a linear combination of these two effects. But what does that mean? First of all let's gain a little insight by looking at the pattern of minus and plus signs assigned to the AB and CD interactions. Figure 14-1 shows the base design in YATES order with the signs for the 4 main factors. To obtain the signs of the interactions, we simply multiply the signs together following ordinary rules of algebra.

A	B	C	D	AB	CD	Response	AB	CD
−	−	−	−	+	+	21	+21	+21
+	−	−	+	−	−	19	−19	−19
−	+	−	+	−	−	20	−20	−20
+	+	−	−	+	+	58	+58	+58
−	−	+	+	+	+	42	+42	+42
+	−	+	−	−	−	41	−41	−41
−	+	+	−	−	−	39	−39	−39
+	+	+	+	+	+	79	+79	+79

Sum for AB 81 Sum for CD 81

Figure 14·1

Since the signs for AB are the same as the signs for CD we can see that the result of summing the responses for these two interactions gives the same result and it is impossible to decide from this experiment which of these effects is producing the effect we find. In fact, it's worse than that. Let's say that there is a real AB effect of +20 and a real CD effect of −10. The resulting effect we would observe in this confounded experiment would be the sum of these two values which would be +10. We would be misled by the result and would have to (as we will) deconfound the effects. Let's continue the example and look at the experiment with the physical values and actual responses.

The experiment is designed and run in random order. The results are presented in Table 14-9 in YATES order.

Table 14·9

A Temp	B Press	C Time	D Conc	Yield
100	14	5	0.5	21
200	14	5	1.0	19
100	28	5	1.0	20
200	28	5	0.5	58
100	14	10	1.0	42
200	14	10	0.5	41
100	28	10	0.5	39
200	28	10	1.0	79 I = ABCD

An analysis of this data produces the YATES ANOVA in Table 14-10. Note that the physical names are attached to the effects. This is the way all analyses should be presented.

Table 14-10

tc	Observation	Sum Square	Half Effect	Measures
(1)	21	12720.1	39.875	Average
a(d)	19	703.125	9.375	Temperature, Pres. x Ti. x Conc.
b(d)	20	666.125	9.125	Pressure, Temp x Ti. x Conc.
ab	58	820.125	10.125	Temp. x Pres., Ti. x Conc.
c(d)	42	861.125	10.375	Time, Temp. x Pres. x Conc.
ac	41	1.125	.375	Temp. x Ti., Pres. x Conc.
bc	39	1.125	−.375	Press. x Ti., Temp x Conc.
abc(d)	79	.125	.125	Concentration, Temp. x Pres. x Ti.

Again, we have underlined the likely effects and have left out the three-factor interactions. The problem with this experiment is the fact that all the two-factor interactions are confused with each other. By judging the size of the effects, it looks like there is a large temperature effect; a large pressure effect; and a large time effect. The concentration effect is very small, and there is an interaction that exists either between temperature and pressure or between time and concentration. To deconfound this set of interactions, we could apply prior knowledge to the problem and choose the likely interaction based on our experience. Based on prior chemical considerations, we could expect a temperature-pressure interaction to take place. However, we do not have any evidence to support this claim.

Since we do not have a definite answer to the question of which interaction is real, we must gather more data. This method is reserved until last since it requires the expenditure of resources. There are two options in this method. We may:

a) run a subset experiment
b) run the other half of the fractional factorial

Because we have some prior knowledge and a possible indication of the temperature-pressure interaction being the likely effect from prior knowledge, we will use this knowledge and run a subset experiment involving only the pressure and temperature factors. This will be run in a 2^2 full factorial design and use 4 treatment combinations. The other option of running the other half of the 2^{4-1} would have used 8 treatment combinations. If we can get the required information for 4 tc's we will be twice as efficient as we would have been with the more conservative approach of running the entire other half.

We will vary temperature and pressure while holding time at its high level and holding concentration at its low level. The design is found in table 14-11 and the analysis in 14-12.

Table 14-11

tc	Temperature	Pressure	Response
(1)	100	14	39
a	200	14	42
b	100	28	40
ab	200	28	81

Table 14-12

tc	Observation	Sum Square	Half Effect	Measures
(1)	39	10201	50.5	--
a	42	484	11	Temperature
b	40	400	10	Pressure
ab	81	361	9.5	Temperature x Pressure

When we compare these results with the results in table 14-10, we can see that the half effects for temperature, pressure and their interaction (in the 10 region) are very close. We conclude that our contention that the interaction between temperature and pressure is valid since we observe a TxP interaction of the same half-effect magnitude as in the 2^{4-1} design. If the 2^2 factorial had not shown similar results to the 2^{4-1} experiment, we would have had to run another 2^2 experiment involving the time and concentration factors.

It is the logical sequence of experiments built on prior information that provides us with an efficient approach to our understanding of a problem and allows us to solve it. When we build on knowledge and use a structured plan of attack, the analyses will point the way to successful experimental interpretation.

PROBLEMS FOR CHAPTER 14

1)

Run #	Treatment Combination	A Temp	B Speed	C Conc	Yield
1	a	170	90	12.5	296
2	c	120	90	27.5	421
3	b	120	110	12.5	351
4	(1)	120	90	12.5	421
5	abc	170	110	27.5	135
6	ab	170	110	12.5	127
7	ac	170	90	27.5	288
8	bc	120	110	27.5	352

a. Put in Yates order

b. Run Yates ANOVA

c. Plot any significant effects

d. Draw Conclusions

2) Run a YATES ANOVA on the following data and after obtaining the half effects, decode back into physical units. Plot any of the significant effects.

Run #	tc	Response (miles/gallon)
1	b	98
2	ac	27
3	ab	46
4	(1)	68
5	bc	103
6	c	71
7	abc	51
8	a	22

	Low(−)	High(+)
A is speed	20 mph	40 mph
B is Temperature	25°F	65°F
C is Octane of Gas	87	91.5

APPENDIX 14

Algorithm: A method to simplify calculations that sometimes confuses understanding, but always gives the correct result.

YATES algorithm: A method used to construct an ANOVA from a 2^k or 2^{k-p} design.

Steps in YATES ANOVA: See detailed instructions pages 187-188 or use computer program, "YATES".

Half-effect: A change in the response over half the range of the factor under study.

Full-effect: A change in the response over the full range of the factor.

YATES ANOVA PROGRAM

```
100 CLS
120 DIM D(128),C(128),S(128),H(128),X(128),FR(128)
140 DIM N$(64)
160 FOR I=1 TO 64
180 READ N$(I)
200 NEXT I
220 DATA AVERAGE,A,B,AB,C,AC,BC,ABC
240 DATA D,AD,BD,ABD,CD,ACD,BCD,ABCD
260 DATA E,AE,BE,ABE,CE,ACE,BCE,ABCE,DE,ADE,BDE,ABDE,CDE,ACDE,BCDE,ABCDE
280 DATA F,AF,BF,ABF,CF,ACF,BCF,ABCF,DF,ADF,BDF,ABDF,CDF,ACDF,BCDF,ABCDF
300 DATA EF,AEF,BEF,ABEF,CEF,ACEF,BCEF,ABCEF,DEF,ADEF,BDEF,ABDEF,CDEF,ACDEF,BCDE
F,ABCDEF
320 PRINT "ANOVA BY THE "
340 PRINT "THE YATES ALGORITHM"
360 PRINT:PRINT
380 INPUT "DO YOU WANT PRINTED OUTPUT (Y/N)",P$
390 INPUT "WHAT IS THE NAME OF THE EXPERIMENT?",NM$
400 PRINT "ENTER THE NUMBER OF FACTORS (K-P)"
420 INPUT P
440 PRINT "ENTER THE NUMBER OF REPLICATES (AT LEAST 1)"
460 INPUT R
480 N=2^P
500 N1=N-1
520 P1=0
540 PRINT " ENTER RESPONSES IN YATES ORDER!!!!"
560 FOR I=1 TO N
580 PRINT "OBSERVATION#";I;
600 D2=0
620 FOR J=1 TO R
640 PRINT "REPLICATE#";J;
660 INPUT D1
680 D2=D2+D1
700 D3=D3+D1*D1
720 NEXT J
740 D(I)=D2
760 NEXT I
780 PRINT
```

```
800 FOR I=1 TO N
820 X(I)=D(I)
840 NEXT I
860 K=0
880 FOR I= 1 TO N1 STEP 2
900 K=K+1
920 I1=I+1
940 C(K)=D(I)+D(I1)
960 NEXT I
980 K=N/2
1000 FOR I=1 TO N1 STEP 2
1020 K=K+1
1040 I1=I+1
1060 C(K)=D(I1)-D(I)
1080 NEXT I
1100 P1=P1+1
1120 IF P1=P THEN 1220
1140 FOR I= 1 TO N
1160 D(I)=C(I)
1180 NEXT I
1200 GOTO 860
1220 FOR I=1 TO N
1240 S(I)=C(I)^2/(2^P*R)
1260 S1=S1+S(I)
1280 DF=1
1300 H(I)=C(I)/(2^P*R)
1320 S2=D3-S1
1340 NEXT I
1360 DFE=R*N-N
1370 IF DFE=0 THEN INPUT "THERE ARE NO DF FOR ERROR. DO YOU HAVE AN OUTSIDE ESTI
MATE OF ERROR";O$
1372 IF LEFT$(O$,1)="Y" THEN INPUT "ENTER ERROR MEAN SQUARE";MSE:GOTO 1400
1374 MSE=S(N)
1375 IF DFE<>0 GOTO 1390
1376 PRINT "SINCE THERE IS NO ESTIMATE OF ERROR"
1377 PRINT "THE HIGHEST ORDER INTERACTION HAS BEEN USED FOR"
1378 PRINT "THE ERROR ESTIMATE":PRINT "PRESS <C> TO CONTINUE"
1379 IF INKEY$<>"C" THEN 1379
1380 IF DFE=0 THEN 1400
1390 MSE=S2/DFE
1400 FOR I=1 TO N:FR(I)=S(I)/MSE:NEXT I
1420 IF P$="Y" THEN GOTO 1770
1440 CLS:PRINT:PRINT
1450 PRINT NM$
1455 PRINT
1460 PRINT "INDEX    TOTAL      SUM OF      HALF                       MEAN
    F"
1480 PRINT "  #  OBSERVATION    SQUARE      EFFECT  MEASURES  DF      SQUARE
    RATIO"
1500 AB$="###  #####.####  #######.####  #####.###  \    \  ## #######.####  #
##.###"
1520 I=1
1540 PRINT USING AB$;1;X(1);S(1);H(1);N$(1)
1560 FOR I=2 TO N
1580 PRINT USING AB$;I;X(I);S(I);H(I);N$(I);DF;S(I);FR(I)
1600 IMOD=I-INT(I/16)*16:IF IMOD<>0 THEN 1660
1620 PRINT "PRESS <RETURN> TO CONTINUE"
1640 MASK$=INKEY$:INPUT " ",MASK$
1660 NEXT I
1680 D4=D3-S(1)
1700 BB$="      \       \ #######.####            ## #######.####"
1720 PRINT USING BB$;"ERROR";S2;DFE;MSE
1740 PRINT USING BB$;"TOTAL";D3-S(1);N*R-1
1760 PRINT:GOTO 2040
1770 LPRINT NM$
1775 LPRINT
1780 LPRINT "INDEX    TOTAL      SUM OF      HALF                       MEAN
    F"
```

```
1800 LPRINT "   #   OBSERVATION     SQUARE      EFFECT  MEASURES  OF       SQUARE
     RATIO"
1820 AB$="###   #####.####  #######.####  #####.###   \      \    ## #######.####  #
##.###"
1840 I=1
1860 LPRINT USING AB$;1;X(1);S(1);H(1);N$(1)
1880 FOR I=2 TO N
1900 LPRINT USING AB$;I;X(I);S(I);H(I);N$(I);DF;S(I);FR(I)
1920 NEXT I
1940 D4=D3-S(1)
1960 BB$="        \       \    #######.####                        ## #######.####"
1980 LPRINT USING BB$;"ERROR";S2;DFE;MSE
2000 LPRINT USING BB$;"TOTAL";D3-S(1);N*R-1
2020 LPRINT
2040 PRINT "DO YOU WANT TO GET MAIN EFFECT PLOT POINTS";
2060 INPUT W$
2080 IF W$="Y" GOTO 2140
2100 IF W$="YES" GOTO 2140
2120 GOTO 2320
2140 PRINT "INDICATE THE INDEX # OF THE MAIN EFFECT FOR PLOT POINTS";
2160 INPUT I4
2180 L1=H(1)-H(I4)
2200 H1=H(1)+H(I4)
2220 IF P$="Y" THEN GOTO 2280
2240 PRINT "PLOT POINTS FOR:";N$(I4);" ARE: LOW";L1;" HIGH";H1
2260 GOTO 2300
2280 LPRINT "PLOT POINTS FOR:";N$(I4);" ARE: LOW";L1;" HIGH",H1
2300 GOTO 1760
2320 PRINT
2340 PRINT "DO YOU WANT TO CREATE A 2-FACTOR INTERACTION TABLE";
2360 INPUT W$
2380 IF W$="Y" GOTO 2440
2400 IF W$="YES" GOTO 2440
2420 END
2440 PRINT "WHAT IS THE NAME OF THE INTERACTION (IE AB)";
2460 INPUT W$
2480 PRINT "ENTER THE INDEX #'S OF THE TERMS IN THE INTERACTION"
2500 PRINT "ENTER 1ST FACTOR (MAIN EFFECT) INDEX #";
2520 INPUT I1
2540 PRINT "ENTER 2ND FACTOR (MAIN EFFECT) INDEX #";
2560 INPUT I2
2580 PRINT "ENTER INTERACTION INDEX #";
2600 INPUT I3
2620 PRINT
2640 IF P$="Y" THEN GOTO 2840
2660 PRINT "INTERACTION TABLE FOR THE ";W$;" INTERACTION"
2680 PRINT "LEVEL OF    LEVEL OF     POINT TO"
2700 PRINT " FACTOR1     FACTOR2       PLOT"
2720 PRINT "    -           -        ";H(1)-H(I1)-H(I2)+H(I3)
2740 PRINT "    +           -        ";H(1)+H(I1)-H(I2)-H(I3)
2760 PRINT "    -           +        ";H(1)-H(I1)+H(I2)-H(I3)
2780 PRINT "    +           +        ";H(1)+H(I1)+H(I2)+H(I3)
2800 PRINT
2820 GOTO 3000
2840 LPRINT:LPRINT:LPRINT "INTERACTION TABLE FOR THE ";W$;" INTERACTION"
2860 LPRINT "LEVEL OF    LEVEL OF     POINT TO"
2880 LPRINT " FACTOR1     FACTOR2       PLOT"
2900 LPRINT "    -           -        ";H(1)-H(I1)-H(I2)+H(I3)
2920 LPRINT "    +           -        ";H(1)+H(I1)-H(I2)-H(I3)
2940 LPRINT "    -           +        ";H(1)-H(I1)+H(I2)-H(I3)
2960 LPRINT "    +           +        ";H(1)+H(I1)+H(I2)+H(I3)
2980 LPRINT
3000 GOTO 2340
```

EXAMPLE FROM TABLE 14-2

INDEX #	TOTAL OBSERVATION	SUM OF SQUARE	HALF EFFECT	MEASURES	DF	MEAN SQUARE	F RATIO
1	2.6000	159.3112	4.462	AVERAGE			
2	3.9000	0.5512	-0.263	A	1	0.5512	0.612
3	4.4000	15.4012	1.387	B	1	15.4012	17.112
4	8.0000	0.0012	0.012	AB	1	0.0012	0.001
5	4.1000	0.5513	-0.263	C	1	0.5513	0.613
6	1.7000	17.7012	-1.488	AC	1	17.7012	19.668
7	7.8000	0.0612	-0.087	BC	1	0.0612	0.068
8	3.2000	2.5313	-0.563	ABC	1	2.5313	2.813
	ERROR	0.0000			0	0.9000	
	TOTAL	36.7988			7		

FLOT POINTS FOR:A ARE: LOW 4.725 HIGH   4.2
PLOT POINTS FOR:B ARE: LOW 3.075 HIGH   5.85

INTERACTION TABLE FOR THE PRESSURE*TIME INTERACTION
LEVEL OF FACTOR1	LEVEL OF FACTOR2	POINT TO PLOT
-	-	3.499999
+	-	5.95
-	+	5.95
+	+	2.45

15

MATRIX ALGEBRA

The YATES method and the general ANOVA techniques we have studied are both algorithms based on a more general system of analysis called regression analysis or the general linear model approach to the solution of modeling problems.

To use the general linear model effectively, some of the rules of matrix algebra need to be understood. This brief chapter will simply show how to manipulate a matrix with no theoretical development of the concepts.

MATRIX DEFINED

A matrix is simply a one, two or n dimensional array of numbers ordered in such a way that we can identify any element by a position number. The position number is called a subscript. In a very simple, one-dimensional matrix (commonly called a vector) we refer to the elements of the array as:

$$X_1, X_2, X_3, X_4 \ldots \ldots X_n \qquad (15\text{-}1)$$

So we can call out the value of the third item of this array by finding X_3. This concept is expecially useful in computer programming when we wish to build a general approach to the solution of a problem and there is an unknown number of values that will change each time the program is used.

The vector may be written as a row (across as shown above) or as a column (up and down).

A column vector looks like this:

$$\begin{matrix} X_1 \\ X_2 \\ X_3 \\ X_4 \\ \cdot \\ \cdot \\ \cdot \\ X_n \end{matrix} \qquad (15\text{-}2)$$

Usually vectors are written in row fashion to conserve space.

The next step in looking at matricies is to look at a two-dimensional array which is usually called a "matrix". Again, the columns are the up-down and the rows are the across arrangements of the values. Now we have a double subscript. The first element of the subscript (usually the letter "i") refers to the row of the matrix. The second element of the subscript (usually "j") refers to the column of the matrix. So the matrix would look like this:

$$\begin{matrix} X_{11} & X_{12} & X_{13} & X_{14} & \cdots & X_{1j} \\ X_{21} & X_{22} & X_{23} & X_{24} & \cdots & X_{2j} \\ X_{31} & X_{32} & X_{33} & X_{34} & \cdots & X_{3j} \\ X_{41} & X_{42} & X_{43} & X_{44} & \cdots & X_{4j} \\ \cdot & \cdot & \cdot & \cdot & & \\ \cdot & \cdot & \cdot & \cdot & & \\ \cdot & \cdot & \cdot & \cdot & & \\ X_{i1} & X_{i2} & X_{i3} & X_{i4} & \cdots & X_{ij} \end{matrix} \qquad (15\text{-}3)$$

The essential parts of matrix manipulation we need to know to solve the equations involved in the general regression approach to experimental analysis are:

1) Matrix Transposition
2) Matrix Multiplication
3) Matrix Inversion

TRANSPOSITION

This is a very simple concept. To transpose a matrix, we just turn the matrix to be transposed on its side. To be more exact, the rows are interchanged with the columns, Given the matrix in Table 15-1 the transpose is shown in 15-2. The symbol for a transpose is X'. This is usually pronouced "X prime". Notice that the matrix symbol is in bold face type.

Table 15-1   Table 15-2

$$X = \begin{matrix} a & b & c \\ d & e & f \\ g & h & i \\ j & k & l \end{matrix} \qquad X' = \begin{matrix} a & d & g & j \\ b & e & h & k \\ c & f & i & l \end{matrix}$$

MULTIPLICATION

While any matrix may be transposed, there are restrictions on which matrices may be multiplied together.   Also, we must realize that the order of multiplicaiton is important. The matrix that is written down first is called the premultiplier matrix and the matrix that follows is called the postmultiplier matrix.   To perform matrix multiplication, the number of columns in the premultiplier matrix must equal the number of rows in the postmultiplier matrix.

If this does not occur, we have an "order mismatch" and the operation cannot be done. When specifying the matrix, we always look to its order which is simply the maximum number of rows and columns. A matrix with 4 rows and 2 columns would be of order 4,2. A matrix with 2 columns and 3 rows would be of order 2,3. The two matrices could be multiplied together since they follow the rule. Table 15-3 shows an example of these two matrices.

Table 15-3

$$A = \begin{matrix} a & b \\ c & d \\ e & f \\ g & h \end{matrix} \qquad B = \begin{matrix} a & b & c \\ d & e & f \end{matrix}$$

a 4 by 2 matrix   a 2 by 3 matrix

To multiply two matrices together, we start with the 1,1 element of the premultiplier matrix and multiply this value times the 1,1 element of the post multiplier matrix. Go next to the 1,2 element of the premultiplying matrix and multiply this times the 2,1 element of the postmultiplying matrix.   Add this result to the previous product. Continue to find products across the first row and down the first column of the matrices and sum these to obtain a single value which becomes the 1,1 element of the resulting matrix.

Using the above A and B matrices with A as the premultiplier, we get the following results:

$a*a + b*d$ which becomes the 1,1 element of the C matrix that results.

To obtain the 1,2 element of the **C** matrix, we stay in row 1 of the premultiplier but move to Column 2 of the postmultiplier.

We repeat the multiplication and addition across the row and down the column which produces the 1,2 element of **C**.

In our example:

$$C_{12} = a*b + b*e$$

The procedure is repeated using row 1 of the premultiplier until there are no more columns left in the postmultiplier matrix.

For our example the first row of **C** looks like this:

$$
\begin{array}{ccc}
a*a + b*d & a*b + b*e & a*c + b*f \\
C_{11} & C_{12} & C_{13}
\end{array}
$$

Having exhausted row one of the premultiplier, we move, as you might suspect, to row two of the premultiplier and repeat the whole thing over again. This is where computers come in handy since they don't tire of repetitive, boring operations. When all the rows of the premultiplier are "used up", the multiplicaiton is finished. The new **C** matrix looks like this now upon completion:

$$
\mathbf{C} =
\begin{array}{ccc}
a*a + b*d & a*b + b*e & a*c + b*f \\
C_{11} & C_{12} & C_{13} \\[2ex]
c*a + d*d & c*b + d*e & c*c + d*f \\
C_{21} & C_{22} & C_{23} \\[2ex]
e*a + f*d & e*b + f*e & e*c + f*f \\
C_{31} & C_{32} & C_{33} \\[2ex]
g*a + h*d & g*b + h*e & g*c + h*f \\
C_{41} & C_{42} & C_{43}
\end{array}
$$

The system used in this procedure is to go across the row and down the column with the subscript of the new row in the resulting matrix being supplied by the row number of the premultiplier matrix and the column number of the resulting matrix being supplied by the column number of the postmultiplier matrix. This is why there must be a match in the order of the matrices being multiplied.

Now let's look at the numerical example of the type we will encounter in the general regression situation. We will start out with a matrix and then transpose this matrix.

The transpose will become the premultiplier matrix and the original matrix will be the postmultiplier matrix.

$$
X = \begin{bmatrix} 1 & 4 & 4 & 9 \\ 1 & 2 & 4 & 9 \\ 1 & 4 & 8 & 9 \\ 1 & 2 & 8 & 5 \\ 1 & 3 & 6 & 5 \end{bmatrix}
\qquad
X' = \begin{bmatrix} 1 & 1 & 1 & 1 & 1 \\ 4 & 2 & 4 & 2 & 3 \\ 4 & 4 & 8 & 8 & 6 \\ 9 & 9 & 9 & 5 & 5 \end{bmatrix}
$$

$$
\begin{bmatrix} 1 & 1 & 1 & 1 & 1 \\ 4 & 2 & 4 & 2 & 3 \\ 4 & 4 & 8 & 8 & 6 \\ 9 & 9 & 9 & 5 & 5 \end{bmatrix}
*
\begin{bmatrix} 1 & 4 & 4 & 9 \\ 1 & 2 & 4 & 9 \\ 1 & 4 & 8 & 9 \\ 1 & 2 & 8 & 5 \\ 1 & 3 & 6 & 5 \end{bmatrix}
=
\begin{bmatrix} 5 & 15 & 30 & 37 \\ 15 & 49 & 90 & 115 \\ 30 & 90 & 196 & 214 \\ 37 & 115 & 214 & 293 \end{bmatrix}
$$

X'	X	$X'X$
Premultiplier	Postmultiplier	Resulting Matrix
4 x 5	5 x 4	4 x 4

In the above example we have taken a 4 x 5 matrix and multiplied it times a 5 x 4 to obtain a 4 x 4 resultant matrix.

MATRIX "DIVISION"

Division is not done directly, but by the *inverse* of multiplication. For this reason the operation is called inverting a matrix. This is one of the most numerically difficult operations in matrix algebra and there are a number of methods used to accomplish this objective. We will simply indicate the concept behind the inverting of a matrix and supply a computer program in 15B to finish the job since no one does this operation by hand any more.

In ordinary arithmetic, we obtain the quotient by dividing the dividend by the divisor. So, if we wished to divide 8 by 2 we put 8 over 2 and obtain the answer of 4. We could obtain the same result in a slightly different manner by multiplying the 8 by the reciprocal or inverse of 2 which is .5. We can reduce all division to multiplication by the inverse of the divisor. This is the idea in matrix algebra and the only way we can accomplish division in this system.

The basic rules to accomplish inversion are:

● Only square matrices may be inverted (i.e. # rows = # columns).
● The matrix may not be ill-conditioned or singular.
● The matrix times it's inverse will produce the identity matrix.

When these conditions exist, then the matrix may be inverted. the symbol for an inverted matrix is a "-1" superscript. So the inverse of A is symbolized by A^{-1}.

The identity matrix (like any identity element in mathematics) is a matrix that will give back the matrix it pre- or post-multiplies. Let's look at an example.

Identity Matrix					A								
1	0	0	0		2	4	6	8		2	4	6	8
0	1	0	0	X	1	3	5	6	=	1	3	5	6
0	0	1	0		4	8	6	2		4	8	6	2
0	0	0	1		3	5	1	6		3	5	1	6

or

2	4	6	8		1	0	0	0		2	4	6	8
1	3	5	6	X	0	1	0	0	=	1	3	5	6
4	8	6	2		0	0	1	0		4	8	6	2
3	5	1	6		0	0	0	1		3	5	1	6

A	Identity Matrix

Figure 15-1

The identity matrix as shown in Figure 15-1 is a diagonal matrix with ones on the diagonal and zeros elsewhere.

The criterion for checking an inverse of a matrix is if the original matrix times its inverse gives the identity matrix, and at the same time the inverse times the original matrix also gives the identity we have the inverse. The trick in inverting the matrix is to convert the original matrix into the identity matrix while changing an identity matrix to the inverse. This is a cumbersome task and not easily done by hand. The computer program in Part B of this chapter does this quite well.

There is one inverse operation that is easily done by hand and is an important in the realm of designed experiments. If we have a diagonal matrix to invert (i.e.: a matrix that has elements only on its diagonal with the remaining elements zeros) the inversion is simply the inverse (or reciprocal) of the diagonal elements.

Original Matrix (A)				Inverse (A^{-1})			
4	0	0	0	¼	0	0	0
0	4	0	0	0	¼	0	0
0	0	4	0	0	0	¼	0
0	0	0	4	0	0	0	¼

Figure 15-2

This introduction to matrix algebra should be sufficient to support the subsequent chapters on the general linear regression approach to statistical analysis problems.

PROBLEMS FOR CHAPTER 15

1) From the following matrix A identify the following elements:

     a. 2,4   _____
     b. 4,2   _____
     c. 4,5   _____
     d. 1,3   _____
     e. 3,3   _____
     f. The number 18 is the ____ row, ____ column.
     g. The number 10 is the ____ row, ____ column.
     h. The number 26 is the ____ row, ____ column.

$$
A = \begin{array}{ccccc}
2 & 4 & 6 & 8 & 10 \\
12 & 14 & 16 & 18 & 20 \\
22 & 24 & 26 & 28 & 30 \\
32 & 34 & 36 & 38 & 40
\end{array}
$$

2) Transpose the matrix found in Problem #1. This will be the A'.

3) Multiply A' times A (A is from Problem #1, A' is from Problem #2).

4) Multiple the following matrix and vector.

$$
\begin{array}{ccccccc}
1 & 2 & 3 & 6 & 3 & 7 & 1 \\
2 & 4 & 6 & 9 & 5 & 9 & 4 \\
4 & 6 & 8 & 2 & 7 & 9 & 9
\end{array}
\quad * \quad
\begin{array}{c}
1 \\
4 \\
9 \\
36 \\
9 \\
49 \\
1
\end{array}
\quad =
$$

5) Invert the following matrices:

$$
X = \begin{array}{cc} 2 & -.6 \\ -1 & .4 \end{array}
\qquad
Y = \begin{array}{cc} 14 & 3 \\ 2 & 10 \end{array}
\qquad
Z = \begin{array}{ccc} 3 & 0 & 0 \\ 0 & 3 & 0 \\ 0 & 0 & 3 \end{array}
$$

APPENDIX 15

Matrix:	An ordered array of numbers.
Subscript:	The order number in a matrix — X_{35} is the number in the third row and fifth column.
Column:	In a two-dimensional matrix, the values arranged vertically (up and down).
Row:	In a two-dimensional matrix, the values arranged horizontally (across).
Vector:	A one-dimensional matrix.
Element:	The number in a matrix.
Postmultiplier:	Second matrix in a left to right multiplication.
Premultiplier:	First matrix in a left to right multiplication.
Identity Matrix:	A matrix with diagonal elements of value 1 and all other elements of value zero. This matrix may premultiply or post multiply another matrix (A) and the rsult will always be the matrix A.
Inverse:	A matrix derived from another matrix (A) such that the result of multiplying the inverse of A (A^{-1}) by A produces the identity matrix I.

$$I \;=\; A^{-1} \;*\; A$$
$$\text{and } I \;=\; A \quad * \; A^{-1}$$

Transpose:	A matrix turned on its side. The rows are interchanged with the columns. The symbol is a "prime" sign. So the transpose of A is symbolized by A'.
Inversion:	Inverting a 2 x 2 matrix.

To invert a 2 x 2 matrix, we need to find the determinant of the matrix. This is accomplished by finding the cross product of the downward diagonals and subtracting the cross product of the upward diagonals. The determinant of matrix X is then:

$$X = \begin{matrix} a & b \\ c & d \end{matrix} \qquad \begin{matrix} D = a*d - c*b \\ \text{where D is the determinant of X} \end{matrix}$$

To complete the inversion, we rearrange the original matrix X by interchanging the positions of the downward diagonals and changing the signs of the upward diagonals. Then we divide the elements of the matrix by the determinant.

$$X^{-1} = \begin{matrix} d/D & -b/D \\ -c/D & a/D \end{matrix} = \begin{matrix} d/a*d-c*b & -b/a*d-c*b \\ -c/a*d-c*b & a/a*d-c*b \end{matrix}$$

A numerical example:

$$X = \begin{matrix} 2 & 3 \\ 5 & 10 \end{matrix} \qquad D = 2*10-3*5 = 5$$

$$X^{-1} = \begin{matrix} 10/5 & -3/5 \\ -5/5 & 2/5 \end{matrix} = \begin{matrix} 2 & -.6 \\ -1 & .4 \end{matrix}$$

16

LEAST SQUARES ANALYSIS

In the realm of statistical inference used to sort the signal from the noise, there is a hierarchy of methods. We have studies these methods from the bottom up. Starting with "t" tests and moving up to ANOVA, there is still one last method to discover. We have seen that "t" tests are restricted to investigations of dichotomies while ANOVA can go beyond the simple comparison of two populations at a time and look at "n" populations with a single risk. The general linear hypothesis based on Least Squares is at the top of the hierarchy and can do anything that ANOVA or "t" tests can plus a lot more.

LEAST SQUARES DEVELOPED

In investigating the relationships between variables, we would like to be able to create an equation that shows the dependence of a response on one or more control factors. Let's start with the simple case that involves only a single x control factor and a single y response. This equation is a mathematical "short hand" that represents a state of nature. If we were interested in learning if there is a dependence between theses factors, we could use the concept of covariance introduced in Chapter 4. Recall the definition of the covariance was:

$$s_{xy} = \frac{\Sigma(x_i - \overline{X}) * (y_i - \overline{Y})}{n-1} \qquad (16\text{-}1)$$

Now this defining formula can be converted into a formula that is easier to compute with. Notice in the defining formula, that the averages of x and y need to be computed and then subtracted from each value of x_i and y_i. This means that all the values of x_i and y_i must be stored somewhere. Also if the values of $\overline{X}$ and $\overline{Y}$ are not rounded properly or have repeating decimals that round poorly, the results of the calculations using equation 16-1 could be in error. Therefore, the following formula which is mathematically equivalent to 16-1 is a better method to obtain the same results.

$$s_{xy} = \frac{n(\Sigma x_i * y_i) - (\Sigma x_i) * (\Sigma y_i)}{n(n-1)} \qquad (16\text{-}2)$$

Let's compute some covariances to get a feel for the kinds of numbers produced.

Table 16-1

	A			B		
	x	y	x*y	x	y	x*y
	1	4	4	10	40	400
	2	6	12	20	60	1200
	3	9	27	30	90	2700
	4	10	40	40	100	4000
Total	10	29	83	100	290	8300

From Example A of Table 16-1 we obtain the following covariances:

$$s_{xy} = \frac{4*(83) - (10)*(29)}{4(4-1)} = 3.5$$

From Example B of Tabel 16-1 we can obtain the following covariance:

$$s_{xy} = \frac{4*(8300) - (100)*(290)}{4(4-1)} = 350$$

Now we were led to believe that the magnitude of the covariance is an indication of the degree of relationship between the variable. We can see that the magnitude of the B example is 10 times that of A. However, if we were to plot the data as in Figure 16-1 we can see that there is no difference is the pattern of the relationship between either A or B. The only difference is in the magnitude of the numbers we are working with. B has a higher covariance because it starts with bigger numbers!

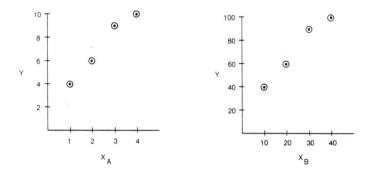

Figure 16-1

The covariance is an <u>unanchored</u> measure of the relationship between the variables. To anchor this relationship, we will scale the covariance by the product of the standard deviations of x and y. This new measure of the relationship will be called the correlation coefficient and it is anchored between −1 and +1.

$$r = \frac{s_{xy}}{s_x * s_y}$$ (16-3)

The correlation for the A example is:

$$r = \frac{3.5}{1.29 * 2.75} = .987$$

The correlation for the B example is:

$$r = \frac{350}{12.9 * 27.5} = .987$$

So we can see that the relationship between the two sets of data is exactly the same. The closer the correlation coefficient approaches the absolute value of 1, the better the degree of relationship between the variables. The correlation coefficient is a first intuitive step in finding the relationships between variables. While it shows us that the degree of relationship, it does not give us the equation or rate of change of y with x. We could look back to Figure 16-1 and draw a "best fit eyeball" line through the data points. This line would have the criteria that it would follow the trend in the data putting as many point below the line as above as it pivots to follow the relationship that, as we can see, is not a perfectly straight line. We shall concentrate only on straight line relationships for the moment and sidestep the question of curving the line to better fit the data. Figure 16-2 shows such an eyeball fit.

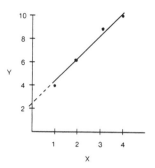

Figure 16-2

The change in y over a unit change in x is called the **slope of y on x**. The place where the line intersects the y axis at a value of zero for x is called the **y intercept**. We could obtain these values from the geometry of Figure 16-2.

Slope = 2.1

Intercept = 2.2

You are probably remembering this from the high school geometry course that presented the concept of the straight line relationship and gave a model for the line as:

$$y = mx + b \quad (16\text{-}4)$$

Where y is the value we are solving for

m is the slope

x is the know value

For our equation: $y = 2.1X + 2.2$

We can "solve" our equation and see how well it predicts the actual values we had. The difference between the actual y value and the predicted value (y) is a measure of how well we have drawn the line. To arrive at this set of values, we will solve the equation for each value of x. Table 16-2 shows these results and compares them with the observed y values to obtain the difference or "residual".

Table 16-2

x	y	y	Residual
1	4	4.3	−0.3
2	6	6.4	−0.4
3	9	8.5	0.5
4	10	10.6	−0.6

Notice that the sum of the residuals is equal to −0.8. It looks like we have biased the position of the "eyeball" line since, if we had indeed drawn it so that there were as many points below the line as above, then the algebriac sum of the differences would be zero. In drawing the line by sight, we can use a trick that will enable us to only have to worry about one of the parameters of the line (the slope). By pivoting the line through the point where the average of x and y occur, we can adjust the slope to obtain the zero sum of the residuals criteria. The average of the x values is 2.5 and the average of the y values is 7.25. Let's try this out and see what happens.

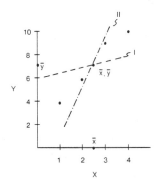

Figure 16-3

We have drawn two lines in Figure 16-3. Both pivot through the average of x and y. Both have a zero sum for the residuals! Both are different!

Table 16-3

LINE #I				LINE #II			
slope = 0.7 intercept = 5.5				slope = 3.0 intercept = −0.5			
x	y	y	residual	x	y	y	residual
1	4	6.2	−2.2	1	4	2.5	−1.5
2	6	6.9	−0.9	2	6	5.5	−0.5
3	9	7.6	1.4	3	9	8.5	0.5
4	10	8.3	1.7	4	10	11.5	1.5
			0.0				0.0

The problem is that there are many lines that can be drawn using the criteria of pivoting throught x and y with a zero algebraic sum of the residuals. We do not have a <u>unique</u> line described by this process. There are other thoughts on the criteria for drawing a line through the data; however, they also lead to ambiguity and many possible lines rather than the unique solution we want.

The criterion generally used to fit a unique line to a set of correlated data (meaning that the x and y come in pairs) is called the method of least squares. In this method, we will fit a line that gives us the smallest sum of the squares of the residuals, while still pivoting through the x, y positions. Now, we could obtain the values for the intercept (called b_0) and the slope (called b_1) by trial and error application of least squares, but this would be a very tedious task.

Instead, we shall use a bit of calculus to find the minimum. By taking the first derivative of the function and set it equal to zero we obtain the minimum. All we need to do is set up a function in terms of the known values and complete the calculus. Let's see what we know about our function and apply this knowledge to our example.

Form of equation: $y = mx + b$

In the terms of b_0 and b_1 this function becomes:

$$y = b_0 + b_1 * X_1 + error \qquad\qquad (16\text{-}5)$$

We have added an error term since we know there is not a perfect straight line relationship between x and y. (Actually, we have not <u>added</u> error, it always existed, we now simply recognize its existence!)

The error is the difference between the actual y value and the predicted y (sumbolized by $\hat{y}$ and pronounced "y hat"). This is what we had called the "residual" before. We can build a table of what we know and what is unknown and then apply the calculus to compute the unknowns.

Table 16-4

x	y	$\hat{y} = b_0 + b_1 x_1$	residual error
1	4	$b_0 + b_1 * 1$	$4 - (b_0 + b_1 * 1)$
2	6	$b_0 + b_1 * 2$	$6 - (b_0 + b_1 * 2)$
3	9	$b_0 + b_1 * 3$	$9 - (b_0 + b_1 * 3)$
4	10	$b_0 + b_1 * 4$	$10 - (b_0 + b_1 * 4)$

Since we want to find a unique line that will fit the data best, we will square the residual error and then take the partial derivatives with respect to the b_0 term and then with respect to the b_1 term. Since we want the sum of these derivatives to be a minimum, we will sum the terms and then having two equations in two unknowns, we can solve for b_0 and b_1. Table 16-5 shows these steps.

Table 16-5

residual error squared	partial derivative with respect to b0	partial derivative with respect to b1
$(4-(b_0+b_1*1))^2$	$-2(4-b_0-b_1*1)$	$-2(1)(4-b_0-b_1*1)$
$(6-(b_0+b_1*2))^2$	$-2(6-b_0-b_1*2)$	$-2(2)(6-b_0-b_1*2)$
$(9-(b_0+b_1*3))^2$	$-2(9-b_0-b_1*3)$	$-2(3)(9-b_0-b_1*3)$
$(10-(b_0+b_1*4))^2$	$-2(10-b_0-b_1*4)$	$-2(4)(10-b_0-b_1*4)$
SUM:	$-58 + 8b_0 + 20b_1$	$-166 + 20b_0 + 60b_1$

Now take the sums of the derivatives and set each equal to zero:

$$-58 + 8b_0 + 20b_1 = 0 \tag{16-6}$$
$$-166 + 20b_0 + 60b_1 = 0 \tag{16-7}$$

Rearrange these equations:

$$8b_0 + 20b_1 = 58$$
$$20b_0 + 60b_1 = 166$$

We have a set of simultaneous linear equations in two unknowns which we may find the solution to by elimination of one of the terms. We will eliminate b_0 by multiplying the second equation by 8/20,

$$8b_0 + 20b_1 = 58$$
$$\frac{8}{20} (20b_0 + 60b_1 = 166)$$

which produces:

$$8b_0 + 20b_1 = 58 \tag{16-8}$$
$$8b_0 + 24b_1 = 66.4 \tag{16-9}$$

subtract 16-8 from 16-9 to give:

$$4b_1 = 8.4$$
$$b_1 = \frac{8.4}{4} = 2.1$$

To solve for b_0 we simply substitute the value of b_1 into either of the original expressions created from the sum of the derivatives. Substituting into 16-8, we obtain:

$$8b_0 + 20\,(2.1) = 58$$
$$8b_0 = 58 - (20\,(2.1))$$
$$b_0 = \frac{16}{8} = 2.0$$

We may now write the least squares equation that described the four pieces of data as follows:

$$Y = 2 + 2.1\,X_1 \tag{16-10}$$

The procedure we have just illustrated obtains the correct least squares equation, but is not the most convenient method of obtaining the results. Let's look into the numbers we have just calculated to see if there is a generalization we can make and somehow set up a simple formula to do the job on a routine basis.

If we look back to Table 16-5 and put the derivatives into an algebraic form we obtain the following more general tabulation of the information.

Table 16-6

Residual Error Squared	Partial Derivative With Repsect to B_0	Partial Derivative With Respect to B_1
$(y - (b_0 + b_1 x))^2$	$-2(y - b_0 - b_1 x)$	$-2(x)(y - b_0 - b_1 x)$
SUM:	$2(-\Sigma y + \Sigma b_0 + \Sigma b_1 x)$	$2(-\Sigma xy + \Sigma x b_0 + \Sigma b_1 x^2)$

The multiplier of 2 may be discarded since it is common to both summations and we may now set these sums equal to zero and rearrange.

$$\Sigma b_0 + \Sigma b_1 x = \Sigma y \tag{16-11}$$

$$\Sigma x b_0 + \Sigma b_1 x^2 = \Sigma xy \tag{16-12}$$

We can use a trick here to help solve these simultaneous equations. The sum of the b_0 is the same as all the b_0's added together, and since b_0 is a constant we may just multiply by the number (n) of b_0's that we have. So $\Sigma b_0 = nb_0$. Using this trick, we can rewrite 16-11 as follows:

$$nb_0 + \Sigma b_1 x = \Sigma y \tag{16-13}$$

Now we will eliminate b_0 by multiplying 16-12 by $n/\Sigma x$ and then subtract   16-13
from this result. These operations are exactly the procedures we used on the
numerical data.

$$nb_0 + \Sigma b_1 x = \Sigma y$$
$$\frac{n}{\Sigma x} \; (\Sigma x b_0 + \Sigma b_1 x2 = \Sigma xy)$$

which produces:

$$nb_0 + \Sigma b_1 x = \Sigma y \qquad\qquad (16\text{-}14)$$
$$nb_0 + \frac{n}{\Sigma x} \Sigma b_1 x2 = \frac{n}{\Sigma x} \Sigma xy \qquad\qquad (16\text{-}15)$$

Subtract 16-14 from 16-15 to give:

$$\frac{n}{\Sigma x} \Sigma b_1 x^2 - \Sigma b_1 x = \frac{n}{\Sigma x} \Sigma xy - \Sigma y$$

We can factor out a b_1 from the left hand part of the expression. This produces:

$$b_1 \left(\frac{n}{\Sigma x} \Sigma x^2 - \Sigma x\right) = \frac{n}{\Sigma x} \Sigma xy - \Sigma y \qquad\qquad (16\text{-}16)$$

Now 16-16 is a pretty messy expression and does not resemble any familiar statistical
expression. Let's see if we can clean it up and make it look like some old "friends".

If we multiply through by $\Sigma x/n$ we obtain:

$$b_1(\Sigma x^2 - \frac{(\Sigma x)^2}{n}) = \Sigma xy - \frac{\Sigma x\Sigma y}{n} \qquad\qquad (16\text{-}17)$$

.....And to be even more clever, we now multiply through by n to get:

$$b_1 (n\Sigma x^2 - (\Sigma x)^2) = n\Sigma xy - \Sigma x\Sigma y \qquad\qquad (16\text{-}18)$$

Solving for b1 we have our general formula for the slope of x on y:

$$b1 = \frac{n\Sigma xy - \Sigma x \Sigma y}{n\Sigma x^2 - (\Sigma x)^2} \qquad (16\text{-}19)$$

Now the numerator in 16-19 is the same as the numerator in expression 16-2 which is the formula for the covariance! The denominator in 16-19 is the same as the numerator in the expression for the variance of x. So, we can see that the solution to the general linear equation is simply the covariance divided by the variance of x. To find b_0 which is really a "centering" factor for average levels of x and y, we need only go to the model and solve for b_0 at $\overline{X}$ and $\overline{Y}$.

$$\overline{Y} = b_0 + b_1\overline{X}$$

$$\text{and...} \qquad b_0 = \overline{Y} - b_1\overline{X} \qquad (16\text{-}20)$$

Another way of looking at the b_0 point is to think of how the regression line pivots through the $\overline{X}$ and $\overline{Y}$ points. The "pivoting" factor is the slope (b_1). If there is no slope then there is no relationship between x and y and the b_0 term is the same as $\overline{Y}$. As the slope becomes larger and larger, the b_0 term gets farther and farther away from the $\overline{Y}$. We should also recognize that because of the "center of gravity" effect of the averages, the b_0 term is also the point on the y axis where x takes on the value of zero.

USING THE FORMULA

Let's go through our numerical example and use the formulas we have just derived.

Table 16-7

x	y	y^2	x*y
1	4	1	4
2	6	4	12
3	9	9	27
4	10	16	40

x = 2.5 y = 7.25 $\Sigma x = 10$ $\Sigma y = 29$ Σx^2 $\Sigma x^*y = 83$ $\Sigma n = 4$

Substituting the proper values into expression 16-19:

$$b_1 = \frac{4(83) - (10)(29)}{4(30) + (10)^2} = \frac{42}{20} = 2.1$$

And by using 16-20 we obtain:

$$b_0 = 7.25 - 2.5 \, (2.1) = 7.25 - 5.25 = 2.0$$

This is the same result that we obtained using the long, drawn-out procedure a few pages back.

THE ROLE OF THE MATRIX

Equations 16-11 and 16-12 form what are called the "normal equations". Now, the term "normal" has nothing to do with the normal distribution function, but means the "usual" equations for the solution by least squares.

Up to now we have worked with a single x variable and the normal equations are not too complicated. However, what happens when there are more variables under study than just an x_1? What if there are two x's or even more? In these cases, the normal equations become larger and larger, and there are more pieces to them. So, if we had two x variables, there would be three equations in three unknowns. If there were 4 x's, there would be 5 equations in 5 unknowns. Note that there is always an extra equation to account for the b_0 or centering factor in our equations. While it is possible to solve such complex algebraic expressions, it is easier to have a more general solution technique for higher order problems involving multiple x factors. This branch of least squares analysis is called multiple regression and is handled systematically by matrix algebra.

Let's look into the normal equations and see what is there. Then we will generalize the quantities into a matrix form that will solve all types of problems by a set of simple rules.

Since we know what is in the simple example that we solved using algebra, we will continue to use these numbers in our investigation of the matrix approach.

Let's rewrite the normal equations again and see if we can view them in terms of a matrix.

$$n \, b_0 + \Sigma x \, b_1 = \Sigma y$$
$$\Sigma x \, b_0 + \Sigma x^2 b_1 = \Sigma xy$$

In the left side of the equations we can see a common set of terms in the b's. Just as in algebra, we can in matrix algebra isolate these terms by dividing through both sides of the equation. Since we will be working with matrix algebra, we cannot really "divide", but can get the same effect by multiplying both sides by the inverse of all the parts that do not include the b's. This gives us the following:

$$\begin{bmatrix} n & \Sigma x \\ \Sigma x & \Sigma x^2 \end{bmatrix}^{-1} * \begin{bmatrix} n & \Sigma x \\ \Sigma x & \Sigma x^2 \end{bmatrix} \begin{bmatrix} b0 \\ b_1 \end{bmatrix} = \begin{bmatrix} n & \Sigma x \\ \Sigma x & \Sigma x^2 \end{bmatrix}^{-1} * \begin{bmatrix} \Sigma y \\ \Sigma xy \end{bmatrix} \tag{16-21}$$

Since the inverse times itself gives the identity matrix, the left side of the equation reduces to the vector of b's which of course are what we are looking for. Now the question is how to generalize the right hand side of the equation. Here we have to be clever and a bit insightful into the form of the equation we are seeking. We need a set of b's which include a b_1 term which is the rate of change in y with x; and we also need a b_0 term which is a centering or averaging factor. The b_1 term comes from the x factors we have. But where can we generate the b_0 term from?

THE DUMMY FACTOR

It is possible to introduce a term into an equation by using what has been called a "dummy factor". In the case of the b_0 term, the dummy factor is simply a column of 1's. We can write the data from our example as follows with the dummy 1's in the first position in a 4 by 2 matrix. We will also write this set of data in transposed form.

$$X = \begin{bmatrix} 1 & 1 \\ 1 & 2 \\ 1 & 3 \\ 1 & 4 \end{bmatrix} \qquad X' = \begin{bmatrix} 1 & 1 & 1 & 1 \\ 1 & 2 & 3 & 4 \end{bmatrix}$$

If we multiply X by X' as follows we get what we are looking for.

$$X' * X = \begin{bmatrix} 4 & 10 \\ 10 & 30 \end{bmatrix} \text{ Which is: } \begin{bmatrix} n & \Sigma x \\ \Sigma x & \Sigma x^2 \end{bmatrix} \tag{16-22}$$

And further, we can get the other vector of values by multiplying X' times the Y response vector as follows:

$$X' * Y = \begin{bmatrix} 1 & 1 & 1 & 1 \\ 1 & 2 & 3 & 4 \end{bmatrix} * \begin{bmatrix} 4 \\ 6 \\ 9 \\ 10 \end{bmatrix} = \begin{bmatrix} 29 \\ 83 \end{bmatrix}$$

$$\text{which is: } \begin{bmatrix} \Sigma y \\ \Sigma xy \end{bmatrix} \tag{16-23}$$

Expressions 16-22 and 16-23 are exactly the parts of expression 16-21 that we were seeking and lead us to the general formula in matrix notation terms for the vector of coefficients, which is the inverse of the x-transpose times x, all times the x-transpose times y.

$$B = (X'X)^{-1} * (X'Y) \tag{16-24}$$

Expression 16-24 is one of the most useful formulas and is the most general approach to finding regression coefficients and the basis for many of the calculations needed for statistical inference.

To find the inverse of the $X'X$ matrix (for this simple 2x2 case) we find the determinant of the matrix by taking the cross product of the downward diagonals and subtracting the cross product of the upward diagonals. So for our general expression we get:

$$\text{determinant of:} \quad \begin{bmatrix} n & \Sigma x \\ \Sigma x & \Sigma x^2 \end{bmatrix} \quad = n * \Sigma x^2 - (\Sigma x)^2$$

Next we take the determinant and use it to divide the original matrix with its downward diagonals interchanged and the signs changed on the upward diagonals. This gives:

$$(X'X)^{-1} = \begin{bmatrix} \dfrac{\Sigma x^2}{n\Sigma x^2 - (\Sigma x)^2} & \dfrac{\Sigma x}{n\Sigma x^2 - (\Sigma x)^2} \\ \\ \dfrac{\Sigma x}{n\Sigma x^2 - (\Sigma x)^2} & \dfrac{n}{n\Sigma x^2 - (\Sigma x)^2} \end{bmatrix} \tag{16-25}$$

It is good practice to do the division last in order to preserve the accuracy of the calculations. So, we will rewrite 16-25 as follows and complete the multiplication with the $X'Y$ to obtain the vector of coefficients.

$$\frac{1}{n\Sigma x^2 - (\Sigma x)^2} \begin{bmatrix} \Sigma x^2 & -\Sigma x \\ -\Sigma x & n \end{bmatrix} * \begin{bmatrix} \Sigma y \\ \Sigma xy \end{bmatrix} = \begin{bmatrix} \Sigma x^2 \Sigma y & -\Sigma x \Sigma xy \\ -\Sigma x & -n\,\Sigma xy \end{bmatrix} \frac{1}{n\Sigma x^2 - (\Sigma x)^2}$$

$$\begin{array}{ccc} \text{A 2 x 2} & \text{A 2 x 1} & \text{A 2 x 1} \\ \text{Matrix} & \text{Matrix} & \text{Matrix} \end{array}$$

Now dividing through by the determinant we begin to see a familiar formula that we derived using the algebraic approach to least squares.

$$\begin{bmatrix} b_0 \\ b_1 \end{bmatrix} = \begin{bmatrix} \dfrac{\Sigma x^2 \Sigma y - \Sigma x \Sigma xy}{n\Sigma x^2 - (\Sigma x)^2} \\ \\ \dfrac{n\Sigma xy - \Sigma x}{n\Sigma x^2 - (\Sigma x)^2} \end{bmatrix} \tag{16-26}$$

The term for b_1 is exactly the same as we obtained from the algebraic approach to the solution of the least squares fit. If we substitute the values from our numerical example into the matrix form of the equation we obtain the same values as before, 2.1 for the slope (b_1) and 2.0 for the intercept (b_0). The advantage of the least squares solution by matrix algebra is of course, the expandability of the formula to more than one x variable.

REGRESSION, ANOVA, AND YATES

Since the least squares regression approach to statistical inference is the most general method, it is important to see how the ANOVA, and particularly the YATES algorithm for ANOVA, are related to this technique. We will take a simple 2^2 factorial design and solve it using the general least squares approach and in doing so, we will see how the algorithm is indeed a simplification of the more general approach to the solution of the problem.

Recall that the design matrix for a two-level factorial can be written in its entirety (including interactions) as an ordered set of "-1's" and "$+1$'s". We have just learned that to include a b_0 term, we need to provide for a dummy variable which is made up of a column of $+1$'s. Therefore, the matrix that represents the X matrix for a 2^2 design is as follows:

$$X = \begin{bmatrix} 1 & -1 & -1 & +1 \\ 1 & +1 & -1 & -1 \\ 1 & -1 & +1 & -1 \\ 1 & +1 & +1 & +1 \end{bmatrix} \tag{16-27}$$

$$Y = \begin{bmatrix} 2 \\ 4 \\ 2 \\ 2 \end{bmatrix} \tag{16-28}$$

In our example, the response vector is given in 16-28. We can solve the ANOVA by the YATES method as found below in Table 16-8.

Table 16-8

	I	II	½Effect	Sum Sq	Measures
2	6	10	2.5	---	Average
4	4	2	.5	1.0	Factor A
2	2	-2	-.5	1.0	Factor B
2	0	-2	-.5	1.0	A*B Interaction

We can also use the general least squares approach to the solution as follows:

Table 16-9

$$X'$$

$$\begin{bmatrix} 1 & 1 & 1 & 1 \\ -1 & +1 & -1 & +1 \\ -1 & -1 & +1 & +1 \\ +1 & -1 & -1 & +1 \end{bmatrix} * $$

$$X$$

$$\begin{bmatrix} 1 & -1 & -1 & +1 \\ 1 & +1 & -1 & -1 \\ 1 & -1 & +1 & -1 \\ 1 & +1 & +1 & +1 \end{bmatrix} = $$

$$X'X$$

$$\begin{bmatrix} 4 & 0 & 0 & 0 \\ 0 & 4 & 0 & 0 \\ 0 & 0 & 4 & 0 \\ 0 & 0 & 0 & 4 \end{bmatrix}$$

$$X'$$

$$\begin{bmatrix} 1 & 1 & 1 & 1 \\ -1 & +1 & -1 & +1 \\ -1 & -1 & +1 & +1 \\ +1 & -1 & -1 & +1 \end{bmatrix} * $$

$$Y$$

$$\begin{bmatrix} 2 \\ 4 \\ 2 \\ 2 \end{bmatrix} = $$

$$X'Y$$

$$\begin{bmatrix} 10 \\ -2 \\ 2 \\ -2 \end{bmatrix}$$

Notice that the final column (column #II) in the YATES is exactly the same as the $X'Y$ result. Also very carefully notice that the $X'X$ matrix is a diagonal matrix (only diagonal elements) with the diagonal elements equal to the number of observations in the design. Now we begin to see the reasons that the YATES method and the ANOVA method <u>can</u> work in the general linear model. The fact that the design is ORTHOGONAL gives us the diagonal $X'X$ matrix. The diagonal matrix is the easiest of all matrices to invert! To do so, we simply take the inverse of each of the diagonal elements. The inverse of the diagonal matrix in our example is then:

$$(X'X)^{-1} = \begin{bmatrix} ¼ & 0 & 0 & 0 \\ 0 & ¼ & 0 & 0 \\ 0 & 0 & ¼ & 0 \\ 0 & 0 & 0 & ¼ \end{bmatrix} \qquad (16\text{-}29)$$

So the solution for the set of b coefficients is simply ¼ of each of the elements of the $X'Y$ matrix.

$$\begin{bmatrix} ¼ & 0 & 0 & 0 \\ 0 & ¼ & 0 & 0 \\ 0 & 0 & ¼ & 0 \\ 0 & 0 & 0 & ¼ \end{bmatrix} * \begin{bmatrix} 10 \\ 2 \\ -2 \\ -2 \end{bmatrix} = \begin{bmatrix} 2.5 \\ .5 \\ -.5 \\ -.5 \end{bmatrix} \qquad (16\text{-}30)$$

Which is exactly the same as the half-effects from the YATES ANOVA! But what about the sums of squares? It is possible to obtain the sum of squares in matrix methods by the following formula:

Sum of Squares $= \mathbf{B}' \, (\mathbf{X}'\mathbf{Y})$

for our example:

$$\begin{bmatrix} 2.5 & .5 & -.5 & -.5 \end{bmatrix} \begin{bmatrix} 10 \\ 2 \\ -2 \\ -2 \end{bmatrix} = \begin{bmatrix} 25 \\ 1 \\ 1 \\ 1 \end{bmatrix}$$

Again, this is exactly the same as we obtained from the YATES ANOVA in Table 16-8. So, the YATES method takes advantage of the orthogonality of the design (which produces the diagonal $\mathbf{X}'\mathbf{X}$ matrix) to simplify the computations. The general ANOVA method follows the same line of thinking to create the sums of squares used to draw inferences in the face of the variability of the data.

As we shall see in the next chapter, we can make use of this common link between the Least Squares Method and the ANOVA techniques to gain a better insight into the nature of the information in the experiments we perform.

PROBLEMS FOR CHAPTER 16

1) Using the algebriac formulas find the slope and intercept for x and y for the following data:

X	Y
5	6
8	3
3	8
5	7
6	5
9	2
10	1

2) Compute the correlation coefficient for Problem #1.

3) Use the Matrix approach to find the slope and intercept for the data found in Problem #1.

4) Use the Matrix approach to find the vector of coefficients for the following multiple regression problems.

X_1	X_2	X_3	y
-1	-1	-1	5
$+1$	-1	-1	6
-1	$+1$	-1	9
$+1$	$+1$	-1	6
-1	-1	$+1$	10
$+1$	-1	$+1$	12
-1	$+1$	$+1$	18
$+1$	$+1$	$+1$	12

APPENDIX 16

Covariance s_{xy} $= \dfrac{n\,(\Sigma x_i * y_i) - (\Sigma x_i) * (\Sigma y_i)}{n(n-1)}$

Correlation coefficient r: Measures the degree of linear dependence between two variables. It is anchored between -1 and $+1$ with the highest dependence indicated as it approaches an absolute value of 1. An r of zero indicates no dependence.

$$r = \frac{s_{xy}}{s_x * s_y}$$

where: s_{xy} is the covariance.

s_x standard deviation of x.

s_y standard deviation of y

General Linear Model: $\hat{Y} = b_0 + b_1 * X_1$

Where $\hat{Y}$ (y hat) is the estimate of the value being predicted.

b_0 is the value of y at $x = 0$ or the y intercept.

b_1 is the change in y due to x or the slope of the line describing the relationship between x and y.

X_1 is the particular value of x we are solving for.

Slope b_1:

$$b_1 = \frac{n\Sigma xy - \Sigma x\, \Sigma y}{n\Sigma x2 - (\Sigma x)^2}$$

intercept:

$b_0 = \bar{Y} - b_1 \bar{X}$ where $\bar{Y}$ and $\bar{X}$ are the averages of x & y

MATRIX FORMULA: $\mathbf{B} = (\mathbf{X'X})^{-1} * (\mathbf{X'Y})$

Where: $\mathbf{X}$ is the matrix of control variables
$\mathbf{Y}$ is the vector of responses
$\mathbf{B}$ is the vector of coefficients

17

PUTTING ANOVA AND LEAST SQUARES TO WORK

Now that we have developed the ANOVA and Least Squares approach to statistical analysis and see the similarities in these two methods, let's find out how we can put these tools to work on an experimental design and analysis problem.

The following problem involving three factors and one response will serve as an example of the steps in the analysis of the central composite design. It will also serve as a general example of the approach to be taken in any statistical analysis of an experimental design. Table 17-1 shows the central composite design for the three factors of Temperature, Concentration, and Speed.

The first step in the analysis will be to run a YATES ANOVA on the factorial portion of the design. This will identify the linear main effects and any of the interactions that are significant. Notice that the "zero" point has been replicated to produce an estimate of experimental error. We shall see later that this replication is important for a second reason. Table 17-2 is the computer generated YATES ANOVA for this problem.

The mean square of the replicates is found by computing the sum of squares for the four data points and dividing by the three degrees of freedom.

$$\text{Sum Square} \quad = \quad 792993 - (\ \underline{\quad 1781 \quad}\ )^2 \quad = 2.75$$
$$\frac{\Sigma x^2 - (\Sigma x)^2 / 4}{4}$$

$$\text{Mean Square} \quad = \quad \frac{2.75}{3} \quad = .917$$

239

Table 17-1

tc	A Temperature	B Concentration	C Speed	(Response) Tensile Strength
(1)	120	30	6	230
a	180	30	6	384
b	120	45	6	520
ab	180	45	6	670
c	120	30	9	180
ac	180	30	9	330
bc	120	45	9	465
abc	180	45	9	612
$-\alpha_a$	100	37.5	7.5	260
$+\alpha_a$	200	37.5	7.5	507
$-\alpha_b$	150	25	7.5	206
$+\alpha_b$	150	50	7.5	689
$-\alpha_c$	150	37.5	5	495
$+\alpha_c$	150	37.5	10	400
zero	150	37.5	7.5	446,445,446,444

Table 17-2

#	OBSERVATION	SUM SQUARE	HALF EFFECT	MEASURES	INDEX #
1	230		423.875	Average	1
2	384	45150.1	75.125	A (Temp.)	2
3	520	163306	142.875	B (Conc.)	3
4	670	6.125	−.875	AB	4
5	180	5886.13	−27.125	C (Speed)	5
6	330	6.125	−.875	AC	6
7	465	10.125	−1.125	BC	7
8	612	.125	.125	ABC	8

The critical F value for 1 and 3 degress of freedom is 10.128 at an alpha risk of .05. using the above error estimate, we find statistically significant effects for the main effects of temperature, concentration and speed. There is also an interaction effect just significant ($F = 11.04$) for the BC interaction which is the concentration*speed factor. The remaining effects are not significant. If we did not have an error estimate, we could have looked at the magnitude of the half effects to judge if there was enough of a change in the response to warrent further work or investigation. In the above case, we would probably have picked the 3 main effects, but would have not judged the interactions as making important contributions.

USING THE HALF EFFECTS

We have shown that the half effects are the same quantity as the regression coefficients. We can use them to illustrate the trends in the experiment by plotting the change in the response as a function of the variables under study. The first half effect (Index #1) measures the average and is located at the "conceptual" zero point in the experiment. We call this "conceptual" since we don't really have a middle experimental point in the 2^k design. In our design, we only have a -1 point and a $+1$ point. Since the half effect is the change in the response over a unit change in the control variable, the half effect measures the change from the center (or zero point) of the experimental space to either the -1 position or the $+1$ position. This is how the half effect gets its name since it is a measure of the change in the response over half the range of the experimental space. Figure 17-1 illustrates this concept for the particular set of data we have been working with. The "x" axis has been laid out in the design unit space from -1 to $+1$ with the zero indicated (but remember we don't have a real data point for the response from this part of the experiment). The "y" axis has the range of the response and the average is highlighted.

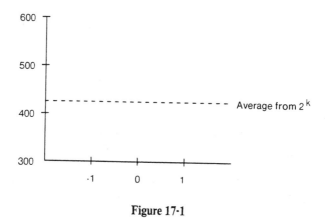

Figure 17-1

We can use Figure 17-1 as a model to plot the three main effects. The responses we plot will represent the average value for the factor under study at the low and high points. In our experiment, we could take the average of the four low values and the average of the four high values and plot them for each factor. We'll do this as an example for Factor C, the speed. Afterwards, we'll show how this same task can be done using the half effects. To find the average low level of Factor C add up the first four responses from Table 17-1 and then divide by 4. The average of the high level of Factor C comes from adding the next four responses from Table 17-1 and dividing this result by 4.

$$\text{Low C} = \underline{230 + 384 + 520 + 670} = 451$$
$$4$$

$$\text{High C} = \underline{180 + 330 + 465 + 612} = 396.75$$
$$4$$

Now let's plot the average level of Factor C at its low and high input points.

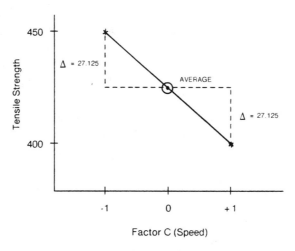

Figure 17-2

Notice that the difference from the average for both points is 27.125. This is exactly the half effect reported in the YATES ANOVA of Table 17-2. Therefore, we can obtain the average points for the main effect plots by simply adding the half effect and subtracting the half effect from the average value of the 2^k design. We can do this for Factors A and B which we plot on one axis in Figure 17-3 along with Factor C.

Points for Factor A (Temperature)

low:	423.875	−	75.125	=	348.75
high:	423.875	+	75.125	=	499.00

Points for Factor B (Concentration)

low:	423.875	−	142.875	=	281.00
high:	423.875	+	142.875	=	566.75

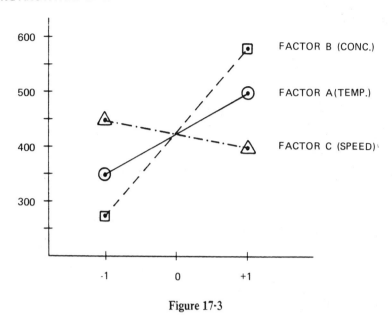

Figure 17-3

From Figure 17-3 we can see the relative effect of the change in the response as a function of the three main factors. In obtaining the points for this plot, we have used the half effects and actually solved a regression equaiton. The equation we have is a result of our YATES Analysis and consists of the significant effects. The full equation is:

Tensile Strength =   423.875 + 75.125 * Temp. (A) + 142.875 * Conc. (B)   (17-1)
                     − 27.125 * Speed (C) − 1.125 * Conc.* Speed (BC)

To obtain the coefficients in 17-1 we simply went to the YATES analysis and picked out the half effects that had significant F values. Now, the coefficients for Temperature, Concentration, and Speed are in terms of the design units $(-1, +1)$ and not in terms of the physical variables. Therefore, when we solve this or any other equation from a YATES analysis, we must put in the correct parameters. The correct parameters for solution are the coded levels of the design units which are -1 for the low level and $+1$ for the high level. When we obtained the points for Figure 17-2 we solved the equation (17-1) using the -1 when we subtracted and the $+1$ when we added the half effect to the average! We also ignored the rest of the equation in solving for just one main effect at a time. Actually by "ignoring" the rest of the equation, we have considered the other factors at their zero level which eliminates them from the computation. To illustrate this point let's write the full equation down and solve for the low level of Factor A (Temp.). To do this we will put in the low level of A (which is a -1) and enter zero for all the other effects.

Tensile Strength $= 423.875 + 75.125*(-1) + 142.875*(0) - 27.125*(0)$ (17-2)
$- 1.125*(0)*(0)$
$= 423.875 - 75.125$
$= 348.75$

So, the rule to subtract to find the low level of a main effect and add to find the high level of an effect has its basis in the solution of the equation formed from the YATES analysis. This concept can now be extended into the solution for the points in the interaction.

PLOTTING INTERACTIONS

Factorial designs were specifically engineered to detect interactions. The analysis of variance will detect significant interactions, but the next step is to plot the functional form of the interaction to gain insight into the nature of the effect. We can obtain the coordinates of the interaction plot by solving the design unit equation from the YATES. In our example, there was a significant BC interaction. To find the points to plot, we solve the equation (17-1) for all the terms involved with this interaction. Since this is a two factor interaction with two levels per factor there will be 4 points to plot. We need to solve for the:

Factor:	B	C
	Low	Low
	High	Low
	Low	High
	High	High

Since Factor A is not involved, equaiton 17-1 reduces down to:

Tensile Strength $= 423.875 + 142.875*$Conc. (B) $- 27.125*$Speed (C)   (17-3)
$- 1.125*B*C$

Again, we have eliminated the factor not under study (in this case Factor A) by solving the equation using the center point of this factor which is zero. Now we solve the remaining equation (17-3) for the design unit levels for Factors B and C. The

Table 17-3

Levels			Substituted Into Equation	Result
B	C	B*C		
-1	-1	$+1$	$423.875 + 142.875*(-1) - 27.125*(-1) - 1.125*(+1)$	307.00
$+1$	-1	-1	$423.875 + 142.875*(+1) - 27.125*(-1) - 1.125*(-1)$	595.00
-1	$+1$	-1	$423.875 + 142.875*(-1) - 27.125*(+1) - 1.125*(-1)$	255.00
$+1$	$+1$	$+1$	$423.875 + 142.875*(+1) - 27.125*(+1) - 1.125*(+1)$	538.50

interaction term (B*C) is found by finding the cross-product of the B and C main factor levels. Tabel 17-3 shows the work with the plottable results.

We can now construct the interaction table that will allow us to plot the interaction.

Table 17-4

		Concentration (B) 30ppm (−)	45ppm (+)
S p e e d (C)	6ips (−)	307	595
	9ips (+)	255	538.5

We not take the points from Table 17-4 and plot them. Since it is possible to form this plot with either of the factors on the "x" axis while the other is held at an isolated level (iso-level), we will plot the results both ways. Sometimes the interaction will "talk to us" in a more meaningful manner if plotted both ways.

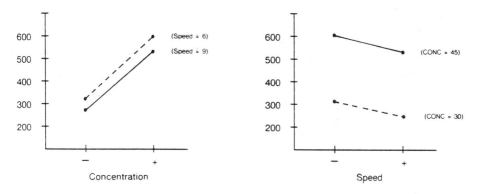

Figure 17-4

The amount of interaction is slight if we use the above plots to make this judgement. However, remember, that the effect was significant in a statistical sense. That is, the lack of parrallelism between the two iso-level lines is enough that when compared with the noise of the experiment we can say that there is non-parallelism. We may, however, judge the effect from a practical point and disregard the interaction based on our knowledge of the process. The lack of parallelism between these two iso-level lines is less than 10% (8.7%) with respect to the speed plot and only 1.6% with respect to the concentration plot. This percent lack of parallelism may be found by taking the ratios of the iso-slopes with the larger slope placed in the numerator. This ratio gives a relative anchored feel for the magnitude of the interaction.

PLOTTING CURVES

So far, the results of our analysis have indicated that there are significant effects for all three main effects and a single two-factor interaction. We still have the "bottom half" of the central composite design to draw upon for more information. The information from this part of the experiment is used to guide our thinking to the correct polynomial model. We will augment out linear plots with the alpha position values to see if a straight line continues or if there is evidence of a curve. If there is a curvature in the data, then there will be a difference between the zero value in the experiment (the one we actually ran a treatement combination on) and the "conceptual" zero that is calculated in the YATES analysis. Let's see if this is the case in our example and then determine why this takes place.

We will plot factors A, B, and C using the -1 and $+1$ points from the YATES analysis which will give us the same points as we plotted in Figurre 17-3. However,in the following figure (17-5) we will add the actual zero point and the two alpha points for each factor.

Figure 17-5 has some strange twists and turns and would lead us to believe that there are cubic effects for the factors under study. What has actually happened, is the following. The average effect from the factorial portion of the experiment (found in the first line of the YATES output) is lower than the actual average value of the four zero points from the composite portion of the experiment. The average effect from the YATES is a mathematical result while the zero point is an actual observation. Why is the zero point bigger than the average? The answer lies in the functional form of the factors in this experiment. In another experiment, the zero point could be smaller than the average. In this experiment, two of the factors show a strong positive slope while the third shows a slight negative slope. There is a tendency with this data for the response to be higher as the factors' levels get bigger. Since the composite portion of the experiment is concentrated around the zero point, the positive effect of the two factors (A & B) is exerted to give a physical increase in the response for the composite treatments. Unfortunately, this does induce some confusion into the graphical analysis of the data as seen in Figure 17-5. This confusion can be removed by "normalizing" the two parts of the experiment to a common zero point. While this normalization could be achieved by either "correcting" the factorial portion or the composite portion, it is more convenient to change the composite values. While some people may argue that this does not reflect reality, remember we are only plotting the data to get a qualitative picture of the functional forms involved. The equation will be generated using the actual data with multiple regression.

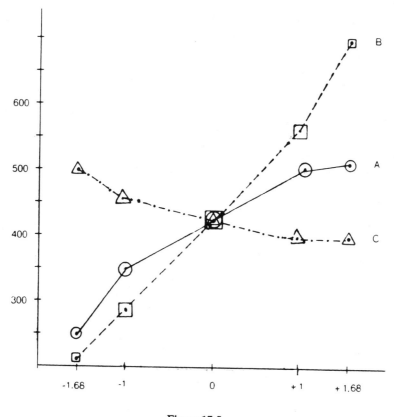

Figure 17-5

Correcting or normalizing the composite (or bottom half) part of the experiment is convenient since we can still use the half effects to find the low and high plot points as described before.

Now let's re-plot Figure 17-5 and use the normalized points from the composite portion. To find the normalized points, we first find the <u>difference</u> between the YATES average and the zero of the composite.

$$\text{Delta} = \text{average (YATES)} - \text{zero (composite)} \qquad (17\text{-}4)$$
$$-21.375 = 423.875 - 445.25$$

To complete the normalization, we <u>add</u> the delta (watch signs) to each point in the composite portion of the design as follows:

Table 17-5

tc	Actual Response	Normalized Response
$-\alpha_a$	260	238.625
$+\alpha_a$	507	485.625
$-\alpha_b$	206	184.625
$+\alpha_b$	689	667.625
$-\alpha_c$	495	473.625
$+\alpha_c$	400	378.625
zero	445.25	423.875

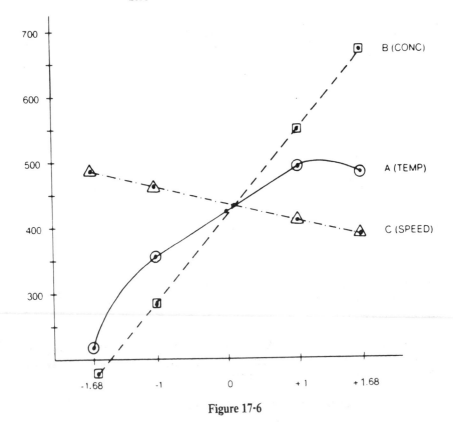

Figure 17-6

We have removed the "wrinkles" from our first plot and now see the functional forms of the polynomials for each of the factors. Factor A, the temperature, is quadratic in nature while B, the concentration, and C, the speed, are both linear. We now propose our model based on the analysis completed. There are three linear main effects, a quadratic (square) for one factor and a single two-factor interaction. The model is:

Tensil Strength = $b_0 + b_1 * Temp + b_2 * Conc. + b_3 * Speed +$ (17-5)
$b_{11} * Temp^2 + b_{23} * Conc. * Speed$

The last step in our analysis is to submit the data to a computer program for analysis. The details of this procedure are reproduced in the appendix of this chapter. The results of the regression produced the following equation:

$TS = -1100.68 + 10.0284 * Temperature - .025 * Temperature^2 +$ (17-6)
$19.9 * Conc. - 14.71 * Speed - 0.10 * Conc. * Speed$

The details of the regression are also found in the appendix. The encouraging aspect of this exercise is the fact that expression 17-6 is very close to the original equation that produced the data for this example. The deviation from reality will of course depend upon the random error of the data.

Besides the computer programs supplied with this book, there are many other commercially available software packages that will produce the same results. SAS, MINITAB, SPSS and BMDP are all in common use on large "main-frame" computers. The programs used here are of course for desk-top "micro" computers.

PROBLEMS FOR CHAPTER 17

1) A YATES analysis was performed on an experiment and produced the following half effects. Plot the effects as follows:

     a)   Main Effect A   c)   Main Effect C
     b)   Interaction A*C   d)   Interaction A*B

half effect	Measure
200	Average
-10	A
20	B
5	AB
15	C
7	AC
0	BC
0	ABC

2) Use the half effect results from the factorial design of Question #1 and augment

the following composite values. Plot each main effect and purpose a model for regression analysis.

<u>Response</u>

$-\alpha_a$	260
$+\alpha_a$	230
$-\alpha_b$	180
$+\alpha_b$	260
$-\alpha_c$	220
$+\alpha_c$	220
Zero	220

APPENDIX 17

Outline of the steps in the analysis of a Central Composite Design:

1)   Run YATES analysis on the factorial portion of the design.

2)   Plot the results from the YATES analysis.

3)   Normalize the composite portion by adding the delta to the composite values of the response.

Delta = Average (YATES) − Zero (Composite)

4)   Plot the results from the entire experiment. Do so by adding the alpha position values of the responses to the plot of the YATES results.

5)   Propose a model for regression analysis.

6)   Prepare the data for regression.

7)   Run the regression.

Plotting results from half-effects. (Note: The YATES computer program will do this for you).

- For main effects, find the low level by subtracting the factor's half effect from the average. For the high level, add the factor's half effect to the average.

- For two factor interactions, set up the equation in design units for the factors in the interaction. Solve the equation for the four points to be plotted.

APPENDIX 17·I
Example of use of Regression program
FILE BUILDER/EDITOR

```
      MENU
<1> BUILD NEW FILE
<2> EDIT EXISTING FILE
<3> VIEW FILE
<4> AUGMENT FILE WITH TRANSFORMATIONS
    OR ADD MORE ROWS OF DATA
<5> END

MAKE SELECTION FROM ABOVE BY #
?1
WHAT'S THE NAME OF YOUR NEW FILE
?CH17EX
HOW MANY ROWS OF DATA
?18
HOW MANY COLUMNS OF DATA
?3
ENTER THE DATA ROW WISE
ROW   1  COL  1  ?120
ROW   1  COL  2  ?30
ROW   1  COL  3  ?6
ROW   2  COL  1  ?180
ROW   2  COL  2  ?30
ROW   2  COL  3  ?6
ROW   3  COL  1  ?120
ROW   3  COL  2  ?45
ROW   3  COL  3  ?6
ROW   4  COL  1  ?180
ROW   4  COL  2  ?45
ROW   4  COL  3  ?6
ROW   5  COL  1  ?120
 ⌐W   5  COL  2  ?30
      5  COL  3  ?9
      6  COL  1  ?180
         COL  2  ?30
        ⌐OL  3  ?9
              1  ?120
              2  ?45
              ⌐  ?9
                 ?180
                  5
```

After loading the program EDITOR and telling the computer to "RUN" the data is entered by simply following the instructions. The X matrix of data is first entered as shown on the left. It is entered row by row.

```
ROW  16   C⌐
ROW  17   COL
ROW  17   COL
ROW  17   COL   3
ROW  18   COL   1
ROW  18   COL   2  ?3,
ROW  18   COL   3  ?7.5
```

```
MAKE SELECTION FROM ABOVE BY #
?3
FILE NAME TO BE VIEWED
?CH17EX
ROWS OF DATA=      18
COLUMNS OF DATA=    3

 1  --    120    30      6
 2  --    180    30      6
 3  --    120    45      6
 4  --    180    45      6
 5  --    120    30      9
 6  --    180    30      9
 7  --    120    45      9
 8  --    180    45      9
 9  --    100   37.5000    7.50000
10     --     200   37.5000    7.50000
11     --     150    25     7.50000
12     --     150    50      7.50000
13     --     150   37.5000    5
14     --     150   37.5000   10
15     --     150   37.5000    7.50000
16     --     150   37.5000    7.50000
17     --     150   37.5000    7.50000
18     --     150   37.5000    7.50000
              FILE BUILDER/EDITOR

          MENU
<1> BUILD NEW FILE
<2> EDIT EXISTING FILE
<3> VIEW FILE
<4> AUGMENT FILE WITH TRANSFORMATIONS
    OR ADD MORE ROWS OF DATA
<5> END

MAKE SELECTION FROM ABOVE BY #
?4
FILE NAME TO BE TRANSFORMED
?CH17EX
ROWS OF DATA=      18   COLS OF DATA=     3
HOW MANY NEW DATA POINTS (ROWS) ARE YOU ADDING  ?0
HOW MANY NEW COLUMNS ARE YOU ADDING
?2
LIST OF TRANSFORMS
<1> LOG(10)
<2> LN
<3> X SQUARED
<4> X CUBED
<5> CROSS PRODUCT OF 2 X'S
<6> 1/X
<7> SQUARE ROOT OF X
<8> SCALE X
<9> ADD A NEW VARIABLE
```

We now view the file to see if it is correct. Since it is correct, we ....

.....Add the proper columns via the transform option (4) of EDITOR.

```
ENTER TRANSFORM CHOICE (IE:#  )
?3
ENTER COLUMN # TO BE TRANSFORMED
?1
THIS WILL BECOME COLUMN:    4
LIST OF TRANSFORMS
<1> LOG(10)
<2> LN
<3> X SQUARED
<4> X CUBED
<5> CROSS PRODUCT OF 2 X'S
<6> 1/X
<7> SQUARE ROOT OF X
<8> SCALE X
<9> ADD A NEW VARIABLE
ENTER TRANSFORM CHOICE (IE:#  )
?5
ENTER COLUMN # TO BE TRANSFORMED
?2
THIS WILL BECOME COLUMN:    5
WHAT'S THE # OF THE OTHER VARIABLE IN THE CROSS PRODUCT?
?3
          FILE BUILDER/EDITOR

          MENU
<1> BUILD NEW FILE
<2> EDIT EXISTING FILE
<3> VIEW FILE
<4> AUGMENT FILE WITH TRANSFORMATIONS
    OR ADD MORE ROWS OF DATA
<5> END

MAKE SELECTION FROM ABOVE BY #
?3
FILE NAME TO BE VIEWED
?CH17EX
ROWS OF DATA=    18
COLUMNS OF DATA=    5
```

We construct an X squared column and a cross product column for our model.

We view the X matrix again with all the columns needed for the model.

```
 1  --      120      30      6      14400      180
 2  --      180      30      6      32400      180
 3  --      120      45      6      14400      270
 4  --      180      45      6      32400      270
 5  --      120      30      9      14400      270
 6  --      180      30      9      32400      270
 7  --      120      45      9      14400      405
 8  --      180      45      9      32400      405
 9  --      100   37.5000   7.50000    10000   281.250
10  --      200   37.5000   7.50000    40000   281.250
11  --      150      25   7.50000    22500   187.500
12  --      150      50   7.50000    22500   375
13  --      150   37.5000      5    22500   187.500
14  --      150   37.5000     10    22500   375
15  --      150   37.5000   7.50000    22500   281.250
16  --      150   37.5000   7.50000    22500   281.250
17  --      150   37.5000   7.50000    22500   281.250
18  --      150   37.5000   7.50000    22500   281.250
```

```
MAKE SELECTION FROM ABOVE BY #
?1
WHAT'S THE NAME OF YOUR NEW FILE
?CH17EY
HOW MANY ROWS OF DATA
?18
HOW MANY COLUMNS OF DATA
?1
ENTER THE DATA ROW WISE
ROW     1   COL     1   ?230
ROW     2   COL     1   ?384
ROW     3   COL     1   ?520
ROW     4   COL     1   ?670
ROW     5   COL     1   ?180
ROW     6   COL     1   ?330
ROW     7   COL     1   ?465
ROW     8   COL     1   ?612
ROW     9   COL     1   ?260
ROW    10   COL     1   ?507
ROW    11   COL     1   ?206
ROW    12   COL     1   ?689
ROW    13   COL     1   ?495
ROW    14   COL     1   ?400
ROW    15   COL     1   ?446
ROW    16   COL     1   ?445
ROW    17   COL     1   ?446
ROW    18   COL     1   ?444
            FILE BUILDER/EDITOR

        MENU
<1> BUILD NEW FILE
<2> EDIT EXISTING FILE
<3> VIEW FILE
<4> AUGMENT FILE WITH TRANSFORMATIONS
    OR ADD MORE ROWS OF DATA
<5> END

MAKE SELECTION FROM ABOVE BY #
?5
```

Now we build the response vector file......

.......and finish our work (5) with the EDITOR.

```
>RUN
15:50   JUL 29  REGRESSION2...
DO YOU WISH TO ENTER A SIMPLE ONE VARIABLE
MODEL, IE.: Y=B(0)+B(1)*X   ?N
YOU SHOULD HAVE PREPARED TWO FILES FOR YOUR REGRESSION
USING THE EDIT PROGRAM.  IF YOU HAVE NOT, HIT BREAK AND
SET UP THESE X AND Y FILES

WHAT IS THE NAME OF YOUR X FILE?
?CH15\7EX
THERE ARE     5 COLUMNS AND    18   ROWS IN THIS FILE
WHAT IS THE NAME OF YOUR Y FILE?
?CH17EY
HOW MANY FACTORS ARE IN YOUR MODEL?(UP TO 28)
?5
  FROM YOUR ORIGINAL INPUT MATRIX WHICH COLUMNS OR FACTORS
ARE INCLUDED IN THE MODEL?  LIST THEM IN THE ORDER OF
MODEL BUILDING
INPUT THE FACTOR'S COLUMN #   ?1
NAME OF FACTOR #   1  ?TEMPERATURE
INPUT THE FACTOR'S COLUMN #   ?4
NAME OF FACTOR #   4  ?TEMP**2
INPUT THE FACTOR'S COLUMN #   ?2
NAME OF FACTOR #   2  ?CONCENTRATION
INPUT THE FACTOR'S COLUMN #   ?3
NAME OF FACTOR #   3  ?SPEED
INPUT THE FACTOR'S COLUMN #   ?5
NAME OF FACTOR #   5  ?CONC*SPEED
ENTER THE NUMBER OF ROWS OF DATA IN YOUR MODEL
?18
DO YOU WANT TO DELETE ANY ROWS OF DATA  ?N
ENTER THE T VALUE FOR DF=   12  ?2.1788


COEFFICIENTS
INTERCEPT B(0)=   -1100.68
TEMPERATURE    10.0284
TEMP**2   -2.51276E-02
CONCENTRATION    19.9107
SPEED   -14.7090
CONC*SPEED  -.100000

ANOVA
TOTAL SUM OF SQUARES:     372802.
REG SUM OF SQ;    372754.  DF=   5  MS=   74550.8
RESIDUAL SUM OF SQUARES:     48.4137  DF=   12  MS=    4.03448
THE OVERALL F RATIO FOR THIS REGRESSION IS:    18478.4

CALCULATED VALUES   INPUT VALUES    RESIDUAL
     231.95867        230.000000     -1.95867
     381.36850        384.000000      2.63150
     521.61850        520.000000     -1.61850
     671.02834        670.000000     -1.02834
     178.83162        180.000000      1.16838
     328.24145        330.000000      1.75855
     463.99145        465.000000      1.00855
     613.40129        612.000000     -1.40129
     259.09263        260.000000      0.90737
     508.10903        507.000000     -1.10903
     206.91162        206.000000     -0.91162
     685.92801        689.000000      3.07199
     492.56735        495.000000      2.43265
     400.27227        400.000000     -0.27227
     446.41981        446.000000     -0.41981
     446.41981        445.000000     -1.41981
     446.41981        446.000000     -0.41981
     446.41981        444.000000     -2.41981


STANDARD ERROR OF THE ESTIMATE=    2.00860


STD. ERROR OF COEFFICIENTS & T TEST VALUES
B(0) STD.ERROR=    22.7401
B    1   .185014  TEMPERATURE    T=   54.2036
B    2   6.13729E-04  TEMP**2    T=  -40.9425
B    3   .478987  CONCENTRATION  T=   41.5682
B    4   2.39494  SPEED   T=  -6.14172
B    5   6.31242E-02  CONC*SPEED  T=  -1.58418

R SQUARED=    .999870
```

Now we do the regression using the PREDICT program. Load "PREDICT" and then RUN.

Follow the questions to set up the correct model.

The "t" value is needed to calculate the confidence intervals on the results.

The ANOVA and residuals check the "goodness" of the equation derived.

The "t" tests check the goodness of each coefficient in the equation.

APPENDIX 17-II

Regression Coefficients From Half Effects

In Table 17-2 the YATES ANOVA gives us the half effects. Now, remember that these values are regression coefficients, but they are in terms of design units. Back in Chapter 4 we showed how the design units were related to physical units. Recall that the design units of a two-level factorial design are derived in general by the following expression:

$$\text{Design Unit} = \frac{X_{level} - \overline{X}_{of\,levels}}{\dfrac{X_{high} - X_{low}}{2}}$$

For the example in Chapter 17 then, the temperature factor would fit into this equation as follows:

$$\text{low design unit} = \frac{120 - 150}{30} = -1$$

$$\text{high design unit} = \frac{180 - 150}{30} = +1$$

The above relationships can be used to decode the design unit half effects into physical unit regression coefficients. You should notice that the regression coefficients in expression 17-6 do not match the half effects in Table 17-1. That's because the coefficients in 17-6 are in physical units and the half effects are in design units (ie: -1 and $+1$). To make the transition from the design units to physical units, we first write the equation down in terms of the half effects from Table 17-2. We will use only the significant terms to keep the math down to a minimum.

The equation is:

$$Y = 423.875 + 75.125 * \text{Temp.} + 142.875 * \text{Conc.} - 27.125 * \text{Speed} - 1.125 * \text{Conc.} * \text{Speed}$$

Now we substitute the design unit expressions into each term.

$$Y = 423.875 + 75.125 * ((T - 150)/30) + 142.875 * ((C - 37.5)/7.5)$$

$$- 27.125 * ((S - 7.5)/1.5)$$

$$- 1.125 * ((C - 37.5)/7.5) * ((S - 7.5)/1.5)$$

$$Y = 423.875 + \frac{75.125\ T - 11268.75}{30} + \frac{142.875\ C - 5357.8125}{7.5}$$

$$- \frac{27.125\ S + 203.4375}{1.5}$$

$$- 1.125 \left(\frac{(C - 37.5) * (S - 7.5)}{11.25} \right)$$

$$Y = 423.875 + 2.504\ T - 375.625 + 19.05\ C - 714.375$$

$$- 18.08\ S + 135.62$$

$$- 1.125 \left(\frac{SC - 37.5\ S - 7.5\ C + 281.25}{11.25} \right)$$

$$Y = 423.875 + 2.504T - 375.625 + 19.05C - 714.375 - 18.08S + 135.62$$
$$- .10SC + 3.75\ S + .75\ C - 28.125$$

Gather up terms:

$$Y = 558.63 + 2.504T + 19.8\ C - 14.33 * S - 0.1 * SC$$

Now this equation is still different from the regression equation found in 17-6. The main source of difference is the lack of the quadratic term for temperature afforded by the use of the data from the composite portion of the experiment. The b_0 term is also different, but this term is always fluctuating since it is a centering factor. This shows the value of the full CCD experiment as opposed to only a two-level experiment.The technique we have just demonstrated shows that it is possible to do a complete regression without the use of a computer! The reason for this is, of course, the fact that the design we have is <u>orthogonal</u>. This orthogonality reduces the really tough (matrix inversion) part of the regression computation to a simple algorithm.

EDITOR PROGRAM

```
10 CLS
15 CLEAR
20 PRINT TAB( 10):"FILE BUILDER/EDITOR"
26 PRINT
30 PRINT TAB( 9): "MENU"
40 PRINT   "<1> BUILD NEW FILE"
50 PRINT "<2> EDIT EXISTING FILE"
55 PRINT "<3> VIEW FILE"
60 PRINT "<4> AUGMENT FILE WITH TRANSFORMATIONS"
65 PRINT "<5> END"
66 PRINT
70 INPUT "MAKE SELECTION FROM ABOVE BY #";S1
80 ON S1 GOTO 100,500,800,900,3000
90 PRINT "TRY AGAIN":GOTO 70
```

```
100 CLS
110 INPUT "WHAT'S THE NAME OF YOUR NEW FILE";B$
120 OPEN "O",1,B$
130 INPUT "HOW MANY ROWS OF DATA";R
140 INPUT "HOW MANY COLUMNS OF DATA"; C
141 PRINT #1,R,C
145 PRINT "ENTER THE DATA ROW WISE"
150 FOR I=1 TO R: FOR J=1 TO C:PRINT "ROW";I;"COL";J;: INPUT X1
160 PRINT #1,X1;:NEXT J:NEXT I
170 CLOSE:GOTO 10
500 CLS
510 INPUT "FILE NAME TO BE EDITED";B$
520 OPEN "I",1,B$
525 INPUT #1,R,C
530 PRINT "ROWS OF DATA=";R
540 PRINT "COLUMNS OF DATA=";C
550 DIM X(R,C)
555 IF S1=3 GOTO 845
560 FOR I=1 TO R:FOR J=1 TO C:INPUT #1,X(I,J)
590 NEXT J:NEXT I
595 CLOSE
600 PRINT "WHICH DATA POINTS DO YOU WANT TO EDIT?"
610 INPUT "ENTER THE ROW # AND THE COL #: R,C";I,K
615 PRINT "THE OLD VALUE IS:";X(I,K)
620 INPUT "NEW VALUE";X(I,K)
630 INPUT "MORE EDITING <YES/NO>"; W$
640 IF LEFT$(W$,1)="Y" THEN 600
645 OPEN "O",1, B$
647 PRINT #1,R,C
650 FOR I=1 TO R:FOR J=1 TO C:PRINT #1,X(I,J):NEXT J:NEXT I
670 CLOSE
680 GOTO 10
800 CLS
830 INPUT "FILE NAME TO BE VIEWED";B$
835 CLOSE
840 GOTO 520
845 PRINT "TO CONTINUE LIST PRESS <RETURN>"
850 FOR I=1 TO R:PRINT :IMOD=I-INT(I/4)*4: PRINT I"--";:FOR J=1 TO C:INPUT #1
I,J):PRINT X(I,J);
855 NEXT J
860 IF IMOD<>0 THEN 870
865 A$=INKEY$:INPUT " ",A$
870 NEXT I
871 PRINT
875 PRINT "PRESS <RETURN> IF YOU ARE FINISHED VIEWING";
876 A$=INKEY$:INPUT " ",A$
880 GOTO 10
900 CLS
910 INPUT "FILE NAME TO BE TRANSFORMED";B$:CLOSE
920 OPEN "I",1,B$
930 INPUT #1,R,C
940 PRINT "ROWS OF DATA=";R;"COLS OF DATA=";C
942 INPUT "ARE YOU ADDING ANY NEW ROWS OF DATA";W$
943 IF LEFT$(W$,1)<>"Y" THEN 950
945 INPUT "HOW MANY NEW ROWS OF DATA";NR
947 GOTO 965
950 INPUT "HOW MANY NEW COLUMNS ARE YOU ADDING";NC
960 C=C+NC
965 IF LEFT$(W$,1)="Y" THEN NC=0:R=R+NR
970 DIM X(R,C)
980 FOR I=1 TO R-NR:FOR J=1 TO C-NC:INPUT #1,X(I,J):NEXT J:NEXT I
985 IF LEFT$(W$,1)="Y" GOTO 2500
990 FOR K=1 TO NC:CLS:PRINT "LIST OF TRANSFORMS"
1000 PRINT "<1> LOG(10)":PRINT "<2> LN"
1010 PRINT "<3> X SQUARED":PRINT "<4> X CUBED"
1020 PRINT "<5> CROSS PRODUCT OF 2 X'S":PRINT "<6> 1/X"
```

```
1030 PRINT "<7> SQUARE ROOT OF X":PRINT "<8> SCALE X"
1040 PRINT   "<9> ADD A NEW VARIABLE"
1050 PRINT:INPUT "ENTER TRANSFORM CHOICE (ie:#  )";S2
1055 IF S2<>9 THEN INPUT "ENTER COLUMN # TO BE TRANSFORMED";S3
1056 PRINT "THIS WILL BECOME COLUMN:";C-NC+K
1057 IF S2=5 THEN INPUT "WHAT'S THE OTHER VARIABLE IN THE CROSS PRODUCT";S4
1058 IF S2=8 THEN INPUT "WHAT IS THE SCALE FACTOR YOU WILL MULTIPLY BY";S8
1059 PRINT "PRESS <RETURN> TO CONTINUE"
1060 A$=INKEY$:INPUT " ",A$
1065 FOR I=1 TO R
1070 ON S2 GOSUB 1200,1300,1400,1500,1600,1700,1800,1900,2000
1080 NEXT I:NEXT K
1090 CLOSE:OPEN "O",1,B$:PRINT #1,R,C
1100 FOR I=1 TO R:FOR J=1 TO C: PRINT #1,X(I,J):NEXT J:NEXT I:PRINT CHR$(26)
1110 GOTO 10
1200 X(I,C-NC+K)=LOG(X(I,S3))/LOG(10):RETURN
1300 X(I,C-NC+K)=LOG(X(I,S3)):RETURN
1400 X(I,C-NC+K)=X(I,S3)*X(I,S3):RETURN
1500 X(I,C-NC+K)=X(I,S3)*X(I,S3)*X(I,S3):RETURN
1600 X(I,C-NC+K)=X(I,S3)*X(I,S4):RETURN
1700 X(I,C-NC+K)=1/X(I,S3):RETURN
1800 X(I,C-NC+K)=SQR(X(I,S3)):RETURN
1900 X(I,C-NC+K)=S8*X(I,S3):RETURN
2000 PRINT "ENTER DATA FOR YOUR NEW VARIABLE"
2010 PRINT"ROW#";I;:INPUT X1
2020 X(I,C-NC+K)=X1:RETURN
2500 PRINT "ENTER NEW DATA"
2510 FOR I=1 TO NR:FOR J=1 TO C
2520 PRINT "ROW#";R-NR+I;"COL#";J;:INPUT X1
2530 X(R-NR+I,J)=X1:NEXT J:NEXT I
2540 GOTO 1090
3000 END
```

REGRESSION PROGRAM

```
90 CLS
100 PRINT TAB(13);"THE PREDICTOR":PRINT TAB(7);"AN EMPIRICAL MODEL BUILDER"
120 PRINT TAB( 9);"BASED ON LEAST SQUARES":PRINT TAB( 15);"REGRESSION"
160 PRINT   "PRESS <RETURN> TO CONTINUE";
180 MASK$=INKEY$:INPUT " ",MASK$
200 CLEAR 400:PRINT CHR$(26)
210 DEFDBL A,P,D,Y,G
215 DEFINT I,J,K
220 PRINT "DO YOU WANT TO CONSTRUCT A SIMPLE ONE"
240 INPUT "FACTOR MODEL, IE.: Y=B(0)+B(1)*X";I$:IF LEFT$(I$,1)="Y" THEN I4=1
280 INPUT "DO YOU WANT TO PRINT RESULTS ON LINE PRINTER";LP$
290 IF I4=1 THEN 520
300 INPUT "WHAT IS THE NAME OF YOUR X FILE";F$
320 OPEN "I",1,F$
340 INPUT #1,R,C
350 PRINT "THIS FILE ";F$;" HAS";R;"ROWS OF DATA AND";C;"COLUMNS OR FACTORS"
360 DIM M(R,C),V(28),Q(125),Y1(R),V$(28)
380 V$(0)="INTERCEPT"
400 FOR I=1 TO R:FOR J=1 TO C:INPUT #1,M(I,J):NEXT J:NEXT I
420 INPUT "WHAT'S THE NAME OF YOUR Y INPUT FILE";E$
440 CLOSE:OPEN "I",1,E$
460 INPUT #1,Y6,Y7
480 FOR I=1 TO R:INPUT #1,Y1(I):NEXT I
500 IF I4<>1 THEN 820
520 INPUT "HOW MANY ROWS (OBSERVATIONS)";R
540 W$="YES":I7=1:PRINT "INDICATE THE NUMBER OF FACTORS"
560 PRINT "IN YOUR SIMPLE MODEL. YOU MAY DO"
580 PRINT "A SECOND ORDER FIT (IE.:X SQUARED)"
600 INPUT "THEN ENTER 3 OTHERWISE ENTER 2";C
```

```
620 Z9=C-1
640 INPUT "WHAT'S THE NAME OF YOUR X FACTOR";V$(1)
660 IF C=3 THEN V$(2)="YOUR X FACTOR SQUARED"
680 PRINT "ENTER YOUR DATA"
700 DIM X#(R,C),A1(R),T#(C,R),P(C,C),NN#(C,C),Y(R),Z#(R),B#(R),G(R),CM#(C,C),SM#
(C),CR#(C,C)
720 FOR I1=1 TO R:PRINT "X(";I1;")";:INPUT T9:PRINT TAB( 14);"Y(";I1;")";:INPU
T Y(I1)
740 X#(I1,1)=1
760 X#(I1,2)=T9
780 IF C=3 THEN X#(I1,3)=T9*T9
800 NEXT I1
820 IF I4=1 THEN 1820
840 INPUT "HOW MANY FACTORS IN YOUR MODEL ";Z9
860 PRINT "FROM YOUR ORIGINAL INPUT MATRIX WHICH "
880 PRINT "FACTORS ARE INCLUDED IN THE MODEL"
900 PRINT "LIST THEM IN  ORDER OF MODEL BUILDING."
920 FOR I=1 TO Z9:INPUT "FACTOR #";V(I):INPUT"FACTOR NAME";V$(I):NEXT I
940 FOR I=1 TO 45
960 Q(I)=0:NEXT I
980 INPUT "DO YOU WANT A B(0) TERM <YES/NO>";W$
1000 INPUT "ENTER THE # OF ROWS LEFT AFTER DELETIONS";R
1020 IF LEFT$(W$,1)="Y" THEN C=Z9+1 ELSE C=Z9
1040 IF LEFT$(W$,1)="Y" THEN I7=1 ELSE I7=0
1060 DIM X#(R,C),Y(R),X(R,C)
1080 IF LEFT$(W$,1)="N" THEN 1120
1100 FOR I=1 TO R:X#(I,1)=1:NEXT I
1120 INPUT "DO YOU WANT TO DELETE ANY ROWS";I$
1130 IF LEFT$(I$,1)<>"Y" THEN 1240
1140 PRINT "(NO MORE THAN 3 CONSECUTIVE ROWS)"
1160 INPUT "ENTER ONE ROW # AT A TIME   END WITH 999";R1
1180 IF R1=999 THEN 1240
1200 Q(R1)=R1
1220 GOTO 1160
1240 INPUT "DO YOU WANT TO SEE THE X MATRIX <YES/NO>";W1$
1241 IF LEFT$(LP$,1)<>"Y" THEN GOTO 1280
1242 IF LEFT$(W1$,1)="Y" THEN LPRINT "THIS IS YOUR MATRIX:"
1280 IF LEFT$(W1$,1)="Y" THEN PRINT "THIS IS YOUR X MATRIX:"
1300 I1=1
1320 FOR I=1 TO R
1330 X(I,1)=X#(I,1)
1331 IF LEFT$(LP$,1)<>"Y" THEN GOTO 1340
1332 IF LEFT$(W1$,1)="Y" AND LEFT$(W$,1)="Y" THEN LPRINT I;X(I,1);
1333 IF LEFT$(W1$,1)="Y" AND LEFT$(W$,1)<>"Y" THEN LPRINT I;
1340 IF LEFT$(W1$,1)="Y"AND LEFT$(W$,1)="Y"THEN PRINT I;X(I,1);
1360 IF LEFT$(W1$,1)="Y" AND LEFT$(W$,1)<>"Y" THEN PRINT I;
1380 IF Q(I1)=0 THEN 1420
1400 I1=I1+1
1420 IF Q(I1)=0 THEN 1460
1440 I1=I1+1
1460 IF Q(I1)=0 THEN 1500
1480 I1=I1+1
1500 FOR I2=1 TO Z9
1520 C1=V(I2)
1540 IF LEFT$(W$,1)="Y" THEN I3=I2+1 ELSE I3=I2
1560 X#(I,I3)=M(I1,C1)
1580 Y(I)=Y1(I1)
1590 X(I,I3)=X#(I,I3)
1591 IF LEFT$(LP$,1)<>"Y" THEN GOTO 1600
1592 IF LEFT$(W1$,1)="Y" THEN LPRINT X(I,I3);
1600 IF LEFT$(W1$,1)="Y" THEN PRINT X(I,I3);
1620 NEXT I2
1640 A$="#######.#######"
1660 I1=I1+1
1670 IF LEFT$(LP$,1)<>"Y" THEN GOTO 1680
1671 IF LEFT$(W1$,1)="Y" THEN LPRINT "Y=";:Y6=Y(I):LPRINT Y6
1680 IF LEFT$(W1$,1)="Y" THEN PRINT "Y=";:Y6=Y(I):PRINT Y6:IMOD=I-INT(I/12)*12
1700 IF IMOD<>0 THEN 1780
1720 IF LEFT$(W1$,1)="Y" THEN PRINT "PRESS <RETURN> TO CONTINUE";
```

```
1740 IF LEFT$(W1$,1)<>"Y" GOTO 1780
1760 MASK$=INKEY$:INPUT " ",MASK$
1780 NEXT I
1800 DIM A1(R),T#(C,R),P(C,C),NN#(C,C),Z#(R),B#(R),G(R)
1810 DIM CM#(C,C),SM#(C),CR#(C,C)
1820 FOR J=1 TO C:FOR I=1 TO R:T#(J,I)=X#(I,J):SM#(J)=SM#(J)+X#(I,J):NEXT I:NEXT
J
1860 PRINT "PRESS <RETURN> TO CONTINUE";
1880 MASK$=INKEY$:INPUT " ",MASK$
1900 CLS:PRINT "COMPUTING: PLEASE WAIR"
1920 S2=0
1940 FOR I=1 TO R:S2=S2+Y(I):NEXT I
1960 D1=S2/R
1980 FOR I=1 TO C:FOR J=1 TO C:P(I,J)=0
2000 FOR K=1 TO R:P(I,J)=P(I,J)+T#(I,K)*X#(K,J):NEXT K:NEXT J:NEXT I
2020 S1=0:S3=0:S4=0
2030 IF I4=1 THEN 2060
2040 INPUT "WANT THE CORRELATION MATRIX";W2$
2060 IF LEFT$(W2$,1)<>"Y" THEN 2200
2100 IF LEFT$(W$,1)="Y" THEN I1=2 ELSE I1=1
2120 IF LEFT$(W$,1)="Y" THEN I2=1 ELSE I2=0
2130 PRINT "THAT WILL TAKE A BIT LONGER"
2140 FOR I=I1 TO C:FOR J=I1 TO C:CM#(I,J)=P(I,J)-((SM#(I)*SM#(J))/R):NEXT J:NEXT
I
2150 IF LEFT$(LP$,1)<>"Y" THEN GOTO 2160
2151 LPRINT:LPRINT "CORRELATION MATRIX INFORMATION:"
2160 FOR I=I1 TO C:FOR J=I1 TO C:CR#(I,J)=CM#(I,J)/(SQR(CM#(I,I)*CM#(J,J))):NEXT
J:NEXT I
2180 PRINT:PRINT "CORRELATION MATRIX INFORMATION:":FOR I=I1 TO C
2185 IF LEFT$(LP$,1)<>"Y" THEN GOTO 2190
2186 LPRINT "FACTOR#";I-I2:FOR J=I1 TO C:W6=CR#(I,J):LPRINT J-I2;W6:NEXT J
2190 PRINT "FACTOR#";I-I2:FOR J=I1 TO C:W6=CR#(I,J):PRINT J-I2;W6:NEXT J
2191 IMOD=II-INT(II/12)*12:IF IMOD<>0 THEN 2195:II=II+1
2192 PRINT "PRESS <RETURN> TO CONTINUE";
2193 MASK$=INKEY$:INPUT " ",MASK$
2195 NEXT I
2200 I1=C:J1=C
2210 PRINT "INVERTING MATRIX"
2215 PRINT "PLEASE WAIT"
2220 GOSUB 4800
2240 C=I1
2260 FOR I=1 TO C:Z#(I)=0
2280 FOR K=1 TO R:Z#(I)=Z#(I)+T#(I,K)*Y(K):NEXT K:NEXT I
2300 FOR I=1 TO C:B#(I)=0
2320 FOR K=1 TO C:B#(I)=B#(I)+NN#(I,K)*Z#(K):NEXT K:NEXT I
2340 G2=0:FOR I=1 TO C:G2=B#(I)*Z#(I)+G2:NEXT I
2360 G2=G2-R*D1*D1
2380 CLS
2400 IF LEFT$(LP$,1)<>"Y" THEN GOTO 2420
2404 LPRINT:LPRINT
2405 LPRINT "RESULTS OF REGRESSION WITH"
2407 LPRINT Z9;"FACTOR(S) AND"
2410 LPRINT R;"OBSERVATIONS":LPRINT
2415 LPRINT "COEFFICIENTS AND YOUR EQUATION:"
2420 PRINT "RESULTS OF REGRESSION WITH"
2440 PRINT Z9;"FACTOR(S) AND"
2460 PRINT R;"OBSERVATIONS":PRINT
2480 PRINT "COEFFICIENTS AND YOUR EQUATION:"
2500 G1=0:FOR I=1 TO R:G1=Y(I)*Y(I)+G1:NEXT I
2520 G1=G1-R*D1*D1
2540 R3#=G1-G2
2560 IF I4=1 THEN Z9=C-1
2580 A$="######.##########   ##  ######.######  ###.###"
2600 FOR I=1 TO C:IF LEFT$(W$,1)<>"Y" THEN I5=I ELSE I5=I-1
2620 IF I4=1 THEN I5=I-1
2630 IF LEFT$(LP$,1)<>"Y" THEN GOTO 2640
2632 LPRINT "B(";I5;")=";:LPRINT USING A$;B#(I);:LPRINT "   ";V$(I5)
2640 PRINT "B(";I5;")=";:PRINT USING A$;B#(I);:PRINT "   ";V$(I5):NEXT I
2660 PRINT "PRESS <RETURN> TO CONTINUE";
```

```
2680 MASK$=INKEY$:INPUT " ",MASK$
2690 PRINT:PRINT
2700 PRINT "ANOVA"
2710 IF LEFT$(LP$,1)<>"Y" THEN GOTO 2720
2711 LPRINT:LPRINT:LPRINT "ANOVA"
2712 LPRINT TAB(15);"SUM OF SQUARES";TAB(31);"DF";TAB(37);"MEAN SQUARE";TAB(51);
"F RATIO"
2713 LPRINT "TOTAL        ";:LPRINT USING A$;G1;R-I7
2714 LPRINT "REGRESSION ";:LPRINT USING A$;G2,Z9;G2/Z9;(G2/Z9)/(R3#/(R-I7-Z9))
2715 LPRINT "RESIDUAL     ";:LPRINT USING A$;R3#,R-I7-Z9;R3#/(R-I7-Z9)
2716 LPRINT
2717 LPRINT "STANDARD ERROR OF THE ESTIMATE: S(Y.X)=";
2718 S5=SQR(ABS(R3#/(R-I7-Z9))):LPRINT S5
2720 PRINT TAB(15);"SUM OF SQUARES";TAB(31);"DF";TAB(37);"MEAN SQUARE";TAB(51);"
F RATIO"
2740 PRINT "TOTAL        ";:PRINT USING A$;G1,R-I7
2760 PRINT "REGRESSION ";:PRINT USING A$;G2,Z9;G2/Z9;(G2/Z9)/(R3#/(R-I7-Z9))
2780 PRINT "RESIDUAL     ";:PRINT USING A$;R3#,R-I7-Z9;R3#/(R-I7-Z9)
2795 PRINT
2800 PRINT "STANDARD ERROR OF THE ESTIMATE: S(Y.X)=";
2820 S5=SQR(ABS(R3#/(R-I7-Z9))):PRINT S5:INPUT "DO YOU WANT RESIDUALS";W1$
2840 IF LEFT$(W1$,1)<>"Y" THEN 3140
2860 FOR J=1 TO R:A1(J)=0
2880 FOR K=1 TO C:A1(J)=A1(J)+X#(J,K)*B#(K):NEXT K:NEXT J
2881 IF LEFT$(LP$,1)<>"Y" THEN GOTO 2900
2882 LPRINT:LPRINT
2883 LPRINT "RUN #  CALCULATED VALUES      INPUT VALUES       RESIDUAL"
2900 PRINT  "RUN #  CALCULATED VALUES      INPUT VALUES       RESIDUAL"
2920 A$=" ###   ######.#####       ######.#####    ######.#####"
2940 FOR J=1 TO R: G(J)=Y(J)-A1(J)
2950 IF LEFT$(LP$,1)<>"Y" THEN GOTO 2960
2951 LPRINT USING A$;J,A1(J),Y(J),G(J)
2960 PRINT USING A$;J,A1(J),Y(J),G(J)
2980 IMOD=J-INT(J/12)*12
3000 IF IMOD<>0 THEN 3060
3020 PRINT "PRESS <RETURN> TO CONTINUE"
3040 MASK$=INKEY$:INPUT " ",MASK$
3060 NEXT J
3100 PRINT "PRESS <RETURN> TO CONTINUE";
3120 MASK$=INKEY$:INPUT " ",MASK$
3140 FOR I=1 TO C:FOR J=1 TO C: P#(I,J)=S5*S5*NN#(I,J):NEXT J:NEXT I
3150 IF LEFT$(LP$,1)<>"Y" THEN GOTO 3180
3154 LPRINT:LPRINT
3155 LPRINT "STANDARD ERROR OF THE COEFFICIENTS"
3180 PRINT "STANDARD ERROR OF THE COEFFICIENTS"
3200 FOR I=1 TO C:IF LEFT$(W$,1)<>"Y" THEN I5=I ELSE I5=I-1
3220 IF I4=1 THEN I5=I-1
3225 A$="#####.########"
3230 IF LEFT$(LP$,1)<>"Y" THEN GOTO 3240
3231 LPRINT "B(";I5;")";:LPRINT USING A$;SQR(P#(I,I))
3240 PRINT "B(";I5;")=";:PRINT USING A$;SQR(P#(I,I))
3260 NEXT I
3280 A$="####.##"
3290 IF LEFT$(LP$,1)<>"Y" THEN GOTO 3300
3291 LPRINT:LPRINT "R SQUARED=";:LPRINT USING A$;G2/G1*100;:LPRINT "%"
3292 LPRINT:LPRINT "MULTIPLE R=";SQR(G2/G1)
3300 PRINT:PRINT "R SQUARED=";:PRINT USING A$;G2/G1*100;:PRINT "%"
3320 PRINT:PRINT "MULTIPLE R=";  SQR(G2/G1)
3360 PRINT "END OF CALCULATIONS":PRINT "PRESS <RETURN> TO CONTINUE";
3380 MASK$=INKEY$:INPUT " ",MASK$
3400 PRINT "YOU HAVE JUST DERIVED A ":PRINT"PREDICTOR EQUATION FOR THE";Z9:PRINT
"FACTOR(S) YOU IDENTIFIED"
3420 PRINT "YOU SHOULD TEST EACH ":PRINT"TERM IN YOUR EQUATION FOR"
3440 PRINT "STATISTICAL SIGNIFICANCE. TO HELP"
3460 PRINT "WITH THIS TEST THE FOLLOWING 'T TESTS'"
3480 PRINT "HAVE BEEN COMPUTED ON EACH TERM:"
3500 IF LEFT$(LP$,1)<>"Y" THEN GOTO 3520
3510 LPRINT:LPRINT
3515 LPRINT "'T' TEST STATISTICS"
```

```
3520 IF LEFT$(W$,1)="Y"THEN P9=2 ELSE P9=1
3540 FOR I=P9 TO C:IF LEFT$(W$,1)<>"Y" THEN I5=I ELSE I5=I-1
3545 A$="####.###"
3550 IF LEFT$(LP$,1)<>"Y" THEN GOTO 3560
3552 LPRINT V$(I5);:LPRINT TAB(30);"T=";
3560 PRINT V$(I5);:PRINT TAB(10);"T=";
3580 A$="####.###"
3590 IF LEFT$(LP$,1)<>"Y" THEN GOTO 3600
3595 LPRINT USING A$;B#(I)/SQR(P(I,I))
3600 PRINT USING A$;B#(I)/SQR(P(I,I)):NEXT I:PRINT
3640 PRINT "PRESS <RETURN> TO CONTINUE";
3660 MASK$=INKEY$:INPUT " ",MASK$
3680 PRINT "IF ANY OF THE 'T' VALUES FALL BELOW "
3700 PRINT "AN ABSOLUTE VALUE OF 2 (-2 TO +2)"
3720 PRINT "YOU SHOULD CONSIDER RERUNNING THE PROBLEM"
3740 PRINT "EXCLUDING THESE FACTORS"
3760 PRINT "PRESS <RETURN> TO CONTINUE";
3780 MASK$=INKEY$:INPUT " ",MASK$
3800 IF LEFT$(W2$,1)<>"Y" THEN 3920
3810 PRINT "WAIT A MOMENT"
3821 IF LEFT$(W$,1)="Y" THEN I1=1 ELSE I1=0
3822 FOR I=I1+1 TO C:FOR J=1+I1 TO C:P(I-I1,J-I1)=CR#(I,J):NEXT J:NEXT I
3824 I1=Z9:C7=1:J1=Z9
3826 GOSUB 4980
3840 CLS:PRINT "HERS'S SOME MORE INFO ON YOUR DATA":PRINT "THE VARIANCE INFLATIO
N FACTORS (VIF'S)"
3860 C=I1+1
3870 IF LEFT$(W$,1)<>"Y" THEN C=Z9
3900 FOR I=1 TO Z9:PRINT "B(";I;")=";:PRINT USING A$;P(I,I):NEXT I
3920 INPUT "DO YOU WISH TO CONTINUE <YES/NO>";W2$
3940 IF LEFT$(W2$,1)="N"  THEN GOTO 4160
3960 PRINT "HERE'S YOUR EQUATION AGAIN":PRINT:PRINT "Y = ";
3980 A$="######.#######"
3990 PRINT USING A$;B#(I)
4000 FOR I=2 TO C:IF LEFT$(W$,1)<>"Y" THEN I5=I ELSE I5=I-1
4020 IF SGN(B#(I))=-1 THEN A1$="   -" ELSE A1$="   +"
4040 IF I>1 THEN PRINT A1$;
4060 PRINT USING A$;ABS(B#(I));:IF I5>=1 OR LEFT$(W$,1)<>"Y" THEN PRINT " * ";V$
(I5)
4080 NEXT I
4100 PRINT:PRINT:INPUT"WANT TO TRY YOUR EQUATION OUT";W2$
4120 DIM XK(C)
4140 IF LEFT$(W2$,1)="Y"GOTO 4180
4160 PRINT "THANK YOU FOR USING THE PREDICTOR":END
4180 PRINT "ENTER THE VALUE FOR EACH FACTOR":XY=0
4200 IF LEFT$(W$,1)="Y" OR  I4=1  THEN CC=1 ELSE CC=0
4220 XK(CC)=1
4230 IF LEFT$(LP$,1)<>"Y" THEN GOTO 4240
4235 LPRINT:LPRINT
4236 LPRINT "FOR THE EQUATION WITH THE FOLOWING SUBSTITUTED VALUES:"
4237 LPRINT
4240 FOR I=P9 TO C:IF LEFT$(W$,1)<>"Y" THEN I5=I ELSE I5=I-1
4260 PRINT V$(I5);:INPUT X8
4265 IF LEFT$(LP$,1)<>"Y" THEN GOTO 4280
4266 LPRINT V$(I5);"=";X8
4280 XK(I)=X8
4300 XY=XY+X8*B#(I):NEXT I
4320 IF LEFT$(W$,1)="Y" THEN XY=XY+B#(1)
4340 FOR I=1 TO C:Z#(I)=0
4360 FOR K=1 TO C:Z#(I)=Z#(I)+XK(K)*NN#(I,K):NEXT K:NEXT I
4380 SC=0:FOR I=1 TO C:SC=Z#(I)*XK(I)+SC:NEXT I
4400 VS=SQR((1+SC)*S5*S5):L6=XY-VS*2:H6=XY+VS*2
4410 IF LEFT$(LP$,1)<>"Y" THEN GOTO 4420
4411 LPRINT:LPRINT "THE PREDICTED VALUE IS:";XY
4412 LPRINT "WITH A 95% CONFIDENCE INTERVAL OF:";
4413 LPRINT L6;"TO";H6
4420 PRINT "THE PREDICTED VALUE IS:";XY
4440 PRINT "WITH A 95% CONFIDENCE INTERVAL OF:";
4460 PRINT L6;"TO";H6
```

```
4480 INPUT "WANT TO TRY ANOTHER <YES/NO>";W2$
4500 IF LEFT$(W2$,1)<>"N" GOTO 4180 ELSE GOTO 4160
4800 DIM A#(I1,I1),AB#(I1,I1)
4980 FOR J=1 TO I1:FOR I=1 TO I1
5000 A#(J,I)=P(I,J)
5020 NEXT I:AB#(J,J)=1:NEXT J
5040 FOR J=1 TO I1:FOR I=J TO I1
5060 IF A#(I,J)<>0 THEN 5120
5080 NEXT I
5100 PRINT "SINGULAR MATRIX":END
5120 FOR K=1 TO I1
5140 S#=A#(J,K):A#(J,K)=A#(I,K):A#(I,K)=S#:S#=AB#(J,K):AB#(J,K)=AB#(I,K):AB#(I,K
)=S#
5160 NEXT K
5180 TT#=1/A#(J,J)
5200 FOR K=1 TO I1
5220 A#(J,K)=TT#*A#(J,K)
5230 AB#(J,K)=TT#*AB#(J,K)
5240 NEXT K
5260 FOR L=1 TO I1
5280 IF L=J THEN 5400
5300 TT#=-A#(L,J)
5320 FOR K=1 TO I1
5340 A#(L,K)=A#(L,K)+TT#*A#(J,K)
5360 AB#(L,K)=AB#(L,K)+TT#*AB#(J,K)
5380 NEXT K
5400 NEXT L
5420 NEXT J
5500 FOR I=1 TO I1:FOR J=1 TO I1
5520 NN#(I,J)=AB#(I,J):P(I,J)=AB#(I,J)
5540 NEXT J:NEXT I
5560 RETURN




READY
>LOAD "PREDICT"
READY
>RUN
              THE PREDICTOR
        AN EMPIRICAL MODEL BUILDER
          BASED ON LEAST SQUARES
              REGRESSION

PRESS <C> TO CONTINUE
DO YOU WANT TO CONSTRUCT A SIMPLE ONE
FACTOR MODEL, IE. ' Y=B(0)+B(1)*X? YES
DO YOU WANT TO PRINT RESULTS ON LINE PRINTER? Y
HOW MANY ROWS (OBSERVATIONS)? 10
INDICATE THE NUMBER OF FACTORS
IN YOUR SIMPLE MODEL. YOU MAY DO
A SECOND ORDER FIT (IE. 'X SQUARED)
THEN ENTER 3 OTHERWISE ENTER 2? 3
WHAT'S THE NAME OF YOUR X FACTOR? TIME
ENTER YOUR DATA
X( 1 )'? 1
                    Y( 1 )'? 3
X( 2 )'? 2
                    Y( 2 )'? 6
X( 3 )'? 3
                    Y( 3 )'? 9
X( 4 )'? 4
                    Y( 4 )'? 16
X( 5 )'? 5
                    Y( 5 )'? 24
X( 6 )'? 6
```

```
X( 7 )·? 7        Y( 6 )·? 38

X( 8 )·? 8        Y( 7 )·? 45

X( 9 )·? 9        Y( 8 )·? 62

X( 10 )·? 10      Y( 9 )·? 78

                  Y( 10 )·? 95
```

RESULTS OF REGRESSION WITH
2 FACTOR(S) AND
10 OBSERVATIONS

COEFFICIENTS AND YOUR EQUATION:
```
B( 0 )=    2.166667
B( 1 )=   -0.292424  TIME
B( 2 )=    0.962121  YOUR X FACTOR SQUARED
```

PRESS <C> TO CONTINUE
ANOVA
```
              SUM OF SQUARES DF    MEAN SQUARE
TOTAL        9242.401147   9
REGRESSION   9225.740541   2    4612.870271
RESIDUAL       16.660606   7       2.380087
```
STANDARD ERROR OF
THE ESTIMATE: S(Y.X)= 1.54275
DO YOU WANT RESIDUALS? Y
```
CALCULATED VALUES   INPUT VALUES  RESIDUAL
        2.83636       3.000000     0.16364
        5.43030       6.000000     0.56970
        9.94848       9.000000    -0.94848
       16.39091      16.000000    -0.39091
       24.75758      24.000000    -0.75758
       35.04848      38.000000     2.95152
       47.26364      45.000000    -2.26364
       61.40303      62.000000     0.59697
       77.46667      78.000000     0.53333
       95.45455      95.000000    -0.45455
```
STANDARD ERROR OF THE COEFFICIENTS
```
B( 0 )=    1.81451
B( 1 )=    0.75782
B( 2 )=    0.06714
```

R SQUARED= 99.82%

MULTIPLE R= .999098
TIME   T= -0.386
YOUR X FACTOR SQUARED T= 14.330

HERE'S YOUR EQUATION AGAIN

```
Y=    2.1666667    -0.2924242 * TIME
 +    0.9621212 * YOUR X FACTOR SQUARED
```

WANT TO TRY YOUR EQUATION OUT? Y
ENTER THE VALUE FOR EACH FACTOR
TIME? 2.5
YOUR X FACTOR SQUARED? 6.25
THE PREDICTED VALUE IS: 7.44886
WITH A 95% CONFIDENCE INTERVAL OF:
 4.05459 TO 10.8431
WANT TO TRY ANOTHER <YES/NO>? Y
ENTER THE VALUE FOR EACH FACTOR
TIME? 4

```
YOUR X FACTOR SQUARED? 16
THE PREDICTED VALUE IS: 16.3909
WITH A 95% CONFIDENCE INTERVAL OF:
 13.0173 TO 19.7645
WANT TO TRY ANOTHER <YES/NO>? N
```

18

ANOVA FOR BLOCKED AND NESTED DESIGNS

In Chapter 8 we introduced the concept of blocking in factorial designs with the purpose of removing an unwanted source of variation. We will now show how such a source of variation will inflate the noise (or error) in an experiment unless it is treated properly. Table 18-1 is a reproduction of the random assignment of acres to the 16 treatment combinations as first found in Chapter 8. We have now added the response, plant growth in inches to allow an analysis.

Table 18-1

RUN #	TC	NITRO %	PHOSP %	POTSH %	TYPE PL	ACRE #	HEIGHT
12	(1)	10	5	5	Corn	3	5.5
2	A	20	5	5	Corn	1	15.0
13	B	10	10	5	Corn	4	9.0
8	AB	20	10	5	Corn	2	12.0
14	C	10	5	10	Corn	4	7.5
4	AC	20	5	10	Corn	1	14.0
1	BC	10	10	10	Corn	1	9.5
9	ABC	20	10	10	Corn	3	10.0
11	D	10	5	5	Tomato	3	3.5
3	AD	20	5	5	Tomato	1	13.0
10	BD	10	10	5	Tomato	3	4.0
15	ABD	20	10	5	Tomato	4	12.0
16	CD	10	5	10	Tomato	4	5.5
6	ACD	20	5	10	Tomato	2	8.5
5	BCD	10	10	10	Tomato	2	4.0
7	ABCD	20	10	10	Tomato	2	9.0

The YATES analysis of variance is shown in Table 18-2. Since there were no replicates, we used the higher order interactions for error mean square estimate. This was done by adding the sums of squares for ABCD, BCD, ACD, ABD, and ABC together and dividing by their combined 5 degrees of freedom.

The results show that nitrogen (A) and the type of vegetable (D) have an effect on the height of the plant, while the other two fertilizer components do not significantly change the height. Remember, in this design the acres were randomly assigned to the treatments. If there is a systematic effect due to acres, then this effect has to show up in the random error. If the error is big, then it will reduce the F ratio and our experiment is reduced in sensitivity.

Table 18-2

OBSERVATION	SUM OF SQUARES	"F"*	HALF EFFECT	MEASURE
5.5000	1260.2500	--.--	8.8750	Average
15.0000	126.5625	47.3**	2.8125	A-Nitrogen
9.0000	0.5625	.2 NS	−0.1875	B - Phosp
12.0000	9.0000	3.4 NS	−0.7500	AB
7.5000	2.2500	.8 NS	−0.3750	C - Potash
14.0000	14.0625	5.3 NS	−0.9375	AC
9.5000	0.5625	--.--	−0.1875	BC
10.0000	1.0000	--.--	0.2500	ABC
3.5000	33.0625	12.4**	−1.4375	D - Type Crop
13.0000	2.2500	--.--	0.3750	AD
4.0000	0.0000	--.--	0.0000	BD
12.0000	10.5625	--.--	0.8125	ABD
5.5000	1.5625	--.--	−0.3125	CD
8.5000	1.0000	--.--	−0.2500	ACD
4.0000	0.2500	--.--	0.1250	BCD
9.0000	0.5625	--.--	0.1875	ABCD

*Pool 3 and 4 factor interactions for error MS = 2.68 $F_{.05,1,5} = 6.6$

The design in Table 18-3 is a reproduction of the blocked experiment found in Chapter 9. We have added the response variable and use a YATES ANOVA for the analysis found in Table 18-4. In the blocked design, we equated the 4 blocks with three degrees of freedom representing the two primary blocks ABC, BCD; and the secondary block AD. This means that the effect of blocks is confounded with these three interactions and we can see an accumulation of sums of squares for each block. If we compare Tables 18-4 and 18-2 we can see that the random assignment of the acres causes a"sprinkling" of the variation due to native fertility over the entire experiment while in the blocked design the acre effects are neatly placed in only 3

Table 18-3

RUN#	TC	NITRO%	PHOSP%	POTSH%	TYPE PL	ABC	BCD	BLOCK#	HEIGHT
12	(1)	10	5	5	Corn	−	+	1	10.0
2	A	20	5	5	Corn	+	−	2	11.5
13	B	10	10	5	Corn	+	+	3	6.0
8	AB	20	10	5	Corn	−	+	4	14.0
14	C	10	5	10	Corn	+	+	3	4.5
4	AC	20	5	10	Corn	−	+	4	12.5
1	BC	10	10	10	Corn	−	−	1	9.5
9	ABC	20	10	10	Corn	+	−	2	11.0
11	D	10	5	5	Tomato	−	+	4	6.5
3	AD	20	5	5	Tomato	+	+	3	8.5
10	BD	10	10	5	Tomato	+	−	2	5.0
15	ABD	20	10	5	Tomato	−	−	1	13.5
16	CD	10	5	10	Tomato	+	−	2	3.5
6	ACD	20	5	10	Tomato	−	−	1	12.5
5	BCD	10	10	10	Tomato	−	+	4	6.0
7	ABCD	20	10	10	Tomato	+	+	3	8.0

Table 18-4

OBSERVATION	SUM OF SQUARES	HALF EFFECT	MEASURE
10.0000	1260.2500	8.8750	Average
11.5000	100.0000	2.5000	A-Nitrogen
6.0000	1.0000	0.2500	B - Phosp
14.0000	0.0000	0.0000	AB
4.5000	4.0000	−0.5000	C - Potash
12.5000	0.0000	0.0000	AC
9.5000	0.0000	0.0000	BC
11.0000	42.2500	−1.6250	ABC - Block
6.5000	16.0000	−1.0000	D - Type Crop
8.5000	0.2500	0.1250	AD - Block
5.0000	0.0000	0.0000	BD
13.5000	0.0000	0.0000	ABD
3.5000	0.0000	0.0000	CD
12.0000	0.0000	0.0000	ACD
6.0000	6.2500	−0.6250	BCD - Block
8.0000	0.0000	0.0000	ABCD

positions. What is more important is the fact that these 3 positions were determined by our choice in the original design and not by chance.

The interpretation of the analysis of the 2^k blocked factorial is shown in Table 18-4. Just as in any YATES ANOVA, the sums of squares and half effects appear opposite the tc identifier for that factor or interaction. So, for instance, Potash (factor C) has a sum of squares of 4 with a half effect of $-.5$. This indicates that increasing potash concentration decreases the height of the crop. Notice that in this example, there are exactly zero effects for any interactins other that the interactions confounded with the blocks. The purpose of this example is to demonstrate the physical and mathematical meaning behind confounding and the effect of blocking. In our next example the data will contain randon error as well as a systematic effect that will be "blocked" out.

COMPLETE RANDOMIZED BLOCK

In this type of experiment all of the possible treatments are present in each block. The analysis is accomplished via an ANOVA. We assume no possible physical interaction between the factor(s) under study and the block. Therefore, there is a simplification of the ANOVA calculations since the interaction of block and factor does not need to be computed. We should comment on the assumption of no interaction between the block and the factor or factors under investigation. The block is usually a nuisance factor such as day-to-day or batch-to-batch variation that we don't wish to study. Further, if there were an interaction, we would be hard pressed to attach a physical meaning to it since the block is usually a factor that varies at random rather than in a fixed, controlled manner. If we do not have control over a factor we can't control the interaction or predict what would happen at another randomly selected "level" of the block. As we shall see in the analysis of a randomized block experiment, the interaction (if any) will end up in the error term and if this interaction is of any substantial magnitude, the error will be inflated and thus reduce the sensitivity of the experiment.

We will now analyze the developer solution design found in Chapter 9. Recall, that we were investigating the effect of two different developer formulations on the density (how black) of the image. Also remember that the entire experiment could not be completed on a single day and we expected to find day-to-day variation creeping into the results. Table 18-5 shows the design which is a randomized block.

Table 18-5

	Developer A		Developer B		
	tc#3	(1.1)	tc#6	(1.2)	
Day #1	tc#7	(1.0)	tc#2	(1.3)	Total Day 1 = 9.3
	tc#1	(1.1)	tc#8	(1.2)	
	tc#4	(1.3)	tc#5	(1.1)	

Table 18-5 (cont.)

	tc#4 (1.2)	tc#7 (1.4)	
Day #2	tc#8 (1.4)	tc#1 (1.5)	Total Day 2 = 10.9
	tc#5 (1.3)	tc#6 (1.4)	
	tc#2 (1.2)	tc#3 (1.5)	

Total Dev. A = 9.6   Total Dev. B = 10.6   Grand Total = 20.2

We could test the analysis as a 1-way ANOVA if we were unaware of the day-to-day source of variation. We shall try that approach and see what happens. We first will compute to total sum of squares.

$$\Sigma_{sq}\ Total \quad = \quad 1.1^2 + 1.0^2 + \dots 1.4^2 + 1.5^2 - \frac{20.2^2}{16} \qquad (18\text{-}1)$$

$$\Sigma_{sq}\ Total \quad = \quad 25.84 - 25.5025 = .3375$$

Next we compute the sum of squares due to the developers:

$$\Sigma_{sq}\ Dev \quad = \quad \left(\frac{(9.6)^2}{8} + \frac{(10.6)^2}{8}\right) - \frac{20.2^2}{16} = .0625 \qquad (18\text{-}2)$$

The error sum of squares is the remaining part of this 1-way ANOVA.

Total	=	Developer Effect + ERROR	(18-3)
.3375	=	.0625 + ERROR	
.275	=	ERROR Sum of Squares	

The ANOVA Table will look like this:

Table 18-6

ANOVA

SOURCE	Σ_{Sq}	df	MS	F	$F_{.05,1,14}$
Developers	.0625	1	.0625	3.18	4.60
Error	.275	14	.0196		
Total	.3375	15			

Since the calculated F is less than the critical F, we fail to reject the null hypothesis and conclude that there is no significant difference between the two developers. However, is this conculsion correct in the light of what we know about the day-to-day variation? If we look closely in Table 18-5 we can see that the variations induced by days is larger than the variation due to developers. In the 1-way ANOVA we treated the day-to-day "factor" as a random source of variation and included its component of variance in the random error. Since day-to-day is systematic and accountable, we are able to extract it from the error sum of squares. To compute the day-to-day variation we simply treat this block effect as if it were another factor as follows:

$$\Sigma_{sq} \text{ Block} = \left(\frac{(9.3)^2}{8} + \frac{(10.9)^2}{8} \right) - \frac{20.2^2}{16} = .16 \qquad (18\text{-}4)$$

The error sum of squares is now the remainder after we remove the developer and block sum of squares from the total.

$$\Sigma_{sq} \text{ Error} = .3375 - (.16 + .0625) = .115 \qquad (18\text{-}5)$$

The ANOVA table now includes blocks and produces a different conclusion.

Table 18-7

<u>ANOVA</u>

SOURCE	Σ_{Sq}	df	MS	F	$F_{.05,1,14}$
Developers	.0625	1	.0625	7.07	4.67
Blocks	.16	1			
Error	.115	13	.00885		
Total	.3375	15			

We now reject the hypothesis that the developers are the same and conclude that developer B produces a highter density than developer A. Now none of the observations have changed, but we draw different conclusions depending on the ANOVA Table we use! Of course we know that the analysis in Table 18-6 is inadequate since we neglected to account for the systematic day-to-day source of change. The day-to-day makes up a large percentage of the "ERROR" sum of squares in Table 18-6. We can compute this percentage by taking the sum of squares for blocks from Table 18-7 and divide it by the "ERROR" sum of squares found in Table 18-6.

$$\frac{.16}{.275} = 58.2\% \qquad (18\text{-}6)$$

Well over 50% of the noise is due to a systematic source which we can extract from the error term and thereby increase the sensitivity of the analysis. Notice that we do <u>not</u> compute on F ratio for the blocks. To do so would be meaningless and only add confusion. The blocks are a source of variation that we simply wish to get rid of. We are not interested in making a study of the daily variation. If we were, then we would have continued to compute the interaction between days and developers. However, from a physical perspective, such an interaction would be difficult to control because days is a qualitative factor over which we have no ability to select or control. The days just happen to us. Now, of course, if we could relate a physical parameter to the day-induce variation then we would be able to control the variation. In such a case we would no longer have a blocked experiment, but a 2 factor factorial. Once again we can see that the analysis depends upon the original intent of the design. The more we put into an experiment, the more we can extract during the analysis.

PAIRED COMPARISON

While ANOVA is the technique used most often to extract information from an experimental design, it is sometimes possible to use a simpler "t" test to do the analysis. The paired comparison experiment was introduced in Chapter 9 with an application aimed at bringing generality into an experimental situation. We could use ANOVA in the analysis of a paired comparison, but the traditional paired "t" test will do nicely at first.

Table 18-8

Car Type	Plain Unleaded	Gas-o-hol	Difference
Chevette	31	34	3
Escort	33	37	4
Toyota	39	38	−1
T-2000	28	30	2
Reliant K	26	27	1
Rabbit	39	43	4
Coup DeVille	18	21	3
Regal	23	26	3
Firebird	14	18	4
Fairmont	18	20	2
	$\bar{X} = 26.9$	29.4	$\bar{d} = 2.5$
	$s = 8.75$	8.46	$S_d = 1.58$

Table 18-8 shows the results of an experiment established to determine the difference between two types of fuel over many types of automobiles. If we were to run a simple "t" test between the averages of the two types of fuel we would find that the variation induced by the 10 different cars would make the error so large, we would not be able to determine a significant effect. This is the same problem we have observed in other blocked designs. The only difference in this case is the fact that the "extra" source of variation (the cars) was purposely put into the experiment to give a broader inference space and make our conclusions about the fuels more general. But in doing so, we have inflated the noise in the experiment. However, the source of the noise is again systematic. We can remove the effect of the cars in the analysis. One way is to concentrate on the response we are really interested in. It's not just the miles per gallon (MPG), but the difference in MPG that is of interest. If we take the _difference_ between the Gas-o-hol and the plain Unleaded, we look at the response that is of interest to us, and remove the inherent variation caused by the differences in cars. In terms of a null and alternative hypothesis, this is:

$$H_0: \quad \delta = \delta_0 = 0 \qquad\qquad (18\text{-}7)$$
$$H_1: \quad \delta > \delta_0 \qquad \text{Where } \delta = \text{difference}$$

We use a single sided alternative since we would hope that the gas-o-hol will produce a better MPG than the plain unleaded gas. If the MPG is no different or less, we will decide to not use the gas-o-hol. The test statistic used in our decision process is similar to the expression used in the simple "t" test of the mean (i.e.: $H_0: \mu = \mu_0$).

$$t = \frac{d - \delta_0}{s_d/\sqrt{n}} \qquad\qquad (18\text{-}8)$$

For our data we calculate:

$$t = \frac{2.5 - 0}{1.58/\sqrt{10}} = 5.0$$

A comparison with the single sided t at the .05 level for 9 degrees of freedom (1.8331) shows that we should reject the null hypothesis. We conclude that gas-o-hol delivers a significantly better MPG rating.

Table 18-9

Car Type	Plain Unleaded	Gas-o-hol	Row Totals
Chevette	31	34	65
Escort	33	37	70
Toyota	39	38	77
T-2000	28	30	58
Reliant K	26	27	53
Rabbit	39	43	82
Coup DeVille	18	21	39
Regal	23	26	49
Firebird	14	18	32
Fairmont	18	20	38
Total	269	294	563 ← Grand Total

The analysis we just completed via the "t" test can also be done using the more general ANOVA approach. We will find the sum of squares due to type of cars (the block); the sum of squares due to fuels and subtract these two sources of variation from the total sum of squares to obtain the "residual" or noise sum of squares. The results are shown in Table 18-10.

The ANOVA gives the same result as the "t" test although it requires more computation. An interesting observation of the calculated "t" and "F" values shows that the F is exactly the square of the t. This is always the case when we have 1df for the numerator of the F distribution.

Table 18-10

ANOVA

SOURCE	Σ_{Sq}	df	MS	F	$F_{.05,1,9}$
Fuels	31.25	1	31.25	25.0	5.1174
Cars (Block)	1322.05	9	–	–	
Residual	11.25	9	1.25		
Total	1364.55	19			

LATIN SQUARE

The same concept we have presented and developed for the blocked experiments holds for the Latin Square design. Recall that this design is able to block on two sources of variation at the same time while investigating one factor. In the example found in Table 18-11, we are interested in drawing inferences about types of films but want to generalize the result by using different pictures. We also wish to remove the influence of variation between observers who will give a rating to the quality of the photographs.

Table 18-11

Block #1 - Picture Content

		Child	Model	Rural	Portrait	Old Man	Food	
	3	75(I)	85(Fj)	80(Ft)	50(Km)	65(A)	88(EK)	433
	6	97(EK)	43(Km)	73(A)	85(Fj)	60(Ft)	65(I)	423
Block #2	1	82(Ft)	67(I)	87(Fj)	97(EK)	37(Km)	75(A)	445
Observer	4	82(A)	87(EK)	42(Km)	67(I)	72(Fj)	65(Ft)	415
	5	95(Fj)	70(Ft)	65(I)	80(A)	80(EK)	43(Km)	433
	2	57(Km)	77(A)	92(EK)	77(Ft)	57(I)	85(Fj)	445
		488	429	429	456	371	421	2594

The ANOVA for the Latin Square follows the same path as other randomized block designs. We find the totals for each level of each block (row, column totals) and the totals for the effect we are investigating. We compute the usual total sum of squares and find the residual sum of squares by difference between the 2 blocks plus the effect and the total.

For our example the calculations are as follows:

$$\Sigma sq \text{ Picture} = \frac{488^2 + 429^2 + 429^2 + 456^2 + 371^2 + 421^2}{6} - \frac{2594^2}{36}$$

$$\Sigma sq \text{ Picture} = 188174 - 186912.11$$
$$= 1261.89$$

$$\Sigma sq \text{ Observers} = \frac{433^2 + 423^2 + 455^2 + 415^2 + 433^2 + 445^2}{6} - \frac{2594^2}{36}$$

$$\Sigma sq \text{ Observers} = 187030.33 - 186912.11$$
$$= 118.22$$

Now we will need to find the sums for each of the 6 types of film used in our experiment. This is done by sweeping down each column and finding the response for each film (there will be only one film per column). So, for the first column we get a 75 for Ilford (I), in column 2 a 67 for Ilford, in column 3 we find a 65 for Ilford, etc. The sum for Ilford is 396. We continue to sum for each film and the results are as follows:

Table 18-12

	Total	$\bar{x}$
Ilford (I)	396	66.0
Kodak (Ek)	541	90.2
Fotomat (Ft)	424	70.7
Agfa (A)	452	75.3
Fiji (Fj)	509	84.8
K-Mart (Km)	272	45.3

$$\Sigma sq \text{ Films} = \frac{396^2 + 541^2 + 424^2 + 452^2 + 509^2 + 272^2}{6} - \frac{2594^2}{36}$$

$$\Sigma sq \text{ Films} = 194440.33 - 186912.11$$
$$= 7528.22$$

$$\text{Total } \Sigma sq = \frac{75^2 + 97^2 + \ldots + 43^2 + 85^2}{1} - \frac{2594^2}{36}$$

$$\text{Total } \Sigma sq = 195840 - 186912.11$$
$$= 8927.89$$

So the residual is the total less the sums of squares of the blocks and the films.

$$\Sigma sq \text{ Residual} = 8927.89 - (1261.89 + 118.22 + 7528.22)$$
$$= 19.56$$

We now summarize this information in the ANOVA table.

Table 18-13

ANOVA

SOURCE	Σ_{Sq}	df	MS	F	$F_{.05,5,20}$
Films	7528.22	5	1505.64	1536	2.599
Block 1 - Pictures	1261.89	5	---	---	
Block 2 - Observers	118.22	5	---	---	
Residual	19.56	20	.98		
Total	8927.89	35			

From the above results there is no question that the films produce different quality images. Notice that we do not test the two block factors since we are not interested in their effects and only compute their sums of squares to remove their influence from the error term. If we had treated this analysis as a 1-way ANOVA with the pictures and observers included in the random noise component, then the residual mean square would have been 46.7 and the F value for the films would have been 161.4 or about an order of magnitude less than we observe in the doubly blocked Latin Square analysis.

While there is still a strong indication of difference between the films from the 1-way ANOVA, we have a "clouded" conclusion due to the large contribution of the picture-to-picture factor.

We complete the analysis of the Latin Square by setting up the shortest significant range (SSR) which will tell us which individual films are different from each other. The standard error is computer and then multiplied times the studentized range statistic.

$$S_{\bar{x}} = \sqrt{\frac{.98}{6}} = .404$$

$$SSR_2 = .404 * 2.95 = 1.2$$

Since all of the means in Table 18-12 are different by more than 1.2, we conclude that all the films are different in image quality.

NESTED DESIGNS

Up to now, we have avoided any reference to a formality used in many books on ANOVA. We have not needed this formality of stating a mathematical model since all of our designs and analyses have had the same trivial underlying model. However, the nested design produces a different type of information than the crossed design and therefore needs a more formal guide to its analysis.

Before we look at the model for the nested design, we should list the models involved with other designs. We'll use the following notation in the construction of the models.

Y   Represents an observation and will be multiple subscripted to show its position in the design matrix.

μ Represents the grand mean of the experiment.

A,B,C...   Represent the factors under study and will be singly subscripted with i, j, k ... etc.

ϵ Represents the random experimental error that is sprinkled over the entire experiment.

For a 1-way (1 factor) experiment the model is then:

$$Y_{ij} = \mu + A_i + \epsilon_{j(i)} \qquad (18\text{-}9)$$

We read the model by saying the observation Y is equal to the grand average plus an effect due to factor A plus error within (or nested) the levels of factor A.

For a 2-way experiment the model is:

$$Y_{ijk} = \mu - A_i + B_j + AB_{ij} + \epsilon_{k(ij)} \qquad (18\text{-}10)$$

Which reads the same way as the 1-way but we have added another dimension (factor B) to our sample space and the interaction between A and B.

We can expand these examples to as many factors as are in need of investigation always adding the new factors, their subscripts and the interactions that are appropriate.

For blocked experiments we do not include terms in the model that depict an interaction between the factors under study and the blocks. So, for a simple randomized block with one factor the model is:

$$Y_{ijk} = \mu + A_i + Block_j + \epsilon_{k(ij)} \qquad (18\text{-}11)$$

And for a Latin Square:

$$Y_{ij} = \mu + A_k + Block1_i + Block2_j + \epsilon_{ij} \qquad (18\text{-}12)$$

In the Latin Square we play a little game with the subscript k. Since this design is only a 2-dimensional array, there really is no dimension k. We of course have superimposed the dimension k over the i rows and j columns. We usually do not "nest" any error in the treatment combinations of the Latin Square, but could do so and then the model would become:

$$Y_{ijl} = \mu + A_k + Block1_i + Block2_j + \epsilon_{l(ij)} \qquad (18\text{-}13)$$

While we may construct mathematical models for our experimental designs that will compactly state what we are testing (a form of an alternative hypothese) we can also use the math model to determine where the sources of variation come from. This is their prime use with nested designs. The math model will lead us to the determination of the expected mean squares (EMS). Since a mean square can be reduced to a variance via the EMS, we can then quantify the sources of variation present in the process under investigation.

In Chapter 10 we had set up a hierarchical or nexted type design that had as its objective the quantification of variation in a coal analysis. Table 18-14 shows the sulphur content of the coal that comes from 3 randomly selected hopper cars, 4 random samples in each car and two analyses per sample. If we were to disregard the three sources of variation, we would compute the overall variation of the 24 pieces of data. This simple calculation is usually the trigger for further work if a specificaiton is not met. In our case, the specificaiton dictated by the EPA states that the sulphur content may not exceed 5%. Now our average is below 5% (4.2), but the standard deviation is nearly 1.5 which (if we can assume a normal distribution) leads up to believe there is 30% of our coal contains sulphur above 5%.

Table 18-14

	Hopper Car #1				Hopper Car #2				Hopper Car #3			
Sample:	1	2	3	4	1	2	3	4	1	2	3	4
Analysis:	1 2	1 2	1 2	1 2	1 2	1 2	1 2	1 2	1 2	1 2	1 2	1 2
Sulphur Content:	2 3	4 4	2 2	2 4	4 4	4 5	3 3	3 5	6 7	5 6	4 6	5 7

$\bar{x} = 4.2$
$S = 1.52$

The question is what can we do about it? We need to first understand where the greatest sources of variation are present. We will do an analysis of the variance to pinpoint the major contributors. This is a real variance analysis, not an analysis of means like we have done before.

For this ANOVA we will "shake up" the hierarchy of our design and find the variance due to the hopper cars, the samples and the analyses. To do so we will

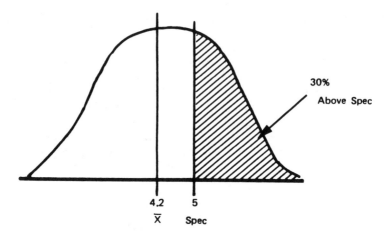

4.2   5
X̄   Spec

Figure 18-1

compute "mini ANOVAS" within each category. We'll start at the bottom of the hierarchy with the analysis to analysis variation. This calculation is nothing new to us since the method has been used in all our other ANOVA calculations to compute the noise or error. We find the sum of each of the two values and the sum of squares of each of the two values.

For Hopper #1, Sample #1 the two analyses were 2 and 3; so we get 5 for the sum, and 13 for the sum of squared values. To get the sum of squares we square the sum and divide by the number of items that made it up (2) and subtract this from the sum of squared values.

$$\Sigma sq = \quad 13 \quad - \quad \frac{5^2}{2} \quad = \quad .5 \qquad (18\text{-}14)$$

We repeat this type of calculation for all combinations of hopper cars and samples (there are 12 such combinations).

Table 18-15

Hopper	Sample	Σsq Analyses
1	1	0.5
	2	0.0
	3	0.0
	4	2.0

Table 18-15 (cont.)

2	1	0.0
	2	0.5
	3	0.0
	4	2.0
3	1	0.5
	2	0.5
	3	2.0
	4	2.0
		10.0

We next move up to the sample to sample variation. <u>Within each Hopper Car</u> we will find the sum for <u>each</u> sample, the sum across samples and the sum for squared samples.

Table 18-16

For Hopper #1:

Sample	Σ	Square
1	5	25
2	8	64
3	4	16
4	6	36
	23	141

$$Ssq = \frac{141}{2} - \frac{23^2}{8} = 4.375$$

For Hopper #2:

Sample	Σ	Square
1	8	64
2	9	81
3	6	36
4	8	64
	31	245

$$Ssq = \frac{245}{2} - \frac{31^2}{8} = 2.375$$

For Hopper #3:

Sample	Σ	Square
1	13	169
2	11	121
3	10	100
4	12	144
	46	534

$$Ssq = \frac{534}{2} - \frac{46^2}{8} = 2.500$$

9.250

Remember in all these calculations, we are applying our general sum of squares formula which says to subtract the squared sum (divided by the number of items in the sum) from the sum of the squares (divided by the number of items in the sum that was squared).

$$\Sigma Sq \quad = \quad \frac{\Sigma X_i^2}{n} \quad - \quad \frac{(\Sigma X_i)^2}{n} \qquad (18\text{-}15)$$

Observe that in Table 18-16 we have applied formula 18-15 individually to each hopper car since Sample #1 in Hopper #1 is a random sample and does not relate to the other Sample #1's. This is the main difference between the analysis of a crossed design and a nested design. After finding the sums of squares in each hopper due to the samples, we sum these sums of squares to obtain the overall (pooled) sum of squares for the sample to sample variation.

There is one last source of variation to compute that arises from different sulphur concentrations found in different hopper cars. We find the sum of each hopper car, square each sum and find the grand sum over all hopper cars. Then apply 18-15.

$$\text{Hopper } \Sigma sq \quad = \quad \frac{23^2 + 31^2 + 46^2}{8} \quad - \quad \frac{100^2}{24} \quad = \quad 34.083 \qquad (18\text{-}16)$$

To check our arithmetic we will compute the total sum of squares in the usual way by squaring each individual observation and summing. Then find the grand sum and then apply expression 18-15.

$$\text{Total } \Sigma sq \quad = \quad \frac{2^2 + 3^2 + ... 5^2 + 7^2}{1} - \frac{100^2}{24} \quad = \quad 53.333$$

We will put all the information into an ANOVA table, but before we do that we will go back to the math model for this components of variance experiment.

$$Y_{ijk} \quad = \quad \mu \; + \; HC_i \; + \; S_{j(i)} \; + \; A_{k(ij)} \qquad (18\text{-}17)$$

This model reads as follows: "The observation Y is equal to the grand mean plus an effect due to the hopper car sampling, plus an effect due to the samples nested within hopper cars (this is how you read the parenthetical subscript) and an effect due to the analyses nested within hopper cars and samples".

If we look back at our design, we see that within each hopper car we have 8 observations. Each observation has a variance associated with it, so we have 8 variance components for cars. Within each car there are 4 samples and within each sample there are 2 observations with a variance associated with each observation. Therefore each sample has 2 variance components. Each analysis is done once so there is only one component of variance for the analysis. If the above allocation of components of variance seems unclear, then it is best to use an algorithm to determine the sources of variation that make up each sum of squares from an experimental design.

The algorithm we shall use utilizes the math model as follows.

Set up column headings by using the subscripts and indicate the number of levels that the subscript represents. Set row headings by using the terms from the math model. Indicate if the factor is Random (R) or Fixed (F) over each column.

Table 18-17

	R	R	R
	$i:3$	$j:4$	$k:2$
HC_i			
$S_{j(i)}$			
$A_{k(ij)}$			

To fill in the body of the table, start in the first column and place the number 1 where the subscript of a nested (in parenthesis) factor matches the column heading subscript.

Table 18-18

	R^*	
	$i:3$	
HC_i		
$S_{j(i)}$	1	STEP 1
$A_{k(ij)}$	1	

Continue in Column 1 and again look for a column-row subscript match. Where a match occurs place a 1 for a Random factor or a 0 (zero) for a Fixed factor. If there is no match, leave the space blank.

---

* A random factor allows the level selection to be made in a random fashion from a population of levels. Most nested designs will incorporate random factors. The error "factor" is always random. If we pick a level with knowledge and purpose, it is Fixed.

Table 18-19

$$R$$
$$i:3$$

HC_i	1	STEP 2
$S_{j(i)}$	1	
$A_{k(ij)}$	1	

Now repeat the same procedure for the remaining columns.

Table 18-20

	R i:3	R j:4	R k:2
HC_i	1		
$S_{j(i)}$	1	1	
$A_{k(ij)}$	1	1	1

In the remaining blank spaces bring down the column heading numerical values.

Table 18-21

	R i:3	R j:4	R k:2
HC_i	1	4	2
$S_{j(i)}$	1	1	2
$A_{k(ij)}$	1	1	1

We will work row-wise to build the EMS and determine the components of variance. We will first want to determine the first row or the Hopper Car (HC) contribution to the variation componets. To do so, cover over (or ignore) the column with the subscript of the factor in question. In the first case, we ignore the first column so Table 18-21 becomes 18-22.

Table 18-22

	R j:4	R k:2
HC_i	4	2
$S_{j(i)}$	1	2
$A_{k(ij)}$	1	1

Look at each row heading. Where ever there is the subscript of the column we have ignored we may multiply the numerical values remaining in that row together to obtain the number of variance components for the row heading. If the factor of the row heading is random then the component is random and is symbolized with a σ^2. If the factor of the row heading is fixed, then the component is symbolized by a $\varnothing$. We have all random factors in our example so they will have σ^2 components. Table 18-23 shows the EMS for the Hopper Car component. Note that the components are all a part of HC. The subscripts on the σ^2's come from the names of the factors.

Table 18-23

	R $j:4$	R $k:2$	EMS
HC_i	4	2	$8\sigma^2_{HC} + 2\sigma^2_S + \sigma^2_A$
$S_{j(i)}$	1	2	
$A_{k(ij)}$	1	1	

The EMS for Hopper Cars is 8 parts due to the cars plus 2 due to samples within the cars and 1 due to the analyses. This means that when we compute the Mean square for HC it is not just a variance due to cars, but includes other sources of variation as well. This occurs because of the way the ANOVA of this hierarchial design sums from the bottom of the hierarchy up and in doing so includes all the lower components of variance in the upper factors. This is not a serious problem and as we shall see we can separate the sum to determine the contribution of each single piece.

We next ignore the second as well as the first column and compute the EMS for all those factors with a j subscript (because both j and i are present for S).

Table 18-24

	R $k:2$	EMS
HC_i	2	$8\sigma^2_{HC} + 2\sigma^2_S + \sigma^2_A$
$S_{j(i)}$	2	$2\sigma^2_S + \sigma^2_A$
$A_{k(ij)}$	1	

At last, we cover all three columns (since the last row has all 3 subscripts represented) and multiply by 1 only for the component that has all 3 subscripts, namely the analysis. Now the EMS calculation is complete and is shown in Table 18-25.

Table 18-25

Source	EMS
Hopper Cars	$8\sigma^2_{HC} + 2\sigma^2_S + \sigma^2_A$
Samples	$2\sigma^2_S + \sigma^2_A$
Analyses	σ^2_A

Now let's go back and build a ANOVA table from the sums of squares we computed from the sulphur experiment. We will place the EMS along with the ANOVA table and then find the single value of the variance for each source.

Table 18-26

ANOVA

Source	Σsq	df	MS	EMS
Hopper Cars	34.083	2	17.044	$8\sigma^2_{HC} + 2\sigma^2_S + \sigma^2_A$
Samples	9.25	9	1.028	$2\sigma^2_S + \sigma^2_A$
Analyses	10.000	12	.833	σ^2_A
Total	53.333	23		

To find the variance of each contributor we will start at the bottom of Table 18-26. The analysis Mean Square is already reported as a single component and is .833 so there is no need to adjust it. However, the samples mean square has a component due to the analyses, so we must subtract .833 (σ^2_A) from the 1.028 ($2\sigma^2_S + \sigma^2_A$) to obtain .995 which is $2\sigma^2_S$. Therefore $1\sigma^2_S$ is .195/2 = 0.0975. The hopper car mean square has a component due to the samples and the analyses so we subtract 1.028 ($2\sigma^2_S + \sigma^2_A$) from 17.044 ($8\sigma^2_{HC} + 2\sigma^2_S + \sigma^2_A$) to get 16.016 which is $8\sigma^2_{HC}$. Therefore $1\sigma^2_{HC}$ is 16.016/8 = 2.002.

We will summarize the above information is an analysis of the variation table.

Table 18-27

Source	EMS (s^2)	% s^2	S	Coeff. of Var. (S/X)*100
Hopper Cars	2.0020	68.3	1.415	33.7%
Samples	0.0975	3.3	.312	7.4%
Analyses	0.8333	28.4	.913	21.7%
Total	2.9328	100.0		

We can see from the % s^2 column that the majority of the variation comes from the hopper cars followed by the analyses. Since the analysis has a better than 25% impact on the variation of the sulphur content we would like to judge if something should be done to improve the method. The coefficient of variation is nearly 22% which by most standards is far too great for such an analytical test method. We would conclude from this experiment that the analysis method will have to be improved by reducing the variability.

USING THE HIERARCHY

Now that we have the variances of the three "stages" in this sampling and measure system, it is possible to compute the standard error of our measurements and determine the number of samples from each stage.

The expression for computing the standard error is expanded to include a component for each stage of the system. For our problem the $S_{\bar{X}}$ is:

$$S_{\bar{X}} = \sqrt{\frac{S^2_{HC}}{i} + \frac{S^2_S}{i*j} + \frac{S^2_A}{i*j*k}} \qquad (18\text{-}18)$$

$$
\begin{aligned}
i &= \# \text{ Cars} \\
j &= \# \text{ Samples} \\
k &= \# \text{ Analyses}
\end{aligned}
$$

If we were to sample 5 cars, with 2 samples in each car and run 2 analyses on each sample, the standard error would be:

$$S_{\bar{X}} = \sqrt{\frac{2.002}{5} + \frac{.0975}{10} + \frac{.8333}{20}} = .672 \qquad (18\text{-}19)$$

If we sample 10 cars, 2 samples per car, but only 1 analysis per sample:

$$S_{\bar{X}} = \sqrt{\frac{2.002}{10} + \frac{.0975}{20} + \frac{.8333}{20}} = .497 \qquad (18\text{-}20)$$

The $S_{\bar{X}}$ from the second (18-20) sampling requires the same number of analyses, but is 26% smaller (which is good) than the .672 of (18-19). We can build a table of standard errors for various combinations of cars, samples and analyses and pick the combination that gives the lowest error with the least cost. In general, the standard error is reduced faster by increasing the sample size of high noise, early (higher) stage components in the hierarchy.

PROBLEMS FOR CHAPTER 18

1. Complete the analysis for the following blocked experiment. The primary blocks are BC and AC.

tc	Response	
(1)	20.4	
a	26.6	A = Type of Fuel (Reg., Prem.)
b	21.3	B = Speed (30 mph, 60 mph)
ab	21.7	C = Type of Automobile (Compact, Mid Size)
c	15.8	Blocks = Driving Conditions
ac	19.2	Response is miles/$
bc	16.2	
abc	14.7	

a) How many block levels were there in this experiment?

b) If the blocks represented various parts of the nation (NE, SE, SW, NW) why do you think blocking was done?

c) Which combination of type of fuel, speed, automobile gets the best economy?

2. Analyze the following experiment. Response is judged degree of goodness of the hamburger served at 4 restaurants. (Scale 0 = Poor, 10 = Good).

Observer	Bill Gray's	Vic & Irv's	Tom's	Don & Bob's
1	8.1	7.6	9.5	9.0
2	9.1	6.1	9.0	8.5
3	7.6	5.5	8.0	7.5
4	3.2	4.2	5.0	4.5
5	7.7	7.8	7.9	7.5
6	5.0	6.0	6.2	6.1
7	9.2	9.9	10.0	9.0
8	7.5	7.0	6.1	8.0
9	6.0	7.0	9.0	7.0
10	7.0	6.5	7.5	7.0

3. If the Latin Square analysis had not been used on the data in Table 18-11, then the mean square for Residual would have been 46.7. In the application of the

SSR using the 46.7 how would the conclusions change in contrast with the SSR conclusions made from the Latin Square Analysis.

4. Compute the ANOVA and draw the appropriate conclusions for the following Latin Square design.

BLOCK 1

		1	2	3	4
	1	17.1 (E)	24.1 (M)	17.5 (C)	27.3 (H)
BLOCK	2	26.1 (H)	23.2 (E)	26.1 (M)	22.2 (C)
2	3	18.3 (C)	25.3 (H)	18.2 (E)	24.1 (M)
	4	25.0 (M)	22.3 (C)	29.1 (H)	25.3 (E)

Block 1 represents regions of the country.

Block 2 represents different drivers.

The factor under study is brands of fuel.

The response is miles per dollar.

E = Exxon   M = Mobil   C = Citgo   H = Hess

5. Apply the appropriate analysis technique to the folowing experiment.

Lab A	Lab B
10.5	10.9
10.7	11.1
5.2	6.1
4.6	5.1
20.8	22.0
25.6	27.1
8.1	8.8
6.2	6.3

The response is particle size and each lab was given the same standard (there were 8 different standards).

6. Compute an ANOVA for the following data on Nitrogen content of a fertilizer:

$$X_{ijk} = \mu + BAG_i + SAMPLE_{j(i)} + ERROR_{k(ij)}$$

BAG:			1				2				3	
SAMPLE:	1	2	3	4	1	2	3	4	1	2	3	4
Rep. 1	8	10	11	8	12	11	10	12	10	9	11	10
Rep. 2	7	9	9	7	11	12	12	11	10	9	9	11
Rep. 3	9	9	10	9	12	11	13	10	9	10	10	12

7. The ANOVA shown below while computed by the computer as if it were a crossed-fixed design came from a random-nested design experiment. Combine the appropriate terms and from the EMS table, compute the variance components, the standard deviation, coefficient of variation and recommend a sampling and evaluation plan. (See appendix for method combining sums of squares and degrees of freedom).

Source	df	Sum of Squares	
A: Sample of Sample	17	1,557,358	
B: Evaluators Within Samples	5	156,816	$\bar{\bar{X}} = 150$
A*B	85	420,816	
Within Evaluators	108	431,925	

a) How many samples, evaluators, replicates were there in the experiment?

b) Write math model.

c) Find EMS.

d) Compute the mean squares for samples and between evaluators.

e) Set up components of variance table.

f) Build a sampling table and recommend the most efficient sampling/evaluation scheme.

APPENDIX 18

1. ANOVA for 2 level blocked factorial is done using the YATES Alogrithm. The block "effects" sums of squares are found in the line with the interactions confounded with blocks. These interactions are therefore not measurable.

2. In a Complete randomized block experiment, the block "factor" is treated as another factor in the ANOVA but the interaction between this "factor" and all others is not computed. Also the F test is not completed on any block "effect".

3. A Latin Square analysis in an extension of the blocked concept. No interaction is computed between the blocks nor between the blocks and the single factor under study.

4. A mathematical model is a formality utilized to identify the sources of either fixed or random variation in the response variable resulting from changes in the control variables. Unlike a regression model, the math model does not seek coefficients, but merely cites the sources of variation. Insight gleaned from the math model helps establish the expected mean square (EMS). (See Appendix 18-1 for more details).

5. Hierarchy in sampling: To determine the standard error which results from sampling a continuous variable at stages or levels, we use the following relationship. We need to know the variance of each stage. This may be determined by a nested experiment.

$$S_{\bar{X}} = \sqrt{\frac{S^2_{TH}}{i} + \frac{S^2_{MH}}{ij} + \frac{S^2_{BH}}{ijk}}$$

Where S_X is the standard error.

S^2_{TH} is variance at top of hierarchy.
i is number of samples at top of hierarchy.
S^2_{MH} is variance at middle of hierarchy.
j is number of samples at middle of hierarchy.
S^2_{BH} is variance at bottom of hierarchy.
k is number of samples at bottom of hierarchy.

APPENDIX 18-1

MORE ON EMS

Besides helping us allocate the components of variance from a nested experiment, the expected mean square is used in determining the proper terms in our F test for significance. We mentioned that math models and EMS turn out to be trivial formalities in most factorial experiments. We will now show why.

For a typical factorial fixed factor experiment, the math model is:

$$X_{ijk} = \mu + A_i + B_j + AB_{ij} + E_{k(ij)}$$

and the EMS Algorithm looks like this:

Table 18A-1

	Fixed $i=a$	Fixed $j=b$	Random $k=n$	EMS
A_i	0	b	n	$bn\varnothing_A + \sigma^2_e$
B_j	a	0	n	$an\varnothing_B + \sigma^2_e$
AB_{ij}	0	0	n	$n\varnothing_{AB} + \sigma^2_e$
$e_{k(ij)}$	1	1	1	σ^2_e

To fill in EMS Algorithm Table:

1. Match rows and columns for subscripts:
    a. All Nested (in parenthesis) subscript matches get a 1.
    b. All Random column heading subscript matches get a 1.
    c. All fixed column heading subscript matches get a zero.

2. All non-match intersections bring down number of levels in factor under study found in column heading. (i.e. column i has a levels; j has b levels, and k has n levels).

3. To compute the EMS from the table, take each factor row wise.
    a. Ignore the column with the matching subscript.
    b. Look to each row that contains the subscript of the factor you are computing EMS for.
    c. Multiply the non-ignored terms of the row.
    d. For fixed factors the EMS is $\varnothing$ (phi) with a subscript of the factor's symbol (ie: $\varnothing_A$).
    e. For random factors the EMS is σ^2 with a subscript of the factor's symbol (ie σ^2_e).

4. Set up F test so the effect is compared to the next lower source of variation. So if the effect is made up of $nb\varnothing_a + \sigma^2_e$ the next lower source of variation is σ^2_e. So the F ratio is $\left(bn\varnothing_a + \sigma^2_e\right)/\sigma^2_e$.

In the fixed model we will always compare our effects to error as the fixed effect EMS Table (18A-1) shows. The random factor EMS is much different, and the F tests are made between main effects and the interaction, plus error as shown in Table 18A-2. The same rules are used to build 18A-2. Note that error is always random.

Table 18A-2

	Fixed $i=a$	Fixed $j=b$	Random $k=n$	EMS
A_i	1	b	n	$bn\sigma^2_A + n\sigma^2_{AB} + \sigma^2_e$
B_j	a	1	n	$an\sigma^2_B + n\sigma^2_{AB} + \sigma^2_e$
AB_{ij}	1	1	n	$n\sigma^2_{AB} + \sigma^2_e$
$e_{k(ij)}$	1	1	1	σ^2_e

A surprising result takes place in a mixed (some random, some fixed) model. Table 18A-3 shows that the random factor is tested against error alone, while the fixed factor is tested against the interaction and error. The symbol for an interaction that is part fixed and part random is expressed as σ^2 rather than $\varnothing$.

Table 18A-3

	Random $i=a$	Fixed $j=b$	Random $k=n$	EMS
A_i	1	b	n	$bn\sigma^2_A + \sigma^2_e$
B_j	a	0	n	$an\varnothing_B + n\sigma^2_{AB} + \sigma^2_e$
AB_{ij}	1	0	n	$n\sigma^2_{AB} + \sigma^2_e$
$e_{k(ij)}$	1	1	1	σ^2_e

The Derivation of Empirical Equations from Statistically Designed Experiments

19

A CASE HISTORY OF AN EXPERIMENTAL INVESTIGATION

We have studied organization, experimental design techniques, and analysis methods. Now is the time to see these concepts at work. In this chapter we will gain experience and learn by doing. We will look at actual experiments and watch the planning, organization, and application of sound experimental methods produce the required information at the least expenditure of resources. This chapter will show us why we design experiments rather than just let information arrive at our doorstep in some haphazard manner.

THE PHASE APPROACH

In Chapter 2 we introduced the concept of sequential or phased experimentation. The idea is to avoid putting all our experimental eggs into one basket for fear that there is a hole in the theory that built the basket. Rather than one big experiment, we work in phases. Each phase builds our knowledge in a systematic way. Table 19-1 is an expanded outline of the phases of experimentation with the types of designs and the analysis techniques appropriate at each phase.

The building block approach: There are 8 steps in the building block approach to experimentation. These steps lead to a *toleranced* specification that produces a quality product that is on target with the least variation at the lowest production and development cost. During the concept phase, and throughout phase zero, we rely on our prior knowledge of the process. In phase I, we sharpen this knowledge with information derived from fractional factorial experiments (CH5). The analysis of the factorial design (CH14) leads us to the next phase (II) where we use multi-level designs (CH6) which when analyzed (CH16 & CH17) produce a process model which we exercise (CH20) to determine process set points *and* tolerances. We then verify our predictions in phase III and issue our final specifications.

Table 19-1

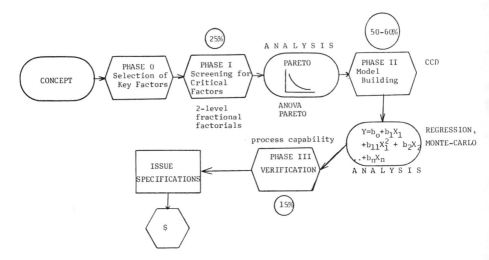

Notice the expenditure of resources circled near each phase. This is a guide for spending that assures good budgetary control *and* valid results.

EXAMPLE ONE — A POPCORN FORMULA

We will look at a comparatively simple experiment first and then a much more complex example. Our first experiment involves the production of a tasty product, popcorn.

Although the manufacturers do <u>not</u> recommend[*] making popcorn in a microwave oven, it is a convenient method of quickly producing a single serving of this food snack.

The concept phase of the experiment, although discovered by chance, needs to be developed to the point where we can obtain a uniform product. We would like our popcorn to pop completely and taste good. The first thing we must do is state a goal.

GOAL: To maximize the yield of popcorn and maintain taste.

---

[*]The story goes that the cooking properties of microwave energy were discovered at a military installation where microwave communication beams were used. A box of unpopped corn got into the beam by accident and popped! Now an entire industry revolves around microwave cooking.

Now it is time to bring our prior knowledge of the process together in such a way that we can write an objective for our experiment. This objective will be the basis for our experimental design.

To bring our knowledge together, we conduct a brainstorming session. To give the reader a better idea of the microwave popcorn process, here's a description of how it works.

A small dish is filled with popcorn and oil. To prevent a mess, a paper lunch bag is fitted over the dish. The bag is cut to fit into the oven and steam vents are cut in the bag. The dish is placed on a trivet to prevent the heat from being drawn off by the oven floor. The oven timer is set and popcorn is usually produced.

During the brainstorming session, a large number of ideas are freely proposed. The team is made up of experts in corn popping and a statistical expert who "runs" the session.

The list of possible variables for the popcorn process from the brainstorming session is as follows:

Table 19-2

Factor	Name	Levels
A	Amount of Popcorn *	1 TBS - 2 TBS
B	Amount of Oil *	1 TBS - 2 TBS
C	Type of Oil *	Olive/Corn
D	Height of Bag *	6 IN - 9 IN
	Phase of the Moon	
E	Number of Holes in Bag *	2 - 4
F	Time of Cooking *	2 MIN - 3.25 MIN
	Trivet (Yes or No)	
	Placement In Oven	
G	Power Level *	Med - High
H	Type of Corn *	Jolly - Orville
	* selected factors	

Notice that for even such a simple problem, we have a large number of factors to consider and control. After the brainstorming session, we use our prior knowledge to select only those factors we believe will have an influence on the popping.

Now we have enough information to write our objective. This objective will lead us to the experimental design that will get us the required information at the least expenditure of resources.

> **OBJECTIVE:**   To test the hypothesis that yield and taste rating are functions of popcorn type and amount, oil type and amount, height of bag, number of holes in bag, cooking time and power.

Since there are 8 factors, we will need at least 8 degrees of freedom (assuming a 2 level experiment) for the single effects and C_2^8 = 28* df for the 2 factor interactions.

This means that for all these effects to be unconfounded, we would need a 2^{k-p} experiment with $28 + 8 = 36$df. The closest integer power of 2 (without rounding down) is 64. With such a design, we would have 27 df in excess over the 36 we need. Therefore, we will discard such a large design and see what a 32 tc design will buy us.

With 32 treatments, we have an $n=5$. Therefore, $p=3$ since $k=8$ (recall $n=k-p$). The 2^{8-3} design is a 1/8 fraction and we will select 3 higher order interactions to "generate" our design. We will pick three of the four factor interactions as follows:

$$F \equiv ABCD$$
$$G \equiv BCDE \qquad (19\text{-}1)$$
$$H \equiv ABDE$$

Which gives the defining contrast of:

$$I \equiv ABCDF, BCDEG, ABDEH, \underline{AEFG}, \underline{CEFH}, \underline{ACGH}, \qquad (19\text{-}2)$$
$$BDFGH$$

This design is a resolution IV since the shortest "word" has four letters, which means that we have 2 factor interactions confounded together. We can get some of the 28 two factor interactions free of other two factor interactions, but not all of them. Since this is a screening experiment, we probably won't find all the factors making major contributions and we can "live" with this.

We could, and will, take this premise one step further to reduce the size of our experiment to only 16 tc's, which is more in line with the resources we have. Such a design would be a 2^{8-4} (1/16 fraction) and is a resolution IV with all 2-factor interactions confounded with each other. Since we have limited resources for the screening phase, this 2^{8-4} should strike a balance between information and resources.

---

*Recall C_2^8 means the combination of 8 items taken 2 at-a-time and is $(8(8-1))/2$.

The generators and defining contrast for this design are as follows:

$$E \equiv ABC$$
$$F \equiv ABD$$
$$G \equiv ACD \qquad (19\text{-}3)$$
$$H \equiv BCD$$

$$I \equiv ABCE, ABDF, ACDG, BCDH, CDEF, BDEG, ADEH, \qquad (19\text{-}4)$$
$$BCFG, ACFH, ABGH, AEFG, BEFH, DFGH,$$
$$CEGH, ABCDEFGH$$

This design is also a resolution IV, but <u>all</u> of the 2 factor interactions are confounded with each other. Again, we suspect that the 8 factor will "collapse" to a lesser number and, in turn, justify the high degree of potential confounding. The justification is, of course, based on the hypothesis that a number of effects will not be important and neither will their interactions. Remember, our objective for this first phase of experimentation is to find the factors that contribute most to the functional relationship. We do not expect to find the best set of conditions amoung the 16 runs that we make. We will find the direction to the best set of conditions.

Before we begin to gather data, let's see if we have all the elements of a good experiment. Our *prior knowledge* has helped gather the factors. We have a clearly stated *Goal* and *Objective*. The *response* variable, yield, is quantitative and precise since it is based on an exact count of the number of popped and unpopped kernels. We will also measure the taste of the popcorn by having an expert give a rating on a 1 to 10 scale. With these elements in place, we are now ready to gather data.

The TOKAYMP program found in Chapter 5 conveniently sets up the table of treatment combinations as shown on the next page:

Table 19-3

Using TOKAYMP computer program to generate the design for the popcorn problem.

```
READY
>RUN
HOW MANY FACTORS(NO MORE THAN 10)? 8
HOW MANY REPLICATES? 1
WHAT IS THE NAME OF FACTOR A?(USE 6 LETTER ABBREV.)
? AMTPC
WHAT IS THE LOW LEVEL OF AMTPC? 1 TBS
WHAT IS THE HIGH LEVEL OF AMTPC? 2T TBS
WHAT IS THE NAME OF FACTOR B?(USE 6 LETTER ABBREV.)
? AMTOIL
WHAT IS THE LOW LEVEL OF AMTOIL? 1 TBS
WHAT IS THE HIGH LEVEL OF AMTOIL? 2 TBS
WHAT IS THE NAME OF FACTOR C?(USE 6 LETTER ABBREV.)
? TYOIL
WHAT IS THE LOW LEVEL OF TYOIL? OLIVE
WHAT IS THE HIGH LEVEL OF TYOIL? CORN
WHAT IS THE NAME OF FACTOR D?(USE 6 LETTER ABBREV.)
? HTBAG
WHAT IS THE LOW LEVEL OF HTBAG? 6 IN
WHAT IS THE HIGH LEVEL OF HTBAG? 9 IN
WHAT IS THE NAME OF FACTOR E?(USE 6 LETTER ABBREV.)
? #HOLES
WHAT IS THE LOW LEVEL OF #HOLES? 2
WHAT IS THE HIGH LEVEL OF #HOLES? 4
WHAT IS THE NAME OF FACTOR F?(USE 6 LETTER ABBREV.)
? TIME
WHAT IS THE LOW LEVEL OF TIME? 2 MIN
WHAT IS THE HIGH LEVEL OF TIME? 3 1/4
WHAT IS THE NAME OF FACTOR G?(USE 6 LETTER ABBREV.)
? POWER
WHAT IS THE LOW LEVEL OF POWER? MEDIUM
WHAT IS THE HIGH LEVEL OF POWER? HIGH
WHAT IS THE NAME OF FACTOR H?(USE 6 LETTER ABBREV.)
? TYPE CORN
WHAT IS THE LOW LEVEL OF TYPE CORN? JOLLY
WHAT IS THE HIGH LEVEL OF TYPE CORN? ORVILLE

.................INFORMATION ANALYSIS...................
THERE ARE 8 MAIN FACTORS AND
28 TWO-FACTOR INTERACTIONS AS EXPECTED INFORMATION.
THEREFORE, TO OBTAIN THIS INFORMATION, YOU
WILL NEED A MINIMUM BASE DESIGN OF
32 RUNS.
THE RECOMMENDED DESIGN IS A: 1  / 8 FRACTIONAL FACTORIAL.


WILL YOU USE THE RECOMMENDED FRACTION? NO
ENTER THE FRACTIONALIZATION ELEMENT FOR THE DESIGN YOU WANT? 4
TO BUILD THE THE DESIGN, ENTER THE NUMBER OF LETTERS
IN THE GENERATOR 'WORD'.  THEN WHEN PROMPTED ENTER
THE INDIVIDUAL LETTERS (ONE AT A TIME) IN THE GENERATOR
USING THE NUMERICAL EQUIVALENTS OF THE LETTERS.
IE: 1=A,2=B,3=C,4=D,5=E
ENTER THE NUMBER OF LETTERS IN GENERATOR # 1 ? 3
ENTER # VALUE FOR LETTER  1 ? 1
ENTER # VALUE FOR LETTER  2 ? 2
ENTER # VALUE FOR LETTER  3 ? 3
ENTER THE NUMBER OF LETTERS IN GENERATOR # 2 ? 3
ENTER # VALUE FOR LETTER  1 ? 1
```

```
ENTER # VALUE FOR LETTER  2 ? 2
ENTER # VALUE FOR LETTER  3 ? 4
ENTER THE NUMBER OF LETTERS IN GENERATOR # 3 ? 3
ENTER # VALUE FOR LETTER  1 ? 1
ENTER # VALUE FOR LETTER  2 ? 3
ENTER # VALUE FOR LETTER  3 ? 4
ENTER THE NUMBER OF LETTERS IN GENERATOR # 4 ? 3
ENTER # VALUE FOR LETTER  1 ? 2
ENTER # VALUE FOR LETTER  2 ? 3
ENTER # VALUE FOR LETTER  3 ? 4
```

We have our experimental plan in Table 19-4. Our first run is 1 TBS Jolly popcorn with 1 TBS Olive Oil in a 6 inch bag with 2 holes at medium power for 2 minutes. The results are shown in Table 19-5 and are somewhat disappointing for this first run. There were only 13 out of 167 (7.8%) popped kernels and they had a poor, oily taste. TC #2 was a bit better at 60.5% and a medium taste. But if we were to look at each run to see which is the best, we miss the whole point of the *experiment*.

Table 19-4

```
2**K-P FRACTIONAL FACTORIAL
      IN RANDOM ORDER
```

RUN #	TC	AMTPC	AMTOIL	TYOIL	HTBAG	#HOLES	TIME	POWER	TYPE CORN
1	(1)	1 TBS	1 TBS	OLIVE	6 IN	2	2 MIN	MEDIUM	JOLLY
2	BD	1 TBS	2 TBS	OLIVE	9 IN	4	2 MIN	HIGH	JOLLY
3	AC	2 TBS	1 TBS	CORN	6 IN	2	3 1/4	MEDIUM	ORVILLE
4	BC	1 TBS	2 TBS	CORN	6 IN	2	3 1/4	HIGH	JOLLY
5	ABCD	2 TBS	2 TBS	CORN	9 IN	4	3 1/4	HIGH	ORVILLE
6	C	1 TBS	1 TBS	CORN	6 IN	4	2 MIN	HIGH	ORVILLE
7	AB	2 TBS	2 TBS	OLIVE	6 IN	2	2 MIN	HIGH	ORVILLE
8	ABC	2 TBS	2 TBS	CORN	6 IN	4	2 MIN	MEDIUM	JOLLY
9	B	1 TBS	2 TBS	OLIVE	6 IN	4	3 1/4	MEDIUM	ORVILLE
10	AD	2 TBS	1 TBS	OLIVE	9 IN	4	2 MIN	MEDIUM	ORVILLE
11	CD	1 TBS	1 TBS	CORN	9 IN	4	3 1/4	MEDIUM	JOLLY
12	D	1 TBS	1 TBS	OLIVE	9 IN	2	3 1/4	HIGH	ORVILLE
13	BCD	1 TBS	2 TBS	CORN	9 IN	2	2 MIN	MEDIUM	ORVILLE
14	ABD	2 TBS	2 TBS	OLIVE	9 IN	2	3 1/4	MEDIUM	JOLLY
15	ACD	2 TBS	1 TBS	CORN	9 IN	2	2 MIN	HIGH	JOLLY
16	A	2 TBS	1 TBS	OLIVE	6 IN	4	3 1/4	HIGH	JOLLY

Table 19-5

Results of the popcorn experiment.

RESPONSES

RUN #	TC	AMTPC	AMTOIL	TYOIL	HTBAG	#HOLES	TIME	POWER	TYPE CORN	% Popped	Taste	Comments
1	(1)	1 TBS	1 TBS	OLIVE	6 IN	2	2 MIN	MEDIUM	JOLLY	7.8	1	smelly
16	A	2 TBS	1 TBS	OLIVE	6 IN	4	3 1/4	HIGH	JOLLY	86.1	1	burned
9	B	1 TBS	2 TBS	OLIVE	6 IN	4	3 1/4	MEDIUM	ORVILLE	25.5	2	smelly
7	AB	2 TBS	2 TBS	OLIVE	6 IN	2	2 MIN	HIGH	ORVILLE	58.6	8	smelly
6	C	1 TBS	1 TBS	CORN	6 IN	4	2 MIN	HIGH	ORVILLE	62.7	8	fluffy
3	AC	2 TBS	1 TBS	CORN	6 IN	2	3 1/4	MEDIUM	ORVILLE	25.8	5	fluffy
4	BC	1 TBS	2 TBS	CORN	6 IN	2	3 1/4	HIGH	JOLLY	89.3	6	burned
8	ABC	2 TBS	2 TBS	CORN	6 IN	4	2 MIN	MEDIUM	JOLLY	4.3	4	soggy
12	D	1 TBS	1 TBS	OLIVE	9 IN	2	3 1/4	HIGH	ORVILLE	83.5	5	burned
10	AD	2 TBS	1 TBS	OLIVE	9 IN	4	2 MIN	MEDIUM	ORVILLE	2.6	6	smelly
2	BD	1 TBS	2 TBS	OLIVE	9 IN	4	2 MIN	HIGH	JOLLY	60.5	3	smelly
14	ABD	2 TBS	2 TBS	OLIVE	9 IN	2	3 1/4	MEDIUM	JOLLY	46.7	4	smelly
11	CD	1 TBS	1 TBS	CORN	9 IN	4	3 1/4	MEDIUM	JOLLY	34.7	3	hard
15	ACD	2 TBS	1 TBS	CORN	9 IN	2	2 MIN	HIGH	JOLLY	66.4	9	small
13	BCD	1 TBS	2 TBS	CORN	9 IN	2	2 MIN	MEDIUM	ORVILLE	0.8	1	small
5	ABCD	2 TBS	2 TBS	CORN	9 IN	4	3 1/4	HIGH	ORVILLE	83.6	8	burned

2**K-P FRACTIONAL FACTORIAL IN YATES ORDER

We must look at the whole result by applying the proper coherent analysis technique. In this case we use the YATES ANOVA and find the results in Tables 19-6 and 19-7.

There are two very large effects, power and time. Both act positively on the yield, but time has a negative effect on taste. This result is not unexpected since the longer time treatments had a tendency to <u>burn</u>, especially at the higher power levels. The interaction graph shown in figure 19-1 displays this effect. The power increase does improve the taste as long as the time does not get excessive and burn the already popped corn. These two big effects account for most of the change in yield and taste. We also see that there is a trade-off between yield and tast. If the yield comes from a combination of high power and longer time, the taste is reduce due to burning.

Table 19-6

Response: Yield

INDEX #	TOTAL OBSERVATION	SUM OF SQUARE	HALF EFFECT	MEASURES	DF
1	7.8000	34123.3300	46.181	AVERAGE	
2	86.1000	5.4056	0.581	A Amt. Corn	1
3	25.5000	0.0056	−0.019	B Amt. Oil	1
4	58.6000	38.7506	1.556	AB	1
5	62.7000	0.8556	−0.231	C Type Oil	1
6	25.8000	36.3006	−1.506	AC	1
7	89.3000	32.7756	−1.431	BC	1
8	4.3000	22.3257	−1.181	ABC # holes	1
9	83.5000	21.8556	1.169	D Bag High	1
10	2.6000	57.3807	1.894	AD	1
11	60.5000	5.1756	0.569	BD	1
12	46.7000	2795.7660	13.219	ABD Time	1
13	34.7000	8.8506	−0.744	CD	1
14	66.4000	12237.8900	27.656	ACD Power	−1
15	0.8000	173.5807	−3.294	BCD Type Corn	
16	83.6000	10.7256	−0.819	ABCD	1
	ERROR	0.0000			0
	TOTAL	15447.6500			15

Table 19-7

Response: Taste (1 = Poor, 10 = Good)

INDEX #	TOTAL OBSERVATION	SUM OF SQUARE	HALF EFFECT	MEASURES	DF
1	1.0000	342.2500	4.625	AVERAGE	
2	1.0000	16.0000	1.000	A Amt. Corn	1
3	2.0000	0.2500	−0.125	B Amt. Oil	1
4	8.0000	4.0000	0.500	AB	1
5	8.0000	12.2500	0.875	C Type Oil	1
6	5.0000	0.0000	0.000	AC	1
7	6.0000	6.2500	−0.625	BC	1
8	4.0000	1.0000	−0.250	ABC # Holes	1
9	5.0000	1.0000	0.250	D Bag High	1
10	6.0000	12.2500	0.875	AD	1
11	3.0000	9.0000	−0.750	BD	1
12	4.0000	2.2500	−0.375	ABD Time	1
13	3.0000	4.0000	−0.500	CD	1
14	9.0000	30.2500	1.375	ACD Power	1
15	1.0000	9.0000	0.750	BCD Type Corn	
16	8.0000	2.2500	0.375	ABCD	1
	ERROR	0.0000			0
	TOTAL	109.7500			15

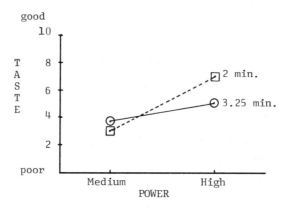

Figure 19-1
Interaction Time and Power

The next biggest effect is caused by type of corn. Unfortunately, in this case, there is a conflict between the two responses. The yield is negatively changed by the type of corn, while the taste is improved with the plus level. It was observed during the experiment that the tastier corn (Orville) was producing bigger morsels than the Jolly.

Now that we have looked at the big effects we need to judge the contribution of the other factors to the results. Both bag height and number of holes had a miniscule effect on the two responses. The amount of corn had a positive effect on taste, but did not change yield. The olive oil had such a smell, that it was decided to use only corn oil in future phases of experimentation.

The screening experiment has pointed the direction for our next phase of work. We shall include power level, time, type of corn, amount of corn, and amount of oil. Now the amount of oil did not show large effects, but prior experience had suggested that this could interact with amount of corn to change yield. Due to the extensive confounding in this experiment, this effect could have been combined with another factor.

PHASE II

In this phase of the experiment we will move our power up to include medium-high and high, but cut the time back a bit to avoid burning at high temperatures. We will still use the same levels of oil and corn and will also continue to compare the two types of popping corn. This results in 5 factors of which most are restricted to only 2 levels. A reasonable design for this number of factors could involve either 8 or 16 runs. The design with 8 treatment combinations has the problem that the single (main) effects are confounded with the 2 factor interactions while the 16 tc design provides information on both single effects and two factor interactions. The two strongest interactions we might expect would be between Power and Time and another between Amount of Oil and Amount of Corn. An infomation analysis tells us that we need 5 df for the 5 single effects and 2 df for the 2 two factor interactions. A design with 8 runs has exactly 7 df but there is a mis-match of the application of the degrees of freedom and at least one of the required inteactions will be confounded with a single effect. (Do Problem #1 to show the reasoning to the above result).

The consideration at hand is to either run the larger design (16 tc's) or live with confounding of the 2^{5-2} or drop a factor to eliminate the confounding. Since we already have strong indications of the power factor's positive influence on both taste and yield we will drop this factor and run a 1/2 fraction on 4 factors which will only require only the 8 tc's that we can afford. This is a practical example of reducing the size of the experiment by eliminating the need for marginal information.

We use the TOKAYMP computer program to set up the design order. The defining contrast for this 2^{4-1} is I≡ABCD.

Table 19-8 shows the factors and levels and Table 19-9 shows the YATES ordered runs with the yield, taste, and a new response "volume" as measured by the number of cups of popped corn per tablespoon of raw corn.

Table 19-8

	FACTOR	LEVELS	
A	Time	2 Min 15 Sec	2 Min 45 Sec
B	Amount of Corn	1 TBS	2 TBS
C	Amount of Oil	1 TBS	2 TBS
D	Type of Corn	Jolly	Orville

The inclusion of new factors (especially a new response) is one of the innovative benefits of sequential experimentation. In the first phase of this experiment, we observed that the Orville corn was bigger. This is an important aspect of popcorn quality and can be measured by the volume metric. While not a statistical consideration, it is important that experimenters use their keen sense of observation throughout all phases of experimentation. Don't let the SED structure put "blinders" on your good engineering judgment.

The results of the second phase of popping (in Table 19-9) show a tighter range of yields than experienced in the first phase. There are some excellent results and we might be inclined to just "pick the winners" at this point.

Table 19-9

```
DEFINING CONTRAST: I=ABCD


            2**K-P FRACTIONAL FACTORIAL
            IN YATES ORDER
                                                            RESPONSES
RUN #    TC        TIME    AMT CRN AMT OIL   TYP CRN    VOL.   YIELD   TASTE

  6     (1)      2M 15S  1 TBS  1 TBS   JOLLY     1.33   60.9     5

  5      A       2M 45S  1 TBS  1 TBS   ORVILLE   2.00   84.0     6

  1      B       2M 15S  2 TBS  1 TBS   ORVILLE   2.00   76.3     7

  4      AB      2M 45S  2 TBS  1 TBS   JOLLY     1.50   77.7     6

  8      C       2M 15S  1 TBS  2 TBS   ORVILLE   1.75   66.7     4

  2      AC      2M 45S  1 TBS  2 TBS   JOLLY     1.50   73.9     3

  3      BC      2M 15S  2 TBS  2 TBS   JOLLY     1.33   66.3     5

  7      ABC     2M 45S  2 TBS  2 TBS   ORVILLE   2.00   81.3     7
```

However, we must look at the experiment as a whole via the ANOVA to detect the trends. We run the YATES analysis on the 3 responses to reveal the following results on volume, yield, and taste.

VOLUME

The largest effect on Volume was the type of corn. Orville produced a half cup more popped corn per tablespoon of raw corn than Jolly. The other effects were much smaller than this major driver and did not conflict with the results for the other two responses. Our conclusion from this volume reponse is to use Orville's popping corn.

YIELD

The yield response showed time to be the biggest single effect followed by type of corn, and then amount of corn, an interaction between time and amount of corn, or (due to confounding) amount of oil and type of corn was next in influence and then the amount of oil.

From physical considerations, it was decided that the time and amount of corn interaction was more likely to be the cause of the difference in yield rather than the amount of oil and type of corn. Again, there were not inconsistencies between the recommendations based on yield and the other two responses. These recommendations are to use 2 minutes, 45 seconds, with 2 tablespoons corn in 1 tablespoon oil, and use Orville's corn.

TASTE

The taste response confirmed the choice of Orville's corn, and showed an interesting interaction between amount of corn and amount of oil.

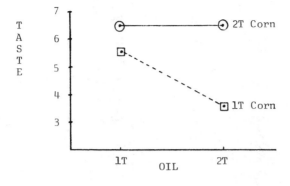

Figure 19-2

Figure 19-2 shows the plot of this interaction which illustrates a sub-additivity. The taste quality drops more than expected when 1 tablespoon of corn is immersed in 2 tablespoons of oil. The problem is that the popped corn comes up soggy and oily when too much oil is used.

The final recommendation based on the complete analysis is as follows:

Table 19-10

FACTOR	LEVEL
Type Corn	Orville
Amount of Corn	2 TBS
Amount of Oil	1 TBS
Time	2 Min, 45 Sec

Now if we look back to TABLE 19-9, we notice that this treatment combination was *not* in the design. This is not an unusual result. Because we have used only a *fraction* of the possible design configurations, it would be unexpected to find the *exact* optimum among the treatment combinations. Instead, we have been given the *direction* to obtain the optimum.

A series of repeated confirmation runs with the optimum formula for microwave popcorn produced the following results:

Table 19-11

RUN #	YIELD	VOLUME	TASTE
1	93.7	2.3	10
2	94.0	2.1	10
3	93.0	2.3	10
4	93.5	2.1	10
5	94.0	2.3	10
6	94.1	2.3	10

The results of the confirmation runs give a consistent and better product than any of the trials in the experiment. This fact again illustrates why the total analysis must be completed on the *whole* design rather than just picking the best run. We have *interpolated* to a result that is better than a simple pick of the "best" tc's in the original design.

EXAMPLE TWO —
A PHOTOGRAPHIC PROCESS

In our first example many of the factors were of a qualitative (non-numeric) nature and it was not necessary to go through the formalities of generating a mathematical model. The simple graphical analysis provided all the insight into the optimization of the process that produced good popcorn. In many other situations like the one we are about to embark upon, the system is more complex and requires a more refined expression of the functional relationships. A mathematical model is a very concise way to accomplish this task. The math model is not the purpose of the experimental effort, but the by-product that will help us accomplish the purpose. It is unfortunate that many statistically oriented experimenters labor to simply create the model and stop short of using it. In the last half of this chapter, we will encounter the various phases of a more complex experiment, create a model and then in Chapter 21 we will put this model to use to engineer quality into the product that the model describes. In this way we become more than statistical engineers, we become quality engineers.

THE CONCEPT PHASE

No experiment can begin without some prior knowledge of the process under investigation. In photographic processing, the exposed film is developed with a specially formulated solution of chemicals, The idea is to convert silver halide crystals that have been exposed to light into black metalic silver. This process is a well-known one that has existed for over 100 years. The real trick is to make the silver image black in proportion to the amount of light striking the film. Also we want the image to be high in its information content and free from unwanted image defects. All of these characteristics may be measured separately by automated equipment or by visual methods. It is further possible to "roll up" the elements of image quality into a single value metric called the IQ (image quality) of the picture. We will use the IQ metric for this example.

Based on prior knowledge of the photographic process, the team of experimenters assembled the following factors at a brainstorming session. Some factors could have an effect on the quality of the developed film and some (like phase of the moon) are the type of factor that comes up at a free-wheeling brainstorming exercise.

Table 19-11

Temperature	Humidity
Ph	Color Of Solution
Agitation	Odor Of Solution
Time Of Development	Speed Of Film Travel
Concentration of Metol	Phase Of The Moon
Concentraction Of Hydroquinone (HQ)	KI Concentration
Day Of the Week	# Of Rolls Of Film
Replenishment Cycle	# Of Weeks Before Change
Type Of Film Being Developed	

There are 17 possible factors listed in Table 19-11. After the brainstorming session, the team rationalized the contribution of each proposed factor and decided what should be kept in the experimental efforts, what should be discarded completely, and what will be held constant. Phase of the moon was discarded as well as the subjective color and smell of the solution. Those factors related to developer solution wear-out were set aside for this part of the effort. It was decided to use new, fresh batches for each trial. Only one type of film was to be developed and a constant type of image would be exposed on it. These decisions reduced the number of factors to a manageable number. Still, further decisions had to be made regarding some factors that are redundant. The agitation and time of development factors became redundant if an automatic processor is used with constantly moving film. It was decided that an automatic processor conforms more to the practice involved with the development of the film in question and therefore, the speed of film travel can replace the agitation and time factors. The above decisions leave us with 7 factors. This is typical of the reduction possible after a brainstorming session. The seven factors are:

Table 19-12

Temperature	Humidity
Ph	Speed Of Travel
Concentration Of Metol	Concentration Of HQ
KI Concentraction	

Up to this point in our experimental design efforts, we have not used a bit of statistics. We have relied upon our prior knowledge of the process to identify the factors influencing the response. We are now ready to state the goal and objective of this experiment.

GOAL: To obtain a maximum IQ (image quality) of 100 with the least variation.

OBJECTIVE: To test the hypothesis that the IQ is a function of Temperature, Ph, Humidity, Speed, and Concentration of: Metol, HQ and KI.

DEFINING THE REQUIRED INFORMATION

The objective concisely states the factors we need to gather information about. If we take the prescribed path in this investigation, an experiment that will identify the quantitative relative importance of the factors is in order. A two-level fractional factorial design is the appropriate screening experiment for this purpose. We now need to determine the most efficient approach to this part in the sequence of experiments. Since we have 7 factors we must allocate the information associated with these 7 factors. There will be one degree of freedom required for each signle factor effect in a two-level design. We should also make provision for the possible two-factor interactions. There will be 21 of these combined effects. Therefore, we will need 28 df in the screening design. The closest 2^{k-p} design would contain 32 treatment combinations and would be based on a 2^5 full factorial.

While we have just defined the required information, we have not balanced our definition of efficiency by looking at the resources necessary to get this information. With 32 treatments (or runs), it will take over 8 months to get the "required" information. From a psychological view, this is just too long. In 8 months, the project could be cancelled or we could just lose interest. Management would probably lose interest sooner and give up on experimental design methods. We have two possible means of cutting the extent of this experiment. We could use a smaller fraction (with more confounding among the factors). We could also attempt to cut down on the actual physical time involved in the running of the tests by reducing the number of rolls of film or possibly using overtime to prepare for the next run in the sequence. It turns out that the original estiamte of a week per run was very conservative and in actuality, it really only takes two days per run. One day to set up the conditions and another to develop and test the film. Now it looks like we can do do two runs a week with a little "breathing space" to spare. The 2^{7-2} would now take 4 months, but a 2^{7-3} could take only 2 months which is more to management's liking.

If we decide to run the 2^{7-3} there will be less information available in the form of the two-factor interactions. In fact, all of the two-factor interactions will be confounded with each other. Here is where some prior knowledge of the process is very important. Of the 21 possible interactions, we would expect only a few interactions to have a large influence on the quality of the development. From basic chemistry we can discount all of the interactions between the humidity factor and the other factors. This eliminates 6 of the 21 bringing the count to only 15 interactions. We could expect a metol-HQ interaction since these two developers tend to super-add in their combined effect. It is now time to look at the statistics of the experimental designs and see exactly the amount of information available in different fractional factorial designs.

Table 19-13

DEFINING CONTRAST: I=ABCE,BCDF,ACDG,ADEF,BDEG,ABFG,CEFG

2**K-P FRACTIONAL FACTORIAL
IN YATES ORDER

RUN #	TC	A TEMPER	B P H	C METOL	D K I	E HUMIDTY	F SPEED	G H Q
6	(1)	LO	LO	LO	LO	LO	LO	LO
5	A	HI	LO	LO	LO	HI	LO	HI
7	B	LO	HI	LO	LO	HI	HI	LO
14	AB	HI	HI	LO	LO	LO	HI	HI
1	C	LO	LO	HI	LO	HI	HI	HI
3	AC	HI	LO	HI	LO	LO	HI	LO
9	BC	LO	HI	HI	LO	LO	LO	HI
15	ABC	HI	HI	HI	LO	HI	LO	LO
12	D	LO	LO	LO	HI	LO	HI	HI
4	AD	HI	LO	LO	HI	HI	HI	LO
8	BD	LO	HI	LO	HI	HI	LO	HI
10	ABD	HI	HI	LO	HI	LO	LO	LO
11	CD	LO	LO	HI	HI	HI	LO	LO
2	ACD	HI	LO	HI	HI	LO	LO	HI
13	BCD	LO	HI	HI	HI	LO	HI	LO
16	ABCD	HI	HI	HI	HI	HI	HI	HI

Table 19-14

DEFINING CONTRAST: I=ABCDF,BCDEG,AEFG

2**K-P FRACTIONAL FACTORIAL
IN YATES ORDER

RUN #	TC	A TEMPER	B P H	C METOL	D K I	E HUMIDTY	F SPEED	G H Q
1	(1)	LO	LO	LO	LO	LO	HI	HI
15	A	HI	LO	LO	LO	LO	LO	HI
8	B	LO	HI	LO	LO	LO	LO	LO
2	AB	HI	HI	LO	LO	LO	HI	LO
30	C	LO	LO	HI	LO	LO	LO	LO
11	AC	HI	LO	HI	LO	LO	HI	LO
4	BC	LO	HI	HI	LO	LO	HI	HI
26	ABC	HI	HI	HI	LO	LO	LO	HI
29	D	LO	LO	LO	HI	LO	LO	LO
31	AD	HI	LO	LO	HI	LO	HI	LO
16	BD	LO	HI	LO	HI	LO	HI	HI
12	ABD	HI	HI	LO	HI	LO	LO	HI
22	CD	LO	LO	HI	HI	LO	HI	HI
9	ACD	HI	LO	HI	HI	LO	LO	HI
32	BCD	LO	HI	HI	HI	LO	LO	LO
21	ABCD	HI	HI	HI	HI	LO	HI	LO
28	E	LO	LO	LO	LO	HI	HI	LO
20	AE	HI	LO	LO	LO	HI	LO	LO
10	BE	LO	HI	LO	LO	HI	LO	HI
18	ABE	HI	HI	LO	LO	HI	HI	HI
6	CE	LO	LO	HI	LO	HI	LO	HI
13	ACE	HI	LO	HI	LO	HI	HI	HI
7	BCE	LO	HI	HI	LO	HI	HI	LO
23	ABCE	HI	HI	HI	LO	HI	LO	LO
25	DE	LO	LO	LO	HI	HI	LO	HI
19	ADE	HI	LO	LO	HI	HI	HI	HI
14	BDE	LO	HI	LO	HI	HI	HI	LO
17	ABDE	HI	HI	LO	HI	HI	LO	LO
24	CDE	LO	LO	HI	HI	HI	HI	LO
5	ACDE	HI	LO	HI	HI	HI	LO	LO
27	BCDE	LO	HI	HI	HI	HI	LO	HI
3	ABCDE	HI	HI	HI	HI	HI	HI	HI

The information available in the two designs may be compared by looking at the defining contrasts printed above each design. In the smaller design (Table 19-13) the defining contrast is made up of only 4-letter words. Due to management considerations, we will probably have to use this design, so we should understand the level of confounding. All of the single effects will be confounded with 3-factor interactions and should not cause a problem. The two-factor interactions will be confounded in sets of 3 as follows:

Table 19-15

$$I = ABCE, BCDF, ACDG, ADEF, BDEG, ABFG, CEFG \text{ (defining contrast)}$$

$$AB = CE = FG$$
$$AC = BE = DG$$
$$BC = AE = DF$$
$$AD = CG = EF$$
$$BD = CF = EG$$
$$CD = BF = AG$$

$$ABCD = DE = AF = BG$$

Now it is time to assign the factors to their exact columns given the pattern of confounding observed in Table 19-15. If we look at the information in Table 19-13, the most likely interaction (Metol-HQ) is CG. CG is confounded with AD and EF. Both of these effects are unlikely to take place, so the design looks pretty good, so far. Since we already stated that none of the efects would interact with the humidity, we can reduce Table 19-15 as follows and make good, information-based judgments about the possibility of the effects taking place.

Table 19-16

$AB = FG$	neither are likely
$AC = DG$	most likely is AC (temp-metol)
$BC = DF$	most likely is BC (PH-metol)
$AD = CG$	most likely is CG (metol-HQ)
$BD = CF$	neither likely
$CD = BF = AG$	none likely to occur
$AF = BG$	most likely AF (temp-speed)

Table 19-16 shows the summary of our expectations on the possibilities of two-factor interactions taking place. We do not go so far as to state the quantitative effects, but only indicate if we would expect or not expect such an effect to take place. We will need the experiment to *quantify* our educated guesses. Based on this up-front analysis, we can safely say that the 1/8 fractional factorial design with only 16 tc's will get us the required information in the short time of 2 months.

ADDING LEVELS

Our design has only identified the factors with low and high levels so far. We now need to add the final pieces of information so the actual tests can be run. Again, prior knowledge of the process helps us set the levels from the "working ranges" over which we know a film will develop. Some of these working levels have come from one factor at a time experiments and some from data gathered over the years. Others have come from chemical considerations.

Table 19-17

FACTOR	NAME	WORKING RANGE	LEVELS
A	Temperature	70 - 90 degrees F	75, 85
B	PH (by alkali)	40 - 80 g/l Alkali	50, 70
C	Metol	8 - 16 g/l	10, 14
D	KI	1 - 5 gl	2, 4
E	Humidity	20 - 80%	30, 70
F	Speed	10 - 20 ips	13, 17
G	Hydroquionone (HQ)	10 - 20 g/l	13, 17

Table 19-18

DEFINING CONTRAST: I=ABCE,BCDF,ACDG,ADEF,BDEG,ABFG,CEFG

2**K-P FRACTIONAL FACTORIAL
IN YATES ORDER

RUN #	TC	A TEMPER	B P H	C METOL	D K I	E HUMIDITY	F SPEED	G H Q
1	(1)	75	50	10	2	30	13	13
7	A	85	50	10	2	70	13	17
4	B	75	70	10	2	70	17	13
15	AB	85	70	10	2	30	17	17
6	C	75	50	14	2	70	17	17
2	AC	85	50	14	2	30	17	13
13	BC	75	70	14	2	30	13	17
14	ABC	85	70	14	2	70	13	13
8	D	75	50	10	4	30	17	17
11	AD	85	50	10	4	70	17	13
16	BD	75	70	10	4	70	13	17
5	ABD	85	70	10	4	30	13	13
10	CD	75	50	14	4	70	13	13
9	ACD	85	50	14	4	30	13	17
3	BCD	75	70	14	4	30	17	13
12	ABCD	85	70	14	4	70	17	17

In selecting the levels, we do not use the entire range for fear of finding combinations that will not work at all. In this example, we have set levels half way between the mid-point of the range and the upper and lower limits. We will see that the choice will be helpful in the second phase of the experiment.

We now use the computer program TOKAYMP to generate the exact design for the factors and levels described in Table 19-17. We will run the 16 tc design plus a center point which will allow us to check for any curved effects in the data and also by replicating this center point we will have a measure of the error in our experiment. Table 19-19 is the design in random order with five repeats of the center point.

In Table 19-19 we show the responses. Now these response values did not appear out of the "blue", but were the result of many hours of carefully controlled

Table 19-19

2**K-P FRACTIONAL FACTORIAL
IN RANDOM ORDER

RUN #	TC	A TEMPER	B P H	C METOL	D K I	E HUMIDITY	F SPEED	G H Q	IMAGE QUALITY
1	(1)	75	50	10	2	30	13	13	72.0
2	AC	85	50	14	2	30	17	13	75.6
3	BCD	75	70	14	4	30	17	13	72.2
4	B	75	70	10	2	70	17	13	68.2
4a	Zero	80	60	12	3	50	15	15	82.2
5	ABD	85	70	10	4	30	13	13	75.2
6	C	75	50	14	2	70	17	17	77.8
7	A	85	50	10	2	70	13	17	79.6
7a	Zero	80	60	12	3	50	15	15	83.4
8	D	75	50	10	4	30	17	17	71.0
9	ACD	85	50	14	4	30	13	17	86.4
9a	Zero	80	60	12	3	50	15	15	84.0
10	CD	75	50	14	4	70	13	13	77.0
11	AD	85	50	10	4	70	17	13	71.8
12	ABCD	85	70	14	4	70	17	17	82.0
12a	Zero	80	60	12	3	50	15	15	83.0
13	BC	75	70	14	2	30	13	17	81.9
14	ABC	85	70	14	2	70	13	13	81.0
15	AB	85	70	10	2	30	17	17	75.9
15a	Zero	80	60	12	3	50	15	15	81.8
16	BD	75	70	10	4	70	13	17	74.6

experimentation over a 2 month period. We have invested a lot of time in the design phase of this effort and now it begins to pay off. The analysis is easily accomplished using the YATES computer program and appears in Table 19-20.

Table 19-20

PHOTO PROCESS ANALYSIS

INDEX #	TOTAL OBSERVATION	SUM OF SQUARE	HALF EFFECT	MEASURES	DF	MEAN SQUARE	F RATIO
1	72.0000	93360.8000	76.388	AVERAGE			
2	79.6000	67.2400	2.050	A Temperature		67.2400	84.050
3	68.2000	0.0025	-0.013	B	1	0.0025	0.003
4	75.9000	0.1600	0.100	AB	1	0.1600	0.200
5	77.8000	129.9599	2.850	C Metol	1	129.9599	162.450
6	75.6000	0.0225	-0.038	AC	1	0.0225	0.028
7	81.9000	0.0400	0.050	BC	1	0.0400	0.050
8	81.0000	0.2025	0.113	ABC	1	0.2025	0.253
9	71.0000	0.2025	-0.113	D	1	0.2025	0.253
10	71.8000	4.4100	0.525	AD Mtl*HQ	1	4.4100	5.513
11	74.6000	1.1025	-0.263	BD	1	1.1025	1.378
12	75.2000	0.0900	-0.075	ABD	1	0.0900	0.113
13	77.0000	1.2100	0.275	CD	1	1.2100	1.513
14	86.4000	81.9026	2.263	ACD HQ	1	81.9026	102.378
15	72.2000	68.8899	-2.075	BCD Speed	1	68.8899	86.112
16	82.0000	0.0225	-0.037	ABCD	1	0.0225	0.028
	ERROR	-0.0078			0	0.8000	
	TOTAL	355.4531			15		

```
PLOT POINTS FOR:A ARE: LOW 74.3375  HIGH   78.4375 Temp.
PLOT POINTS FOR:C ARE: LOW 73.5375  HIGH   79.2375 Metol
PLOT POINTS FOR:ACD ARE: LOW 74.125 HIGH   78.65   HQ
PLOT POINTS FOR:BCD ARE: LOW 78.4625 HIGH           74.3125 Speed
```

```
INTERACTION TABLE FOR THE METOL*HQ INTERACTION
LEVEL OF     LEVEL OF    POINT TO
FACTOR1      FACTOR2      PLOT
 _  Metol     _   HQ     71.8
 +            -          76.44999
 -            +          75.275
 +            +          82.025
```

Let us examine the ANOVA. First, because of the replicaiton of the center point, we have an estimate of error which is 0.8 with 4 degrees of freedom. The critical F value for 1 and 4 degrees of freedom at the 10% risk level is 4.5448. Five of the effects exceed this critical level and have been marked and identified with their physical names. We can display the relative importance of the factors with a "Pareto chart" as shown in Figure 19-3. While a number of metrics could be used for the y-axis of this Pareto analysis, we will use the % sum of squares. This is computed by taking the total sum of squares and dividing it into the sum of squares for each significant effect.

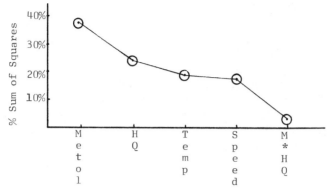

Figure 19-3
A Pareto Plot

The five effects shown above account for 99.2% of the variation in the IQ. Note that there is a steady, decreasing contribution as we add more factors. If we had plotted all of the factors instead of just the significant ones, we would have observed an exponential decay function between % contribution and the factor. This is the sort of thing Pareto (an Italian economist) observed when he plotted the wealth of individuals in his nation vs the number of people holding that wealth. There were the rich few and the many poor. We have found the *vital* few factors among the *trivial* many.

THE SECOND PHASE

The importance of the analysis we have just completed lies in the reduction of the number of factors for the next phase of experimentation. We know that there will be a next phase since we suspect a curved relatioship with at least one of the variables. This is indicated by the fact that since the average of the factorial (76.381) differs significantly from the average of the 5 replicates (82.9). We can test for significance by a simple "t" test of the mean.

$$t = \frac{82.9 - 76.4}{.8 /\sqrt{5}} \qquad \frac{6.5}{.4} = 16.25$$

Now we have a choice to make concerning the remaining experimentation. We may use a central composite design if we can get five levels for each of the factors. If we can't, then a Box-Behnkin three level would be an alternative. If we use the CCD, we could simply just run the alpha star points, since the factorial portion is already completed. In many situations this is a very economical way of running a sequence of experiments. Caution must be exercised, to be sure that nothing has changed between the two phases of experimentation to bias the results. By running the center point replicates in the first phase we have a way of checking for a change, since additional replicates will be run during the alpha star point tests. We will take the more efficient route and just add the alpha star points to the original set of data. We will also add 3 more replicates of the center point to check for commonality between the two halves of the experiment. We will of course run the new tests in random order. Table 19-21 shows the runs and the results. We will use the extremes of the working ranges for the levels in the alpha points. Note that when we picked the plus and minus levels in the fractional factorial, we did so to allow the alpha distance to be ± 2 in the design units. This may seem to be fortuitous, but is a demonstration of good statistical engineering based on our prior knowledge of the process.

Table 19-21

RUN#	TC	TEMP	METOL	SPEED	HQ	QUALITY
11	$-\alpha_a$	70	12	15	15	50.7
10	$+\alpha_a$	90	12	15	15	61.0
7	$-\alpha_b$	80	8	15	15	78.2
4	$+\alpha_b$	80	16	15	15	87.0
3	$-\alpha_c$	80	12	10	15	88.3
6	$+\alpha_c$	80	12	20	15	76.9
2	$-\alpha_d$	80	12	15	10	77.6
9	$+\alpha_d$	80	12	15	20	88.4
1	zero	80	12	15	15	83.9
5	zero	80	12	15	15	82.1
8	zero	80	12	15	15	82.8

After running the 11 additional test that form the alpha start points of the CCD, we first check the average of the zero points from phase II against the average of the zero points form the factorial portion of the first phase. We find that there is no significant difference. Had there been a significant difference, then we could have "normalized" one of the sets of data to the other to avoid bias inthe complete analysis.

PLOTTING THE RESULTS

By following the procedures of Chapter 17, we are able to construct the following function plot. This plot shows that there is a quadratic effect for the temperature and linear effects for the other three factors. Since we have an indication of an interaction between the Metol and Hydroquinone, we also plot its function.

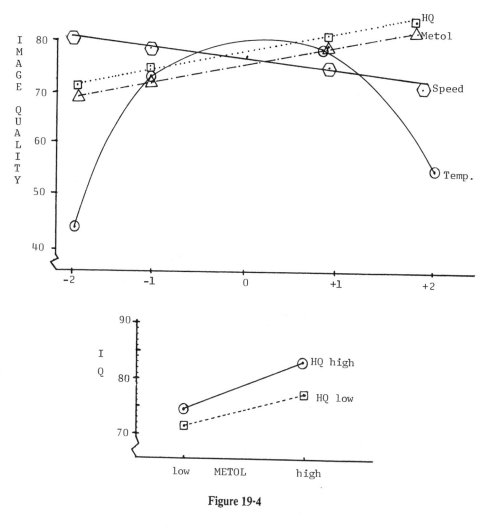

Figure 19-4

CONSTRUCTING THE MODEL

We are now in a position to propose a model for consideration. Our proposal will include 4 linear terms, an interaction cross-product and a quadratic (second order) term.

$$IQ = b_0 + b_1*Temp. + b_2*Metol + b_3*Speed + b_4*HQ + b_{11}*Temp^2 + b_{24}* Metol*HQ \quad (19\text{-}5)$$

We now take all the data from the factorial portion of the experiment and the composite portion as well as the center points and use the regression computer program to obtain the coefficients for our model.

Table 19-22

```
COEFFICIENTS
INTERCEPT B(0)=    -1661.49
TEMP     43.3517
METOL    -.652083
SPEED    -1.08246
HQ   -.466228
TEMPSQ   -.268167
M*HQ    .131250

ANOVA
TOTAL SUM OF SQUARES:      1924.71
REG SUM OF SQ;     1911.75   DF=     6  MS=    318.625
RESIDUAL SUM OF SQUARES:       12.9636  DF=    25   MS=     .518546
THE OVERALL F RATIO FOR THIS REGRESSION IS:      614.459

STANDARD ERROR OF THE ESTIMATE=      .720101


STD. ERROR OF COEFFICIENTS & T TEST VALUES
B(0) STD.ERROR=     34.6432
B    1   .841933   TEMP    T=    51.4906
B    2   .679084   METOL    T=   -.960240  ←
B    3   6.74436E-02  SPEED   T=   -16.0498
B    4   .544271   HQ   T=  -.856611  ←
B    5   5.25887E-03  TEMPSQ  T=   -50.9932
B    6   4.50063E-02  M*HQ   T=    2.91626
```

When we examine the model and the significance of the coefficients that have been determined in the physical units of the problem, we see that two of the single effects involved in the interaction have "t" test values less than the critical value of 2.05. Now there could be two approaches to resolving this problem. We could eliminate the single effects and retain the interaction, but this would produce an "improper polynomial" since we would have the higher order term without the single effects. We will take the other alternative and eliminate the interaction effect from the model. Using this simplified model we run the regression analysis. These results (Table 19-23) show that all the factors are significant. The difficulty we have observed in this regression is a function of the small interaction effect and the fact that when working with physical units, there is a slight loss of othogonality between interaction effects and the single effects making up the interaction. Another way to obtain the regression equation would be to derive the coefficients in design units and then decode the design unit coefficients into physical coefficients. In the above example, there really will be no difference in the result of either analysis method since the interaction effect is so slight. So while prior knowledge gives us reason to believe that there is an interaction between the Metol and the HQ, for this response and this particular set of levels, it would be best to leave the interaction out of the equation.

Table 19-23

```
COEFFICIENTS
INTERCEPT B(0)=    -1685.11
TEMP    43.3517
METOL    1.31667
SPEED   -1.08246
HQ    1.10877
TEMPSQ  -.268167


ANOVA
TOTAL SUM OF SQUARES:      1924.71
REG SUM OF SQ;    1907.34  DF=     5  MS=     381.468
RESIDUAL SUM OF SQUARES:      17.3736  DF=     26   MS=      .668217
THE OVERALL F RATIO FOR THIS REGRESSION IS:      570.875
DO YOU WANT RESIDUALS     ?Y
```

CASE #	CALCULATED VALUES	INPUT VALUES	RESIDUAL
1	71.33487	72.000000	0.66513
2	80.21996	79.600000	-0.61996
3	67.00504	68.200000	1.19496
4	75.89013	75.900000	0.00987
5	76.70680	77.800000	1.09320
6	76.72171	75.600000	-1.12171
7	81.03662	81.900000	0.86338
8	81.05154	81.000000	-0.05154
9	71.44013	71.000000	-0.44013
10	71.45504	71.800000	0.34496
11	75.76996	74.600000	-1.16996
12	75.78487	75.200000	-0.58487
13	76.60154	77.000000	0.39846
14	85.48662	86.400000	0.91338
15	72.27171	72.200000	-0.07171
16	81.15680	82.000000	0.84320
17	51.68333	50.700000	-0.98333
18	60.58333	61.000000	0.41667
19	77.68333	78.200000	0.51667
20	88.21667	87.000000	-1.21667
21	88.36228	88.300000	-0.06228
22	77.53772	76.900000	-0.63772
23	77.40614	77.600000	0.19386
24	88.49386	88.400000	-0.09386
25	82.95000	83.900000	0.95000
26	82.95000	82.100000	-0.85000
27	82.95000	82.800000	-0.15000
28	82.95000	82.200000	-0.75000
29	82.95000	83.400000	0.45000
30	82.95000	84.000000	1.05000
31	82.95000	83.000000	0.05000
32	82.95000	81.800000	-1.15000

```
STANDARD ERROR OF THE ESTIMATE=     .817445

STD. ERROR OF COEFFICIENTS & T TEST VALUES
B(0) STD.ERROR=      38.2360
B    1    .955747   TEMP   T=     45.3589
B    2   8.34302E-02  METOL    T=    15.7817
B    3   7.65608E-02  SPEED    T=   -14.1385
B    4   7.65608E-02  HQ   T=    14.4822
B    5   5.96978E-03  TEMPSQ   T=   -44.9207
R SQUARED=     .990973
```

Our final equation in then:

$$IQ = -1685.11 + 43.3517*Temp - .268167*Temp^2 + 1.31667*Metol + 1.10877*HQ - 1.0825*Speed$$

At this point we probably would congratulate ourselves for the fine job of finding the equation that describes our process. BUT we have only accomplished our objective. There is more work to do. Now we must complete the task and take care of the GOAL. Our goal is to get an image quality of 100. None of the experimental runs produced an IQ of 100. However, we have the power in the form of our equation to find the combination of the factors to achieve the IQ of 100. All we have to do is solve the equation to get this value.

By inspection, we can see that to get the highest IQ, we will have to put in the higher levels of Metol and HQ. The speed will have to be reduced because of its negative coefficient. The temperature has a quadratic term, so other than plotting the function, we can use some very simple calculus to find the maximum of this function. We take the partial derivative with respect to the temperature (all the other terms drop out) and set this equal to zero.

$$\frac{dIQ}{dt} = dt(43.3517t - .268167t^2) = 43.3517 - 2(.26816t)$$

...and setting this equal to zero $43.3517 - .53633t = 0$

which becomes: $.53633t = 43.3517$

$$t = \frac{43.3517}{.53633} = 80.82$$

We will now solve the equation for the optimum levels of each of the four factors. We will use Temperature at 80.82, Metol at 16 g/l, HQ at 20 g/l and the speed will be held at 10 ips. Putting these values into the equation we get:

$$IQ = -1685.11 + 43.3517*80.82 - .268167*80.82^2 + 1.31667*16 + 1.10877*20 - 1.0825*10$$
$$IQ = -1685.11 + 3503.6844 - 1751.6326 + 21.067 + 22.1754 - 10.825$$

$$IQ = 99.36$$

The 99.36 is very close (acutally close enough) to the goal of 100. We have now completed our work and have produced a formula for a product that meets the targeted quality goals and we have a process equation to allow trouble shooting when problems arise in the future. However, we are still not finished in our quest for a quality product. We have not yet asked the question concerning the variability of the product. We know that it is almost impossible to make a product without variation, but is there a way of finding out how much tolerance may be allowed in the factors that influence the product quality? The next chapter will show the way to answer that important question. We will revisit this photographic process in the last chapter and make our equation work even harder for us and with a greater impact on quality.

A FINAL NOTE

While we have found 4 of the 7 factors that have an influence on the IQ response, we must realize that the other factors must be included in the formulation of the developer. Since KI, Alkaki (Ph control) and humidity did not influence the IQ, we may use any level of these that fit other constraints, such as cost. Therefore, given a cost consideration, we would put the chemical factors in at their lowest levels and let the humidity change as it will with the weather. Information on factors that do not have an influence on the process is sometimes as important as information on factors that have a functional relationship with the response. We should never consider factors that "drop out" of the equation as negative information. On the contrary, this kind of information is very valuable.

PROBLEMS FOR CHAPTER 19

1. Show why all the 7 effects (5 single and 2 two-factor interactions) cannot be obtained with a 2^{5-2} fractional factorial design as discussed in the popcorn experiment, phase II.

2. Show how dropping the power factor solves the confounding problem in the second phase of the popcorn experiment.

3. Run the YATES ANOVA on the 3 responses in Table 19-8 to confirm the findings reported in the conclusions.

4. If temperature and humidity were likely to interact as well as Ph and Metol, would the design shown in Table 19-13 be adequate? State your reasons and suggest a way to get around this difficulty.

5. Compute the error mean square from the replicates in Table 19-19.

6. Solve the modeling problem described on the next page. Use the simulation computer program supplied to generate the responses.

A SIMULATED PROBLEM

PHOTOGRAPHIC EMULSION

Response: Image Quality (0-100)

Controlling
Variables:

Grams/liter of $AgNO_3$	5 to 15
Grams/liter of Gelatine	20 to 40
Grams/liter of KBr	5 to 15
Grams/liter of KI	1 to 5
Temperature	90° to 120°
Relative Humidity	50 to 80%
Speed of Dumping	Fast (1) Slow (0)
Length of mixing	5 to 20 minutes
Size of Batch	1 to 10 liters

Costs: $500/ treatment combination

Gains: $2000/ unit increase over the 50 mark

Your job is to find the model and the equation for the
above process and then use this model to specify the
levels of chemicals and process conditions with their
functional tolerances.

PROGRAM TO GENERATE RESPONSES

```
90 DIM N$(9)
100 PRINT "ENTER THE VALUES OF YOUR EMULSION FORMULATION"
110 FOR I=1 TO 9
115 READ N$(I)
120 DATA   AGNO3, GELATINE,KBR,KI TEMP
140 DATA   RH,SPEED, MIXTIME,BATCHSIZE
150 NEXT I
160 DIM X(9)
170 FOR I=1 TO 9
180 PRINT N$(I);
185 INPUT X(I)
186 NEXT I
220 Y=-4*X(1)+X(3)*X(4)+10*X(5)-.05*X(5)**2+10*X(7)-465
240 Y1=Y
260 R1=0
300 FOR J=1 TO 6
320 R=RND(Y)-.5
340 R=R*15
360 R1=R1+R
380 Y=R
400 NEXT J
420 PRINT "IMAGE QUALITY=";Y1+(R1/6)
440 PRINT "MORE? IF SO ENTER 1"
460 INPUT M
480 IF M=1 THEN 170
500 END
>


RUN
15:42   FEB 22   EMULSION1...
ENTER THE VALUES OF YOUR EMULSION FORMULATION
AGNO3   ?7.5
GELATINE  ?30
KBR    ?7.5
KI   ?2.5
TEMP   ?105
RH  ?65
SPEED   ?.5
MIXTIME   ?12.5
BATCHSIZE   ?5
IMAGE QUALITY=   27.7681
MORE? IF SO ENTER 1
?

     500 HALT
```

PART V

Utilization of Empirical Equations

20

MONTE CARLO SIMULATION

Monte Carlo is a famous gambling commune in the small, 368 acre country of Monaco. The broad field of statistics displays some of its underpinnings by naming a probabilistic technique after this city where the laws of chance are a way of life and a way of living.

Monte Carlo Simulation is a technique that in its simplest form allows us to look at a portion or a whole of a real situation and ask the question "what if". Since even simple problems have many "what ifs" or branch points, we would like to see the most likely (expected value) results as a consequence of trying all the combinations of branches. Besides the expected value, we would also like to know how much variation is involved in our predictions. This information can be used to build confidence in our prediction (with low variation) or unconfidence (for large variation). The probabilistic part of Monte Carlo Simulation establishes the degree of variability which produces the level of confidence in our prediction.

SIMULATION

The simulation part of the Monte Carlo technique is done using the equation we have derived via designed experiments. Simulation itself is a common daily practice in many of the things we tackle and accomplish. To illustrate, think of a trip to the grocery store. We usually have a shopping list. The list is the model of what we intend to buy at the store. If we know the store, we may even have the list arranged in a specific order so we go through the store in a systematic manner. This system might have the forethought and consideration to move through the store in such a way to fill the shopping basket with the frozen and meat items last to avoid the possibility of thawing or spoilage.

Another illustration of mapping a plan of action via simulation is the effort we invest when planning a vacation trip. The extent and degree of planning depends on the goal of the vacation. For a camping trip to the mountains, our goal is to get there as fast as possible with the least traffic and small towns along the way. If we are touring the country or a section of the country, we <u>want</u> to move more slowly to savor the climate and the surroundings.

In both cases, we search out a model (which is a road atlas) and go over alternate routes to accomplish our goal. We even might write an itinerary for the longer trip which includes places to visit and where to stay each night. There are many examples of simulation that we take for granted, but are a large part of our daily lives.

COMBINING SIMUATIONS AND PROBABILITIES

Let's go back to the grocery store illustration and build it into a Monte Carlo example. We want to know how much money to bring to the store to finance a party. We would like to buy specific brand names, but have at least one alternative brand as a back-up. Further, we know the prices of the items and the chances of the items being on the shelf. Our <u>model</u> is simply a map of the store with the prices. The <u>chances</u> are our beliefs in a product's availability. Here's a listing of the products, prices, and chances:

Table 20-1

Product	Price	Quality	Chances (p)	Primary (P)/ Backup (B)
Lite Potato Chips	1.19	4	.75	P
Potato Frills	1.39	4	.85	B1
Corn Chips	1.69	4	.65	B2
Clam Dip	1.98	3	.45	P
Onion Dip	1.59	3	.70	B1
Vegetable Dip	.98	3	.90	B2
Canada Dry Ginger Ale	1.19	4	.95	P
Generic Ginger Ale	.99	4	.80	B1
Schweppes	1.59	4	.50	B0
7-Up	1.19	4	.90	P
Sprite	1.29	4	.80	B1
Mellow Yellow	1.20	4	.60	B2
Miller	2.89	8	.75	P
Bud	2.99	8	.85	B1
Schlitz	2.99	8	.75	B2

If we were able to obtain all the primary items our grocery bill would look like the following:

```
4    @    1.19
          4.79
3    @    1.98
          5.94
4    @    1.19
          4.76
4    @    1.19
          4.76
8    @    2.89
          23.12

TOTAL    $43.34
```

Figure 20-1

If we were to go through the entire set of possible purchases then the most costly bill would come to $48.14; and the least costly would be $39.54. We can prepare for the worst and take $50.00 or hope for the least costly and take $40.00. This approach, of course, has not taken the probabilities into account. We would like to know what the expected cost will be. To do so, we would have to go to the store a great number of times to experience the shopping. We would also have to give a lot of parties to do this. So instead of actually going to the store, we simulate a great number of shopping trips. A computer provides a convenient mechanism to act out this simulation. The BASIC program on the next page "goes to the store" for us and "buys" our party supplies as many times as we tell it, and finds the average expenditure as well as the standard deviation of our spending. The program is really no more complicated than a series of instructions to buy a primary item and if it is not available, to buy the first back-up or second back-up. The page after the program code shows the program in action.

The simulation of the shopping trip found in table 20-3 has given us an average cost of about $42.50. Notice that while the mean value is fairly stable over many such simulations (trials), the variation does fluctuate. We would expect less fluctuation in both the mean value and the variation as the sample size increases. However as the sample size goes up, the computing time increases. A typical 10,000 trial run would take 40 minutes. There are faster computers than the turtle I own, and their existence has been justified by extensive Monte Carlo simulations

Table 20-2

```
100 REM SIMULATION OF A SHOPPING TRIP "SIMSHOP"
105 CLEAR 300
110 REM THE "DIM" SETS THE SPACE UP FOR OUR VARIABLES:
115 REM I=ITEM PRICE; P=PROBABILITY; Q=QUANTITY; N$=NAMES
120 DIM I(5,3),P(5,3),Q(5),N$(5,3)
125 DATA 1.19,1.39,1.69,1.98,1.59,.98,1.19,.99,1.59,1.19,1.29,1.29,2.89,2.99,2.99
126 DATA .75,.85,.65,.45,.70,.90,.95,.80,.50,.90,.80,.60,.75,.85,.75
127 DATA 4,3,4,4,8
128 DATA CHIPS,FRILLS,CORN CHIPS,CLAM DIP,ONION DIP,VEGETABLE DIP,CANADA DRY
129 DATA GENERIC,SCHWEPPS,7-UP,SPRITE,MELLOW YELLOW,MILLERS,BUD,SCHLITZ
130 FOR J=1 TO 5:FOR K=1 TO 3
132 READ I(J,K):NEXT K:NEXT J
135 FOR J=1 TO 5:FOR K=1 TO 3
137 READ P(J,K):NEXT K:NEXT J
140 FOR J=1 TO 5:READ Q(J):NEXT J
143 FOR J=1 TO 5:FOR K=1 TO 3
145 READ N$(J,K):NEXT K:NEXT J
150 PRINT "HOW MANY SHOPPING TRIALS";
151 INPUT N
152 PRINT "WANT TO SEE EACH TRIAL PRINTED <Y/N>";
153 INPUT Z$
157 S=0:S1=0
160 FOR I1=1 TO N
165 C=0
166 IF Z$="N" GOTO 170
167 PRINT "BUY ";
170 FOR J=1 TO 5
180 FOR K=1 TO 3
190 R=RND(0)
200 IF R<=P(J,K) GOTO 215
210 NEXT K
212 IF Z$="Y" THEN PRINT "NOTHING ";
213 GOTO 240
215 IF Z$="N" GOTO 230
220 PRINT N$(J,K);" ";
230 C=C+I(J,K)*Q(J)
240 NEXT J
242 IF Z$="N" GOTO 250
245 PRINT
250 S=C+S
260 S1=C*C+S1
270 NEXT I1
280 A=S/N
290 S2=SQR((S1-(S*S)/N)/(N-1))
300 PRINT "AVERAGE COST=";A;"STD. DEV.=";S2
310 END
```

Now, why should we bother with Monte Carlo when in many cases (including our shopping spree example), it is possible to make a direct calculation based on probability of the expected cost. Table 20-4 does an <u>exact</u> calculation by combining probabilities and gives an expected cost of $42.41. This expected cost is what we had observed in the last of the 1000 trail runs in Table 20-3 using Monte Carlo. The other 1000 Trial Run (#1) comes within 4¢ of the truth and as the sample size increases, the chances of the Monte Carlo hitting the exact value increases. So, while the Monte Carlo takes a "brute force" wack at finding the expected value of the response, it can get there. The direct calculation method has the advantage of always getting the expected value. There is an advantage of Monte Carlo, however, that is neither

Table 20-3

```
HOW MANY SHOPPING TRIALS? 10
WANT TO SEE EACH TRIAL PRINTED <Y/N>? Y
BUY CHIPS CLAM DIP CANADA DRY 7-UP MILLERS
BUY CHIPS ONION DIP CANADA DRY 7-UP MILLERS
BUY CHIPS ONION DIP CANADA DRY SPRITE BUD
BUY CHIPS CLAM DIP CANADA DRY 7-UP MILLERS
BUY CHIPS VEGETABLE DIP CANADA DRY 7-UP MILLERS
BUY CHIPS ONION DIP CANADA DRY SPRITE MILLERS
BUY CHIPS CLAM DIP CANADA DRY 7-UP MILLERS
BUY CHIPS CLAM DIP CANADA DRY 7-UP MILLERS
BUY CHIPS CLAM DIP CANADA DRY 7-UP MILLERS
BUY CHIPS VEGETABLE DIP CANADA DRY 7-UP MILLERS
AVERAGE COST= 42.549 STD. DEV.= 1.2341
READY
>RUN
HOW MANY SHOPPING TRIALS? 1000
WANT TO SEE EACH TRIAL PRINTED <Y/N>? N
AVERAGE COST= 42.45   STD. DEV.= 2.18
READY
>RUN
HOW MANY SHOPPING TRIALS? 10
WANT TO SEE EACH TRIAL PRINTED <Y/N>? N
AVERAGE COST= 42.41   STD. DEV.= 1.99
READY
>RUN
HOW MANY SHOPPING TRIALS? 10
WANT TO SEE EACH TRIAL PRINTED <Y/N>? N
AVERAGE COST= 41.63   STD. DEV.= 1.71
READY
>RUN
HOW MANY SHOPPING TRIALS? 10
WANT TO SEE EACH TRIAL PRINTED <Y/N>? N
AVERAGE COST= 42.38   STD. DEV.= 1.67
READY
>RUN
HOW MANY SHOPPING TRIALS? 10
WANT TO SEE EACH TRIAL PRINTED <Y/N>? N
AVERAGE COST= 42.39   STD. DEV.= 1.41
READY
>RUN
HOW MANY SHOPPING TRIALS? 10
WANT TO SEE EACH TRIAL PRINTED <Y/N>? N
AVERAGE COST= 42.19   STD. DEV.= 2.26
READY
>RUN
HOW MANY SHOPPING TRIALS? 10
WANT TO SEE EACH TRIAL PRINTED <Y/N>? N
AVERAGE COST= 40.2 STD. DEV.= 7.22
READY
>RUN
HOW MANY SHOPPING TRIALS? 1000
WANT TO SEE EACH TRIAL PRINTED <Y/N>? N
AVERAGE COST= 42.41   STD. DEV.= 2.74
```

statistical nor mathematical in nature. It is a psychological advantage. What we do in a Monte Carlo is exactly what happens in real life. Therefore, we can explain what we have done more easily to the end users of the analysis who may not understand probabilities. Another prime reason for Monte Carlo is the fact that sometimes we neither have the proper distribution function for the probabilities or the funciton is too complex to determine how to combine the various functions in a reasonable time frame.

Table 20-4

Direct Calculation

Type	Prob.		Cost	Kind		Number		Expected Cost
Chips	.75	*	1.19	(Lite)	*	4	=	4.92
	.2125	*	1.39	(Frills)				
	.024375	*	1.69	(Corn)				
	.013125	*	0.00					
Dip	.45	*	1.98	(Clam)	*	3	=	4.95
	.385	*	1.59	(Onion)				
	.1485	*	.98	(Vege.)				
	.0165	*	0.00					
Ginger Ale	.95	*	1.19	(C.D.)	*	4	=	4.68
	.04	*	.80	(Gen)				
	.005	*	1.59	(Schwepps)				
	.005	*	0.00					
Lemon Drink	.90	*	1.19	(7-Up)	*	4	=	4.76
	.08	*	1.29	(Sprite)				
	.012	*	1.29	(M.Y.)				
	.008	*	0.00					
Beer	.75	*	2.89	(Mill)	*	8	=	23.10
	.2125	*	2.99	(Bud)				
	.028125	*	2.99	(Sch)				
	.009375	*	0.00					

Total Expected Cost $42.41

The Direct Calculation Method works like this: Our first choice for chips has a 75% chance of getting into our basket. If it is not available (which is 25% of the time) we will look for Frills which has an 85% chance of being bought. So the P of looking for Frills (.25) and the P of getting Frills is .25 * .85 - .2125. If Lite and Frills are both not availabe (.25 * .15), then we purchase corn chips if they are available (.65). There is the probability that there will be no chip item and we spend nothing (and have a poor chipless party).

It is for these reasons that we will tend to use Monte Carlo rather than exact calculation methods. The results speak for themselves and the method, although tedious, simulates the situation in a clear, straightforward manner.

APPLICATION TO MORE COMPLEX SITUATIONS

Our example on buying party items at a store serves to lay the ground work for more complex and useful applicaitons of the Monte Carlo method. In the application of simulation to an emperical equation, we are usually interested in obtaining an expected (average) value and a variation about this expected value. We will follow the same general procedure for a Monte Carlo simulation with an emperical equation as we followed for the shopping example. With the equation our model is the equation and all we need to do is run the equation with various input levels of the factors in the equation.

To illustrate, let's use a very simple additive equation that says the height of an assembly is equal to piece #A plus part #B.

$$Y_{Height} \quad = \quad A + B \qquad\qquad (20\text{-}1)$$

$$\text{Where} \quad \begin{array}{lll} A & = & 2 \\ B & = & 3 \end{array} \qquad \begin{array}{lll} S_A & = & .1 \\ S_B & = & .2 \end{array}$$

Again, this example is simple enough to solve in closed form. The average height of Y will simply be A + B or 5 units. The standard deviation is the square root of the sum of the variances (S^2). So we find this to be:

$$S_Y \quad = \quad \sqrt{.1^2 + .2^2} \quad = \quad .22361 \qquad\qquad (20\text{-}2)$$

Using Monte Carlo methods we will exercise our equation N times for samples from the A population and the B population. When we solved the problem in 20-1 and 20-2 using the closed form method we did not assume any distribution function. With Monte Carlo, we must decide on the distribution of the components in the equation. We will look at 2 distributions: a uniform (all values have an equal chance) and a normal distribution (extreme values have a lower chance). We will also look at a "true" random Monte Carlo and a discrete simulation.

We will compare the outputs of each distribution method to see if any differences exist.

We already understand how the "true" Montel Carlo method reaches into each distribution at random and picks a piece and then makes the assembly. The discrete method, on the other hand, picks a specific combination of pieces from the two populations in a factorial design manner. Then the expectation of the event (assembly) is weighted by the probability of the pieces that were selected. In this way, the discrete method combines the closed form concept with simulation techniques. Let's look at the various outputs for the 4 methods/ distributions.

Table 20-6

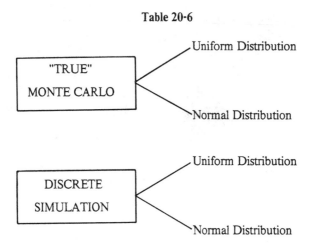

Table 20-7

Method	Distribution	Code #	Mean	Std. Dev.	# Trials
True Monte Carlo	Uniform	TU	5.0166	0.38956	1000
True Monte Carlo	Normal	TN	5.005	0.22714	1000
Discrete	Uniform	DU	5.000	0.45185	49
Discrete	Normal	DN	5.000	0.22314	49

To better visualize each of the 4 simulation procedures, we will use Figure 20-2. Note that the distribution shapes are the same despite the change in simulation techniques. The only difference we see is how the sampling is done. In the Monte Carlo method, we have a continuous distribution and all positions in the distribution have a chance of being selected for the assembly. In the discrete method only seven values may be chosen.

The results in Table 20-7 show that the uniform distribution has a broader variation then the normal. This is expected since the resultant distribution of two uniforms is broader than the combination of two normals. The normal distribution gives standard deviation values very close to the closed form solution to this simple problem and

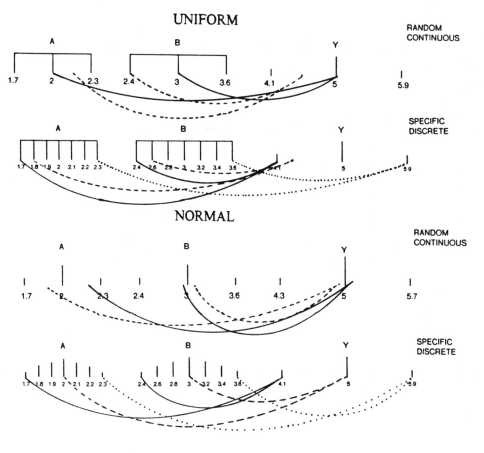

Figure 20-2

there is a closer agreement between the random and discrete methods using a normal than when we use a uniform.

Since the discrete method using a normal assumption produces an equivalent result with the random method with fewer trials, we conclude that for small numbers of variables (under 5), the discrete method has a computational advantage over the random method. However, with a 7 level discrete simulation, the number of combinations grows rapidly beyond 5 factors ($7^5 = 16807$). We can get around this problem by using a 3 level fractional factorial. To approximate a normal distribution based variance for the resulting distribution of Y, we transform the standard deviations of the input distribution by a factor of $\sqrt{3/2} * S$. Table 20-8 shows the 9 calculations that give a standard deviation very close to the normal distribution value.

The frequency distribution pattern of Y is, however, not normal in shape. The interesting aspect of this 3 level design application is the fact that 3 level designs can be easily fractionalized so that a discrete simulation can be accomplished with very few runs. This use of 3 level designs for simulation is a common application in Japan where traditional Monte Carlo methods are in lesser use.

Table 20-8

A	B	Y		
1.878	2.756	4.634		
2.000	2.756	4.756	A:	$\tilde{X} = 2$
2.122	2.756	4.878		$S = .1$
1.878	3.000	4.878		$\sqrt{3/2}*S = .122$
2.000	3.000	5.000		
2.122	3.000	5.122	B:	$\bar{X} = 3$
1.878	3.244	5.122		$S = .2$
2.000	3.244	5.122		$\sqrt{3/2}*S = .244$
2.122	3.244	5.366		

$$\bar{Y} = 5.000$$
$$S_Y = .23625$$

We will next apply (in Chapter 21) these simulation methods to the equation for the photographic process that we derived in Chapter 19.

PROBLEMS FOR CHAPTER 20

1. Write all the detailed steps for preparing a breakfast of bacon, eggs, buttered toast, orange juice, and coffee.

2. With your computer, generate 100 normally distributed random numbers with mean zero and a standard deviation of one. Plot a frequency distribution of the 100 values.

3. Use the table you generated in #2 or, if you do not have a computer, use Table 20-9   to run a Monte Carlo simulation of the following problem. Use 10 trials and do this problem manually.

Factor	Dist.	$\overline{X}$	$\underline{S}$
A	Normal	2.5	.15
B	Normal	1.0	.05
C	Normal	.5	.01

$$Y = 2A + B - 3C$$

APPENDIX 20

SUMMARY OF MONTE CARLO METHODS

METHOD	HOW	ADVANTAGES	DISADVANTAGES
1) Random Selection ("True Monte Carlo")	Reach into the populations and "grab" samples. Assemble the samples using the equation. Repeat many time (1,000 to 100,000).	Realistic. Frequency distributions look "right".	Slow. Requires massive computer power.
2) Discrete Selection (Full Factorial)	Pick only certain (by design) values. Assemble in a factorial fashion using the equation.	Fast for small numbers of factors. Gives proper $\overline{Y}$ and S.	Frequency distribution of the result (Y) does not look right.
3) Discrete Selection (3 Level Factorial or 3^{k-p} Fractional Factorial)	Use 3 level factorial to pick values. For a normal distribution, standard deviation, use $\sqrt{3/2}$*S as $\pm$ value from nominal value.	Very fast for even large number of factors.	Frequency distribution of the result (Y) does not look right.

Methods of computing Random Normal Numbers given Uniform Random Numbers.

$$\text{Random Normal} = \overline{X} + \sqrt{-2*\text{Log}_e(RU)}*\text{COS}(2\pi*RU)*S$$

Where $\overline{X}$ = Average
         S   = Std. Dev.
        RU = Random Uniform (On 0 to 1 Interval)

Note: Compute COS in radians.

Reference: Box, G.E.P. and Muller, M.E.; A Note on the Generation of Random Normal Deviates, Ann. Math. Stat., Vol. 29 (1958), P610.

Table 20-9

XII.4 RANDOM NORMAL NUMBERS, $\mu = 0$, $\sigma = 1$

01	02	03	04	05	06	07	08	09	10
0.464	0.137	2.455	−0.323	−0.068	0.296	−0.288	1.298	0.241	−0.957
0.060	−2.526	−0.531	−0.194	0.543	−1.558	0.187	−1.190	0.022	0.525
1.486	−0.354	−0.634	0.697	0.926	1.375	0.785	−0.963	−0.853	−1.865
1.022	−0.472	1.279	3.521	0.571	−1.851	0.194	1.192	−0.501	−0.273
1.394	−0.555	0.046	0.321	2.945	1.974	−0.258	0.412	0.439	−0.035
0.906	−0.513	−0.525	0.595	0.881	−0.934	1.579	0.161	−1.885	0.371
1.179	−1.055	0.007	0.769	0.971	0.712	1.090	−0.631	−0.255	−0.702
−1.501	−0.488	−0.162	−0.136	1.033	0.203	0.448	0.748	−0.423	−0.432
−0.690	0.756	−1.618	−0.345	−0.511	−2.051	−0.457	−0.218	0.857	−0.465
1.372	0.225	0.378	0.761	0.181	−0.736	0.960	−1.530	−0.260	0.120
−0.482	1.678	−0.057	−1.229	−0.486	0.856	−0.491	−1.983	−2.830	−0.238
−1.376	−0.150	1.356	−0.561	−0.256	−0.212	0.219	0.779	0.953	−0.869
−1.010	0.598	−0.918	1.598	0.065	0.415	−0.169	0.313	−0.973	−1.016
−0.005	−0.899	0.012	−0.725	1.147	−0.121	1.096	0.481	−1.691	0.417
1.393	−1.163	−0.911	1.231	−0.199	−0.246	1.239	−2.574	−0.558	0.056
−1.787	−0.261	1.237	1.046	−0.508	−1.630	−0.146	−0.392	−0.627	0.561
−0.105	−0.357	−1.384	0.360	−0.992	−0.116	−1.698	−2.832	−1.108	−2.357
−1.339	1.827	−0.959	0.424	0.969	−1.141	−1.041	0.362	−1.726	1.956
1.041	0.535	0.731	1.377	0.983	−1.330	1.620	−1.040	0.524	−0.281
0.279	−2.056	0.717	−0.873	−1.096	−1.396	1.047	0.089	−0.573	0.932
−1.805	−2.008	−1.633	0.542	0.250	−0.166	0.032	0.079	0.471	−1.029
−1.186	1.180	1.114	0.882	1.265	−0.202	0.151	−0.376	−0.310	0.479
0.658	−1.141	1.151	−1.210	−0.927	0.425	0.290	−0.902	0.610	2.709
−0.439	0.358	−1.939	0.891	−0.227	0.602	0.873	−0.437	−0.220	−0.057
−1.399	−0.230	0.385	−0.649	−0.577	0.237	−0.289	0.513	0.738	−0.300
0.199	0.208	−1.083	−0.219	−0.291	1.221	1.119	0.004	−2.015	−0.594
0.159	0.272	−0.313	0.084	−2.828	−0.439	−0.792	−1.275	−0.623	−1.047
2.273	0.606	0.606	−0.747	0.247	1.291	0.063	−1.793	−0.699	−1.347
0.041	−0.307	0.121	0.790	−0.584	0.541	0.484	−0.986	0.481	0.996
−1.132	−2.098	0.921	0.145	0.446	−1.661	1.045	−1.363	−0.586	−1.023
0.768	0.079	−1.473	0.034	−2.127	0.665	0.084	−0.880	−0.579	0.551
0.375	−1.658	−0.851	0.234	−0.656	0.340	−0.086	−0.158	−0.120	0.418
−0.513	−0.344	0.210	−0.735	1.041	0.008	0.427	−0.831	0.191	0.074
0.292	−0.521	1.266	−1.206	−0.899	0.110	−0.528	−0.813	0.071	0.524
1.026	2.990	−0.574	−0.491	−1.114	1.297	−1.433	−1.345	−3.001	0.479
−1.334	1.278	−0.568	−0.109	−0.515	−0.566	2.923	0.500	0.359	0.326
−0.287	−0.144	−0.254	0.574	−0.451	−1.181	−1.190	−0.318	−0.094	1.114
0.161	−0.886	−0.921	−0.509	1.410	−0.518	0.192	−0.432	1.501	1.068
−1.346	0.193	−1.202	0.394	−1.045	0.843	0.942	1.045	0.031	0.772
1.250	−0.199	−0.288	1.810	1.378	0.584	1.216	0.733	0.402	0.226
0.630	−0.537	0.782	0.060	0.499	−0.431	1.705	1.164	0.884	−0.298
0.375	−1.941	0.247	−0.491	−0.665	−0.135	−0.145	−0.498	0.457	1.064
−1.420	0.489	−1.711	−1.186	0.754	−0.732	−0.066	1.006	−0.798	0.162
−0.151	−0.243	−0.430	−0.762	0.298	1.049	1.810	2.885	−0.768	−0.129
−0.309	0.531	0.416	−1.541	1.456	2.040	−0.124	0.196	0.023	−1.204
0.424	−0.444	0.593	0.993	−0.106	0.116	0.484	−1.272	1.066	1.097
0.593	0.658	−1.127	−1.407	−1.579	−1.616	1.458	1.262	0.736	−0.916
0.862	−0.885	−0.142	−0.504	0.532	1.381	0.022	−0.281	−0.342	1.222
0.235	−0.628	−0.023	−0.463	−0.899	−0.394	−0.538	1.707	−0.188	−1.153
−0.853	0.402	0.777	0.833	0.410	−0.349	−1.094	0.580	1.395	1.298

```
100 DIM X(6),F(7),S(6),Z(6,7)
101 FOR I=1 TO 7:READ F(I):NEXT I
102 DATA .44,5.4,24.2,39.89,24.2,5.4,.44
103 S2=0
104 S3=0
105 F1=0
110 REM THIS IS AN SCF PROGRAM WHICH SIMULATES A PROCESS
111 REM AND GIVES THE PARAMETERS OF THE JOINT
112 REM DISTRIBUTION FUNCTION RESULTING FROM
113 REM THE FACTORS UNDER STUDY.
114 REM UNLESS OTHERWISE CHANGED, THE FUNCTIONS
115 REM ARE CONSIDERED NORMAL.
116 REM N IS THE NUMBER OF FACTORS IN THE EQUATION WHICH
117 REM IS AT LINE 160. LINES 150-155 CONTROL THE START
118 REM OF THE LOOPS LINES 210-215 THE ENDS. 165 HAS FREQUENCY.
119 PRINT "TYPE IN THE NUMBER OF FACTORS"
120 INPUT N
125 PRINT "AT EACH QUESTION MARK TYPE IN THE MEAN AND STD DEV OF EACH FACTOR"
130 FOR I=1 TO N
131 PRINT "FACTOR";I
132 INPUT X(I),S(I)
135 Z(I,1)=X(I)-3*S(I)
140 FOR J=2 TO 7
145 Z(I,J)=Z(I,J-1)+S(I)
146 NEXT J
147 NEXT I
150 FOR J1=1 TO 7
151 FOR J2=1 TO 7
152 FOR J3=1 TO 7
153 FOR J4=1 TO 7
154 FOR J5=1 TO 7
155 FOR J6=1 TO 7
160 Y=Z(1,J1)+Z(2,J2)+Z(3,J3)+Z(4,J4)+Z(5,J5)+Z(6,J6)
165 P=F(J1)*F(J2)*F(J3)*F(J4)*F(J5)*F(J6)
170 Y1=Y*P
180 S2=S2+Y1
190 S3=S3+(Y^2)*P
200 F1=F1+P
210 NEXT J6
211 NEXT J5
212 NEXT J4
213 NEXT J3
214 NEXT J2
215 NEXT J1
220 B=S2/F1
225 D=(F1*S3-S2^2)/F1^2
226 D=SQR(D)
230 D1=3*D
235 R1=B-D1
236 R2=B+D1
240 PRINT " THE MEAN=";B;"WITH STD DEV=";D
241 PRINT " THREE SIGMA VALUES:"
245 PRINT " LOWER VALUE=";R1;"UPPER VALUE=";R2
250 PRINT "IF YOU WISH TO CONTINUE TYPE 1  TO STOP TYPE 2"
260 INPUT T
265 IF T=1 THEN 103
270 END
```

Example of the use of this table:

If the variable you have has a mean of X and a standard deviation of s, then multiply s by the value found in this table and add the mean (X) to the result. Be sure to watch the proper sign!
so, if $X = 4$ and $s = .5$ and we choose ar random normal # from column 06 and row 10 (-0.736), then:

$$\text{our number} = (-0.736 * .5) + 4 = -.368 + 4 = 3.632$$

21

CASE HISTORY COMPLETED – THE UTILIZATION
OF THE EQUATION

If we were to simply derive the equation for a process, pat ourselves on the back for a good, efficient job and then quit, we would have done only half the job of infusing quality into our efforts. Once the equation is developed and <u>verified</u>, we need to exercise it. This is less a job for experimental design and more an effort for the engineer and therefore has been left out of most books on experimental design. However, it is probably the most important aspect of the proof of the pudding phase of the experimental effort. In Chapter 19 we derived an equation describing a photographic process. In Chapter 20 we learned that any equation could be put through its paces via simulation. We shall now take that photographic processing solution equation and see what makes it tick.

We have already solved the equation to determine the best mid-point operating conditions for the significant influencing factors. Recall that the equation was:

$$IQ = -1685.11 + 43.3517*Temp - .268167*Temp^2 + 1.31667*Metol + 1.10877*HQ - 1.0877*Speed$$

Midpoint values are:

Temperature	80.82^0
Metol	16 g/l
HQ	10 g/l
Speed	10 ips

When we used the above values, the IQ (image quality) of the process was computed at 100, which was our goal. However, the ultimate goal of quality is to achieve the target value and do so consistently. We realize that it would be impossible to hold a temperature of 80.82 all the time. To do so would require very expensive feed-back control systems. To be able to weigh the chemicals to their exact specifications would also be impossible and would impose a restriction on the production process that is too costly. A speed of exactly 10 ips may be accomplished with another system, but again, this is an imposition that a production process usually can't afford. What we need is a toleranced specification. That is a mid-point with a degree of slop around it. This is a common practice in most industry. However, the practice of deriving the degree of variation printed on the specification is not often practiced in a scientific or even economic manner.

First we must realize that the tolerance on the components must be related to the customer's requirements. Quality products meet customer needs in a consistent manner. In other words, a quality product is on target with little variation. We must first determine the target and then understand the amount of variation tolerable. In the photographic processing process, the target value is determined by market research. We must know what level of image quality is required by the customer. We must also know what level of deviation from the target value will cause customer dissatisfaction.

We will use the following market research information to set the product "specs." on the processing example.

The Image Quality should not fall below 95 IQ units.

Further, the distribution shall follow a normal density function.

The above specification could be interpreted to mean (incorrectly) that the mean level shall be at 95. But if there is any variation in the process in the downward direction, the spec. would be violated since we would produce a product below the 95 lower limit. We already know how to get to the IQ of 100, but we don't know how much variation in the four critical parts is tolerable. This is where the simulation techniques come in handy. We will make systematic changes in the levels of the critical parts and study their effect on the overall IQ of the process. We will try two approaches to this simulation. One will be the traditional Monte-Carlo random method and the other will be to make changes according to a pattern based on an orthogonal experimental design.

RANDOM METHOD

While there are many ways of accomplishing the same goals using Monte-Carlo concepts, we will in this instance use the very simple method that was the basis for homework problem 20-2. Instead of using a manual selection of the random normal numbers, we will use a self-contained computer program. The program is shown below. It is written in BASIC and should run without modification on most computers. It is set up to allow data to be generated for control chart plotting. If you are not familiar with the concept of a control chart, the idea is to study a series of outputs and observe if the averages of selected groups stay within the "natural" variation of the process. We will not use the subgroup feature of this simulation program for this exercise, but will use only the final mean and standard deviation summary statistics.

```
10 INPUT "HOWMANY CONTROL PARAMETERS IN YOUR PROCESS";N5
20 INPUT "HOW MANY SUBGROUPS FOR THE CONTROL CHART";T1
30 INPUT "HOW MANY ITEMS PER SUBGROUP";I1
40 DIM P(N5,2),ND(100),X(N5)
50 CLS:PRINT "PLEASE WAIT"
60 FOR I=1 TO 100:READ ND(I):NEXT
70 DATA .906,-.513,-.525,.595,.881,-.934,1.579,.161,-1.885,.371
80 DATA 1.179,-1.055,.007,.769,.971,.712,1.09,-.631,-.255,-.702
90 DATA -1.501,-.488,-.162,-.136,1.033,.203,.448,.748,-.423,-.432
100 DATA -.69,.756,-1.618,-.345,-.511,-2.051,-.457,-.218,.857,-.465
110 DATA 1.372,.225,.378,.761,.181,-.736,.96,-1.53,-.26,.12
120 DATA -1.787,-.261,1.237,1.046,-.508,-1.63,-.146,-.392,-.627,.561
130 DATA -.105,-.357,-1.384,.36,-.992,-.116,-1.698,-2.832,-1.108,-2.357
140 DATA -1.339,1.827,-.959,.424,.969,-1.141,-1.041,.362,-1.726,1.956
150 DATA 1.041,.535,.731,1.377,.983,-1.33,1.62,-1.04,.524,-.281
160 DATA .279,-2.056,.717,-.0872,-1.096,-1.396,1.047,.089,-.573,.932
170 FOR I=1 TO N5:PRINT "ENTER CONTROL PARAMETER#";I;:INPUT "MEAN,STD. DEV.";P(I,1),P(I,
171 NEXT
175 S=0:SS=0
180 FOR I=1 TO T1:LPRINT "SUBGROUP #";I;
190 FOR J=1 TO I1
200 FOR K=1 TO N5:R=RND(100):IF R=0 THEN R=1
210 X(K)=P(K,1)+(ND(R)*P(K,2)):NEXT K
220 REM insert equations here
230 REM of the form Y=b0 + b1*X(i),etc.
240 REM be sure to use Y for the response and X(I) for the
250 REM control parameter where I=1,2,3,...N5(the max #)
260 REM
270 REM PLACE AN "LPRINT Y;" STATEMENT AFTER EACH EQUATION
280 Y=-1685.11+43.3517*X(1)-.268167*X(1)*X(1)+1.31667*X(2)
290 Y=Y+1.10877*X(3)-1.0877*X(4)
300 REM X(1)=TEMP;X(2)=METOL;X(3)=HQ;X(4)=SPEED
305 LPRINT Y;
307 S=S+Y:SS=SS+Y*Y
400 NEXT J
405 LPRINT
410 NEXT I
412 N=T1*I1
415 XB=S/N:SD=SQR((SS-(S*S/N))/(N-1))
420 LPRINT "AVERAGE=";XB;" STD. DEV= ";SD
430 END


RUN
HOWMANY CONTROL PARAMETERS IN YOUR PROCESS? 4
HOW MANY SUBGROUPS FOR THE CONTROL CHART? 30
HOW MANY ITEMS PER SUBGROUP? 5
PLEASE WAIT
ENTER CONTROL PARAMETER# 1 MEAN,STD. DEV.? 80.82,2
ENTER CONTROL PARAMETER# 2 MEAN,STD. DEV.? 16,1
```

```
ENTER CONTROL PARAMETER# 3 MEAN,STD. DEV.? 20,1
ENTER CONTROL PARAMETER# 4 MEAN,STD. DEV.? 10,.5
SUBGROUP # 1    99.5515   98.7544   95.9842   95.6807   97.3152
SUBGROUP # 2    101.46    96.8615   95.322    95.9716   99.5437
SUBGROUP # 3    96.9206   101.337   99.114    101.301   95.7245
SUBGROUP # 4    94.5057   96.7225   102.019   96.1188   94.8025
SUBGROUP # 5    97.0107   91.2351   99.2045   100.555   96.9142
SUBGROUP # 6    97.3023   99.9789   99.0049   98.954    97.4788
SUBGROUP # 7    98.6155   95.0559   96.0882   100.106   100.237
SUBGROUP # 8    100.956   95.7584   93.3523   98.7142   98.8754
SUBGROUP # 9    97.5197   97.205    100.752   97.9323   98.5902
SUBGROUP # 10   98.5751   98.9951   99.5575   98.1043   95.5077
SUBGROUP # 11   97.6339   100.049   97.3577   95.3903   98.7323
SUBGROUP # 12   100.718   94.2333   96.9287   100.628   98.8617
SUBGROUP # 13   99.8793   96.6062   93.7636   98.1597   96.8421
SUBGROUP # 14   98.2243   96.4327   98.5757   97.0331   99.9074
SUBGROUP # 15   95.7789   98.0143   99.6979   99.5597   101.601
SUBGROUP # 16   99.9215   95.7105   97.2558   100.152   99.1338
SUBGROUP # 17   93.1559   96.6529   95.0774   98.5918   94.2058
SUBGROUP # 18   99.858    92.6254   98.3126   102.238   96.2764
SUBGROUP # 19   98.5789   94.643    95.662    101.708   96.7508
SUBGROUP # 20   98.6286   99.6073   98.1834   95.7139   100.409
SUBGROUP # 21   98.5661   93.9715   97.5985   93.4244   96.4026
SUBGROUP # 22   98.3465   96.6059   101.886   98.0382   100.101
SUBGROUP # 23   99.4775   95.6577   97.4865   95.924    94.1272
SUBGROUP # 24   95.1356   98.6068   93.7305   98.3915   97.8989
SUBGROUP # 25   100.472   95.9466   97.1509   99.1034   97.1135
SUBGROUP # 26   97.317    97.0724   97.5238   99.161    96.2158
SUBGROUP # 27   97.063    96.9964   98.1644   87.8535   96.6358
SUBGROUP # 28   97.3111   99.6696   100.189   96.1636   97.7747
SUBGROUP # 29   95.8236   97.5378   97.0323   100.44    98.0947
SUBGROUP # 30   98.4104   99.3991   94.8669   98.2455   101.771
AVERAGE= 97.6714  STD. DEV= 2.3017


PLEASE WAIT
ENTER CONTROL PARAMETER# 1 MEAN,STD. DEV.? 80.82,1
ENTER CONTROL PARAMETER# 2 MEAN,STD. DEV.? 16,.5
ENTER CONTROL PARAMETER# 3 MEAN,STD. DEV.? 20,.5
ENTER CONTROL PARAMETER# 4 MEAN,STD. DEV.? 10,.25
SUBGROUP # 1    98.977    99.8454   98.5446   97.8393   96.8351
SUBGROUP # 2    99.1929   99.3894   97.5113   99.1199   99.5946
SUBGROUP # 3    97.5385   98.4896   99.1595   100.13    98.6102
SUBGROUP # 4    97.5404   99.6814   99.0945   99.9114   100.583
SUBGROUP # 5    99.3558   99.2254   99.5981   100.095   99.5283
SUBGROUP # 6    100.353   99.1386   97.8767   98.0769   98.8124
SUBGROUP # 7    98.1814   99.7941   98.9351   98.6371   99.8552
SUBGROUP # 8    98.4184   98.6619   98.684    98.6154   98.0363
SUBGROUP # 9    96.9485   100.679   97.5291   100.144   97.6329
SUBGROUP # 10   99.7853   97.1573   98.9168   99.8201   99.324
SUBGROUP # 11   100.428   99.1925   97.7352   97.6152   99.0598
SUBGROUP # 12   99.7966   97.4408   99.6137   97.7453   97.532
SUBGROUP # 13   100.502   96.773    98.6655   99.3239   97.9999
SUBGROUP # 14   99.5457   99.7773   99.5768   97.4714   99.2979
SUBGROUP # 15   97.095    98.9426   99.6162   99.1111   98.3513
SUBGROUP # 16   99.7493   98.4198   98.4282   97.4813   98.5958
```

```
SUBGROUP # 17    98.6781    99.4712    99.3712    100.385    99.6866
SUBGROUP # 18    99.3191    99.6774    98.8695    98.5843    99.6862
SUBGROUP # 19    98.5236    98.5688    98.2744    97.5391    98.6961
SUBGROUP # 20    98.4614    98.731     98.4533    98.3644    99.7472
SUBGROUP # 21    96.9089    99.209     99.1061    100.044    96.981
SUBGROUP # 22    98.1516    99.0346    96.681     97.9182    98.3812
SUBGROUP # 23    98.8111    97.9997    100.287    101.263    98.903
SUBGROUP # 24    98.9694    100.115    98.9527    100.483    99.1807
SUBGROUP # 25    98.2496    99.8325    100.06     99.1815    101.238
SUBGROUP # 26    100.304    100.25     99.7159    99.9922    99.1689
SUBGROUP # 27    98.4197    98.7148    99.5273    96.9862    99.4713
SUBGROUP # 28    100.039    99.8336    99.7191    99.9524    97.7149
SUBGROUP # 29    99.6989    98.5933    97.8834    97.9223    98.0034
SUBGROUP # 30    98.6414    100.426    98.3411    98.8461    98.7405
AVERAGE= 98.9215    STD. DEV= .98521


PLEASE WAIT
ENTER CONTROL PARAMETER# 1 MEAN,STD. DEV.? 80,.5
ENTER CONTROL PARAMETER# 2 MEAN,STD. DEV.? 16,.75
ENTER CONTROL PARAMETER# 3 MEAN,STD. DEV.? 20,.75
ENTER CONTROL PARAMETER# 4 MEAN,STD. DEV.? 10,.25.

SUBGROUP # 1     101.098    98.8049    99.9889    98.631     99.9171
SUBGROUP # 2     98.9302    98.0878    97.356     99.1109    100.444
SUBGROUP # 3     98.8492    100.31     100.812    97.6882    99.4985
SUBGROUP # 4     100.587    99.2141    100.72     98.4294    100.206
SUBGROUP # 5     97.8418    99.9764    100.134    98.9764    95.9068
SUBGROUP # 6     100.359    99.1493    98.1985    100.01     99.3603
SUBGROUP # 7     97.066     97.7923    98.5227    97.6796    101.277
SUBGROUP # 8     96.6977    98.2868    99.8869    97.7363    99.5549
SUBGROUP # 9     99.541     100.1      99.1896    98.6666    99.0575
SUBGROUP # 10    98.0571    99.1016    100.394    99.8651    100.555
SUBGROUP # 11    99.0715    98.4325    98.2998    100.585    98.5948
SUBGROUP # 12    100.491    98.7641    97.555     98.0167    95.8002
SUBGROUP # 13    100.562    100.178    96.9096    100.217    98.8085
SUBGROUP # 14    100.167    95.2914    99.6368    98.1229    97.8476
SUBGROUP # 15    99.9524    100.161    98.3394    97.4013    97.7706
SUBGROUP # 16    99.3565    99.3908    99.4274    98.0914    99.2487
SUBGROUP # 17    102.096    100.011    99.3564    97.8812    99.6381
SUBGROUP # 18    97.7441    98.0417    99.555     99.163     99.3545
SUBGROUP # 19    97.2346    100.587    96.2071    99.6332    99.821
SUBGROUP # 20    99.0916    99.7258    99.3912    99.2348    95.8973
SUBGROUP # 21    99.9521    99.2966    97.8592    99.9511    96.8687
SUBGROUP # 22    100.526    100.623    98.3843    98.6253    98.3161
SUBGROUP # 23    97.6741    101.158    96.4877    98.3349    97.4576
SUBGROUP # 24    98.8414    100.161    98.8078    99.4246    98.4662
SUBGROUP # 25    96.7889    97.7184    101.21     100.375    101.757
SUBGROUP # 26    96.6779    97.5675    97.8159    100.431    99.1291
SUBGROUP # 27    101.103    98.2739    99.1332    99.5868    98.5411
SUBGROUP # 28    95.5414    100.648    101.299    99.0597    99.5396
SUBGROUP # 29    100.002    97.3859    100.124    99.8952    100.013
SUBGROUP # 30    100.688    96.7388    100.818    97.4311    96.5653
AVERAGE= 98.9924    STD. DEV= 1.3745
```

In the program, lines 70-160 hold the random normal values from a distribution with a mean of zero and a standard deviation of one. We will "reach into" this population and sample a value for each of our 4 control parameters. The actual mean and standard deviation will depend upon the mean and standard deviation of the parameter and the random value picked. This is exactly like the homework problem, only we have automated the process. After all 4 parameter values have been selected, the equation is activated and a response is generated. We will continue this process of selecting the random values and apply them to the parameters and then solve the equation until we have satisfied the required number of trails. This is exactly what would have happened in running the photographic process, except we do it with an equation rather than the real chemicals and process settings. The following table (21-1) shows a summary of the simulation work and the final settings that accomplish the goal of IQ greater than 95.

Table 21-1

TEMP MEAN/SD	METOL MEAN/SD	HQ MEAN/SD	SPEED MEAN/SD	SAMPLE SIZE	IQ AVERAGE	STANDARD DEVIATION
80.82 2.0	16 1.0	20 1.0	10 0.5	150	97.7	2.30
80.82 1.0	16 0.5	20 0.5	10 0.25	150	98.9	1.0
80 0.5	16 0.75	20 0.75	10 0.25	150	99.0	1.37

The last trial with a mean of 99 and a standard deviation of 1.37 will give a lower 3s level of 94.9 which is close enough to the specification of 95. The first Monte-Carlo trail represented low cost tolerances and the selection of the tolerances was made based on the prior knowledge of the photographic process. Such knowledge is very important in making the first set of trail runs in such a simulation. The educated guessing of the subsequent tolerances is based on the knowledge and an observation of the previous run. In the second trial, we cut the tolerances in half and got a greater reduction in the overall IQ standard deviation than we may have expected. We had "over corrected" and the last run brought us back to the right set of conditions. Had we tried to do this in a production environment, we would have had to run nearly 500 rolls of film through the process with exact control of the conditions to observe the results that we obtained with only a small amount of computer time and a little bit of programming effort. The combined use of simulation techniques and the results of empirical equations derived from statistically designed experiments pays real dividends in shortening schedules, giving us the quality products the customer desires.

ANOTHER APPROACH

While the Monte-Carlo approach will give us the answers we desire, there is a certain amount of guess-work involved in using the random process in simulating the parameter set-points and especially the variation around these set points. The problem is recognized by the experts in the field of simulation and there are far more sophisticated computer routines for doing the job than the simple one we just used. Some of these programs have "sensitivity" analysis built in to point to the parameters that have the greatest influence on the output variable. Of course, as the simulation programs become more complex, they take longer to run and require bigger and bigger computer resources. What is worse is the involvement in the programming and the learning required to run these monster programs. No matter how complex the simulation program, we must remember that it is only a tool to help up make a good decision. I have seen some efforts become so involved with the tool that the users forget about the real problem.

As experimental designers, we should have realized that we have always had the most powerful method for simulation and *rational* reduction of variance in the product or process design. The purpose of a Monte-Carlo simulation is to make purposeful changes in the input parameters to see how these changes effect the output. This is exactly the same purpose a designed experiment has! While the Monte-Carlo method will give us the good news or the bad news of meeting or not meeting the desired goal, it can't do much more. It does not tell us which of the parameters has an influence on the variation. A Monte-Carlo is almost like a one-factor-at-a-time test. It lacks a method of analysis. On the other hand, a designed experiment is capable of being analyzed. We can determine which parameters have an influence on the output. We can determine the magnitude as well as the identity of these factors. In our second look at the photo process simulation, we will not use random samples of the parameters, but we will use fixed levels. We will use an orthogonal experimental design to generate variation and then analyze the results of this design to determine how much each factor contributes to the variation in the response variable.

[NOTE: It would be unfair for this author to claim authorship for the following technique. Professor Genichi Taguchi of Japan first introduced this concept in his works related to quality engineering. I am grateful to have learned this method from him.]

In Chapter 7 we introduced the idea of 3-level orthogonal designs. We said that they would become useful in later applications. The time has arrived to put these designs to work in a simulation exercise. While other designs will do an adequate job, the 3-level design is particularly well-suited because it provides a nominal (mid-point) and an excursion on both sides of this nominal. We can (as we indicated in Chapter 19) even simulate a normal distribution from such a uniform pattern by a clever transform of the parameter's standard deviation.

To expedite the use of designed experiments in such simulation situations, a special computer program that builds the design and creates the responses is provided. The next few pages give the BASIC code for this. With proper modification of the input and output statements, this program will run on most computer systems. Besides the program, you will need input files for the orthogonal 3-level designs. These are given in the appendix to this chapter.

We will use a 3^{4-1} design for this exercise. This is called an L27 orthogonal array (OA) since it can also be related to a Latin Square design (the "L" stands for Latin).

While we have cautioned against the use of Latin squares as fractional factorial designs, a 3-level design does not consume the degrees of freedom as rapidly as the 4 or 5 level Latin Squares. With the design we are about to use, we find that the confounding is minimal. Also, we do not have any interactions in our model, so we need not worry about anything except single effects.

To use the program and the experimental design approach to simulation, we will simply answer the questions asked by the program. This program has been built for a simulation beyond the scope of this chapter, but a portion of the power of the method can be used by cleverly answering the first few questions.

Let's take each major question and see what's behind the answer. The program first asks how many factors in the "inner array". We simple answer with the number of control parameters in our equation. The concept of an inner array and outer array is a subject for another book on Taguchi's methods. After naming the factors, we then designate which type of L design we will use for this problem. We name the L27 and then input the same values for all 3 levels of each of the parameters. This is done to skirt around the more extensive use of the program. It is the "outer array" that will be providing the simulation for us and it is also an L27. We do not have any "noise factors". A noise factor is an uncontrolled factor that influences the response. Again this is another valuable concept of the Taguchi method.

We now enter the low cost tolerances in the form of standard deviation when asked by the program. Setting up the exact design is a matter of picking the "right" columns from the L27 array. For now, we will simply say that columns 1, 2, 5 and 9 are the right ones that will avoid confounding. We pick the same columns in this case for both the inner and outer arrays. We opt to see the outer array, since this will be the output we need for analysis.

```
 90 DIM A(36,13),B(36,13),F(20,3),N$(20),P(20),S(20),U(20),V(20),X(36,13
),Y(36,13)
100 REM EQOPT
110 REM EQUATION OPTIMIZER
120 PRINT "TO USE THIS PROGRAM YOU MUST INSERT YOUR EQUATION AT LINE 20
00"
130 PRINT "IF YOU HAVE NOT DONE SO, TYPE: EXIT";
140 INPUT Z$
150 IF Z$="EXIT" GOTO 1360
160 PRINT "HOW MANY FACTORS WILL YOU VARY IN YOUR INNER ARRAY";
170 INPUT I1
171 FOR I= 1 TO I1
172 PRINT "NAME OF FACTOR #";I;
173 INPUT N$(I)
174 NEXT I
180 PRINT "ENTER THE NAME OF YOUR INNER ARRAY DESIGN MATRIX (IE L9,L27,
L36,ETC)";
190 INPUT Z$
200 OPEN Z$ TO:1,INPUT
210 INPUT:1,R1,C1
220 FOR I=1 TO I1
230 FOR J=1 TO 3
240 PRINT "ENTER NUMERICAL VALUE";
250 PRINT "FOR";N$(I);"LEVEL#";J;
260 INPUT F(I,J)
270 NEXT J
280 NEXT I
290 PRINT "ENTER THE NAME OF THE OUTER ARRAY";
300 INPUT Z$
310 OPEN Z$ TO:2,INPUT
320 INPUT:2,R2,C2
330 PRINT "DO YOU HAVE OUTER ARRAY NOISE FACTORS";
340 INPUT Z$
350 IF Z$="N" GOTO 425
360 IF Z$="NO" GOTO 425
370 PRINT "HOW MANY NOISE FACTORS";
380 INPUT N1
390 FOR I=I1+1 TO I1 +N1
400 PRINT "NAME OF NOISE FACTOR#";I-I1;"AND NOMINAL LEVEL"
410 INPUT N$(I),F(I,2)
420 NEXT I
422 GOTO 430
425 N1=0
430 FOR I=1 TO   I1+N1
440 PRINT "IS THE TOLERANCE FOR";N$(I);"A PERCENTAGE";
450 INPUT Z$
460 IF Z$="Y" GOTO 530
470 IF Z$="YES" GOTO 530
480 PRINT "THEN THE TOLERANCE IS A STD. DEV."
490 PRINT "ENTER STD. DEV. FOR";N$(I);
500 INPUT S1
510 S(I)=S1*1.2247
520 GOTO 550
530 PRINT "ENTER % TOLERANCE FOR";N$(I);
540 INPUT P(I)
550 NEXT I
600 PRINT "******* SELECTING THE EXACT DESIGN *******"
610 PRINT "I N N E R    A R R A Y"
620 FOR I=1 TO I1
630 PRINT "TO WHICH COLUMN # OF THE ORIGINAL (BASE) DESIGN MATRIX"
640 PRINT "SHOULD";N$(I);"BE ASSIGNED";
650 INPUT V(I)
```

```
660 NEXT I
670 FOR I=1 TO R1
680 FOR J=1 TO C1
690 INPUT:1,A(I,J)
700 NEXT J
710 NEXT I
720 PRINT "ENTER NAME OF FILE TO BE CREATED FOR ANALYSIS OF THE INNER A
RRAY"
730 INPUT Z$
740 CLOSE:1
750 OPEN Z$ TO:1,PRINTOVER
755 PRINT :1,R1,I1
760 FOR I=1 TO R1
770 FOR J=1 TO I1
780 T1=V(J)
790 X(I,J)=A(I,T1)
795 PRINT:1,X(I,J)
800 NEXT J
810 NEXT I
820 PRINT
830 PRINT "O U T E R      A R R A Y "
835 FOR I=1 TO I1+N1
840 PRINT "TO WHICH COLUMN # OF THE ORIGINAL DESIGN MATRIX"
850 PRINT "SHOULD";N$(I);"BE ASSIGNED";
860 INPUT V(I)
870 NEXT I
875 PRINT "DO YOU WANT TO SEE THE OUTER ARRAYS";
876 INPUT O$
880 FOR I=1 TO R2
890 FOR J=1 TO C2
900 INPUT:2,B(I,J)
905 NEXT J
910 NEXT I
915 CLOSE:2
920 FOR I=1 TO R2
925 FOR J=1 TO I1+N1
930 T1=V(J)
935 Y(I,J)=B(I,T1)
940 NEXT J
945 NEXT I
946 PRINT
947 FOR I=1 TO I1
948 PRINT N$(I);
949 NEXT I
950 PRINT
951 FOR I=1 TO R1
952 PRINT
953 I5=2
955 FOR J= 1 TO I1
960 IF X(I,J)=2 GOTO 990
965 IF X(I,J)=3 GOTO 1010
970 V(J)=F(J,1)
975 PRINT TAB(I5),V(J);
980 GOTO 1030
990 V(J)=F(J,2)
1000 PRINT TAB(I5),V(J);
1005 GOTO 1030
1010 V(J)=F(J,3)
1020 PRINT TAB(I5),V(J);
1030 NEXT J
1040 FOR J1=I1+1 TO I1+N1
1045 V(J1)=F(J1,2)
```

```
1050 NEXT J1
1051 PRINT
1054 A1=0
1055 A2=0
1056 A3=0
1060 FOR K=1 TO R2
1070 FOR L=1 TO I1+N1
1080 IF S(L)>0 GOTO 1180
1090 T1=V(L)*P(L)*.01
1100 IF Y(K,L)=2 GOTO 1140
1110 IF Y(K,L)=3 GOTO 1160
1120 U(L)=V(L)-T1
1130 GOTO 1250
1140 U(L)=V(L)
1150 GOTO 1250
1160 U(L)=V(L)+T1
1170 GOTO1250
1180 IFY(K,L)=2 GOTO 1220
1190 IF Y(K,L)=3 GOTO 1240
1200 U(L)=V(L)-S(L)
1210 GOTO 1250
1220 U(L)=V(L)
1230 GOTO 1250
1240 U(L)=V(L)+S(L)
1250 IF O$="N" GOTO 1253
1251 IF O$="NO" GOTO 1253
1252 PRINT U(L);
1253 NEXT L
1260 GO SUB 2000
1270 A1=R+A1
1280 A2=R*R+A2
1285 A3=A3+1/(R*R)
1290 NEXT K
1300 FOR L=1 TO I1+N1
1310 U(L)=V(L)
1320 NEXT L
1330 GOSUB 2000
1332 S1=SQR((A2-(A1*A1/R2))/(R2-1))
1335 S2=20*LGT(ABS(R)/S1)
1337 PRINT
1340 PRINT "NOM FOR TC#";I;R;"STD DEV=";S1
1343 PRINT "TYPE N S/N=";S2
1346 PRINT "TYPE S S/N=";-10*LGT((1/R2)*A2)
1348 PRINT "TYPE B S/N=";-10*LGT((1/R2)*A3)
1350 NEXT I
1360 END
2000 R=-1685.11+43.3517*U(1)-.268167*U(1)*U(1)
2001 R=R+1.31667*U(2)+1.10877*U(3)-1.0877*U(4)
2005 PRINT "IQ=";R
2020 RETURN
```

ANOVA OF THE RESULTS

Table 21-2 shows the changes in the four control parameters and the solution of the photo process equation after each treatment combination. We now take each of the 27 responses and do a simple ANOVA which is shown in Table 21-3. The results in this table will help us appreciate the power of a fixed experimental design over the random Monte-Carlo approach.

First, look at the bottom line, Total Sum of Squares. If we divide this by 26 df (the total number of df in this L27 design), we obtain the variance of the 27 observations. The square root of this variance is 2.19172, the same value reported as the standard deviation in Table 21-2. This is not surprising, but very important. If the total is made up of the parts, we should be able to dissect the total to find which of the parameters have contributed to the overall variation. Remember, the variation induced into the response (the IQ) came only from the variation in the purposely induced variation of the four control parameters. There is no experimental error since we are solving an equation. If we add up the individual sums of squares, we should get the total of 124.897 (it does add up!).

The important result of the above observation is the fact that we can now determine the fractional contribution of each control parameter to the total. With this knowledge, we can determine the amount of reduction required to meet our goal and set the tolerances on the control parameters from a rational, numerical base.

The next step is to find the fraction (or percent if you multiply by 100) of the total sum of squares for each control factor. This is shown in Table 21-4.

Table 21-4

FACTOR	CONTRIBUTION
Temperature	.295 (29.5%)
Metol	.375 (37.5%)
HQ	.226 (26.6%)
Speed	.064 (6.4%)

Now let's look at out spec on IQ. If we can attain a value of 100 and the lower limit for 3 standard deviations is 95, we need a standard deviation of 5/3 or 1.67 to accomplish of goal. Our current standard deviation is 2.19. Since variances are additive (standard deviations are not) we will square these values and find the amount of reduction required to attain the goal.

```
TO USE THIS PROGRAM YOU MUST INSERT YOUR EQUATION AT LINE 2000
IF YOU HAVE NOT DONE SO, TYPE: EXIT    ?
HOW MANY FACTORS WILL YOU VARY IN YOUR INNER ARRAY   ?4
NAME OF FACTOR #    1    ?TEMP
NAME OF FACTOR #    2    ?METOL
NAME OF FACTOR #    3    ?HQ
NAME OF FACTOR #    4    ?SPEED
ENTER THE NAME OF YOUR INNER ARRAY DESIGN MATRIX (IE L9,L27,L36,ETC)   ?L27
ENTER NUMERICAL VALUE    FOR    TEMP   LEVEL#    1   ?80
ENTER NUMERICAL VALUE    FOR    TEMP   LEVEL#    2   ?80
ENTER NUMERICAL VALUE    FOR    TEMP   LEVEL#    3   ?80
ENTER NUMERICAL VALUE    FOR    METOL    LEVEL#   1   ?16
ENTER NUMERICAL VALUE    FOR    METOL    LEVEL#   2   ?16
ENTER NUMERICAL VALUE    FOR    METOL    LEVEL#   3   ?16
ENTER NUMERICAL VALUE    FOR    HQ LEVEL#    1   ?20
ENTER NUMERICAL VALUE    FOR    HQ LEVEL#    2   ?20
ENTER NUMERICAL VALUE    FOR    HQ LEVEL#    3   ?20
ENTER NUMERICAL VALUE    FOR    SPEED    LEVEL#   1   ?10
ENTER NUMERICAL VALUE    FOR    SPEED    LEVEL#   2   ?1-\0
ENTER NUMERICAL VALUE    FOR    SPEED    LEVEL#   3   ?10
ENTER THE NAME OF THE OUTER ARRAY    ?L27
DO YOU HAVE OUTER ARRAY NOISE FACTORS    ?N
IS THE TOLERANCE FOR  TEMP   A PERCENTAGE   ?N
THEN THE TOLERANCE IS A STD. DEV.
ENTER STD. DEV. FOR   TEMP   ?2
IS THE TOLERANCE FOR   METOL    A PERCENTAGE   ?N
THEN THE TOLERANCE IS A STD. DEV.
ENTER STD. DEV. FOR    METOL   ?1
IS THE TOLERANCE FOR  HQ  A PERCENTAGE   ?N
THEN THE TOLERANCE IS A STD. DEV.
ENTER STD. DEV. FOR   HQ  ?1
IS THE TOLERANCE FOR  SPEED   A PERCENTAGE   ?N
THEN THE TOLERANCE IS A STD. DEV.
ENTER STD. DEV. FOR   SPEED   ?.5
******* SELECTING THE EXACT DESIGN *******
I N N E R    A R R A Y
TO WHICH COLUMN # OF THE ORIGINAL (BASE) DESIGN MATRIX
SHOULD TEMP  BE ASSIGNED    ?1
TO WHICH COLUMN # OF THE ORIGINAL (BASE) DESIGN MATRIX
SHOULD  METOL   BE ASSIGNED    ?2
TO WHICH COLUMN # OF THE ORIGINAL (BASE) DESIGN MATRIX
SHOULD  HQ BE ASSIGNED   ?5
TO WHICH COLUMN # OF THE ORIGINAL (BASE) DESIGN MATRIX
SHOULD  SPEED   BE ASSIGNED    ?9
ENTER NAME OF FILE TO BE CREATED FOR ANALYSIS OF THE INNER ARRAY
?PPFILE

O U T E R    A R R A Y
TO WHICH COLUMN # OF THE ORIGINAL DESIGN MATRIX
SHOULD  TEMP   BE ASSIGNED    ?1
TO WHICH COLUMN # OF THE ORIGINAL DESIGN MATRIX
SHOULD  METOL   BE ASSIGNED    ?2
TO WHICH COLUMN # OF THE ORIGINAL DESIGN MATRIX
SHOULD  HQ BE ASSIGNED    ?5
TO WHICH COLUMN # OF THE ORIGINAL DESIGN MATRIX
SHOULD  SPEED   BE ASSIGNED    ?9
DO YOU WANT TO SEE THE OUTER ARRAYS   ?Y
```

Table 21-2

TEMP		METOL	HQ	SPEED		
80	16	20	10 Nominals			
77.5506		14.7753	18.7753	9.38765	IQ=	94.1191
77.5506		14.7753	20	10	IQ=	94.8110
77.5506		14.7753	21.2247	10.6123	IQ=	95.5028
77.5506		16	18.7753	10	IQ=	95.0656
77.5506		16	20	10.6123	IQ=	95.7574
77.5506		16	21.2247	9.38765	IQ=	98.4475
77.5506		17.2247	18.7753	10.6123	IQ=	96.0121
77.5506		17.2247	20	9.38765	IQ=	98.7021
77.5506		17.2247	21.2247	10	IQ=	99.3939
80		14.7753	18.7753	10	IQ=	96.1519
80		14.7753	20	10.6123	IQ=	96.8437
80		14.7753	21.2247	9.38765	IQ=	99.5338
80		16	18.7753	10.6123	IQ=	97.0984
80		16	20	9.38765	IQ=	99.7884
80		16	21.2247	10	IQ=	100.480
80		17.2247	18.7753	9.38765	IQ=	100.043
80		17.2247	20	10	IQ=	100.735
80		17.2247	21.2247	10.6123	IQ=	101.427
82.4494		14.7753	18.7753	10.6123	IQ=	94.9669
82.4494		14.7753	20	9.38765	IQ=	97.6569
82.4494		14.7753	21.2247	10	IQ=	98.3488
82.4494		16	18.7753	9.38765	IQ=	97.9115
82.4494		16	20	10	IQ=	98.6034
82.4494		16	21.2247	10.6123	IQ=	99.2952
82.4494		17.2247	18.7753	10	IQ=	98.8580
82.4494		17.2247	20	10.6123	IQ=	99.5498
82.4494		17.2247	21.2247	9.38765	IQ=	102.240

NOM FOR TC#   2   99.1223 STD DEV=   2.19172

We will take the required variance of $1.67^2 = 2.7889$ and divide it by the current variance $2.19^2 = 4.80$. This gives a .58 reduction factor which is a little less than a halving of the variation. How can we get the current variance down to 58% of its value? We will have to cut the variation in each of the control parameters. This is what we did in the random Monte-Carlo case, but we did not know which were the major contributors. We could plot a Pareto chart of the situation to communicate, but the real power comes from the following concept.

$$.58 = \left[\left(\frac{1}{T} \right)^2 * .295 + \left(\frac{1}{M} \right)^2 * .375 + \left(\frac{1}{H} \right)^2 * .266 + \left(\frac{1}{S} \right)^2 * .064 \right]$$

Σ Reduce Variance $= \Sigma$ weighted fraction reducitons

[NOTE: Since the weights are for variances, we square the reduction of the standard deviation.]

Table 21-3

```
ANALYSIS FOR ORTHOGONAL ARRAY (3 LEVEL) DESIGNS
ENTER THE ARRAY FILE NAME    ?PPFILE
THIS DESIGN HAS    27   ROWS AND   4  COLUMNS.

HOW MANY FACTORS DID YOU VARY IN YOUR EXPERIMENT  ?4
WHAT IS THE NAME OF FACTOR #   1  ?TEMP
WHAT IS THE NAME OF FACTOR #   2  ?METOL
WHAT IS THE NAME OF FACTOR #   3  ?HQ
WHAT IS THE NAME OF FACTOR #   4  ?SPEED
ENTER RESPONSE FILE NAME   ?PPFILEY

EFFECT:   TEMP  SUMS   AVERAGES
LEVEL    1    867.811    96.4235
LEVEL    2    892.101    99.1224
LEVEL    3    887.430    98.6034

LINEAR SUM OF SQ=     21.3836
QUADRATIC SUM SQ=     15.5316


EFFECT:   METOL   SUMS  AVERAGES
LEVEL    1    867.935    96.4372
LEVEL    2    882.447    98.0497
LEVEL    3    896.961    99.6623

LINEAR SUM OF SQ=     46.8060
QUADRATIC SUM SQ=      1.85185E-08


EFFECT:   HQ  SUMS  AVERAGES
LEVEL    1    870.226    96.6918
LEVEL    2    882.448    98.0497
LEVEL    3    894.669    99.4077

LINEAR SUM OF SQ=     33.1909
QUADRATIC SUM SQ=      1.85185E-10


EFFECT:   SPEED   SUMS   AVERAGES
LEVEL    1    888.442    98.7158
LEVEL    2    882.448    98.0497
LEVEL    3    876.453    97.3837

LINEAR SUM OF SQ=      7.98534
QUADRATIC SUM SQ=      2.96296E-09


TOTAL SUM OF SQUARES=    124.897
```

We now have an expression that we can exercise in a flexible way to determine the most economic allocation of the tolerances on the control parameters. There is no single solution to the above expression. But we can see that the speed has a small contribution to the total, so it could be left at its present tolerance. We also know that the control of the temperature is more difficult than control of the weight of the chemicals. We will try the following solution to the equation. Leave T and S at the present level of tolerance which means make the values of T and S equal to 1 (no fractional reduction of temperature and speed). If we make M equal to 2 (we cut the standard deviation of Metol in half) then since we are reducing the fraction of the variance, we will effectively reduce the .375 by 1/4. The contribution of the Temperature, Speed and Motel comes to .453 after reducing the Metol by 1/2. This leaves a remainder of .125 for the HQ. Since HQ is a .266 contributor, we will have to cut the standard deviation of HQ by 1/1.46. Therefore, the value of H is 1.46. This translates to the following set of specs.:

Temperature	80, 2
Metol	16, .5
HQ	20, .7
Speed	10, .5

A confirmation of this set of conditions shows that we meet our target. This is a different set of operating tolerances then we obtained from the random Monte-Carlo method. These conditions are more economical than the previous set. Notice that the Speed has very little effect and does not have to be controlled as tightly as the Monte-Carlo method trial suggested. Of course, if the .25 speed tolerance was too tight, we would have gone back and tried a different setting. But if there had been no complaint, then we would have imposed a spec that was too tight for no real reason! Monte-Carlo methods are good as simulations of the situation, but because they only tell if a process will work and not *why* it works, they are not sufficient. The experimental design approach to finding the sensitivity of parameter tolerances on the process response is a more structured and engineering oriented appraoch to rational specifications.

APPENDIX 21
THREE USEFUL 3-LEVEL ORTHOGONAL ARRAYS

```
?L27
ROWS OF DATA=      27
COLUMNS OF DATA=    13

 1   --   1  1  1  1  1  1  1  1  1  1  1  1  1
 2   --   1  1  1  1  2  2  2  2  2  2  2  2  2
 3   --   1  1  1  1  3  3  3  3  3  3  3  3  3
 4   --   1  2  2  2  1  1  1  2  2  2  3  3  3
 5   --   1  2  2  2  2  2  2  3  3  3  1  1  1
 6   --   1  2  2  2  3  3  3  1  1  1  2  2  2
 7   --   1  3  3  3  1  1  1  3  3  3  2  2  2
 8   --   1  3  3  3  2  2  2  1  1  1  3  3  3
 9   --   1  3  3  3  3  3  3  2  2  2  1  1  1
10   --   2  1  2  3  1  2  3  1  2  3  1  2  3
11   --   2  1  2  3  2  3  1  2  3  1  2  3  1
12   --   2  1  2  3  3  1  2  3  1  2  3  1  2
13   --   2  2  3  1  1  2  3  2  3  1  3  1  2
14   --   2  2  3  1  2  3  1  3  1  2  1  2  3
15   --   2  2  3  1  3  1  2  1  2  3  2  3  1
16   --   2  3  1  2  1  2  3  3  1  2  2  3  1
17   --   2  3  1  2  2  3  1  1  2  3  3  1  2
18   --   2  3  1  2  3  1  2  2  3  1  1  2  3
19   --   3  1  3  2  1  3  2  1  3  2  1  3  2
20   --   3  1  3  2  2  1  3  2  1  3  2  1  3
21   --   3  1  3  2  3  2  1  3  2  1  3  2  1
22   --   3  2  1  3  1  3  2  2  1  3  3  2  1
23   --   3  2  1  3  2  1  3  3  2  1  1  3  2
24   --   3  2  1  3  3  2  1  1  3  2  2  1  3
25   --   3  3  2  1  1  3  2  3  2  1  2  1  3
26   --   3  3  2  1  2  1  3  1  3  2  3  2  1
27   --   3  3  2  1  3  2  1  2  1  3  1  3  2


?L9
ROWS OF DATA=      9
COLUMNS OF DATA=    4

 1   --   1  1  1  1
 2   --   1  2  2  2
 3   --   1  3  3  3
 4   --   2  1  2  3
 5   --   2  2  3  1
 6   --   2  3  1  2
 7   --   3  1  3  2
 8   --   3  2  1  3
 9   --   3  3  2  1
```

		L18							
1	--		1	1	1	1	1	1	1
2	--		1	2	2	2	2	2	2
3	--		1	3	3	3	3	3	3
4	--		2	1	1	2	2	3	3
5	--		2	2	2	3	3	1	1
6	--		2	3	3	1	1	2	2
7	--		3	1	2	1	3	2	3
8	--		3	2	3	2	1	3	1
9	--		3	3	1	3	2	1	2
10	--		1	1	3	3	2	2	1
11	--		1	2	1	1	3	3	2
12	--		1	3	2	2	1	1	3
13	--		2	1	2	3	1	3	2
14	--		2	2	3	1	2	1	3
15	--		2	3	1	2	3	2	1
16	--		3	1	3	2	3	1	2
17	--		3	2	1	3	1	2	3
18	--		3	3	2	1	2	3	1

TABLE 1
Areas under Normal Curve

z	0.00	0.01	0.02	0.03	0.04	0.05	0.06	0.07	0.08	0.09
−3.4	0.0003	0.0003	0.0003	0.0003	0.0003	0.0003	0.0003	0.0003	0.0003	0.0002
−3.3	0.0005	0.0005	0.0005	0.0004	0.0004	0.0004	0.0004	0.0004	0.0004	0.0003
−3.2	0.0007	0.0007	0.0006	0.0006	0.0006	0.0006	0.0006	0.0005	0.0005	0.0005
−3.1	0.0010	0.0009	0.0009	0.0009	0.0008	0.0008	0.0008	0.0008	0.0007	0.0007
−3.0	0.0013	0.0013	0.0013	0.0012	0.0012	0.0011	0.0011	0.0011	0.0010	0.0010
−2.9	0.0019	0.0018	0.0017	0.0017	0.0016	0.0016	0.0015	0.0015	0.0014	0.0014
−2.8	0.0026	0.0025	0.0024	0.0023	0.0023	0.0022	0.0021	0.0021	0.0020	0.0019
−2.7	0.0035	0.0034	0.0033	0.0032	0.0031	0.0030	0.0029	0.0028	0.0027	0.0026
−2.6	0.0047	0.0045	0.0044	0.0043	0.0041	0.0040	0.0039	0.0038	0.0037	0.0036
−2.5	0.0062	0.0060	0.0059	0.0057	0.0055	0.0054	0.0052	0.0051	0.0049	0.0048
−2.4	0.0082	0.0080	0.0078	0.0075	0.0073	0.0071	0.0069	0.0068	0.0066	0.0064
−2.3	0.0107	0.0104	0.0102	0.0099	0.0096	0.0094	0.0091	0.0089	0.0087	0.0084
−2.2	0.0139	0.0136	0.0132	0.0129	0.0125	0.0122	0.0119	0.0116	0.0113	0.0110
−2.1	0.0179	0.0174	0.0170	0.0166	0.0162	0.0158	0.0154	0.0150	0.0146	0.0143
−2.0	0.0228	0.0222	0.0217	0.0212	0.0207	0.0202	0.0197	0.0192	0.0188	0.0183
−1.9	0.0287	0.0281	0.0274	0.0268	0.0262	0.0256	0.0250	0.0244	0.0239	0.0233
−1.8	0.0359	0.0352	0.0344	0.0336	0.0329	0.0322	0.0314	0.0307	0.0301	0.0294
−1.7	0.0446	0.0436	0.0427	0.0418	0.0409	0.0401	0.0392	0.0384	0.0375	0.0367
−1.6	0.0548	0.0537	0.0526	0.0516	0.0505	0.0495	0.0485	0.0475	0.0465	0.0455
−1.5	0.0668	0.0655	0.0643	0.0630	0.0618	0.0606	0.0594	0.0582	0.0571	0.0559
−1.4	0.0808	0.0793	0.0778	0.0764	0.0749	0.0735	0.0722	0.0708	0.0694	0.0681
−1.3	0.0968	0.0951	0.0934	0.0918	0.0901	0.0885	0.0869	0.0853	0.0838	0.0823
−1.2	0.1151	0.1131	0.1112	0.1093	0.1075	0.1056	0.1038	0.1020	0.1003	0.0985
−1.1	0.1357	0.1335	0.1314	0.1292	0.1271	0.1251	0.1230	0.1210	0.1190	0.1170
−1.0	0.1587	0.1562	0.1539	0.1515	0.1492	0.1469	0.1446	0.1423	0.1401	0.1379
−0.9	0.1841	0.1814	0.1788	0.1762	0.1736	0.1711	0.1685	0.1660	0.1635	0.1611
−0.8	0.2119	0.2090	0.2061	0.2033	0.2005	0.1977	0.1949	0.1922	0.1894	0.1867
−0.7	0.2420	0.2389	0.2358	0.2327	0.2296	0.2266	0.2236	0.2206	0.2177	0.2148
−0.6	0.2743	0.2709	0.2676	0.2643	0.2611	0.2578	0.2546	0.2514	0.2483	0.2451
−0.5	0.3085	0.3050	0.3015	0.2981	0.2946	0.2912	0.2877	0.2843	0.2810	0.2776
−0.4	0.3446	0.3409	0.3372	0.3336	0.3300	0.3264	0.3228	0.3192	0.3156	0.3121
−0.3	0.3821	0.3783	0.3745	0.3707	0.3669	0.3632	0.3594	0.3557	0.3520	0.3483
−0.2	0.4207	0.4168	0.4129	0.4090	0.4052	0.4013	0.3974	0.3936	0.3897	0.3859
−0.1	0.4602	0.4562	0.4522	0.4483	0.4443	0.4404	0.4364	0.4325	0.4286	0.4247
−0.0	0.5000	0.4960	0.4920	0.4880	0.4840	0.4801	0.4761	0.4721	0.4681	0.4641
0.0	0.5000	0.5040	0.5080	0.5120	0.5160	0.5199	0.5239	0.5279	0.5319	0.5359
0.1	0.5398	0.5438	0.5478	0.5517	0.5557	0.5596	0.5636	0.5675	0.5714	0.5753
0.2	0.5793	0.5832	0.5871	0.5910	0.5948	0.5987	0.6026	0.6064	0.6103	0.6141
0.3	0.6179	0.6217	0.6255	0.6293	0.6331	0.6368	0.6406	0.6443	0.6480	0.6517
0.4	0.6554	0.6591	0.6628	0.6664	0.6700	0.6736	0.6772	0.6808	0.6844	0.6879
0.5	0.6915	0.6950	0.6985	0.7019	0.7054	0.7088	0.7123	0.7157	0.7190	0.7224
0.6	0.7257	0.7291	0.7324	0.7357	0.7389	0.7422	0.7454	0.7486	0.7517	0.7549
0.7	0.7580	0.7611	0.7642	0.7673	0.7704	0.7734	0.7764	0.7794	0.7823	0.7852
0.8	0.7881	0.7910	0.7939	0.7967	0.7995	0.8023	0.8051	0.8078	0.8106	0.8133
0.9	0.8159	0.8186	0.8212	0.8238	0.8264	0.8289	0.8315	0.8340	0.8365	0.8389
1.0	0.8413	0.8438	0.8461	0.8485	0.8508	0.8531	0.8554	0.8577	0.8599	0.8621
1.1	0.8643	0.8665	0.8686	0.8708	0.8729	0.8749	0.8770	0.8790	0.8810	0.8830
1.2	0.8849	0.8869	0.8888	0.8907	0.8925	0.8944	0.8962	0.8980	0.8997	0.9015
1.3	0.9032	0.9049	0.9066	0.9082	0.9099	0.9115	0.9131	0.9147	0.9162	0.9177
1.4	0.9192	0.9207	0.9222	0.9236	0.9251	0.9265	0.9278	0.9292	0.9306	0.9319
1.5	0.9332	0.9345	0.9357	0.9370	0.9382	0.9394	0.9406	0.9418	0.9429	0.9441
1.6	0.9452	0.9463	0.9474	0.9484	0.9495	0.9505	0.9515	0.9525	0.9535	0.9633
1.7	0.9554	0.9564	0.9573	0.9582	0.9591	0.9599	0.9608	0.9616	0.9625	0.9633
1.8	0.9641	0.9649	0.9656	0.9664	0.9671	0.9678	0.9686	0.9693	0.9699	0.9706
1.9	0.9713	0.9719	0.9726	0.9732	0.9738	0.9744	0.9750	0.9756	0.9761	0.9767
2.0	0.9772	0.9778	0.9783	0.9788	0.9793	0.9798	0.9803	0.9808	0.9812	0.9817
2.1	0.9821	0.9826	0.9830	0.9834	0.9838	0.9842	0.9846	0.9850	0.9854	0.9857
2.2	0.9861	0.9864	0.9868	0.9871	0.9875	0.9878	0.9881	0.9884	0.9887	0.9890
2.3	0.9893	0.9896	0.9898	0.9901	0.9904	0.9906	0.9909	0.9911	0.9913	0.9916
2.4	0.9918	0.9920	0.9922	0.9925	0.9927	0.9929	0.9931	0.9932	0.9934	0.9936
2.5	0.9938	0.9940	0.9941	0.9943	0.9945	0.9946	0.9948	0.9949	0.9951	0.9952
2.6	0.9953	0.9955	0.9956	0.9957	0.9959	0.9960	0.9961	0.9962	0.9963	0.9964
2.7	0.9965	0.9966	0.9967	0.9968	0.9969	0.9970	0.9971	0.9972	0.9973	0.9974
2.8	0.9974	0.9975	0.9976	0.9977	0.9977	0.9978	0.9979	0.9979	0.9980	0.9981
2.9	0.9981	0.9982	0.9982	0.9983	0.9984	0.9984	0.9985	0.9985	0.9986	0.9986
3.0	0.9987	0.9987	0.9987	0.9988	0.9988	0.9989	0.9989	0.9989	0.9990	0.9990
3.1	0.9990	0.9991	0.9991	0.9991	0.9992	0.9992	0.9992	0.9992	0.9993	0.9993
3.2	0.9993	0.9993	0.9994	0.9994	0.9994	0.9994	0.9994	0.9995	0.9995	0.9995
3.3	0.9995	0.9995	0.9995	0.9996	0.9996	0.9996	0.9996	0.9996	0.9996	0.9997
3.4	0.9997	0.9997	0.9997	0.9997	0.9997	0.9997	0.9997	0.9997	0.9997	0.9998

NORMAL TABLE

TABLE 2

CRITICAL VALUES OF STUDENT·S t DISTRIBUTION

α ν	IIb - Two Tail Critical Values						
	0.50	0.25	0.10	0.05	0.025	0.01	0.005
1	1.00000	2.4142	6.3138	12.706	25.452	63.657	127.32
2	0.81650	1.6036	2.9200	4.3027	6.2053	9.9248	14.089
3	0.76489	1.4226	2.3534	3.1825	4.1765	5.8409	7.4533
4	0.74070	1.3444	2.1318	2.7764	3.4954	4.6041	5.5976
5	0.72669	1.3009	2.0150	2.5706	3.1634	4.0321	4.7733
6	0.71756	1.2733	1.9432	2.4469	2.9687	3.7074	4.3168
7	0.71114	1.2543	1.8946	2.3646	2.8412	3.4995	4.0293
8	0.70639	1.2403	1.8595	2.3060	2.7515	3.3554	3.8325
9	0.70272	1.2297	1.8331	2.2622	2.6850	3.2498	3.6897
10	0.69981	1.2213	1.8125	2.2281	2.6338	3.1693	3.5814
11	0.69745	1.2145	1.7959	2.2010	2.5931	3.1058	3.4966
12	0.69548	1.2089	1.7823	2.1788	2.5600	3.0545	3.4284
13	0.69384	1.2041	1.7709	2.1604	2.5326	3.0123	3.3725
14	0.69242	1.2001	1.7613	2.1448	2.5096	2.9768	3.3257
15	0.69120	1.1967	1.7530	2.1315	2.4899	2.9467	3.2860
16	0.69013	1.1937	1.7459	2.1199	2.4729	2.9208	3.2520
17	0.68919	1.1910	1.7396	2.1098	2.4581	2.8982	3.2225
18	0.68837	1.1887	1.7341	2.1009	2.4450	2.8784	3.1966
19	0.68763	1.1866	1.7291	2.0930	2.4334	2.8609	3.1737
20	0.68696	1.1848	1.7247	2.0860	2.4231	2.8453	3.1534
21	0.68635	1.1831	1.7207	2.0796	2.4138	2.8314	3.1352
22	0.68580	1.1816	1.7171	2.0739	2.4055	2.8188	3.1188
23	0.68531	1.1802	1.7139	2.0687	2.3979	2.8073	3.1040
24	0.68485	1.1789	1.7109	2.0639	2.3910	2.7969	3.0905
25	0.68443	1.1777	1.7081	2.0595	2.3846	2.7874	3.0782
26	0.68405	1.1766	1.7056	2.0555	2.3788	2.7787	3.0669
27	0.68370	1.1757	1.7033	2.0518	2.3734	2.7707	3.0565
28	0.68335	1.1748	1.7011	2.0484	2.3685	2.7633	3.0469
29	0.68304	1.1739	1.6991	2.0452	2.3638	2.7564	3.0380
30	0.68276	1.1731	1.6973	2.0423	2.3596	2.7500	3.0298
40	0.68066	1.1673	1.6839	2.0211	2.3289	2.7045	2.9712
60	0.67862	1.1616	1.6707	2.0003	2.2991	2.6603	2.9146
120	0.67656	1.1559	1.6577	1.9799	2.2699	2.6174	2.8599
∞	0.67449	1.1503	1.6449	1.9600	2.2414	2.5758	2.8070
ν	0.25	0.125	0.05	0.025	0.0125	0.005	0.0025
α	IIa - One Tail Critical Values						

TABLE 3

NUMBER OF OBSERVATIONS FOR t-TEST OF DIFFERENCE BETWEEN TWO MEANS

The entries in this table show the number of observations needed in a t-test of the significance of the difference between two means in order to control the probabilities of the errors of the first and second kinds at α and β respectively.

Value of $D = \delta/\sigma$	Level of t-test 0.01					Level of t-test 0.02					Level of t-test 0.05					Level of t-test 0.1				
Single-sided test $\alpha=$ / Double-sided test $\alpha=$	0.005 / 0.01					0.01 / 0.02					0.025 / 0.05					0.05 / 0.1				
$\beta=$	0.01	0.05	0.1	0.2	0.5	0.01	0.05	0.1	0.2	0.5	0.01	0.05	0.1	0.2	0.5	0.01	0.05	0.1	0.2	0.5
0.05																				
0.10																				
0.15																				
0.20																				137
0.25															124					88
0.30										123					87					61
0.35					110					90					64				102	45
0.40					85					70				100	50			108	78	35
0.45				118	68				101	55			105	79	39		108	86	62	28
0.50				96	55			106	82	45		106	86	64	32		88	70	51	23
0.55			101	79	46		106	88	68	38		87	71	53	27	112	73	58	42	19
0.60		101	85	67	39		90	74	58	32	104	74	60	45	23	89	61	49	36	16
0.65		87	73	57	34	104	77	64	49	27	88	63	51	39	20	76	52	42	30	14
0.70	100	75	63	50	29	90	66	55	43	24	76	55	44	34	17	66	45	36	26	12
0.75	88	66	55	44	26	79	58	48	38	21	67	48	39	29	15	57	40	32	23	11
0.80	77	58	49	39	23	70	51	43	33	19	59	42	34	26	14	50	35	28	21	10
0.85	69	51	43	35	21	62	46	38	30	17	52	37	31	23	12	45	31	25	18	9
0.90	62	46	39	31	19	55	41	34	27	15	47	34	27	21	11	40	28	22	16	8
0.95	55	42	35	28	17	50	37	31	24	14	42	30	25	19	10	36	25	20	15	7
1.00	50	38	32	26	15	45	33	28	22	13	38	27	23	17	9	33	23	18	14	7

Level of t-test

Number of observations ($D = \delta/\sigma$, rows; β = columns).

Level of t-test = 0.01   (Single-sided test $\alpha = 0.005$; Double-sided test $\alpha = 0.01$)

Value of $D = \delta/\sigma$	$\beta=0.01$	$\beta=0.05$	$\beta=0.1$	$\beta=0.2$	$\beta=0.5$
1.1	24	19	16	14	9
1.2	21	16	14	12	8
1.3	18	15	13	11	8
1.4	16	13	12	10	7
1.5	15	12	11	9	7
1.6	13	11	10	8	6
1.7	12	10	9	8	6
1.8	12	10	9	8	6
1.9	11	9	8	7	6
2.0	10	8	8	7	5
2.1	10	8	7	7	
2.2	9	8	7	6	
2.3	9	7	7	6	
2.4	8	7	7	6	
2.5	8	7	6	6	
3.0	7	6	6	5	
3.5	6	5	5		
4.0	6				

Level of t-test = 0.02   (Single-sided test $\alpha = 0.01$; Double-sided test $\alpha = 0.02$)

Value of $D = \delta/\sigma$	$\beta=0.01$	$\beta=0.05$	$\beta=0.1$	$\beta=0.2$	$\beta=0.5$
1.1	21	16	14	12	8
1.2	18	14	12	10	7
1.3	16	13	11	9	6
1.4	14	11	10	9	6
1.5	13	10	9	8	6
1.6	12	10	9	7	5
1.7	11	9	8	7	
1.8	10	8	7	7	
1.9	10	8	7	6	
2.0	9	7	7	6	
2.1	8	7	6	6	
2.2	8	7	6	5	
2.3	8	6	6		
2.4	7	6	6		
2.5	7	6	6		
3.0	6	5	5		
3.5	5				
4.0					

Level of t-test = 0.05   (Single-sided test $\alpha = 0.025$; Double-sided test $\alpha = 0.05$)

Value of $D = \delta/\sigma$	$\beta=0.01$	$\beta=0.05$	$\beta=0.1$	$\beta=0.2$	$\beta=0.5$
1.1	18	13	11	9	6
1.2	15	12	10	8	5
1.3	14	10	9	7	
1.4	12	9	8	7	
1.5	11	8	7	6	
1.6	10	8	7	6	
1.7	9	7	6	5	
1.8	8	7	6		
1.9	8	6	6		
2.0	7	6	5		
2.1	7	6			
2.2	7	6			
2.3	6	5			
2.4	6				
2.5	6				
3.0	5				

Level of t-test = 0.1   (Single-sided test $\alpha = 0.05$; Double-sided test $\alpha = 0.1$)

Value of $D = \delta/\sigma$	$\beta=0.01$	$\beta=0.05$	$\beta=0.1$	$\beta=0.2$	$\beta=0.5$
1.1	15	11	9	7	5
1.2	13	10	8	6	
1.3	11	8	7	6	
1.4	10	8	7	5	
1.5	9	7	6		
1.6	8	6	6		
1.7	8	6	5		
1.8	7	6			
1.9	7	5			
2.0	6				
2.1	6				
2.2	6				
2.3	5				

TABLE 4

NUMBER OF OBSERVATIONS FOR t-TEST OF MEAN

The entries in this table show the numbers of observations needed in a t-test of the significance of a mean in order to control the probabilities of errors of the first and second kinds at α and β respectively.

Value of $D = \dfrac{\delta}{\sigma}$	Level of t-test																			
	0·01					0·02					0·05					0·1				
Single-sided test / Double-sided test	$\alpha = 0.005$ / $\alpha = 0.01$					$\alpha = 0.01$ / $\alpha = 0.02$					$\alpha = 0.025$ / $\alpha = 0.05$					$\alpha = 0.05$ / $\alpha = 0.1$				
$\beta =$	0·01	0·05	0·1	0·2	0·5	0·01	0·05	0·1	0·2	0·5	0·01	0·05	0·1	0·2	0·5	0·01	0·05	0·1	0·2	0·5
0·05																				
0·10																				
0·15																				122
0·20										139					99					70
0·25					110					90				128	64			139	101	45
0·30				134	78				115	63			119	90	45		122	97	71	32
0·35			125	99	58			109	85	47		109	88	67	34	129	90	72	52	24
0·40		115	97	77	45		101	85	66	37	117	84	68	51	26	99	70	55	40	19
0·45		92	77	62	37	110	81	68	53	30	93	67	54	41	21	78	55	44	33	15
0·50	100	75	63	51	30	90	68	55	43	25	76	54	44	34	18	63	45	36	27	13
0·55	83	63	53	42	26	75	55	46	36	21	63	45	37	28	15	52	38	30	22	11
0·60	71	53	45	36	22	63	47	39	31	18	53	38	32	24	13	44	32	26	19	9
0·65	61	46	39	31	20	55	41	34	27	16	46	33	27	21	12	37	28	22	17	8
0·70	53	40	34	28	17	47	35	30	24	14	40	29	24	19	11	32	24	19	15	8
0·75	47	36	30	25	16	42	31	27	21	13	35	26	21	16	10	28	21	17	13	7
0·80	41	32	27	22	14	37	28	24	19	12	31	22	19	15	9	25	19	15	12	6
0·85	37	29	24	20	13	33	25	21	17	11	28	21	17	13	8	22	17	14	11	6
0·90	34	26	22	18	12	29	23	19	16	10	25	19	16	12	7	20	15	13	10	5
0·95	31	24	20	17	11	27	21	18	14	9	23	17	14	11	7	18	14	11	9	5
1·00	28	22	19	16	10	25	19	16	13	9	21	16	13	10	6	16	13	11	8	5

Level of t-test

Value of $D = \delta/\sigma$	0·01					0·02					0·05					0·1				
Single-sided test ($\alpha =$)	0·005					0·01					0·025					0·05				
Double-sided test ($\alpha =$)	0·01					0·02					0·05					0·1				
$\beta =$	0·01	0·05	0·1	0·2	0·5	0·01	0·05	0·1	0·2	0·5	0·01	0·05	0·1	0·2	0·5	0·01	0·05	0·1	0·2	0·5
1·1	42	32	27	22	13	38	28	23	19	11	32	23	19	14	8	27	19	15	12	6
1·2	36	27	23	18	11	32	24	20	16	9	27	20	16	12	7	23	16	13	10	5
1·3	31	23	20	16	10	28	21	17	14	8	23	17	14	11	6	20	14	11	9	5
1·4	27	20	17	14	9	24	18	15	12	8	20	15	12	10	6	17	12	10	8	4
1·5	24	18	15	13	8	21	16	14	11	7	18	13	11	9	5	15	11	9	7	4
1·6	21	16	14	11	7	19	14	12	10	6	16	12	10	8	5	14	10	8	6	4
1·7	19	15	13	10	7	17	13	11	9	6	14	11	9	7	4	12	9	7	6	3
1·8	17	13	11	10	6	15	12	10	8	5	13	10	8	6	4	11	8	7	5	
1·9	16	12	11	9	6	14	11	9	8	5	12	9	7	6	4	10	7	6	5	
2·0	14	11	10	8	6	13	10	9	7	5	11	8	7	6	4	9	7	6	4	
2·1	13	10	9	8	5	12	9	8	7	5	10	8	6	5	3	8	6	5	4	
2·2	12	10	8	7	5	11	9	7	6	4	9	7	6	5		8	6	5	4	
2·3	11	9	8	7	5	10	8	7	6	4	9	7	6	5		7	5	5	4	
2·4	11	9	8	6	5	10	8	7	6	4	8	6	5	4		7	5	4	4	
2·5	10	8	7	6	4	9	7	6	5	4	8	6	5	4		6	5	4	3	
3·0	8	6	6	5	4	7	6	5	4	3	6	5	4	4		5	4	3		
3·5	6	5	5	4	3	6	5	4	4		5	4	4	3		4	3			
4·0	6	5	4	4		5	4	3			4	4	3			4				

TABLE 5

CRITICAL VALUES OF THE F DISTRIBUTION

$\alpha = 0.10$

numerator

$v_2 \backslash v_1$	1	2	3	4	5	6	7	8	9	10	12	15	20	24	30	40	60	120	∞
1	39.864	49.500	53.593	55.833	57.241	58.204	58.906	59.439	59.858	60.195	60.705	61.220	61.740	62.002	62.265	62.529	62.794	63.061	63.328
2	8.5263	9.0000	9.1618	9.2434	9.2926	9.3255	9.3491	9.3668	9.3805	9.3916	9.4081	9.4247	9.4413	9.4496	9.4579	9.4663	9.4746	9.4829	9.4913
3	5.5383	5.4624	5.3908	5.3427	5.3092	5.2847	5.2662	5.2517	5.2400	5.2304	5.2156	5.2003	5.1845	5.1764	5.1681	5.1597	5.1512	5.1425	5.1337
4	4.5448	4.3246	4.1908	4.1073	4.0506	4.0098	3.9790	3.9549	3.9357	3.9199	3.8955	3.8689	3.8443	3.8310	3.8174	3.8036	3.7896	3.7753	3.7607
5	4.0604	3.7797	3.6195	3.5202	3.4530	3.4045	3.3679	3.3393	3.3163	3.2974	3.2682	3.2380	3.2067	3.1905	3.1741	3.1573	3.1402	3.1228	3.1050
6	3.7760	3.4633	3.2888	3.1808	3.1075	3.0546	3.0145	2.9830	2.9577	2.9369	2.9047	2.8712	2.8363	2.8183	2.8000	2.7812	2.7620	2.7423	2.7222
7	3.5894	3.2574	3.0741	2.9605	2.8833	2.8274	2.7849	2.7516	2.7247	2.7025	2.6681	2.6322	2.5947	2.5753	2.5555	2.5351	2.5142	2.4928	2.4708
8	3.4579	3.1131	2.9238	2.8064	2.7265	2.6683	2.6241	2.5893	2.5612	2.5380	2.5020	2.4642	2.4246	2.4041	2.3830	2.3614	2.3391	2.3162	2.2926
9	3.3603	3.0065	2.8129	2.6927	2.6106	2.5509	2.5053	2.4694	2.4403	2.4163	2.3789	2.3396	2.2983	2.2768	2.2547	2.2320	2.2085	2.1843	2.1592
10	3.2850	2.9245	2.7277	2.6053	2.5216	2.4606	2.4140	2.3772	2.3473	2.3226	2.2841	2.2435	2.2007	2.1784	2.1554	2.1317	2.1072	2.0818	2.0554
11	3.2252	2.8595	2.6602	2.5362	2.4512	2.3891	2.3416	2.3040	2.2735	2.2482	2.2087	2.1671	2.1230	2.1000	2.0762	2.0516	2.0261	1.9997	1.9721
12	3.1765	2.8068	2.6055	2.4801	2.3940	2.3310	2.2828	2.2446	2.2135	2.1878	2.1474	2.1049	2.0597	2.0360	2.0115	1.9861	1.9597	1.9323	1.9036
13	3.1362	2.7632	2.5603	2.4337	2.3467	2.2830	2.2341	2.1953	2.1638	2.1376	2.0966	2.0532	2.0070	1.9827	1.9576	1.9315	1.9043	1.8759	1.8462
14	3.1022	2.7265	2.5222	2.3947	2.3069	2.2426	2.1931	2.1539	2.1220	2.0954	2.0537	2.0095	1.9625	1.9377	1.9119	1.8852	1.8572	1.8280	1.7973
15	3.0732	2.6952	2.4898	2.3614	2.2730	2.2081	2.1582	2.1185	2.0862	2.0593	2.0171	1.9722	1.9243	1.8990	1.8728	1.8454	1.8168	1.7867	1.7551
16	3.0481	2.6682	2.4618	2.3327	2.2438	2.1783	2.1280	2.0880	2.0553	2.0281	1.9854	1.9399	1.8913	1.8656	1.8388	1.8108	1.7816	1.7507	1.7182
17	3.0262	2.6446	2.4374	2.3077	2.2183	2.1524	2.1017	2.0613	2.0284	2.0009	1.9577	1.9117	1.8624	1.8362	1.8090	1.7805	1.7506	1.7191	1.6856
18	3.0070	2.6239	2.4160	2.2858	2.1958	2.1296	2.0785	2.0379	2.0047	1.9770	1.9333	1.8868	1.8368	1.8103	1.7827	1.7537	1.7232	1.6910	1.6567
19	2.9899	2.6056	2.3970	2.2663	2.1760	2.1094	2.0580	2.0171	1.9836	1.9557	1.9117	1.8647	1.8142	1.7873	1.7592	1.7298	1.6988	1.6659	1.6308
20	2.9747	2.5893	2.3801	2.2489	2.1582	2.0913	2.0397	1.9985	1.9649	1.9367	1.8924	1.8449	1.7938	1.7667	1.7382	1.7083	1.6768	1.6433	1.6074
21	2.9609	2.5746	2.3649	2.2333	2.1423	2.0751	2.0232	1.9819	1.9480	1.9197	1.8750	1.8272	1.7756	1.7481	1.7193	1.6890	1.6569	1.6228	1.5862
22	2.9486	2.5613	2.3512	2.2193	2.1279	2.0605	2.0084	1.9668	1.9327	1.9043	1.8593	1.8111	1.7590	1.7312	1.7021	1.6714	1.6389	1.6042	1.5668
23	2.9374	2.5493	2.3387	2.2065	2.1149	2.0472	1.9949	1.9531	1.9189	1.8903	1.8450	1.7964	1.7439	1.7159	1.6864	1.6554	1.6224	1.5871	1.5490
24	2.9271	2.5383	2.3274	2.1949	2.1030	2.0351	1.9826	1.9407	1.9063	1.8775	1.8319	1.7831	1.7302	1.7019	1.6721	1.6407	1.6073	1.5715	1.5327
25	2.9177	2.5283	2.3170	2.1843	2.0922	2.0241	1.9714	1.9292	1.8947	1.8658	1.8200	1.7708	1.7175	1.6890	1.6589	1.6272	1.5934	1.5570	1.5176
26	2.9091	2.5191	2.3075	2.1745	2.0822	2.0139	1.9610	1.9188	1.8841	1.8550	1.8090	1.7596	1.7059	1.6771	1.6468	1.6147	1.5805	1.5437	1.5036
27	2.9012	2.5106	2.2987	2.1655	2.0730	2.0045	1.9515	1.9091	1.8743	1.8451	1.7989	1.7492	1.6951	1.6662	1.6356	1.6032	1.5686	1.5313	1.4906
28	2.8939	2.5028	2.2906	2.1571	2.0645	1.9959	1.9427	1.9001	1.8652	1.8359	1.7895	1.7395	1.6852	1.6560	1.6252	1.5925	1.5575	1.5198	1.4784
29	2.8871	2.4955	2.2831	2.1494	2.0566	1.9878	1.9345	1.8918	1.8568	1.8274	1.7808	1.7306	1.6759	1.6465	1.6155	1.5825	1.5472	1.5090	1.4670
30	2.8807	2.4887	2.2761	2.1422	2.0492	1.9803	1.9269	1.8841	1.8490	1.8195	1.7727	1.7223	1.6673	1.6377	1.6065	1.5732	1.5376	1.4989	1.4564
40	2.8354	2.4404	2.2261	2.0909	1.9968	1.9269	1.8725	1.8289	1.7929	1.7627	1.7146	1.6624	1.6052	1.5741	1.5411	1.5056	1.4672	1.4248	1.3769
60	2.7914	2.3932	2.1774	2.0410	1.9457	1.8747	1.8194	1.7748	1.7380	1.7070	1.6574	1.6034	1.5435	1.5107	1.4755	1.4373	1.3952	1.3476	1.2915
120	2.7478	2.3473	2.1300	1.9923	1.8959	1.8238	1.7675	1.7220	1.6843	1.6524	1.6012	1.5450	1.4821	1.4472	1.4094	1.3676	1.3203	1.2646	1.1926
∞	2.7055	2.3026	2.0838	1.9449	1.8473	1.7741	1.7167	1.6702	1.6315	1.5987	1.5458	1.4871	1.4206	1.3832	1.3419	1.2951	1.2400	1.1686	1.0000

denominator

F DISTRIBUTION

α = 0.05

numerator

v_2 \ v_1	1	2	3	4	5	6	7	8	9	10	12	15	20	24	30	40	60	120	∞
1	161.45	199.50	215.71	224.58	230.16	233.99	236.77	238.88	240.54	241.88	243.91	245.95	248.01	249.05	250.09	251.14	252.20	253.25	254.32
2	18.513	19.000	19.164	19.247	19.296	19.330	19.353	19.371	19.385	19.396	19.413	19.429	19.446	19.454	19.462	19.471	19.479	19.487	19.496
3	10.128	9.5521	9.2766	9.1172	9.0135	8.9406	8.8868	8.8452	8.8123	8.7855	8.7446	8.7029	8.6602	8.6385	8.6166	8.5944	8.5720	8.5494	8.5265
4	7.7086	6.9443	6.5914	6.3883	6.2560	6.1631	6.0942	6.0410	5.9988	5.9644	5.9117	5.8578	5.8025	5.7744	5.7459	5.7170	5.6878	5.6581	5.6281
5	6.6079	5.7861	5.4095	5.1922	5.0503	4.9503	4.8759	4.8183	4.7725	4.7351	4.6777	4.6188	4.5581	4.5272	4.4957	4.4638	4.4314	4.3984	4.3650
6	5.9874	5.1433	4.7571	4.5337	4.3874	4.2839	4.2066	4.1468	4.0990	4.0600	3.9999	3.9381	3.8742	3.8415	3.8082	3.7743	3.7398	3.7047	3.6688
7	5.5914	4.7374	4.3468	4.1203	3.9715	3.8660	3.7870	3.7257	3.6767	3.6365	3.5747	3.5108	3.4445	3.4105	3.3758	3.3404	3.3043	3.2674	3.2298
8	5.3177	4.4590	4.0662	3.8378	3.6875	3.5806	3.5005	3.4381	3.3881	3.3472	3.2840	3.2184	3.1503	3.1152	3.0794	3.0428	3.0053	2.9669	2.9276
9	5.1174	4.2565	3.8626	3.6331	3.4817	3.3738	3.2927	3.2296	3.1789	3.1373	3.0729	3.0061	2.9365	2.9005	2.8637	2.8259	2.7872	2.7475	2.7067
10	4.9646	4.1028	3.7083	3.4780	3.3258	3.2172	3.1355	3.0717	3.0204	2.9782	2.9130	2.8450	2.7740	2.7372	2.6996	2.6609	2.6211	2.5801	2.5379
11	4.8443	3.9823	3.5874	3.3567	3.2039	3.0946	3.0123	2.9480	2.8962	2.8536	2.7876	2.7186	2.6464	2.6090	2.5705	2.5309	2.4901	2.4480	2.4045
12	4.7472	3.8853	3.4903	3.2592	3.1059	2.9961	2.9134	2.8486	2.7964	2.7534	2.6866	2.6169	2.5436	2.5055	2.4663	2.4259	2.3842	2.3410	2.2962
13	4.6672	3.8056	3.4105	3.1791	3.0254	2.9153	2.8321	2.7669	2.7144	2.6710	2.6037	2.5331	2.4589	2.4202	2.3803	2.3392	2.2966	2.2524	2.2064
14	4.6001	3.7389	3.3439	3.1122	2.9582	2.8477	2.7642	2.6987	2.6458	2.6021	2.5342	2.4630	2.3879	2.3487	2.3082	2.2664	2.2230	2.1778	2.1307
15	4.5431	3.6823	3.2874	3.0556	2.9013	2.7905	2.7066	2.6408	2.5876	2.5437	2.4753	2.4035	2.3275	2.2878	2.2468	2.2043	2.1601	2.1141	2.0658
16	4.4940	3.6337	3.2389	3.0069	2.8524	2.7413	2.6572	2.5911	2.5377	2.4935	2.4247	2.3522	2.2756	2.2354	2.1938	2.1507	2.1058	2.0589	2.0096
17	4.4513	3.5915	3.1968	2.9647	2.8100	2.6987	2.6143	2.5480	2.4943	2.4499	2.3807	2.3077	2.2304	2.1898	2.1477	2.1040	2.0584	2.0107	1.9604
18	4.4139	3.5546	3.1599	2.9277	2.7729	2.6613	2.5767	2.5102	2.4563	2.4117	2.3421	2.2686	2.1906	2.1497	2.1071	2.0629	2.0166	1.9681	1.9168
19	4.3808	3.5219	3.1274	2.8951	2.7401	2.6283	2.5435	2.4768	2.4227	2.3779	2.3080	2.2341	2.1555	2.1141	2.0712	2.0264	1.9796	1.9302	1.8780
20	4.3513	3.4928	3.0984	2.8661	2.7109	2.5990	2.5140	2.4471	2.3928	2.3479	2.2776	2.2033	2.1242	2.0825	2.0391	1.9938	1.9464	1.8963	1.8432
21	4.3248	3.4668	3.0725	2.8401	2.6848	2.5727	2.4876	2.4205	2.3661	2.3210	2.2504	2.1757	2.0960	2.0540	2.0102	1.9645	1.9165	1.8657	1.8117
22	4.3009	3.4434	3.0491	2.8167	2.6613	2.5491	2.4638	2.3965	2.3419	2.2967	2.2258	2.1508	2.0707	2.0283	1.9842	1.9380	1.8895	1.8380	1.7831
23	4.2793	3.4221	3.0280	2.7955	2.6400	2.5277	2.4422	2.3748	2.3201	2.2747	2.2036	2.1282	2.0476	2.0050	1.9605	1.9139	1.8649	1.8128	1.7570
24	4.2597	3.4028	3.0088	2.7763	2.6207	2.5082	2.4226	2.3551	2.3002	2.2547	2.1834	2.1077	2.0267	1.9838	1.9390	1.8920	1.8424	1.7897	1.7331
25	4.2417	3.3852	2.9912	2.7587	2.6030	2.4904	2.4047	2.3371	2.2821	2.2365	2.1649	2.0889	2.0075	1.9643	1.9192	1.8718	1.8217	1.7684	1.7110
26	4.2252	3.3690	2.9751	2.7426	2.5868	2.4741	2.3883	2.3205	2.2655	2.2197	2.1479	2.0716	1.9898	1.9464	1.9010	1.8533	1.8027	1.7488	1.6906
27	4.2100	3.3541	2.9604	2.7278	2.5719	2.4591	2.3732	2.3053	2.2501	2.2043	2.1323	2.0558	1.9736	1.9299	1.8842	1.8361	1.7851	1.7307	1.6717
28	4.1960	3.3404	2.9467	2.7141	2.5581	2.4453	2.3593	2.2913	2.2360	2.1900	2.1179	2.0411	1.9586	1.9147	1.8687	1.8203	1.7689	1.7138	1.6541
29	4.1830	3.3277	2.9340	2.7014	2.5454	2.4324	2.3463	2.2782	2.2229	2.1768	2.1045	2.0275	1.9446	1.9005	1.8543	1.8055	1.7537	1.6981	1.6377
30	4.1709	3.3158	2.9223	2.6896	2.5336	2.4205	2.3343	2.2662	2.2107	2.1646	2.0921	2.0148	1.9317	1.8874	1.8409	1.7918	1.7396	1.6835	1.6223
40	4.0848	3.2317	2.8387	2.6060	2.4495	2.3359	2.2490	2.1802	2.1240	2.0772	2.0035	1.9245	1.8389	1.7929	1.7444	1.6928	1.6373	1.5766	1.5089
60	4.0012	3.1504	2.7581	2.5252	2.3683	2.2540	2.1665	2.0970	2.0401	1.9926	1.9174	1.8364	1.7480	1.7001	1.6491	1.5943	1.5343	1.4673	1.3893
120	3.9201	3.0718	2.6802	2.4472	2.2900	2.1750	2.0867	2.0164	1.9588	1.9105	1.8337	1.7505	1.6587	1.6084	1.5543	1.4952	1.4290	1.3519	1.2539
∞	3.8415	2.9957	2.6049	2.3719	2.2141	2.0986	2.0096	1.9384	1.8799	1.8307	1.7522	1.6664	1.5705	1.5173	1.4591	1.3940	1.3180	1.2214	1.0000

denominator

TABLE 5

F DISTRIBUTION

α = 0.01

numerator

denominator v_2 \ v_1	1	2	3	4	5	6	7	8	9	10	12	15	20	24	30	40	60	120	∞
1	4052.2	4999.5	5403.3	5624.6	5763.7	5859.0	5928.3	5981.6	6022.5	6055.8	6106.3	6157.3	6208.7	6234.6	6260.7	6286.8	6313.0	6339.4	6366.0
2	98.503	99.000	99.166	99.249	99.299	99.332	99.356	99.374	99.388	99.399	99.416	99.432	99.449	99.458	99.466	99.474	99.483	99.491	99.501
3	34.116	30.817	29.457	28.710	28.237	27.911	27.672	27.489	27.345	27.229	27.052	26.872	26.690	26.598	26.505	26.411	26.316	26.221	26.125
4	21.198	18.000	16.694	15.977	15.522	15.207	14.976	14.799	14.659	14.546	14.374	14.198	14.020	13.929	13.838	13.745	13.652	13.558	13.463
5	16.258	13.274	12.060	11.392	10.967	10.672	10.456	10.289	10.158	10.051	9.8883	9.7222	9.5527	9.4665	9.3793	9.2912	9.2020	9.1118	9.0204
6	13.745	10.925	9.7795	9.1483	8.7459	8.4661	8.2600	8.1016	7.9761	7.8741	7.7183	7.5590	7.3958	7.3127	7.2285	7.1432	7.0568	6.9690	6.8801
7	12.246	9.5466	8.4513	7.8467	7.4604	7.1914	6.9928	6.8401	6.7188	6.6201	6.4691	6.3143	6.1554	6.0743	5.9921	5.9084	5.8236	5.7372	5.6495
8	11.259	8.6491	7.5910	7.0060	6.6318	6.3707	6.1776	6.0289	5.9106	5.8143	5.6668	5.5151	5.3591	5.2793	5.1981	5.1156	5.0316	4.9460	4.8588
9	10.561	8.0215	6.9919	6.4221	6.0569	5.8018	5.6129	5.4671	5.3511	5.2565	5.1114	4.9621	4.8080	4.7290	4.6486	4.5667	4.4831	4.3978	4.3105
10	10.044	7.5594	6.5523	5.9943	5.6363	5.3858	5.2001	5.0567	4.9424	4.8492	4.7059	4.5582	4.4054	4.3269	4.2469	4.1653	4.0819	3.9965	3.9090
11	9.6460	7.2057	6.2167	5.6683	5.3160	5.0692	4.8861	4.7445	4.6315	4.5393	4.3974	4.2509	4.0990	4.0209	3.9411	3.8596	3.7761	3.6904	3.6025
12	9.3302	6.9266	5.9526	5.4119	5.0643	4.8206	4.6395	4.4994	4.3875	4.2961	4.1553	4.0096	3.8584	3.7805	3.7008	3.6192	3.5355	3.4494	3.3608
13	9.0738	6.7010	5.7394	5.2053	4.8616	4.6204	4.4410	4.3021	4.1911	4.1003	3.9603	3.8154	3.6646	3.5868	3.5070	3.4253	3.3413	3.2548	3.1654
14	8.8616	6.5149	5.5639	5.0354	4.6950	4.4558	4.2779	4.1399	4.0297	3.9394	3.8001	3.6557	3.5052	3.4274	3.3476	3.2656	3.1813	3.0942	3.0040
15	8.6831	6.3589	5.4170	4.8932	4.5556	4.3183	4.1415	4.0045	3.8948	3.8049	3.6662	3.5222	3.3719	3.2940	3.2141	3.1319	3.0471	2.9595	2.8684
16	8.5310	6.2262	5.2922	4.7726	4.4374	4.2016	4.0259	3.8896	3.7804	3.6909	3.5527	3.4089	3.2588	3.1808	3.1007	3.0182	2.9330	2.8447	2.7528
17	8.3997	6.1121	5.1850	4.6690	4.3359	4.1015	3.9267	3.7910	3.6822	3.5931	3.4552	3.3117	3.1615	3.0835	3.0032	2.9205	2.8348	2.7459	2.6530
18	8.2854	6.0129	5.0919	4.5790	4.2479	4.0146	3.8406	3.7054	3.5971	3.5082	3.3706	3.2273	3.0771	2.9990	2.9185	2.8354	2.7493	2.6597	2.5660
19	8.1850	5.9259	5.0103	4.5003	4.1708	3.9386	3.7653	3.6305	3.5225	3.4338	3.2965	3.1533	3.0031	2.9249	2.8442	2.7608	2.6742	2.5839	2.4893
20	8.0960	5.8489	4.9382	4.4307	4.1027	3.8714	3.6987	3.5644	3.4567	3.3682	3.2311	3.0880	2.9377	2.8594	2.7785	2.6947	2.6077	2.5168	2.4212
21	8.0166	5.7804	4.8740	4.3688	4.0421	3.8117	3.6396	3.5056	3.3981	3.3098	3.1729	3.0299	2.8796	2.8011	2.7200	2.6359	2.5484	2.4568	2.3603
22	7.9454	5.7190	4.8166	4.3134	3.9880	3.7583	3.5867	3.4530	3.3458	3.2576	3.1209	2.9780	2.8274	2.7488	2.6675	2.5831	2.4951	2.4029	2.3055
23	7.8811	5.6637	4.7649	4.2635	3.9392	3.7102	3.5390	3.4057	3.2986	3.2106	3.0740	2.9311	2.7805	2.7017	2.6202	2.5355	2.4471	2.3542	2.2559
24	7.8229	5.6136	4.7181	4.2184	3.8951	3.6667	3.4959	3.3629	3.2560	3.1681	3.0316	2.8887	2.7380	2.6591	2.5773	2.4923	2.4035	2.3099	2.2107
25	7.7698	5.5680	4.6755	4.1774	3.8550	3.6272	3.4568	3.3239	3.2172	3.1294	2.9931	2.8502	2.6993	2.6203	2.5383	2.4530	2.3637	2.2695	2.1694
26	7.7213	5.5263	4.6366	4.1400	3.8183	3.5911	3.4210	3.2884	3.1818	3.0941	2.9579	2.8150	2.6640	2.5848	2.5026	2.4170	2.3273	2.2325	2.1315
27	7.6767	5.4881	4.6009	4.1056	3.7848	3.5580	3.3882	3.2558	3.1494	3.0618	2.9256	2.7827	2.6316	2.5522	2.4699	2.3840	2.2938	2.1984	2.0965
28	7.6356	5.4529	4.5681	4.0740	3.7539	3.5276	3.3581	3.2259	3.1195	3.0320	2.8959	2.7530	2.6017	2.5223	2.4397	2.3535	2.2629	2.1670	2.0642
29	7.5976	5.4205	4.5378	4.0449	3.7254	3.4995	3.3302	3.1982	3.0920	3.0045	2.8685	2.7256	2.5742	2.4946	2.4118	2.3253	2.2344	2.1378	2.0342
30	7.5625	5.3904	4.5097	4.0179	3.6990	3.4735	3.3045	3.1726	3.0665	2.9791	2.8431	2.7002	2.5487	2.4689	2.3860	2.2992	2.2079	2.1107	2.0062
40	7.3141	5.1785	4.3126	3.8283	3.5138	3.2910	3.1238	2.9930	2.8876	2.8005	2.6648	2.5216	2.3689	2.2880	2.2034	2.1142	2.0194	1.9172	1.8047
60	7.0771	4.9774	4.1259	3.6491	3.3389	3.1187	2.9530	2.8233	2.7185	2.6318	2.4961	2.3523	2.1978	2.1154	2.0285	1.9360	1.8363	1.7263	1.6006
120	6.8510	4.7865	3.9493	3.4796	3.1735	2.9559	2.7918	2.6629	2.5586	2.4721	2.3363	2.1915	2.0346	1.9500	1.8600	1.7628	1.6557	1.5330	1.3805
∞	6.6349	4.6052	3.7816	3.3192	3.0173	2.8020	2.6393	2.5113	2.4073	2.3209	2.1848	2.0385	1.8783	1.7908	1.6964	1.5923	1.4730	1.3246	1.0000

TABLE 6

Table E.1 Upper 5-Percent Points of Studentized Range q*

n_2	p** 2	3	4	5	6	7	8	9	10	11	12	13	14	15	16	17	18	19	20
1	18.0	26.7	32.8	37.2	40.5	43.1	45.4	47.3	49.1	50.6	51.9	53.2	54.3	55.4	56.3	57.2	58.0	58.8	59.6
2	6.09	8.28	9.80	10.89	11.73	12.43	13.03	13.54	13.99	14.39	14.75	15.08	15.38	15.65	15.91	16.14	16.36	16.57	16.77
3	4.50	5.88	6.83	7.51	8.04	8.47	8.85	9.18	9.46	9.72	9.95	10.16	10.35	10.52	10.69	10.84	10.98	11.12	11.24
4	3.93	5.00	5.76	6.31	6.73	7.06	7.35	7.60	7.83	8.03	8.21	8.37	8.52	8.67	8.80	8.92	9.03	9.14	9.24
5	3.61	4.54	5.18	5.64	5.99	6.28	6.52	6.74	6.93	7.10	7.25	7.39	7.52	7.64	7.75	7.86	7.95	8.04	8.13
6	3.46	4.34	4.90	5.31	5.63	5.89	6.12	6.32	6.49	6.65	6.79	6.92	7.04	7.14	7.24	7.34	7.43	7.51	7.59
7	3.34	4.16	4.68	5.06	5.35	5.59	5.80	5.99	6.15	6.29	6.42	6.54	6.65	6.75	6.84	6.93	7.01	7.08	7.16
8	3.26	4.04	4.53	4.89	5.17	5.40	5.60	5.77	5.92	6.05	6.18	6.29	6.39	6.48	6.57	6.65	6.73	6.80	6.87
9	3.20	3.95	4.42	4.76	5.02	5.24	5.43	5.60	5.74	5.87	5.98	6.09	6.19	6.28	6.36	6.44	6.51	6.58	6.65
10	3.15	3.88	4.33	4.66	4.91	5.12	5.30	5.46	5.60	5.72	5.83	5.93	6.03	6.12	6.20	6.27	6.34	6.41	6.47
11	3.11	3.82	4.26	4.58	4.82	5.03	5.20	5.35	5.49	5.61	5.71	5.81	5.90	5.98	6.06	6.14	6.20	6.27	6.33
12	3.08	3.77	4.20	4.51	4.75	4.95	5.12	5.27	5.40	5.51	5.61	5.71	5.80	5.88	5.95	6.02	6.09	6.15	6.21
13	3.06	3.73	4.15	4.46	4.69	4.88	5.05	5.19	5.32	5.43	5.53	5.63	5.71	5.79	5.86	5.93	6.00	6.06	6.11
14	3.03	3.70	4.11	4.41	4.64	4.83	4.99	5.13	5.25	5.36	5.46	5.56	5.64	5.72	5.79	5.86	5.92	5.98	6.03
15	3.01	3.67	4.08	4.37	4.59	4.78	4.94	5.08	5.20	5.31	5.40	5.49	5.57	5.65	5.72	5.79	5.85	5.91	5.96
16	3.00	3.65	4.05	4.34	4.56	4.74	4.90	5.03	5.15	5.26	5.35	5.44	5.52	5.59	5.66	5.73	5.79	5.84	5.90
17	2.98	3.62	4.02	4.31	4.52	4.70	4.86	4.99	5.11	5.21	5.31	5.39	5.47	5.55	5.61	5.68	5.74	5.79	5.84
18	2.97	3.61	4.00	4.28	4.49	4.67	4.83	4.96	5.07	5.17	5.27	5.35	5.43	5.50	5.57	5.63	5.69	5.74	5.79
19	2.96	3.59	3.98	4.26	4.47	4.64	4.79	4.92	5.04	5.14	5.23	5.32	5.39	5.46	5.53	5.59	5.65	5.70	5.75
20	2.95	3.58	3.96	4.24	4.45	4.62	4.77	4.90	5.01	5.11	5.20	5.28	5.36	5.43	5.50	5.56	5.61	5.66	5.71
24	2.92	3.53	3.90	4.17	4.37	4.54	4.68	4.81	4.92	5.01	5.10	5.18	5.25	5.32	5.38	5.44	5.50	5.55	5.59
30	2.89	3.48	3.84	4.11	4.30	4.46	4.60	4.72	4.83	4.92	5.00	5.08	5.15	5.21	5.27	5.33	5.38	5.43	5.48
40	2.86	3.44	3.79	4.04	4.23	4.39	4.52	4.63	4.74	4.82	4.90	4.98	5.05	5.11	5.17	5.22	5.27	5.32	5.36
60	2.83	3.40	3.74	3.98	4.16	4.31	4.44	4.55	4.65	4.73	4.81	4.88	4.94	5.00	5.06	5.11	5.15	5.20	5.24
120	2.80	3.36	3.69	3.92	4.10	4.24	4.36	4.47	4.56	4.64	4.71	4.78	4.84	4.90	4.95	5.00	5.04	5.09	5.13
∞	2.77	3.32	3.63	3.86	4.03	4.17	4.29	4.39	4.47	4.55	4.62	4.68	4.74	4.80	4.84	4.89	4.93	4.97	5.01

* From J. M. May, "Extended and Corrected Tables of the Upper Percentage Points of the Studentized Range," *Biometrika*, vol. 39 (1952), pp. 192–193. Reproduced by permission of the trustees of *Biometrika*.

** p is the number of quantities (for example, means) whose range is involved. n_2 is the degrees of freedom in the error estimate.

Table E.2 Upper 1-Percent Points of Studentized Range q

n_2*	p* 2	3	4	5	6	7	8	9	10	11	12	13	14	15	16	17	18	19	20
1	90.0	135	164	186	202	216	227	237	246	253	260	266	272	227	282	286	290	294	298
2	14.0	19.0	22.3	24.7	26.6	28.2	29.5	30.7	31.7	32.6	33.4	34.1	34.8	35.4	36.0	36.5	37.0	37.5	37.9
3	8.26	10.6	12.2	13.3	14.2	15.0	15.6	16.2	16.7	17.1	17.5	17.9	18.2	18.5	18.8	19.1	19.3	19.5	19.8
4	6.51	8.12	9.17	9.96	10.6	11.1	11.5	11.9	12.3	12.6	12.8	13.1	13.3	13.5	13.7	13.9	14.1	14.2	14.4
5	5.70	6.97	7.80	8.42	8.91	9.32	9.67	9.97	10.24	10.48	10.70	10.89	11.08	11.24	11.40	11.55	11.68	11.81	11.93
6	5.24	6.33	7.03	7.56	7.97	8.32	8.61	8.87	9.10	9.30	9.49	9.65	9.81	9.95	10.08	10.21	10.32	10.43	10.54
7	4.95	5.92	6.54	7.01	7.37	7.68	7.94	8.17	8.37	8.55	8.71	8.86	9.00	9.12	9.24	9.35	9.46	9.55	9.65
8	4.74	5.63	6.20	6.63	6.96	7.24	7.47	7.68	7.87	8.03	8.18	8.31	8.44	8.55	8.66	8.76	8.85	8.94	9.03
9	4.60	5.43	5.96	6.35	6.66	6.91	7.13	7.32	7.49	7.65	7.78	7.91	8.03	8.13	8.23	9.32	8.41	8.49	8.57
10	4.48	5.27	5.77	6.14	6.43	6.67	6.87	7.05	7.21	7.36	7.48	7.60	7.71	7.81	7.91	7.99	8.07	8.15	8.22
11	4.39	5.14	5.62	5.97	6.25	6.48	6.67	6.84	6.99	7.13	7.25	7.36	7.46	7.56	7.65	7.73	7.81	7.88	7.95
12	4.32	5.04	5.50	5.84	6.10	6.32	6.51	6.67	6.81	6.94	7.06	7.17	7.26	7.36	7.44	7.52	7.59	7.66	7.73
13	4.26	4.96	5.40	5.73	5.98	6.19	6.37	6.53	6.67	6.79	6.90	7.01	7.10	7.19	7.27	7.34	7.42	7.48	7.55
14	4.21	4.89	5.32	5.63	5.88	6.08	6.26	6.41	6.54	6.66	6.77	6.87	6.96	7.05	7.12	7.20	7.27	7.33	7.39
15	4.17	4.83	5.25	5.56	5.80	5.99	6.16	6.31	6.44	6.55	6.66	6.76	6.84	6.93	7.00	7.07	7.14	7.20	7.26
16	4.13	4.78	5.19	5.49	5.72	5.92	6.08	6.22	6.35	6.46	6.56	6.66	6.74	6.82	6.90	6.97	7.03	7.09	7.15
17	4.10	4.74	5.14	5.43	5.66	5.85	6.01	6.15	6.27	6.38	6.48	6.57	6.66	6.73	6.80	6.87	6.94	7.00	7.05
18	4.07	4.70	5.09	5.38	5.60	5.79	5.94	6.08	6.20	6.31	6.41	6.50	6.58	6.65	6.72	6.79	6.85	6.91	6.96
19	4.05	4.67	5.05	5.33	5.55	5.73	5.89	6.02	6.14	6.25	6.34	6.43	6.51	6.58	6.65	6.72	6.78	6.84	6.89
20	4.02	4.64	5.02	5.29	5.51	5.69	5.84	5.97	6.09	6.19	6.29	6.37	6.45	6.52	6.59	6.65	6.71	6.76	6.82
24	3.96	4.54	4.91	5.17	5.37	5.54	5.69	5.81	5.92	6.02	6.11	6.19	6.26	6.33	6.39	6.45	6.51	6.56	6.61
30	3.89	4.45	4.80	5.05	5.24	5.40	5.54	5.65	5.76	5.85	5.93	6.01	6.08	6.14	6.20	6.26	6.31	6.36	6.41
40	3.82	4.37	4.70	4.93	5.11	5.27	5.39	5.50	5.60	5.69	5.77	5.84	5.90	5.96	6.02	6.07	6.12	6.17	6.21
60	3.76	4.28	4.60	4.82	4.99	5.13	5.25	5.36	5.45	5.53	5.60	5.67	5.73	5.79	5.84	5.89	5.93	5.98	6.02
120	3.70	4.20	4.50	4.71	4.87	5.01	5.12	5.21	5.30	5.38	5.44	5.51	5.56	5.61	5.66	5.71	5.75	5.79	5.83
∞	3.64	4.12	4.40	4.60	4.76	4.88	4.99	5.08	5.16	5.23	5.29	5.35	5.40	5.45	5.49	5.54	5.57	5.61	5.65

* p is the number of quantities (for example, means) whose range is involved. n_2 is the degrees of freedom in the error estimate.

TABLE 7

Coefficients of Orthogonal Polynomials

n	Polynomial	X=1	2	3	4	5	6	7	8	9	10	ΣZ^2	λ
2	Linear	-1	1									2	2
3	Linear	-1	0	1								2	1
	Quadratic	1	-2	1								6	3
4	Linear	-3	-1	1	3							20	2
	Quadratic	1	-1	-1	1							4	1
	Cubic	-1	3	-3	1							20	10/3
5	Linear	-2	-1	0	1	2						10	1
	Quadratic	2	-1	-2	-1	2						14	1
	Cubic	-1	2	0	-2	1						10	5/6
	Quartic	1	-4	6	-4	1						70	35/12
6	Linear	-5	-3	-1	1	3	5					70	2
	Quadratic	5	-1	-4	-4	-1	5					84	3/2
	Cubic	-5	7	4	-4	-7	5					180	5/3
	Quartic	1	-3	2	2	-3	1					28	7/12
7	Linear	-3	-2	-1	0	1	2	3				28	1
	Quadratic	5	0	-3	-4	-3	0	5				84	1
	Cubic	-1	1	1	0	-1	-1	1				6	1/6
	Quartic	3	-7	1	6	1	-7	3				154	7/12
8	Linear	-7	-5	-3	-1	1	3	5	7			168	2
	Quadratic	7	1	-3	-5	-5	-3	1	7			168	1
	Cubic	-7	5	7	3	-3	-7	-5	7			264	2/3
	Quartic	7	-13	-3	9	9	-3	-13	7			616	7/12
	Quintic	-7	23	-17	-15	15	17	-23	7			2184	7/10
9	Linear	-4	-3	-2	-1	0	1	2	3	4		60	1
	Quadratic	28	7	-8	-17	-20	-17	-8	7	28		2772	3
	Cubic	-14	7	13	9	0	-9	-13	-7	14		990	5/6
	Quartic	14	-21	-11	9	18	9	-11	-21	14		2002	7/12
	Quintic	-4	11	-4	-9	0	9	4	-11	4		468	3/20
10	Linear	-9	-7	-5	-3	-1	1	3	5	7	9	330	2
	Quadratic	6	2	-1	-3	-4	-4	-3	-1	2	6	132	1/2
	Cubic	-42	14	35	31	12	-12	-31	-35	-14	42	8580	5/3
	Quartic	18	-22	-17	3	18	18	3	-17	-22	18	2860	5/12
	Quintic	-6	14	-1	-11	-6	6	11	1	-14	6	780	1/10

TABLE 8

PERCENTILE POINTS FOR Q-TEST, FOR EQUAL DEGREES OF FREEDOM ν, AND FOR p SAMPLES

p	$\nu = 1$ .99	$\nu = 1$ .999	$\nu = 2$ .99	$\nu = 2$ .999	$\nu = 3$ .99	$\nu = 3$ .999	$\nu = 4$ .99	$\nu = 4$ .999
3	*	*	.863	*	.757	.919	.684	.828
4	.920	*	.720	.898	.605	.754	.549	.675
5	.828	*	.608	.773	.512	.644	.443	.552
6	.744	.949	.539	.690	.430	.546	.369	.461
7	.671	.865	.469	.606	.372	.471	.318	.394
8	.609	.793	.412	.537	.325	.411	.276	.342
9	.576	.750	.371	.481	.287	.363	.244	.300
10	.528	.694	.333	.433	.257	.324	.218	.267
12	.448	.598	.276	.358	.211	.265	.179	.217
14	.391	.522	.234	.303	.178	.222	.151	.181
15	.365	.490	.217	.280	.165	.205	.140	.167
16	.343	.460	.202	.261	.154	.190	.130	.155
18	.304	.409	.178	.228	.135	.165	.114	.135
20	.273	.367	.158	.202	.120	.146	.101	.119
22	.246	.332	.142	.180	.108	.130	.090	.106
24	.224	.302	.129	.162	.098	.117	.082	.096
26	.206	.276	.118	.148	.090	.107	.075	.087
28	.190	.254	.108	.135	.082	.098	.069	.080
30	.176	.234	.100	.124	.075	.090	.064	.074
32	.163	.218	.093	.115	.070	.083	.060	.068
36	.143	.189	.082	.100	.062	.072	.052	.060
40	.127	.167	.072	.088	.055	.064	.047	.053
45	.111	.145	.063	.076	.048	.055	.041	.046
50	.098	.127	.056	.067	.043	.049	.037	.041
60	.080	.102	.045	.053	.035	.039	.030	.033
64	.074	.094	.042	.049	.033	.037	.028	.031

*These entries exceeded 1 using the approximating distribution. Since $Q \geq 1$, they are omitted.

TABLE 8

	$\nu = 5$		$\nu = 6$		$\nu = 8$		$\nu = 10$	
p	.99	.999	.99	.999	.99	.999	.99	.999
3	.631	.760	.593	.708	.539	.633	.512	.596
4	.498	.608	.461	.558	.413	.490	.383	.446
5	.399	.490	.368	.446	.328	.388	.303	.351
6	.334	.407	.307	.368	.271	.318	.250	.288
7	.284	.345	.261	.311	.230	.268	.212	.242
8	.246	.298	.226	.268	.199	.231	.184	.209
9	.217	.261	.199	.235	.176	.202	.162	.183
10	.194	.232	.178	.208	.157	.179	.145	.163
15	.123	.145	.113	.131	.101	.113	.094	.103
20	.090	.104	.083	.094	.074	.082	.069	.075
30	.058	.065	.053	.059	.048	.052	.045	.048
40	.042	.047	.039	.043	.035	.038	.033	.035
50	.033	.036	.031	.033	.028	.030	.026	.028
60	.027	.029	.025	.027	.023	.024	.022	.023

	$\nu = 12$		$\nu = 14$		$\nu = 16$		$\nu = 20$	
p	.99	.999	.99	.999	.99	.999	.99	.999
3	.486	.558	.466	.530	.451	.508	.429	.476
4	.362	.415	.347	.393	.335	.375	.319	.351
5	.287	.326	.275	.308	.265	.295	.252	.276
6	.236	.267	.227	.253	.219	.242	.209	.226
7	.201	.225	.192	.213	.186	.204	.178	.191
8	.174	.194	.167	.184	.162	.176	.154	.166
9	.154	.170	.148	.162	.143	.155	.136	.146
10	.137	.152	.132	.144	.128	.138	.122	.130
15	.089	.097	.086	.092	.083	.089	.080	.084
20	.066	.070	.063	.067	.062	.065	.059	.062
30	.043	.045	.042	.043	.040	.042	.039	.040
40	.032	.033	.031	.032	.030	.031	.029	.030
50	.025	.026	.024	.025	.024	.025	.023	.024
60	.021	.022	.020	.021	0.20	.020	.019	.020

For $\nu > 60$, calculate $p\nu(pq-1)$ and compare with χ^2 with $(p-1)$ degrees of freedom in Appendix 7.

TABLE 9

Coefficients $\{a_{n-i+1}\}$ for the W test for normality,

for n = 2(1)50

i \ n	2	3	4	5	6	7	8	9	10
1	0.7071	0.7071	0.6872	0.6646	0.6431	0.6233	0.6052	0.5888	0.5739
2		.0000	.1677	.2413	.2806	.3031	.3164	.3244	.3291
3			.0000	.0875	.1401	.1743	.1976	.2141
4				.0000	.0561	.0947	.1224
5					.0000	.0399

i \ n	11	12	13	14	15	16	17	18	19	20
1	0.5601	0.5475	0.5359	0.5251	0.5150	0.5056	0.4968	0.4886	0.4808	0.4734
2	.3315	.3325	.3325	.3318	.3306	.3290	.3273	.3253	.3232	.3211
3	.2260	.2347	.2412	.2460	.2495	.2521	.2540	.2553	.2561	.2565
4	.1429	.1586	.1707	.1802	.1878	.1939	.1988	.2027	.2059	.2085
5	.0695	.0922	.1099	.1240	.1353	.1447	.1524	.1587	.1641	.1686
6	0.0000	0.0303	0.0539	0.0727	0.0880	0.1005	0.1109	0.1197	0.1271	0.1334
7		.0000	.0240	.0433	.0593	.0725	.0837	.0932	.1013
8			.0000	.0196	.0359	.0496	.0612	.0711
9				.0000	.0163	.0303	.0422
10					.0000	.0410

i \ n	21	22	23	24	25	26	27	28	29	30
1	0.4643	0.4590	0.4542	0.4493	0.4450	0.4407	0.4366	0.4328	0.4291	0.4254
2	.3185	.3156	.3126	.3098	.3069	.3043	.3018	.2992	.2968	.2944
3	.2578	.2571	.2563	.2554	.2543	.2533	.2522	.2510	.2499	.2487
4	.2119	.2131	.2139	.2145	.2148	.2151	.2152	.2151	.2150	.2148
5	.1736	.1764	.1787	.1807	.1822	.1836	.1848	.1857	.1864	.1870
6	0.1399	0.1443	0.1480	0.1512	0.1539	0.1563	0.1584	0.1601	0.1616	0.1630
7	.1092	.1150	.1201	.1245	.1283	.1316	.1346	.1372	.1395	.1415
8	.0804	.0878	.0941	.0997	.1046	.1089	.1128	.1162	.1192	.1219
9	.0530	.0618	.0696	.0764	.0823	.0876	.0923	.0965	.1002	.1036
10	.0263	.0368	.0459	.0539	.0610	.0672	.0728	.0778	.0822	.0862
11	0.0000	0.0122	0.0228	0.0321	0.0403	0.0476	0.0540	0.0598	0.0650	0.0697
12		.0000	.0107	.0200	.0284	.0358	.0424	.0483	.0537
13			.0000	.0094	.0178	.0253	.0320	.0381
14				.0000	.0084	.0159	.0227
15					.0000	.0076

TABLE 9

Coefficients $\{a_{n-i+1}\}$ for the W test for normality,

for n = 2(1)50 (cont.)

n i	31	32	33	34	35	36	37	38	39	40
1	0.4220	0.4188	0.4156	0.4127	0.4096	0.4068	0.4040	0.4015	0.3989	0.3964
2	.2921	.2898	.2876	.2854	.2834	.2813	.2794	.2774	.2755	.2737
3	.2475	.2463	.2451	.2439	.2427	.2415	.2403	.2391	.2380	.2368
4	.2145	.2141	.2137	.2132	.2127	.2121	.2116	.2110	.2104	.2098
5	.1874	.1878	.1880	.1882	.1883	.1883	.1883	.1881	.1880	.1878
6	0.1641	0.1651	0.1660	0.1667	0.1673	0.1678	0.1683	0.1686	0.1689	0.1691
7	.1433	.1449	.1463	.1475	.1487	.1496	.1505	.1513	.1520	.1526
8	.1243	.1265	.1284	.1301	.1317	.1331	.1344	.1356	.1366	.1376
9	.1066	.1093	.1118	.1140	.1160	.1179	.1196	.1211	.1225	.1237
10	.0899	.0931	.0961	.0988	.1013	.1036	.1056	.1075	.1092	.1108
11	0.0739	0.0777	0.0812	0.0844	0.0873	0.0900	0.0924	0.0947	0.0967	0.0986
12	.0585	.0629	.0669	.0706	.0739	.0770	.0798	.0824	.0848	.0870
13	.0435	.0485	.0530	.0572	.0610	.0645	.0677	.0706	.0733	.0759
14	.0289	.0344	.0395	.0441	.0484	.0523	.0559	.0592	.0622	.0651
15	.0144	.0206	.0262	.0314	.0361	.0404	.0444	.0481	.0515	.0546
16	0.0000	0.0068	0.0131	0.0187	0.0239	0.0287	0.0331	0.0372	0.0409	0.0444
17			.0000	.0062	.0119	.0172	.0220	.0264	.0305	.0343
18					.0000	.0057	.0110	.0158	.0203	.0244
19							.0000	.0053	.0101	.0146
20									.0000	.0049

n i	41	42	43	44	45	46	47	48	49	50
1	0.3940	0.3917	0.3894	0.3872	0.3850	0.3830	0.3808	0.3789	0.3770	0.3751
2	.2719	.2701	.2684	.2667	.2651	.2635	.2620	.2604	.2589	.2574
3	.2357	.2345	.2334	.2323	.2313	.2302	.2291	.2281	.2271	.2260
4	.2091	.2085	.2078	.2072	.2065	.2058	.2052	.2045	.2038	.2032
5	.1876	.1874	.1871	.1868	.1865	.1862	.1859	.1855	.1851	.1847
6	0.1693	0.1694	0.1695	0.1695	0.1695	0.1695	0.1695	0.1693	0.1692	0.1691
7	.1531	.1535	.1539	.1542	.1545	.1548	.1550	.1551	.1553	.1554
8	.1384	.1392	.1398	.1405	.1410	.1415	.1420	.1423	.1427	.1430
9	.1249	.1259	.1269	.1278	.1286	.1293	.1300	.1306	.1312	.1317
10	.1123	.1136	.1149	.1160	.1170	.1180	.1189	.1197	.1205	.1212
11	0.1004	0.1020	0.1035	0.1049	0.1062	0.1073	0.1085	0.1095	0.1105	0.1113
12	.0891	.0909	.0927	.0943	.0959	.0972	.0986	.0998	.1010	.1020
13	.0782	.0804	.0824	.0842	.0860	.0876	.0892	.0906	.0919	.0932
14	.0677	.0701	.0724	.0745	.0765	.0783	.0801	.0817	.0832	.0846
15	.0575	.0602	.0628	.0651	.0673	.0694	.0713	.0731	.0748	.0764
16	0.0476	0.0506	0.0534	0.0560	0.0584	0.0607	0.0628	0.0648	0.0667	0.0685
17	.0379	.0411	.0442	.0471	.0497	.0522	.0546	.0568	.0588	.0608
18	.0283	.0318	.0352	.0383	.0412	.0439	.0465	.0489	.0511	.0532
19	.0188	.0227	.0263	.0296	.0328	.0357	.0385	.0411	.0436	.0459
20	.0094	.0136	.0175	.0211	.0245	.0277	.0307	.0335	.0361	.0386
21	0.0000	0.0045	0.0087	0.0126	0.0163	0.0197	0.0229	0.0259	0.0288	0.0314
22		.0000	.0042	.0081	.0118	.0153	.0185	.0215	.0244
23				.0000	.0039	.0076	.0111	.0143	.0174
24						.0000	.0037	.0071	.0104
25								.0000	.0035

TABLE 10

Percentage points of the W test for n = 3(1)50

n	0.01	0.02	0.05	0.10	Level 0.50	0.90	0.95	0.98	0.99
3	0.753	0.756	0.767	0.789	0.959	0.998	0.999	1.000	1.000
4	.687	.707	.748	.792	.935	.987	.992	.996	.997
5	.686	.715	.762	.806	.927	.979	.986	.991	.993
6	0.713	0.743	0.788	0.826	0.927	0.974	0.981	0.986	0.989
7	.730	.760	.803	.838	.928	.972	.979	.985	.988
8	.749	.778	.818	.851	.932	.972	.978	.984	.987
9	.764	.791	.829	.859	.935	.972	.978	.984	.986
10	.781	.806	.842	.869	.938	.972	.978	.983	.986
11	0.792	0.817	0.850	0.876	0.940	0.973	0.979	0.984	0.986
12	.805	.828	.859	.883	.943	.973	.979	.984	.986
13	.814	.837	.866	.889	.945	.974	.979	.984	.986
14	.825	.846	.874	.895	.947	.975	.980	.984	.986
15	.835	.855	.881	.901	.950	.975	.980	.984	.987
16	0.844	0.863	0.887	0.906	0.952	0.976	0.981	0.985	0.987
17	.851	.869	.892	.910	.954	.977	.981	.985	.987
18	.858	.874	.897	.914	.956	.978	.982	.986	.988
19	.863	.879	.901	.917	.957	.978	.982	.986	.988
20	.868	.884	.905	.920	.959	.979	.983	.986	.988
21	0.873	0.888	0.908	0.923	0.960	0.980	0.983	0.987	0.989
22	.878	.892	.911	.926	.961	.980	.984	.987	.989
23	.881	.895	.914	.928	.962	.981	.984	.987	.989
24	.884	.898	.916	.930	.963	.981	.984	.987	.989
25	.888	.901	.918	.931	.964	.981	.985	.988	.989
26	0.891	0.904	0.920	0.933	0.965	0.982	0.985	0.988	0.989
27	.894	.906	.923	.935	.965	.982	.985	.988	.990
28	.896	.908	.924	.936	.966	.982	.985	.988	.990
29	.898	.910	.926	.937	.966	.982	.985	.988	.990
30	.900	.912	.927	.939	.967	.983	.985	.988	.900
31	0.902	0.914	0.929	0.940	0.967	0.983	0.986	0.988	0.990
32	.904	.915	.930	.941	.968	.983	.986	.988	.990
33	.906	.917	.931	.942	.968	.983	.986	.989	.990
34	.908	.919	.933	.943	.969	.983	.986	.989	.990
35	.910	.920	.934	.944	.969	.984	.986	.989	.990
36	0.912	0.922	0.935	0.945	0.970	0.984	0.986	0.989	0.990
37	.914	.924	.936	.946	.970	.984	.987	.989	.990
38	.916	.925	.938	.947	.971	.984	.987	.989	.990
39	.917	.927	.939	.948	.971	.984	.987	.989	.991
40	.919	.928	.940	.949	.972	.985	.987	.989	.991
41	0.920	0.929	0.941	0.950	0.972	0.985	0.987	0.989	0.991
42	.922	.930	.942	.951	.972	.985	.987	.989	.991
43	.923	.932	.943	.951	.973	.985	.987	.990	.991
44	.924	.933	.944	.952	.973	.985	.987	.990	.991
45	.926	.934	.945	.953	.973	.985	.988	.990	.991
46	0.927	0.935	0.945	0.953	0.974	0.985	0.988	0.990	0.991
47	.928	.936	.946	.954	.974	.985	.988	.990	.991
48	.929	.937	.947	.954	.974	.985	.988	.990	.991
49	.929	.937	.947	.955	.974	.985	.988	.990	.991
50	.930	.938	.947	.955	.974	.985	.988	.990	.991

TABLE 11

GENERATORS FOR 2-LEVEL FRACTIONAL FACTORIAL DESIGNS

Number of Factors k	Fractionalization Element p	Number of Runs	Confounded Single Effect in Generator	Interaction(s) in Generator
3	1	4	C	AB (12)
4	1	8	D	ABC (123)
5	1	16	E	ABCD (1234)
5	2	8	D E	AB (12) AC (13)
6	1	32	F	ABCDE (12345)
6	2	16	E F	ABC (123) BCD (234)
6	3	8	D E F	AB (12) AC (13) BC (23)
7	1	64	G	ABCDEF (123456)
7	2	32	F G	ABCD (1234) ABDE (1245)
7	3	16	E F G	ABC (123) BCD (234) ACD (124)
7	4	8	D E F G	AB (12) AC (13) BC (23) ABC (123)
8	1	128	H	ABCDEFG(1234567)
8	2	64	G H	ABCD (1234) ABEF (1256)
8	3	32	F G H	ABC (123) ABD (124) BCDE (2345)
8	4	16	E F G H	BCD (234) ACD (134) ABC (123) ABD (124)

TABLE 11

GENERATORS FOR 2-LEVEL FRACTIONAL FACTORIAL DESIGNS

Number of Factors k	Fractionalization Element p	Number of Runs	Confounded Single Effect in Generator	Interaction(s) in Generator
9	2	128	H	ACDFG (13467)
			J	BCEFG (23567)
9	3	64	G	ABCD (1234)
			H	ACEF (1356)
			J	CDEF (3456)
9	4	32	F	BCDE (2345)
			G	ACDE (1345)
			H	ABDE (1245)
			J	ABCE (1235)
9	5	16	E	ABC (123)
			F	BCD (234)
			G	ACD (134)
			H	ABD (124)
			J	ABCD (1234)
10	3	128	H	ABCG (1237)
			J	BCDE (2345)
			K	ACDF (1346)
10	4	64	G	BCDF (2346)
			H	ACDF (1346)
			J	ABDE (1245)
			K	ABCE (1235)
10	5	32	F	ABCD (1234)
			G	ABCE (1235)
			H	ABDE (1245)
			J	ACDE (1345)
			K	BCDE (2345)
10	6	16	E	ABC (123)
			F	BCD (234)
			G	ACD (134)
			H	ABD (124)
			J	ABCD (1234)
			K	AB (12)

TABLE 11

GENERATORS FOR 2-LEVEL FRACTIONAL FACTORIAL DESIGNS

Number of Factors k	Fractionalization Element p	Number of Runs	Confounded Single Effect in Generator	Interaction(s) in Generator
11	5	64	G	CDE (345)
			H	ABCD (1234)
			J	ABF (126)
			K	BDEF (2456)
			L	ADEF (1456)
11	6	32	F	ABC (123)
			G	BCD (234)
			H	CDE (345)
			J	ACD (134)
			K	ADE (145)
			L	BDE (245)

REFERENCES

1. National Bureau of Standards (1957), *Fractional Factorial Experiment Designs for Factors at Two Levels*. U.S. Department of Commerce.

2. Davies, O. L. (1956), *Design and Analysis of Industrial Experiments*. 2nd edition. Hafner Publishing Co., New York.

3. Box, G.E.P., W.G. Hunter, and J.S. Hunter (1978), *Statistics for Experimenters*. Wiley, New York.

4. Hicks, C.R. (1973), *Fundamental Concepts in the Design of Experiments*. 2nd edition. Holt, Rinehart and Winston, New York.

5. Montgomery, D. C. (1984), *Design and Analysis of Experiments*. 2nd edition. Wiley, New York.

Index

Agriculture, 88
Algorithm, 197, 207
Alias, 47
Alpha risk, 138, 147
Alpha star, 68
Alternative hypothesis, 137, 140, 162
ANOVA, 162
  assumptions, 183
  computer programs, 190, 193
  for Latin Square, 275
  table, 166

Balanced, 77, 171
Beta risk, 138, 147
Blocking, 88, 97, 98, 107, 267
Box-Behnken, 75, 86
Brainstorming, 15, 299, 311
  guide to, 18

Calculus, 224
CCD, 67, 72, 106

[CCD]
  analysis, 239
Centering factor, 257
Central Composite Design, 67
  example, 319
Central limit theorem, 139
Coding, 29, 38
Coefficients, 322
Combinations, 43
Components of variance, 113, 282
Conceptual zero, 241
Confounded, 25, 90, 99
Confounding, 46, 53, 75, 315
  rules, 47
Control chart, 111, 345
Correction factor, 165, 198
Correlated pairs, 100, 108
Correlation coefficient, 223, 237
Cost, 43
Covariance, 28, 38, 221, 237
Crossed factor, 109, 110, 115
Cross-product, 245
Curvature, 246

Curved relationship, 319
Curvilinear, 116
Customer's requirements, 344
Cycle (in EVOP), 119

Decode, 256
Deconfounding effects, 203
Defining contrast, 46, 54
    example, 300
Degree of freedom, 45, 53, 167
Degree of variation, 345
Delta functional, 70
Delta star, 70
Dependence, 221
Derivative, 324
Design rules, 80
Design units, 28, 38, 243, 256
df, 45, 53
Diagonal matrix, 217
Dummy factor, 232

Efficiency, 4, 10, 36
EMS, 279, 285
Engineer quality, 310
Equation, 249
Error estimate, 268
Error limit, 121
Errors, 4
Evolutionary operations, 116
EVOP, 116
    computer program, 131
    rules, 129
    worksheet, 130
Expected Mean Square, 279
Expected value, 337
Experiment, 4
Experimental error, 239

Factor, 25, 162
    fixed, 109, 114, 283

Factorial, 27
Fisher-Behrens, 151
Fractional factorial, 45
    computer program, 54
Fractionalization element, 47, 80, 92
Functional specifications, 111
Fundamental defining contrast, 80, 87

Generalize, 100
General linear model, 197, 212
Generator, 46, 54
Goal, 11, 13, 298, 312, 324
    of quality, 343

Half effect, 198, 208, 241, 243, 256
Hierarchial design, 112
Homogeneous variance, 183
Hypothesis testing, 136, 154

Identity (I), 46
Independence, 88
Independent error, 183
Inference space, 100
Information, 43, 45
    analysis, 307, 312
Inner array, 351
Interaction, 34, 38, 110, 172
    degrees of freedom, 174
    plot, 244
    sum of squares, 172
    table, 245
Iso level, 34
Iso plot, 245

Japan, 340

Knowledge of the process, 245

Lab bench, 11
Latin square, 101, 108, 350
  analysis, 275
  mis-use, 105
Least squares, 221
Level, 24, 25, 162
Linear combinations, 78

Magnitude estimation, 104
Magnitude of effect, 240
Management, 312
Mathematical model, 277
Matrix, 212, 213
  inversion, 213, 216, 219
  multiplication, 213, 214
  transposition, 213, 219
Method of least squares
Model, 331
Modulus algebra, 46, 93
Monte Carlo, 331, 335, 344

Natural variation, 144
Negative information, 115, 325
Nested, 110, 115
  analysis, 278
Noise factors, 351
Non-linear, 62
Normal equations, 231
Normal distribution, 337
Normality test, 185
Normalized response, 248
Nuisance factor, 270
Nuisance variable, 92, 99
Null hypothesis, 137, 140

Objective, 11, 13, 300, 312, 324
One factor at a time, 23
One-way ANOVA, 162
Operating characteristic curve, 158

Operating characteristic curve, 158
Operating tolerances, 358
Order mis-match, 214
Organize, 11
  form, 21
Orthogonal, 68, 257, 344
  design, 28, 38
  experiment, 349
  polynomial coefficients, 179
Outer array, 350
Outside estimate of error, 201

Paired comparison, 100, 108, 273
Pareto chart, 318
Phase, 119
Phases of experimentation, 16, 297
Pocket calculator, 166
Polynomial, 63, 179
  model, 246
Pooled variance, 163, 165
Postmultiplier, 214, 219
Practical importance, 170, 178
Preliminary sample, 148
Premultiplier, 214, 219
Primary blocks, 92, 97, 268
Prime directive (EVOP), 116
Prior knowledge, 12, 349
Probability, 135
Process, 4, 9
Proper polynomial, 63
Psychological, 335
Psychology, 15

Quadratic, 63
Quality, 3
  goals, 324
  products, 348
Quantification of errors, 109

Random
   effect, 114
   error, 110
   factor, 283
Randomize, 32, 39
Randomized block
Regression
   analysis, 212
   coefficients, 256
   computer program, 259
Relationship, 223
Replicate, 26
Replication, 110, 239
Residual, 224
Resolution, 52
Resources, 4
Response, 4, 13
Restrictions on randomization, 98
Risk, 136
Rotatable, 68

Sample size, 142
Sampling stages, 287
Screening, 17, 71
   experiment, 306, 312
Secondary block, 94, 97
Second order, 63
Selecting levels, 317
Sequential analysis, 307
Shapiro-Wilk, 185
Shortest significant range, 175
Signal to noise ratio, 150
Significant, 141, 170
Simulation, 331, 333, 344
Skepticism, 72
Slope of y on x, 224
Sources of variation, 279
SSR, 189, 277
Standard error of the mean, 139

Statistic, 6
Statistical analysis, 135
Student 't', 140
Studentized range, 176
Sub-additivity, 313
Sum over, 33
Super-additivity, 36, 313

Taguchi, 349, 350
Test, 3, 5, 10
Tolerances, 354, 358
Treatment combination (tc), 24, 25, 31
Troubleshoot, 4
Truth table, 138
Type I error, 138
Type II error, 138

Uniform, 337

Variance, 354
   analysis, 279
Variation, 135
   table, 286
Vector, 212

Weighing experiment, 44
Working range, 69

YATES
   ANOVA, 197, 208, 239
   ANOVA (example), 305
   computer program, 209
   order, 30, 32
   rules, 197